EARLY IRISH SATIRE

ROISIN MCLAUGHLIN

SCHOOL OF CELTIC STUDIES
DUBLIN INSTITUTE FOR ADVANCED STUDIES

ISBN 978-1-85500-207-4

Typeset in the School of Celtic Studies

Printed by Dundalgan Press, Dundalk, Co. Louth

2008

for

Sally, Lila and Joe

Contents

Acknowledgements

I am very grateful to Liam Breatnach and Fergus Kelly, who read drafts of this work and made many important suggestions and corrections in the course of preparing it for publication. I would also like to thank Caoimhín Breatnach, Neil McLeod, Damian McManus and Jürgen Uhlich for their help and advice on various aspects of the work. Some of the material was read at a seminar on *Mittelirische Verslehren* III in the School of Celtic Studies at the Dublin Institute for Advanced Studies during 2005–2008 and I thank the participants for their comments and suggestions. I alone am responsible for any errors.

I am grateful to Stephen McCullagh who designed the cover and finalised the work for the printers. The cover design shows an illustration from D ii 2, folio 34^{r}, which is reproduced by kind permission of the Royal Irish Academy.

Research for some of the material was funded by the Irish Research Council for the Humanities and Social Sciences.

Abbreviations

AL	R. Atkinson, W. N. Hancock, W. M. Hennessy, T. O'Mahony and A. G. Richey (eds), *Ancient Laws of Ireland* 1–6 (Dublin 1865–1901).
Ann. Conn.	A. Martin Freeman (ed.), *Annála Connacht: The Annals of Connacht* (Dublin 1944, reprinted 1983).
AU	William M. Hennessy and B. MacCarthy (eds), *Annála Uladh: Annals of Ulster* 1–4 (Dublin 1887–1901, reprinted 1998).
Auraic.	George Calder, *Auraicept na n-Éces: The Scholars' Primer* (Edinburgh 1917).
CIH	D. A. Binchy (ed.), *Corpus Iuris Hibernici.* 6 vols (Dublin 1978).
Companion	Liam Breatnach, *A Companion to the Corpus Iuris Hibernici* (Early Irish Law Series 5, Dublin 2005).
Corm Y	Kuno Meyer, 'Sanas Cormaic', *Anecdota from Irish Manuscripts* 4 (1912) 1–128.
Corp. Gen.	Michael A. O'Brien (ed.), *Corpus Genealogiarum Hiberniae* (Dublin 1962, reprinted 1976).
DIL	*Dictionary of the Irish Language* and *Contributions to a Dictionary of the Irish Language* (Dublin 1913–75).
Dinneen	Patrick S. Dinneen, *Foclóir Gaedhilge agus Béarla* (Dublin 1927, reprinted 1992).
EIV	Kim McCone, *The Early Irish Verb* (Maynooth 1987).

Fodlai Aíre	*Fodlai Aíre* Tract on Satire (Chapter 2 of the present work).
FM	John O'Donovan (ed.), *Annála Ríoghachta Éireann: Annals of the Kingdom of Ireland by the Four Masters, from the Earliest Period to the Year 1616.* 7 vols (Dublin 1848–51).
GOI	Rudolf Thurneysen, *A Grammar of Old Irish* (Dublin 1946, reprinted 1981).
IGT	Osborn Bergin, *Irish Grammatical Tracts* V, supplement to *Ériu* 17 (1955).
IT	Whitley Stokes and Ernst Windisch, *Irische Texte mit Übersetzungen und Wörterbuch* 1–4 (Leipzig 1880–1909).
LL	R. I. Best, O. Bergin, M. A. O'Brien and A. O'Sullivan, *The Book of Leinster.* 6 vols (Dublin 1954–83).
LU	R. I. Best and O. Bergin, *Lebor na hUidre: Book of the Dun Cow* (Dublin 1929, reprinted 1992).
Met. Dind.	E. J. Gwynn (ed.), *The Metrical Dindshenchas* 1–5, Todd Lecture Series 8–12 (Dublin 1903–1935).
MV	Rudolf Thurneysen, 'Mittelirische Verslehren', *Irische Texte* 3, 1. Heft (Leipzig 1891) 1–182. An edition of four mediaeval metrical tracts, numbered *MV* I, *MV* II, *MV* III and *MV* IV. Thurneysen's numbering is followed here.
O'Dav.	Whitley Stokes, 'O'Davoren's Glossary', *Archiv für celtische Lexikographie* 2 (1904) 197–504.
Ó Dónaill	N. Ó Dónaill, *Foclóir Gaeilge-Béarla* (Báile Átha Cliath 1977).
O'Mulc.	Whitley Stokes, 'O'Mulconry's Glossary', *Archiv für celtische Lexikographie* 1 (1900) 232–324, 473–81.
PRIA	*Proceedings of the Royal Irish Academy* (Dublin 1936–).
RC	*Revue Celtique* (Paris 1870–1934).

RIA Cat.	T. F. O'Rahilly, Kathleen Mulchrone and others, *Catalogue of Irish Manuscripts in the Royal Irish Academy* Fasciculi 1-28 (Dublin 1926–70).
SG	K. McCone, D. McManus, C. Ó Háinle, N. Williams and L. Breatnach, *Stair na Gaeilge in Ómós do Pádraig Ó Fiannachta* (Maigh Nuad 1994).
TBC	Ernst Windisch, *Die altirische Heldensage Táin Bó Cúalnge nach dem Buch von Leinster* (Leipzig 1905).
Tecosca Cormaic	Kuno Meyer, *The Instructions of King Cormac mac Airt,* Todd Lecture Series 15 (Dublin 1909).
Thes.	Whitley Stokes and John Strachan, *Thesaurus Palaeohibernicus.* 2 vols (Cambridge 1901–3).
TIG	Whitley Stokes (ed.), 'The Annals of Tigernach (1)', *RC* 16 (1895) 374–419; 'The Annals of Tigernach (2)', *RC* 17 (1896) 6–33, 116–263, 337–420; 'The Annals of Tigernach (3)', *RC* 18 (1897) 9–58, 150–303, 374–91 (reprinted 2 vols, Llannerch, Wales 1993).
Triads	Kuno Meyer, *The Triads of Ireland,* Todd Lecture Series 13 (Dublin 1906).
UR	Liam Breatnach, *Uraicecht na Ríar: the Poetic Grades in Early Irish Law* (Early Irish Law Series 2, Dublin 1987).
YBL	Robert Atkinson, *The Yellow Book of Lecan: a Collection of Pieces (Prose and Verse) in the Irish Language, in Part Compiled at the End of the Fourteenth Century.* Photo-lithographic reproduction (Dublin 1896).
ZCP	*Zeitschrift für celtische Philologie* (Halle, Tübingen, 1897–).

1. Introduction

"Good name in man and woman, dear my lord,
Is the immediate jewel of their souls:
Who steals my purse, steals trash — 'tis something-nothing,
'Twas mine, 'tis his, and has been slave to thousands —
But he that filches from me my good name
Robs me of that which not enriches him
And makes me poor indeed".
(*Othello*, Act III, Scene III).

The importance of reputation in early Ireland is reflected in the concept of *lóg n-enech* 'honour-price'. This established the amount of compensation due to a person in the event of an injury and also acted as a measure of his status in a hierarchical society (Kelly 1988, 8 ff.). Operating within such a society, the poet wielded considerable power through his ability to praise and satirise: just as a person's honour could be enhanced through praise, so his standing in society could be diminished through satire.

The purpose of the present work is to make available a range of material from the Old and Middle Irish periods which gives an overview of the nature and function of satire in early Ireland.[1] The work began as an edition of an Old Irish tract on the classification of satire (beginning *Cis lir fodlai aíre?* 'How many divisions of satire are there?'; hereafter *Fodlai Aíre*) which has been edited in diplomatic form by Meroney (1950, 199–212). In view of the important function of satire as a legal sanction, it was decided to include an edition of the Old Irish heptad on satire. Aside from the *Fodlai Aíre* tract, relatively few satires have been preserved from

[1] Some material, including passages cited in the Introduction and Notes on the editions, has not been translated before. Where previous translations exist, I note only those cases where my translation differs significantly.

the Early Irish period and so it was decided to provide editions of satirical stanzas which are cited as metrical illustrations in a Middle Irish tract on metres known as *Mittelirische Verslehren* III (hereafter *MV* III). This is one of four metrical tracts (Thurneysen 1891, 1-182) which together constitute an important source of information on Old and Middle Irish rhyming syllabic verse.[2] Although the satires are not drawn from a homogeneous text and are cited out of context, they nevertheless provide the modern reader with an insight into the forms and themes of Early Irish satire and the language of invective.[3]

Some of the material edited below has been discussed by Mercier in *The Irish Comic Tradition* (1962, 105-27), a work which provides a useful overview of satire and parody in Ireland ranging from the early period to the works of Swift and Joyce. Several of the satires from *MV* III are cited in the standard works on metrics by Meyer (1909) and Murphy (1961) and a number has also been edited by Meyer with English and German translations (1917 and 1919 respectively). The reader is also referred to important contributions by L. Breatnach (1988, 2004, 2006), McCone (1989), Meroney (1949, 1950, 1953), Ó Cathasaigh (1986) and Robinson (1912).

The book is divided into four chapters. Chapter 1 takes the form of a general overview of legal and literary aspects of satire. Chapter 2 is an edition of the *Fodlai Aíre* tract, including a discussion of the manuscript transmission and an examination of other systems of classification. Chapter 3 is an edition of the Old Irish heptad on satire, accompanied by later glosses and commentary. Chapter 4, which forms the bulk of the work, is a miscellany of eighty-six satirical stanzas extracted from *MV* III. These have been numbered consecutively for ease of reference and have been classified according to subject matter and form as follows:

1) Satires and curses (nos. 1-30).[4]

2) Invectives, which are further classified into four types:

Type A: a series of abusive epithets in the vocative in which the subject is addressed by name (nos. 31-49).

Type B: a series of abusive epithets in the vocative in which the subject remains anonymous or is at most identified with a particular place (nos. 50-6).

[2] For a discussion of the contents of the four tracts see Ó hAodha (1991, 207-10).

[3] Although my aim has been to include all satires in *Mittelirische Verslehren* III, some may have escaped my attention due to the difficult nature of the material.

[4] Nos. 21, 22 and 27 are curses.

Type C: a series of abusive epithets in the nominative in which the subject is named (nos. 57-79).

Type D: a series of abusive epithets in the nominative in which the subject remains anonymous or is at most identified with a particular place (nos. 80-6).

Legal Aspects of Satire

The reciprocal nature of the relationship between the poet and his patron in Early Irish society, whereby the poet received a reward (*dúas*) in exchange for his praise poem (*dúan*), is described by Watkins (1976, 270) as '... a moral and ideological necessity. For only the poet could confer on the patron what he and his culture valued more highly than life itself: imperishable fame...'. The concept is aptly illustrated by the phrase *eochair dúaisi dúana* (Meyer 1908, 270 q. 5): 'the key of recompense is poems'. This relationship existed within the framework of a hierarchical and aristocratic society, where attributes such as nobility, wealth and generosity were highly valued (Kelly 1988, 7-10, 139-40). A ninth-century panegyric in the *Codex Sancti Pauli* addressed to Áed mac Díarmata illustrates the concept of praise in exchange for reward. Here the poet praises his patron's lineage and generosity, stating that *a molad maissiu máenib, lúaidfidir láedib limmsa* (*Thes.* ii, 295 q. 3): 'praising him is more beautiful than treasures, it will be sung in lays by me'. Praise is clearly viewed as being more valuable and enduring than material treasures, since it confirms the patron's status in society. Such a belief is reflected in the well-known assertion by Cú Chulainn that fame and glory are preferable to longevity: *Amra bríg canco rabur acht óenlá ⁊ óenadaig ar bith acht co marat m'airscéla ⁊ m'imthechta dimm ési* 'It is a wonderful thing if I am but one day and one night in the world provided that my fame and my deeds live after me' (C. O'Rahilly 1967, 26 ll. 961-2).[5]

This reciprocal relationship had its negative manifestation in the form of satire, the use of which as a powerful legal sanction on the part of the poets is well documented in the laws and literature. It is stated in the heptads, for example, that a king who tolerates satire forfeits his honour-price and consequently his right to rule: [*A*] *Tait .uii. rig la feine na dligh dire na logh enech ... ri foluing air no aire ...* 'There are seven kings in Irish law who are not entitled to compensation

[5] Ó Cathasaigh (2005, 295 ff.) discusses this statement by Cú Chulainn in the context of the encomiastic tradition as reflected in saga literature.

or honour-price... a king who tolerates satire or satirising' (*CIH* i 14.34-15.3).[6] The laws differentiate between justified and unjustified satire, stating that a person who suffered unjustified satire was entitled to payment of his honour-price as compensation (Kelly 1988, 137-9). They also distinguish between the formal, legal satire of the *fili* 'poet' and that of the *cáinte* 'satirist', who was reviled by both secular and ecclesiastical authorities (McCone 1989, 127-31; 1990, 225-8).

Fear of satire is illustrated by the belief that it was capable of causing physical injury or death and there are numerous references to this effect in the literature and laws of the Old and Middle Irish periods, where metaphors of weapons, lacerating and cutting are frequent. In *Bretha Nemed Toísech*, for example, satire is portrayed as a verbal blade which wounds cheeks: *Ro fóebra fúamann / fó thuinn tethnatar, / ro dúisced fuil / fora grúaide gnúis, / conid fodirc inna rus / ro mbríathraib bíth.* 'Verbal blades have cut beneath his skin, blood has been aroused onto his cheeks [and] face, so that it is evident in his countenance that he has been wounded by words' (L. Breatnach 1998, 42). As noted by Mercier (1962, 107), the modern-day maxim that 'sticks and stones will break my bones but names will never hurt me', often uttered in an attempt to lessen the hurt and embarrassment caused by nicknames or ridicule, would have provided little comfort to the victim of satire in early Ireland. A belief in the power of words to cause actual harm is expressed in the *Collectio Canonum Hibernensis*, where it is stated that false accusations are as dangerous as physical injuries: *Nemo peritorum et prudentium putet, quod minus sit periculum in verbis linguae mentiendo, quam manibus sanguinem effundendo* (Wasserschleben 1885, 68 Cap. 16): 'No wise or learned person would think that there would be less danger in lying by word of mouth than in shedding blood by hand'. The compiler of a passage of legal material on false accusation incorporates a similar citation to emphasise the harm which can be caused by false words: [*N*]*emo peritorum ⁊ prudentium dubitare debet quod sangis efunditur uerbis ⁊ linga sicut ⁊ mainibus cum anmis* [*leg. armis*] *efunndi uidetur .i. ni toimnenn nach neolach combadh lugha do pecad gao i mbriathraib ina todhail ḟola ó laim* 'No wise or learned person should doubt that blood is shed by words and tongue as it is seen to be shed by hands with weapons, i.e. no knowledgeable person thinks that

[6] When quoting from *CIH*, the abbreviations for *dano, no, uero* and *immorro* are expanded silently. Note that two of the Middle Irish satires edited in Chapter 4 below are directed against kings: *Rí Connacht, cenn tamain* 'The king of Connacht, a block-head' no. 68; *Rí Cera, Cú Chonnacht* 'The king of Cera, Cú Chonnacht' no. 71. No. 63 is directed against a king's son: *Mac ríg na nDése* 'The son of the king of the Dési'.

false words are any less of a sin than shedding blood by hand' (*CIH* iv 1383.9-11).[7] Just as the words of a false accusation could cause harmful consequences for the victim, so the words of a satire were believed to be capable of inflicting both physical and social damage.

The poet's power to use satire as a legal sanction is illustrated in a passage in *Bretha Nemed Dédenach*: *Ní roich colainn coimdílsi n-einech. Óenchairde fon Eilg n-áragar. It é ind filid do-bongat cáin n-enech, dáig na crích n-imderg imná bí giall ná comurradas, coro fuiglea cách día giall grúaide frisna fileda ar omun a n-aíre.* 'The body is not as vulnerable as the face/honour. A single treaty is enforced throughout Ireland. It is the poets who enforce the regulation of honour, because of [the existence of] the hostile territories without exchange of hostages and joint citizenship (lit. 'around which there is neither hostage nor joint citizenship'), so that everyone submits to the poets for fear of their satire, having their cheeks/honour as hostage (lit. 'by means of the hostage of his cheek')' (L. Breatnach 2004, 26–7). A similar description of satire as a poet's weapon which was effective beyond the boundaries of the *túath* is found in Middle Irish commentary on *Uraicecht Becc*: ... *is e taidbeas a seodu eigni doib amuig i fail i tincaidter renda aer 7 na tincaidter renda airm* 'it is he who levies the penalty for their forcibly removed chattels for them outside where barbs of satires are responded to and where barbs of weapons are not' (L. Breatnach 1984, 190). Further evidence of the belief in the poet's power to cause harm can be seen in the satires edited in Chapter 4 below, where we find invectives with metrical names such as *bricht nathrach Néde* 'Néde's venomous incantation' no. 46, as well as sentiments such as *ro mela mo mallacht*! 'may my curse grind him!' no. 71. A belief in the power of satire to maim and kill lasted well into the Early Modern Irish period and the Annals of Connacht for the year 1414, for example, record the death of the Lord Lieutenant, John Stanley, as a result of satire. The threat of satire was also used alongside the threat of clerical sanctions to enforce a treaty between Ó Domhnaill of Tír Chonaill and Tadhg Ó Conchobhair concerning Sligo Castle in 1539 (M. Carney 1943, 289; Ó Cathasaigh 1986, 15).[8]

The poet's power was not absolute, however, and the commentary on *Uraicecht Becc* cited above continues with the statement that the lord was

[7] This text consists of Old Irish (and one Latin) extracts with later glosses and commentary (*Companion* 62-3). For the Latin citation see Ó Corráin, Breatnach and Breen (1984, 433 no. 58) and Bracken (1995, 192).

[8] For a discussion of satire in the seventeenth and eighteenth centuries see Ó Briain (2006).

responsible for enforcing the poet's claim for payment in cases where threats of satire were ignored: ... *is e toibdes loigidecht a naisdi doib i fail i tincaiter renda airm 7 na tincaiter renda aeiri* '... it is he who levies the payment of their metres for them where barbs of weapons are responded to and barbs of satire are not' (L. Breatnach 1984, 190). Poets were also obliged to ensure that their compositions were of a high standard in terms of both metre and content, and they could only request the reward appropriate for a particular metre. *Bretha Nemed Dédenach* contains a versified list specifying the appropriate rewards for poems in various types of metres, ranging in value from a grown heifer for a poem composed in *dían* metre to a chariot worth one *cumal* for a composition in *anamain* metre (*CIH* iii 1119.28–32; see Kelly 1988, 45).[9] A Middle Irish poem on different types of metres by Cellach úa Rúanada, who died in 1079, reflects the importance attached to accuracy in poetical compositions: *Casbairdne chass chumaide / is brass ma ros-binnige, / noco chóir a cammḟige / dar cenn n-óir iss indile* (Thurneysen 1912, 77 §12): 'Complex, well-formed *casbairdne*, it is powerful if you harmonise it; it is not proper to construct it falsely for the sake of gold and wealth'. The law tract *Di Astud Chirt ocus Dligid* includes the *fili díupartach* 'fraudulent poet' among a list of *nemed*, or privileged, grades whose status is degraded because of improper behaviour, stating that: *dlegar do cach filid nemdiubairtce aircedail* 'non-fraudulence of composition is due from every poet' (*CIH* i 234.6–7). In the Middle Irish glosses on this section, *fili díupartach* is glossed *.i. fili beires diubairt neich ar ae, ara abairt, ara dan* 'i.e. a poet who defrauds someone by [his] composition, by his utterance, by his poem' (*CIH* i 234.10–11). A version of this passage in the Old Irish introduction to the *Senchas Már* explains *fili díupartach* by the etymological glosses *.i. urain-epertach, beires diubairt .i. adbal-eibertach .i. cuingis ni* 'i.e. excess-speaking, he who makes a supplication, i.e. great-speaking, i.e. he who seeks something' (*CIH* ii 352.21).[10] Commentary on the passage states that the penalty for demanding an excessive reward is the same as that for composing an unlawful satire: *IN fili dano connaig forcraidh a duaisi no agras in mét na dlighinn no doni air nindligthech, is a letheneclann dibhas ime gach ernaile dibh fri cach naon chena coruice in tres fecht, 7 a laneneclann uero on*

[9] A version of this passage is cited in *MV* II §93 (Watkins 1963, 233).

[10] In the etymological gloss, the element *díu-* is glossed by *adbal* 'great' and *airáin* 'excess'. Cf. *athgabail ... im diubud nuire .i. aní ata a n-adbul-tebe na huire* 'Distraint ... concerning the digging of a grave, i.e. that which is in the great cutting of the grave' (*Cethairślicht Athgabálae*, *CIH* v 1698.16, 25). *Urain-epertach* is a standard etymological gloss on *díupart* when used in the contractual sense of over-payment (McLeod 1992, 182 §48).

tres fecht amach 'The poet, moreover, who demands an excessive reward, or who sues for the amount he is not entitled to, or who composes an unlawful satire, it is his half honour-price which each one of those categories diminishes concerning him with respect to each one, moreover, until the third time, and [it is] his full honour-price, truly, from the third time onwards' (*CIH* vi 2091.8–11).

According to *Gúbretha Caratniad*, a poet is not entitled to payment for false praise, since this is equivalent to satire: ... *ar bo molad ngoa fri*[*s*]-*suid aír* 'denn es war ein falsches Lob, das einem Schmählied gleichkam' (Thurneysen 1925, 309 §4).[11] A Middle Irish gloss on the text indicates that false praise could constitute a form of mockery: *.i. mad ar chuitbiud do-gnether, a letheneclann dó ind. 7 cethramthu .uii. cumal, madicain docan– aur– in sin* 'Wenn es zum Spotte gemacht wird, erhält er (der Verspottete) seinen halben Ehrenpreis dafür. Und (er erhält) das Viertel von 7 *cumal*, wenn dieses in der Ferne gesungen wird'.[12] The last few words of the gloss are corrupt, and Thurneysen suggests reading *mad i céin do-cantar* 'if it is from afar that it is recited'. A similar description is found in the heptad on satire: *áer ó bard benar / bís i céin canar* 'A satire which is composed by a bard who is far away and which is recited'; see p. 88 below. A further safeguard against the misuse of satire existed in the form of *trefocul*, a formal warning procedure which poets were expected to follow prior to the composition of a lawful satire. This was a poem of mixed praise and satire, warning the victim of his offence (*UR* 139; L. Breatnach 1988, 17–19; 2004, 25–6). It was also illegal for the poet to satirise someone after his request had been granted, as stated in the fragmentary law tract *Ántéchtae*: *Ni bi aer iar logad .i. ar ni bi aer don fili iar tabairt do loighi a aisti reime, no iarna logad do do neoch logh a aisti* 'There is no satire after conceding, i.e. for there is no satire by the poet after the reward for his poem has already been given to him, or after the reward for his poem has been conceded by someone to him' (*CIH* iv 1238.36–1239.4–5). Praise was believed to negate the ill effects of the satire and so the remedy for unjustified satire was the composition of a palinode or praise poem, as stated in *Bretha Nemed Toísech*: *Do-renar aor a molad, ar as íreiu ro-siad aor oldas an moladh* 'Satire is compensated for by means of praise, for satire reaches further than praise' (*UR* 37 l. 15; see also Watkins 1962, 117 and Kelly 1988, 138).

11 '... for it was false praise which was equivalent to satire'. For an example of false praise (*tár molta*) see *Fodlai Aíre* tract §12.

12 'i.e. if it is for mockery that it is done, his half honour-price [is due] to him in that case: and one quarter of seven *cumals* [is due] if it is from afar that it is recited'.

Literary Satire

There are many accounts in the literature of poets abusing their powers of satire in order to extort gifts or favours from their victims. Aithirne, for example, uses the threat of satire as a means of extorting both wealth and sexual favours in the tales *Tochmarc Luaine ocus Aided Athairne* (L. Breatnach 1980, 12 §14) and *Talland Étair* (Ó Domhnaill 2005, 52; Stokes 1887, 48). The satirist is often portrayed as demanding an object which he knows his victim is forbidden to part with and then using his refusal as an excuse to revile him. This behaviour is reflected in anecdotes concerning Dallán Forgaill, who asks for the brooch or shield of the king Áed mac Ainmire (Stokes 1899, 138; Joynt 1941, ll. 36 ff.), and Néde, who demands the knife of Caíar, the king of Connacht.[13] Similarly, the satirist Redg seeks Cú Chulainn's sword in *Táin Bó Cúalnge* (C. O'Rahilly 1967, ll. 1806–10).

A well-known satire in Early Irish literature is that by Cairpre mac Étaíne against Bres mac Elatha in the saga *Cath Maige Tuired* (Gray 1982, 34 §39), where it is described as the first satire composed in Ireland.[14] Ó Cathasaigh (1986) outlines the similarities between a poet's satire and a saint's curse by comparing this verse with Patrick's cursing of Bécán, recounted in an anecdote in *Acallam na Senórach*. Both satires take the form of a curse or spell incorporating the victim's name and both bring about the deposal of an unrighteous ruler. Other types of satire are illustrated in the *Fodlai Aíre* tract on the divisions of satire, edited in Chapter 2 below. As well as unrhymed forms such as *aisnéis* 'narration' and *ail* 'reproach', this tract identifies ten divisions of versified satire ranging from *mac bronn* 'son of womb', which is performed in secret, to *lánáer* 'full satire', which identifies the victim by name, lineage and abode. Other forms include *dallbach* 'innuendo', *tár n-aíre* 'outrage of satire', *tár molta* 'outrage of praise' and *tamall molta* 'touch of praise', each of which is illustrated by an example. *Bretha Nemed Dédenach* cites two satiric verses to illustrate types of satire known as *áer co ndath molta* 'satire with the colour of praise' and *molad co ndath aíre* 'praise with the colour of satire' (*CIH* iii 1112.13–23).[15]

[13] For the satire composed by Néde see no. 21 below.

[14] See also McCone (1989). Apologues concerning the satires composed against Áed mac Ainmire, Caíar and Bres mac Elatha are also found in a threat of satire by the sixteenth century poet Tadhg (mac Dáire) Mac Bruaideadha (McLaughlin 2005, 39–41).

[15] For the example of *áer co ndath molta* see p. 37. The first two lines of the verse illustrating *molad co ndath aíre* are translated on p. 26.

Despite the many references to satire in the literature and laws, however, the number of examples which have been preserved from the Old and Middle Irish periods is relatively small. This is hardly surprising, since the subject of a satire is unlikely to go to any great lengths to preserve it, unlike the recipient of a praise poem. R. A. Breatnach (1941–42, 242) observes that this is also the case in the Early Modern Irish period and suggests that it is partly due to the fact that satire 'depends for its success on the hearer or reader's being acquainted with the subject and familiar with the circumstances'. The satires from *MV* III edited in Chapter 4 below would have served primarily as illustrative examples of various types of metre and their content may have been of secondary importance to the compiler of the tract and to subsequent scribes. It is fortunate that they have survived, albeit out of context, as they provide the modern reader with a valuable insight into the nature of Early Irish satire and the often difficult and obscure language and imagery of abuse.

Themes in Miscellany of Mediaeval Irish Satires

Many of the satires cited as metrical examples in *MV* III do not ridicule any particular failing, but consist simply of a series of insulting epithets in the nominative or vocative cases and may more properly be termed 'invective'. The *Concise Oxford Dictionary of Literary Terms* defines this as 'the harsh denunciation of some person or thing in abusive speech or writing, usually by a succession of insulting epithets', citing the following example from Shakespeare's *Timon of Athens*: "you most smiling, smooth, detested parasites / courteous destroyers, affable wolves, meek bears / you fools of fortune, trencher friends, time's flies / cap and knee slaves, vapours and minute-jacks" (*Timon of Athens*, act iii scene vi.) Satire, by contrast, ridicules specific characteristics or behaviour, being defined in the *Concise Oxford Dictionary of Literary Terms* s.v. as 'a mode of writing that exposes the failings of individuals, institutions or society to scorn or ridicule'. In the present edition of satires from *MV* III, the invectives have been classified according to whether or not the subject is directly addressed and named and four types have been identified. They constitute a specific genre of satire, the most noteworthy features of which are metrical complexity, the use of unusual and often otherwise poorly attested vocabulary, the absence of finite verbs, the frequent use of animal imagery and the identification of the subject with specific categories of individuals, such as members of low-status occupations or foreigners. They also tend to be of a general nature and seldom convey a single unifying theme or criticise a specific vice.

A number of satires incorporate, or consist entirely of, a series of negative statements, often ridiculing the subject's lack of wealth or talent. The repetition in these verses is formulaic in effect and, like the repetition of the subject's name in both praise poetry and satire, may well be a stylistic device. In the following examples, the similarity between the first lines of nos. 6, 7 and 17 is particularly striking: *Nochon fuil a maín co demin . . . / ní ró a dochur i Maig Femin* no. 6; *Nochon fuil a maín immaig / nochon fuil a maín anonn / nochon fuil a maín anall* no. 7; *Ní fuilet a maíne / nocho mó a-tá a maisse / nocho mór a géire: / nocho déine acht braisse* no. 17; *Nocho mac fir threbair, / nocho thaille i ferunn: / nocho raga im degaid, /nocho raga remum* no. 18; *Nocho gairit a merugud . . . / nochon fúarus a gelugud . . . / nocho chosmail a chlothaige . . .* no. 29; *Nocho Gilla Cellaig etir / nocho cenn for sallaib . . . / nocho finna ar gúaire / cullaig allaid . . . / nocho Gilla Cellaig acaib* no. 64. A similar stylistic device is employed by the sixteenth-century poet Aonghus Ó Dálaigh in a satire against the noble families of Ireland : *Ní raibh lúadh a n-Éirinn air, / 'S ní raibh iomrádh a n-Albain; / do rine mé leas Uí Fhlainn, / Níor bh-fheas é muna n-aorfainn!* 'In Eirinn he was not noticed, Neither was he spoken of in Alba; I have promoted O Flyn's welfare, He would remain unknown had I not satirized him' (O'Donovan 1852, 42).

The attributes which are praised by the panegyric poet are those which are highly esteemed by society, namely wealth and generosity, nobility of birth and physical prowess. Conversely, we find that opposing characteristics such as meanness, low birth, cowardice and physical defects are those ridiculed by the satirist. The Old Irish wisdom text *Tecosca Cormaic* (§32) provides an insight into the characteristics which were deemed to form a *forus cuitbeda* 'basis of mockery'. These include being proud, lazy, feeble, dull, niggardly, timorous and tedious, vices and follies which are well represented in the corpus of satirical material in *MV* III.[16] Black (2001, xxiii) describes the code of satire in 18th century Scottish Gaelic poems as 'reverse imagery', stating that it is '. . . a more or

[16] The metrical tracts *MV* I and II (Thurneysen 1891, 1–66) also contain a number of satires. Four satiric verses cited in *MV* I (§§48–9, 52, 56) have been edited and translated by Ó hAodha (1991, 240 nos. 36–7; 241 no. 40; 242 no. 44 respectively). Six of the illustrative examples cited in *MV* II are satirical: §20 (see no. 3 below); §89 (Meyer 1919, no. 75; see no. 26 below); §103 is also found in *CIH* iii 1112.19–23 (see Dillon 1932, 51); §120 (Meyer 1919, no. 70); §133 is a threat of satire (Meyer 1919, no. 76; McCone 1989, 129–30); §134.

less systematic inversion of praise motifs. Just as the good chief is generous, hospitable and brave, portrayed as a handsome man drinking wine or hunting deer, and likened to an eagle or lion, so the object of satire is mean, inhospitable and cowardly, portrayed as an ugly man eating food or scavaging on a dunghill, and likened to a crawling insect, a toad, a hedgehog, or a smelly burrowing animal such as a badger'. It will be seen that many similar images occur in our poems.

Subjects are criticised for a variety of faults, such as being lazy and incompetent (no. 10). By addressing the victim of no. 28 as *a díultad Día Belltaine* 'you refusal on May Day', the poet apparently satirises the fact that he has failed to carry out certain contractual obligations, since May Day was traditionally the time for entering into contracts (Danaher 1972, 86). This verse is also of interest in that it refers to the testimony of a third party: *Teist do-beir Cú Arad ort / tú labar, olc, / eltaide, etránach!* 'The account which Cú Arad gives of you [is that] you are boastful, wicked, pasty and interfering'. In no. 11, on the other hand, it is merely stated that it was not excessive to satirise the grandson of Conall and the son of Cenn Fáelad since they were guilty of wrongdoing against the son of Dubán. Similarly, the poet states in no. 13 that he has acted reasonably in satirising the grandson of Cú Buide, adding that this is his first time to employ satire. The subject of no. 15 is described as being infested with lice, an image which occurs elsewhere in our poems. Four verses express the wish to cause injury or death. No. 71 states: *Rí Cera, Cú Chonnacht, / ro mela mo mallacht* 'The king of Cera, Cú Chonnacht, may my curse grind him!', while in no. 22 the poet asks: *Cá rét ná teilciub cen terce / do sceirtiud a lecne líath lomda?* 'What thing will I not cast freely in order to peel away his bare, grey cheeks?'. His answer is that he will cast a thorn or a knife at his victim in order to wound him: *Delg scíad nó scían co n-eim chongna, / ic lot ladra Lachtnán!* 'A thorn of a thorn bush or a knife with a handle of horn, wounding Lachtnán's fist!'. No. 21, which is cited in *MV* III in a corrupt and fragmentary form, and no. 27 are curses. Some satires end with a reference in the final lines to a weapon, sharp implement, fire or injury and this may be a deliberate stylistic device: *gebid ina chenn in crann* 'let you assail him with the stick' no. 7; *coro benur air* 'so that I may strike [it] against him' no. 9; *do gelugud galluirge* 'as a result of having been brightened by a foreign club' no. 16; *a chennide chrannáin chrín etir crithre* 'you old wooden helmet among flames' no. 34; *tairnge tarathair i tidle* 'the point of an auger into bunches of corn-stalks' no. 57; *bos fo gerrga nglas* 'a palm under a blue dart' no. 59; *gáe ro chorrmaid tria chrú i cranngail* 'a spear-head which has broken sharply through his wound in a spear-shaft' no. 69; *asa maid carr i mbí fuil!* 'out of which bursts a bloody scab!' no. 79; *gall cen chenn* 'a headless foreigner' no. 81.[17]

As noted earlier, the invectives in *MV* III seldom ridicule a specific vice or failing, the subject in most cases being subjected to a tirade of general abuse with no unifying theme. In some instances, however, a particular theme may be discerned or a reason for satire implied in the course of a stream of insulting epithets. Some examples are *etronn ro memaid* 'we have quarrelled' no. 39, *cella do chobair* 'churches help you' (i.e. you are a beggar) no. 42 and *a glas cam / fo gáir Gall* 'you crooked bolt at the battle-cry of foreigners' (i.e. you are a coward) no. 44.

Meanness and Inhospitality

The panegyric poet often praises his subject's generosity by using imagery and metaphors relating to feasting. The author of *MV* III §28, for example, praises Ethne, the daughter of Domnall, by contrasting her generosity in dispensing mead with her neighbours' meanness (Meyer 1917, 45; 1919 no. 40). Conversely, meanness and a lack of hospitality are common themes in both satiric prose and verse.[18] The author of *MV* I §48 complains that: *Is caingen / bith frisin les n-imdaingen, / ocus gairm neich 'na dorus; / ra-fhromus* 'It is a troublesome business to be at the very solid rampart and to call somebody to the entrance: I have tried it' (Ó hAodha 1991, 240 no. 36). In *MV* II §89, the complaint concerns the meagre rations provided by Crundmáel: *Nīrb ingnad / i tig Chrundmāil cāilfinnach / salann for arān cen imm: / is menand / rosecc feōil a muintire / amal ṡeccas rūsc imm chrann* (Meyer 1919, no. 75): 'It would be no wonder in Crundmáel's house of shaggy wattle-work [to get] salt on bread without butter: it is clear the flesh of his household has dried up as bark dries up around a tree'.[19] In a similar vein, the illustration of *aisnéis* 'narration' in the *Fodlai Aíre* tract (§2) takes the form of a *cáinte*'s reply that he does not require salt for his paltry meal: *ar ním thá ní fora scerter acht ma scerter for mo thengaid irecc. Nícon écen: is coirt cenae* 'for I have not anything on which it may be sprinkled, unless it is sprinkled directly on my tongue. It is not necessary: it's bark already'. Complaints about inhospitality also form the basis of the satires in §§3, 8 and 11 of the tract. Allusions to meanness in the satires in *MV* III include: *díltad dona* 'wretched refusal'

[17] I am grateful to Neil McLeod for drawing this feature to my attention.

[18] For examples in prose tales see *Cath Maige Tuired* (Gray 1982, 34 §39) and *Aislinge Meic Con Glinne* (Jackson 1990, 4 ll. 118 ff.).

[19] A slightly different version of this stanza is cited in *MV* III §192; see no. 26 below.

no. 65; *bert fleda for longabail, linn deidblénach drolmánach* 'a load for a feast [carried] on a bare fork, weak ale on the handles of a vat' no. 67; *Dál re díbe drúth Durlais* 'A tryst with stinginess is the fool of Durlas' no. 73.

Name and Lineage

The hierarchical nature of Early Irish society is reflected in the law tracts, where a clear distinction is drawn between different grades in terms of their contractual capacity, entitlement to sick-maintenance and compensation for injury (Kelly 1988, 7–12). Consequently, the panegyric poet often extols his subject by praising his nobility of birth and lineage, as in a ninth-century panegyric addressed to Áed mac Díarmata: *aue ... na ríg di chlandaib Cualann* 'a descendant ... of the kings of the clans of Cualu' (q. 5); *in gas fine cen dídail* 'the scion of a family without reproach' (q. 6); *di chlaind chéit rig ceit rignae* 'of the children of a hundred kings, of a hundred queens' (q. 7); *drengaitir dreppa dáena* 'fine (genealogical) ladders are climbed' (q. 8) (*Thes.* ii, 295).

Ó hAodha (1991, 230–1 note 82) observes that a number of metrical illustrations in *MV* I which begin with the subject's name also end with the name of one of his ancestors and he suggests that these may be opening verses. The stanzas in question are drawn from panegyric poems and this may have been a device employed by the poet to affirm his patron's lineage and status in society. *MV* I §6, for example, begins with the subject's name and concludes with the name of his father: *Donnchad dia-n-fich domun daigthech; /... comairdirc fri hÉirinn n-ollguirm / ainm maic Domnaill, Donnchad* 'Donnchad through whom a fiery world seethes ... the name of the son of Domnall, Donnchad, is as renowned as great-blue Ireland' (Ó hAodha 1991, 225 no. 1).[20] By contrast, the subjects of the satires in *MV* III are often anonymous, or else there is insufficient information to establish their identities with any degree of certainty. In some instances, of course, this may be due to the fact that the verses have been extracted from longer poems and are cited out of context. A further complication is that it is sometimes difficult to establish whether a name is a genuine personal name, a nickname or simply an adjective. In no. 62 below, for example, I translate *methmac Muiredaig* as 'the degenerate son of Muiredach', whereas Thurneysen (1912, 86) suggests that *meth* could be either a personal name or an adjective. He also suggests (*ibid.*,

[20] For other examples see *ibid.*, 229 no. 10, 230 no. 13, 232 no. 17, 238 no. 32. L. Breatnach (1989, 27 note on §1; 2006, 77) suggests that incorporating the names of the subject's father and grandfather may have been a convention in praise poetry.

86–7) that *lorcán* nos. 8, 19, *máelscolb* no. 43, *thigaill* no. 46 and *mairbthine* no. 55 may be personal names. Other instances where it is difficult to establish the correct form of a personal name, or even to decide if we are dealing with real names or nicknames, are *úa Scélín* no. 33, *Goll Mena* no. 66, and *úa Mesen* no. 70.

There is evidence that the incorporation of the victim's name was an important element in certain types of satire, while in other types he remained anonymous. The *Fodlai Aíre* tract states that *lánáer* 'full satire' must contain the victim's name, as well as information about his lineage and where he lives: *ainm 7 us 7 domgnas* 'name and lineage and abode' (§15). This contrasts with the various types of *dallbach* 'innuendo' illustrated in the tract (§§6–9), the main characteristic of which is anonymity: *ní fess cía dia ndéntar sainriud* 'it is not known for whom exactly it is composed' (§6). The importance of naming the victim is illustrated by an anecdote which recounts how Aithirne was unable to compose a satire against a certain man because he found it impossible to incorporate into his composition the name *Sethor Ethor Othor Sele Dele Dreng Gerce Mec Gerce Ger Ger Dír Dír* (Thurneysen 1918, 398–9).[21] In the case of the invectives from *MV* III edited below, the subject is named in 75% (Types A and C) and is anonymous in 25% (Types B and D).[22] This suggests that naming the victim, either directly or through the use of a nickname, may well have been an important element in this particular type of satire.

In cases where the subjects are identified, they are generally named at the beginning, the exceptions being nos. 7, 41, 43, 46, 60, 61. In six instances, the name is repeated: *Lachtnán* twice (beginning and end) no. 22; *A meic uí Chuinn* twice (beginning of both couplets) no. 42; *Gilla Cellaig* four times (beginning and end of both sections) no. 64; *Dúngal* twice (beginning of both sections) no. 76; *Goll Gabra* twice (beginning of both couplets) no. 77; *Finn* twice (beginning and end) no. 79. Note also the epithet *A drúith na hAlla* no. 53, which is repeated three times. There are three examples of subjects being insulted in terms of their lineage: *a uí airim brocṡalaig* 'you grandson of a ploughman [who is] filthy like a badger' no. 40; *a uí chúic patán pellbuide* 'you descendant of five yellow-furred leverets' no. 52; *mac don gabainn glasléith* 'a son of the wan, grey smith' no. 74.

[21] The passage is also translated by Koch and Carey (1997, 53). For other examples of satires and curses incorporating the victim's name see Ó Cathasaigh (1986, 11–12).

[22] Type A invective (victim named) $^{19}/_{56}$ = 34%; Type B invective (victim anonymous) $^{7}/_{56}$ = 12.5%; Type C invective (victim named) $^{23}/_{56}$ = 41%; Type D invective (victim anonymous) $^{7}/_{56}$ = 12.5%.

Nicknames and Mockery

The *Fodlai Aíre* tract (§3) classifies *lesainm* 'nickname' as a type of *ail* 'reproach', emphasising its permanent nature: *ail lesanmae lenas do neuch* 'the permanence of a nickname which sticks to someone'. The tract cites as an example the nickname *Cell Chorrfesse* 'Church of the Wretched Meal', stating that this was bestowed on the church of Les Mór as a result of its niggardly treatment of guests and that it stuck to it permanently. *Lesainm lenas* 'a nickname which sticks' is one of seven types listed in the heptad on satire, and it was clearly viewed as a serious offence since it entailed the payment of compensation not only to the victim of name-calling, but also to his kinsmen.[23] Since a nickname often alludes to physical defects, it is not surprising to find *lesainm* associated in legal texts and glossaries with types of satire such as *nóad ainme* 'making known a blemish' and *tuba n-ainme* 'taunting with a blemish'. Drawing attention to a person's actual or supposed physical or social shortcomings was also an offence. A citation in *O'Dav.* §1287 defines *nóad* as *.i. athnugud no urdarcugud, ut est noudh ainmhe .i. leasainm* 'i.e. renewing or making conspicuous *ut est* making known a blemish, i.e. nickname'.[24] The connection between nicknames and physical blemishes is further illustrated by the pairing of *tuba n-ainme* and *lesainm* in glosses and commentary. *Cethairṡlicht Athgabálae* classifies *ainmed* 'lampooning' as a *cin tengad* 'an offence of tongue' and it is explained by the glossator as *.i. in tuba nainme no in lesanmad* 'i.e. the taunting with a blemish or the nickname' (*CIH* ii 403.18; 404.3). Commentary on *Bretha Étgid* classifies *air 7 lesainm* 'satire and nickname' as *eitged mbriathar* 'verbal negligence' (*CIH* i 251.22). Glosses on *Bretha Nemed Toísech* allude to the practice of pointing to one's own features in order to mock a defect in someone else's. Here the phrase *ni gonae gruaidhe goaibh anṡoís ná súil na srúbh, ná smech smiotghno* 'You are not to wound cheeks with spears of satire nor eye nor snout nor chin with mimicry' (*CIH* iii 1134.33–4)[25] is glossed as follows: *guilliudh*[26] *.i. ní tharda tú mér for do* (about 8 letters lost) *súil*

[23] Kelly (1988, 137, note 91) suggests that *lesainm lenas* could also be read as *lesainm lénas* 'a nickname which wounds'.

[24] Stokes translates *noudh ainmhe* as 'intensifying a blemish'.

[25] The citation is found in the complete copy of *Bretha Nemed Toísech* at *CIH* vi 2218.27–8. The passage is translated into Modern Irish and discussed by L. Breatnach (1988, 11).

[26] The only example of this word in *DIL* is from *O'Mulc.* §678: *guilliud .i. gosilliud.* Stokes (*ibid.*, 308, s.v. *guilliud*) translates 'mislooking? blinding of an eye?', suggesting that it is derived from *goll .i. caoch.* The gloss *gosilliud,* however, seems to interpret *guilliud* as a compound of *gó–* 'false' and *silliud* 'look, glance'.

nech ele .i. camadh a srubh .i. ní tharda tú mér for do ṡróin más olc srón nech ele (about 11 letters lost) *sibh mér for bhar smech ge ma smiotach smech nech ele .i. ní thugae do laimh ar do* (about 11 letters lost) *dbhidh mása smiotach smech an fir ele. Smit .i. cluas. gnó .i. cuidbhuidh .i. cuidbiodh de* (about 12 letters lost) *aignedh amhail mhaothán a chlúaisi* 'squinting (?), i.e. you are not to bring a finger onto your ... the other person's eye, i.e. a bend in a snout, i.e. you are not to bring a finger onto your nose if the other person's nose is bad (crooked) ... a finger onto your chin if the other person's chin might be broken (?),[27] i.e. you are not to bring your hand onto your ... if the other man's chin is broken (?). *Smit,* i.e. an ear. *Gnó,* i.e. mockery, i.e. mockery ... nature, like the cartilage (tip) of his ear' (*CIH* iii 1135.17–22).

While the text of the glosses is partly illegible, the general sense of mimicry is quite clear. The etymological gloss *smit .i. cluas* and the reference to the cartilage of the ear are of interest in the context of mockery, since an identical gloss is found in *Auraicept na nÉces* in a passage describing a procedure known as *briamon smetrach: Berla na filed so .i. in gne deidinach i*[*s*] *sund .i. bri .i. briathar, mon .i. cleas, 7 smit .i. cluas, 7 forrach .i. rigi: no bri .i. briathar, 7 mon .i. cleas, 7 smetrach .i. smit forrach .i. co forrgidis neach. Cleas bratharda* [recte *briatharda*][28] *sin donidis na filid oc ecnuch .i. smit a cluaisi do gabail ina laimh .i. amal nac*[*h*] *fil cnaim sund ni raib eneach iconti egnaigeas in fili* 'This is the Language of the Poets that is, the last kind here, to wit, *bri,* word; *mon,* feat; and *smit,* ear, and *forrach,* that is stretching; or, *bri,* word, and *mon,* feat, and *smetrach,* that is, ear-lobe compression, that it, that they might injure some one. A verbal trick is that which the poets used to do in satirising, viz., to take the lobe of his ear in his hand, that is, as no bone exists there, the individual whom the poet satirises could have no honour' (*Auraic.* ll. 1328–35).

The process of *briamon smetrach* has been discussed by Hull (1940, 327), who states that: '... the poets of ancient Ireland seem to have

[27] In a passage in *Bretha Déin Chécht* dealing with compensation for wounds to various parts of the body, the adjective *smitach* is used to describe an injury to the chin (*smech*): *IS .u. setaib saidid smech smitaig* 'With five *séoit* one levies [the punishment for] a broken (?) chin'(Binchy 1966, 42 §33). Binchy, op. cit., 63, suggests that *smitach* is related to (Modern Irish) *smioda* 'piece, fragment', although he notes that there are no early attestations of the noun. Neil McLeod has suggested (personal comment) that since the five *séoit* penalty is the standard fine for bloodshed, this points to a cut to the chin rather than a fracture of the lower jaw. For a discussion of this section of *Bretha Déin Chécht* see McLeod (2000b, 388–9).

[28] Calder translates 'brotherly'. The version in the Yellow Book of Lecan contains the superior reading *cleas briatharda* 'a verbal feat' (*Auraic.* 1917, ll. 4646–7).

possessed a *nemthes* or special privilege which enabled them to coerce a person who denied them any request that they might demand by means of a process called *Briamon Smethrach.* This process the poets apparently exercised in the following manner: They grasped the lobe of their ear which they then rubbed between their fingers or pulled, and, at the same time, according to the testimony of Cormac, they regarded the person whom they were seeking to constrain by their malediction ... The act of rubbing the earlap, therefore, might be said to be a strong reproach bordering upon an insult, the evil effects of which the victim could only counteract by granting the demands of the perpetrator'. *Briamon smetrach* is not mentioned in the text of *Bretha Nemed Toísech* itself, however, and it is impossible to establish if there is any connection between this process and the glosses.

Further evidence that mockery was considered to be a serious offence is found in heptad 7, where it is stated that a woman was allowed to divorce her husband if he satirised her and caused her to be mocked: ... *ben fora fuirme a celi tinchur naire co mbi namat fuirre .i. cu mbidh cach ag fanamut fuithe* '... a woman upon whom her husband inflicts the application (?) of a satire so that she is mocked, i.e. so that everyone mocks her' (*CIH* i 47.30).[29] Commentary on *Cáin Íarraith* implies that *tuba n-ainme* and *lesainm* were considered to be as serious as causing a physical injury: *Mic na ngrad feini 7 na ngrad flatha, slan a mbualudh 7 a cainiud, acht narub tubhu nainme no lesainm, no cu ria cneid for corp* 'Sons of the lay grades and of the noble grades, striking them and reviling them is immune from liability, except for taunting with a blemish or a nickname or leaving a wound on the body' (*CIH* v 1761.17–18). The two terms also occur together in commentary on the heptad on satire, where they are listed among five types which entail payment of full honour-price; see gloss 15, p. 92. *Bretha Déin Chécht* states that causing facial disfigurement entails the payment of additional compensation, since the injured person must suffer embarrassment every time attention is drawn to the blemish in public: *Trummu tresa turgabail ... basith cert cumal cach mbel nodifoclatar fib firdal* 'Graver and more violent (?) is the raising [of a blemish in the face?] ... An exact *cumal* from every mouth that publishes it [the blemish] in the presence of an assembly' (Binchy 1966, 40 §31).[30] Similarly,

[29] *Tinchor* is normally used of property brought into a marriage and it is difficult to interpret its meaning in the present context. It may refer to a husband employing someone to satirise his wife.

[30] Cf. also *la cumail cech aonuig. la set cach aidbriuda ima ruide rus* 'together with [further payments of] a *cumal* for every assembly and a *sét* for every advertisement for which [his]

a passage in *Míadślechtae* specifies the penalty for a wound to the face of a bishop and states that a *cumal* is due for drawing attention to this blemish in public: ... *7 adgaire nainme i sochaide co cenn teora mbliadnae o suidhiudh anunn, is cumal ind mana dilge* '... and drawing attention to (?) a blemish in a crowd until the end of three years from then on, a *cumal* is to be paid for it unless he waives it' (*CIH* ii 588.20).[31] A king was expected to be free from blemishes, and any type of physical impairment could result in the loss of sovereignty (Kelly 1988, 19). The tale *Echtra Fergusa maic Léti*, for example, recounts how it was feared that the king would be taunted on account of a facial blemish: ... *arna beth druth na hoinmid ann arna toirbeitis a ainme ina inchaib* '... so that there should be neither fool nor half-wit therein lest these should cast his blemish in the king's face'; ... *dobi a an(a)im fria enechsom* '... she taunted him to his face with his blemish' (Binchy 1952, 38 §§7, 8).[32] An anecdote in the life of Saint Moling includes a stanza which might be described as *tuba n-ainme* 'taunting with a blemish', although it is referred to in the text as *epaid* 'a spell'. After Moling's eye had been injured by a splinter of wood, he met a demon disguised as a student. The demon remarked upon his injury and then recited the following verse, which had the effect of making the blemish worse: *Mol muilind fot súil. craeb cuilind fot súil, / cach imnedh it gruaidh / grip ingnech fot súil* 'A millshaft under thine eye: a holly-branch under thine eye; every trouble in thy cheek; a taloned griffin under thine eye!' (Stokes 1906, 280–1). Charles-Edwards (2000, 25–6) draws attention to the giving of nicknames ridiculing physical defects to rivals in a contest for kingship and notes that: 'If a *forainm* could be made to stick — and here a friendly poet acting as satirist could work wonders — the person's reputation would be fatally besmeared'. On the other hand, a number of kings are described in the annals as *cáech* 'the one-eyed', *dall* 'the blind', *bacach* 'the lame' and *got* 'the stammerer', which suggests that blemishes may not always have been a bar to sovereignty (Jaski 2000, 86).

In *Bretha Nemed Dédenach*, the offence of *epert ainme* 'telling of a blemish' is included alongside satire and taunting in a list of offences which

---

cheek blushes' (*ibid.*, 62 §31). Binchy defines *aidbriud* as 'drawing attention (by a third party) to a blemish which has resulted from a previous injury and thus shaming the victim in public'. Ó Corráin (1984, 164) is of the opinion that this section of text refers to injuries to clerics of high status, noting a parallel passage in the *Canones Hibernenses.* For a discussion of how laughter can function as a form of condemnation in Early Irish literature see O'Leary (1991).

[31] This is based on a passage in the penitentials (Bieler 1963, 170 §3).

[32] See also Charles-Edwards (2000, 106–7).

entail the payment of full honour-price: *Cair cis lir dos-liad* [*leg. do-sliad*] *lánlógh enech lá Féine? áor, eitech, airbhire, liudh gaide gniomh nád áirithe, liudh misgeoil dia rús ruicther, eíbirt ainmhe la feirg*[*leg. feirge*] *foisgiobudh; as-reanar lánlógh enech ainmhe, amhail bidh e rofearadh* 'How many things incur full honour-price in Irish law? Satire, refusal, taunting, an accusation of theft — a deed which is not certain — spreading a defamatory story by which a face is reddened, telling of a defect with receding of anger; full honour-price for the blemish is paid as though it were he (i.e. the person telling) who had caused it' (*CIH* iii 1123.22–4).[33] The passage is cited in a text on false accusation, where the phrase *aibert ainme la ferge foscibadh* is glossed *.i. co scipann a tonn riasan nimderga* 'i.e. so that his wave [of anger] recedes before the shame' (*CIH* iv 1382.37).[34] The gloss suggests that ridiculing or revealing another person's defect could arise as a form of defensive behaviour in the course of an argument or heated exchange.

As well as physical defects, a wide range of personal and social circumstances could give rise to taunting and the calling of nicknames. Commentary on *Cóic Conara Fugill* lists eight 'insulting words' and states that full honour-price is to be paid for taunting someone with these. The lists comprises six physical defects (*claime* 'leprosy', *leime* 'impotence', *buidre* 'deafness', *caíche* 'being one-eyed, blind in one eye', *baccaige* 'lameness' and *talmaidecht* 'epilepsy') and two social conditions (*tuilidecht* 'illegitimacy' and *fuichecht* 'cuckoldry'): *Ocht sarbriathra sár gen meth. / i ndlegur lanlog enech / fuichi do tuba re nech. / do-ní ogul don airech. / Inann leis 's a bheith a cacht. / tuilidecht no talmaidecht / claime lime lathar ngle. / coiche buidhri bacaide* 'Acht Beleidigungsworte — Beleidigung ohne Fehl —, für welche voller Ehrenpreis geschuldet wird: jemand 'Hahnrei' zu schelten, das macht einen Freigeborenen heftig. Es dünkt ihn dasselbe, als wäre er ein Sklave: 'Bastardtum' oder 'Epilepsie', 'Aussatz (Räude)', 'Impotenz' — eine deutliche Absicht —, 'Einäugigkeit (Blindheit)', 'Taubheit', 'Lahmheit'' (Thurneysen

[33] A version cited in a text on false accusation (*CIH* iv 1382.34) reads *aiteach* 'reproach, reviling (?)' instead of *eitech* 'refusal'.

[34] The phrase is given as *aibertar ainme la feirg foscibadh .i. co scipann a tonn rias an iumderga* (preceded by a query) in *DIL* s.v. *scibid* 'moves' (col. 93, l. 43), and the reader is referred to *scipaid* 'snatches, sweeps'. There is no meaning given in *DIL* s.v. *foisgiobudh* and I translate this as 'receding', a meaning which is suggested by the gloss *.i. co scipann.* Stokes (1889, 89 note 3) suggests that the form *foscibset* in the phrase *7 foscibset na tonda for culo* 'and the waves withdrew' seems to be a scribal error for *roscibset*, which is found as a variant. The occurrence of the verbal noun *foisgiobudh* in *Bretha Nemed Dédenach*, however, provides evidence of the existence of such a compound.

1925b, 35 §39).[35] A gloss on this passage is of interest in that it draws a distinction between known and secret defects, stating that only half honour-price is due if the person being insulted is known to suffer from the condition: *Ainme sin na rabadar fair no ce ro batar fair nocon fes a mbeith fair conas foreill triana tuba friss uair nocon fuill acht letheiric a tuba na n-ainme forreilli.* 'Those are blemishes which were not upon him, or even if they were upon him, it was not known that they were upon him until he revealed them through taunting him with them. For there is only half honour-price for taunting with the visible defects'.[36] A similar distinction is made in a text on false accusation: *.i. ainibh sin na fuil ar duine, no ma ta, nochan forreill* 'that is a blemish which is not upon a person, or if it is, it is not visible' (*CIH* iv 1382.38–9).

A distinction between known and unknown defects is also found in a passage dealing with the loss of honour-price which consists of Old Irish citations and Middle Irish commentary. The main factor to be taken into consideration here is whether or not the person responsible for taunting knows that his victim suffers from the defect being ridiculed. If he does not know this for certain, then he must pay a penalty irrespective of whether or not his victim suffers from the condition. If, on the other hand, it is known that the person being taunted suffers from the defect, then the penalty is reduced. This contrasts with the modern-day concept of political correctness, since it would be considered particularly offensive to mock someone who suffered from a physical disability or who was in some way socially disadvantaged. It does, however, agree with the modern law of slander in most jurisdictions, which holds that truth is normally a defence. The passage in question states: *Gach gnim a fuil eneclann .i. tuilidhacht ⁊ futhacht ⁊ claim ⁊ leime ⁊ buidhre ⁊ caiche ⁊ bacaidh ⁊ talmaidhacht, is .uii. cumala smacht cacha hainme (?) dibh do radh fris mana fes a mbeth fair, ce beth gingo beth fair; laneneclann ina .c.cantain, ⁊ letheneclann in[a] hathcantain no dia mbeith a follsaigacht. Ma na lesanmanna .ii. na ferfadar (?)*[37] *.i. brachsuile ⁊ cortighi ⁊ brenanálaigi, is cumal*

[35] 'Eight insulting words — an insult without fail — for which full honour-price is due: to taunt someone with cuckoldry makes the nobleman angry. It is the same to him as being in bondage: illegitimacy or epilepsy, leprosy, impotence — a clear intention — being one-eyed, deaf, lame'. The text is found at *CIH* iii 1031.12–14.

[36] I give the text of the gloss from NLI MS G138 37a1–4; see *Catalogue of Irish Manuscripts in the National Library of Ireland*, Fasc. 4 (Ní Shéaghdha 1977, 84). This is a more faithful copy of *Cóic Conara Fugill* than the copy by Tadhg Ó Neachtain in H 1. 15 (Thurneysen 1925b, 35 §39 gloss 4); see *Companion* 234.

[37] The version in *CIH* iii 1100. 8 reads *na feastar* 'which may not be known'.

smacht a raiti fri nech 7 a laneneclann no[38] *mana festar, cia beth ginco beth; dia festar, is lethcumal 7 cethraime* 'Every deed for which there is honour-price, i.e. [to taunt a person with] illegitimacy and cuckoldry and leprosy and impotence and deafness and being blind in one eye and lameness and epilepsy: seven *cumals* is the penalty for taunting him with each of those blemishes if it is not known that he suffers from them, whether or not he does. There is full honour-price for the first utterance and half honour-price for repetition or if it has become public knowledge. In the case of the other nicknames which are not ... i.e. being squint-eyed (?) and swarthiness and having bad breath, there is a penalty of one *cumal* for taunting someone with these and his full honour-price if it is not known [that he suffers from the condition], whether or not he does. If it is known, the penalty is half a *cumal* and one quarter [honour-price]' (*CIH* iv 1229.34–41).[39]

Claime 'leprosy, scabies' occurs twice in abusive epithets in our poems. The subject of no. 62 is described as *breccar claime i cinn* 'mangy spots on a head', while the victim of no. 77 is described as *tragna co cossaib clama ar cnocán* 'a corncrake with mangy feet on a mound'. Other references to physical appearance include *a mellṡrón mataid* 'you pug-nose of a dog' no. 38, *a bél chaillige caíche* 'you mouth of a one-eyed hag' no. 49 and *a chossa cromma crebair* 'you crooked feet of a woodcock' no. 49.

Evidence of the shame attached to circumstances such as illegitimacy and cuckoldry is found in other sources. *Cáin Ḟuithirbe* states that the measures which a lord may use to avenge attacks upon his honour include *áerailche i ngrúaidib* 'satirical invectives in cheeks', *rád n-ainmech* 'a statement pointing out a blemish' and *immammus cenéoil* 'impugning descent' (L. Breatnach 1986, 39). *Rád n-ainmech* is glossed *.i. leasainm, no 'a tuiliche'* 'i.e. a nickname, or "his bastardy"' (*CIH* iii 764.13). The penalty for accusing someone of being illegitimate is outlined in *Cethairṡlicht Athgabálae*: *athgabail .u.thi ... im guliud mec a orb*[40] *.i. imamus ceneoil do denam de dus in astaibther, no tuillide do rad ris .i. co festar in fir, is airi ata for .u.thi .i. ina rad tuilithe fris, a fis ima fir fa ngo, ar is leth in fir, lan ina go* 'Distraint with a stay of five days ... for the false accusation of a son with regard to his patrimony, i.e. to impugn his descent in order to find out if it will

[38] Binchy, note s, suggests omitting *no*.

[39] Similar passages are found in *CIH* iii 1015.14–21 and 1100.2–10. A citation from *Bretha Nemed Dédenach* (*Cis lir dosli lanlogh enech mo corp*) is written in the margin of the version in *CIH* iii 1015.14 (note h); see p. 19 above. *CIH* 1100.8 reads *brachairecht* instead of *brachsuile* and Binchy, note h, suggests reading *brocairecht*, for which see p. 246 below.

[40] The version in *CIH* v 1695.10 reads *i norbae*.

be substantiated or calling him a bastard, i.e. in order that it might be known if it is true, it is for that reason that it is with a stay of five days, i.e. for calling him a bastard, for knowing if it is true or false, because it is half if it is true, full if it is false' (*CIH* ii 391.29; 391.35–392.1). As in the case of mocking physical defects, the penalty is less serious if the person being reproached is illegitimate. Illegitimacy is also given as an example of an accusation which would be shameful to a cleric: *.i. tuilithe do radh reis, no gait do liu fair* 'i.e. to call him a bastard or to accuse him of theft' (*CIH* iv 1383.1).[41]

An indication of the social stigma caused by cuckoldry is found in a citation in *O'Dav.* §935: *Fuiche .i. on ceo imdergtha aderar, ut est gugairm fuchachta .i. dobeir ceo n-imdergtha fair* '"A cuckold", i.e. from the mist of shaming it is said, *ut est* a false name of cuckoldry, i.e. he puts upon him a mist of shaming'. It is stated in *Tecosca Cormaic* §31 that *sognaid cách co fuichecht* 'Everyone is decorous until he is cuckolded'.[42] According to heptad 49, a cuckold (*fer fuichi*) is disqualified from giving evidence, although this is presumably only in a case involving the man who cuckolded him (*CIH* i 45.1–3; see Kelly 1988, 206). This is also stated in *Aibidil Luigne maic Éremóin*: *écond cach fuithi* (Meyer 1906–07, 228 l. 90): 'every cuckold is legally incompetent'.

Not all nicknames are derogatory, of course, and some simply reflect a person's occupation. *Echuir* 'Key', *Tochur* 'Meeting' and *Teagmong* 'Arrival' are the names of the doorkeepers in *Togail Bruidne Da Derga* (Knott 1936, l. 1344) and these names accurately reflect their role in greeting guests. Other examples of this type of nickname are less flattering, however, as in the case of the names of dispensers given in the *Triads* §231 as *cúacroessach* 'hollow-gulleted' and *bolcśronach brocóiti*. Kelly (1997, 335) translates the latter as 'swollen-nosed bragget-swigger', suggesting (note 141) that the 'implication seems to be that this type of dispenser is helping himself generously to his employer's liquor'.[43]

[41] For a modern example of satirising a person through accusations of illegitimacy or theft see Williams (1980, 61–2).

[42] Meyer translates 'till he commits adultery'. A gloss in 23 N 23 p. 23 suggests that cuckoldry is the intended meaning, however: *.i. soghnaoieach no so-ghnéach cách go dul d'fior eile chúm a mhná* 'i.e. everyone is well-mannered or of good kind (?) until another man goes to his wife'; see O'Don. Supp. *s.v. Fuichecht.*

[43] For other examples of such names see C. Breatnach (1996, 52 §7 and note).

Physical Weakness and Cowardice

Physical prowess and valour are common themes in panegyric poetry, with metaphors of warfare and animal imagery often being used to portray the strength and bravery of the subject. *MV* I §26 describes its subject as *dín slúaig* 'protector of a host', *garg rinn* 'rough spearpoint', *lán fergae* 'fullness of anger' and *fáel crú, cú chúan Nad Corba* 'blood of wolves, the hound of the packs of Nia Coirb' (Ó hAodha 1991, no. 17).[44] Similarly, the subject of *MV* III §103 is addressed as *a rith mara buirb tar brúachaib* 'du Sturz des wilden Meeres über Küsten'[45] (Meyer 1919, no. 29).

In marked contrast, the victim of no. 75 below is described not as a fierce and valorous warrior but as *láech ic íarraid lomma is imme* 'a warrior asking for a sip of milk and butter' and *láir is láech ic léim íar n-escur uirre* 'a mare with a warrior jumping onto her after falling off'. Other references to physical weakness and cowardice include: *Uch, a lorcáin, isat lac!* 'Alas, you little mite, you are weak!' no. 8; *a charpat lenaim liúin* 'you gum of a pathetic child' no. 34; *a drúith chaíl ar clocthaig, / a rann lem sech lecnaib* 'you puny fool on a belfry, you [body-]part softer than cheeks' no. 37; *a lenaim laic: / beca do bossa, / cáela do chossa* 'you weak child, small are your hands, skinny your feet' no. 39; *a chrúachaide lenaim laic* 'you swollen stomach of a weak child' no. 49; *A mír do duine* 'you bit of a man' no. 51; *deidblén ac dul i lluing* 'a weakling going into a ship' no. 61.

Low Status

Many satires allude to the low status of the victim. In no. 1 below, for example, the poet satirises his victim as follows: *Ro-cúala / ní tabair eochu ar dúana; / do-beir a n-í is dúthaig dó — / bó* 'I have heard he does not give horses in exchange for poems; he gives what is natural for him — a cow'. This could be taken to mean simply that he is miserly and does not give due payment for a poem, but only something of lesser value (a cow). A more likely interpretation, however, is that he does not give payment for praise poems simply because he is of low status (a *bóaire*) and therefore unworthy of praise: he gives instead a cow in base clientship to his lord.[46] The subject of no. 20 is described as *inar*

[44] Cf. also *is garg do rinn* 'your spear is fierce' *MV* I §10 (*ibid.*, no. 6) and *A Dorchaidi delbchathaig* 'O Dorchaide of warlike appearance' *MV* I §15 (*ibid.*, no. 10).

[45] 'you rush of the fierce sea across borders'.

[46] A cow was the standard render from the *bóaire* to his lord and Thurneysen has suggested that the name *bóaire* derives from this (Binchy 1979, 77). A similar stanza is found

odar 'a dun-coloured tunic', while the victim of no. 51 is addressed as *a inair uidir* 'you dun-coloured tunic'. This is probably an allusion to their lowly status, since dun-coloured clothing is associated with commoners in Middle Irish commentary on *Cáin Íarraith*: *Etach duibh 7 fubaidhe 7 odhur 7 lachtna do maccaibh na ngradh feine* 'black and yellowish and dun and grey clothing for the sons of freemen' (*CIH* i 82.3–4; see Kelly 1997, 263).[47] The Old Irish text outlines a threefold division: *fo miadh caich étidh a maic ota fear miudbu co righ; étiudh lachtnuidh 7 buidi. 7 dub 7 find do macuibh aithiuch, étiudh dearg 7 glas 7 dond do macuiph airiuch, étiudh corcrudh 7 gorm do macuibh righ* 'his son's clothing is according to each person's rank, from *fer midboth* to king: grey and yellow and black and white clothing for the sons of commoners, red and green and brown for the sons of noblemen, purple and blue for the sons of kings' (*CIH* v 1759.12–3). Such an association may also explain the frequent use of the adjectives *buide* 'yellow' and *odor* 'dun' in our poems.

A common form of insult is to associate the victim with a particular occupation, such as a ploughman, storyteller, jester or musician. In no. 62, for example, the son of Muiredach is satirised by being described as *mesce chírmaire* 'as drunk as a comb-maker (lit. 'drunkenness of a comb-maker)' and *crossán líath ic linn* 'a grey-haired jester at ale'. No. 50 addresses its anonymous victim as *a fetánaig, / a chornaire, a chléraige / ... a scélaige* 'You piper, you horn-player, you wandering musician ... you storyteller'. The subject of no. 82 is described as *muccaid íar maidm a charann* 'a swine-herd with a broken leg'. This is a double insult, since he is portrayed as a person of base status who is also useless because he is unable to perform even the lowly function of herding pigs. In no. 2, the son of Cú Aba is portrayed as being incompetent at everything except the simple and menial tasks of sifting flour and door-keeping. There are also a number of allusions to poverty and scrounging, for example: *a bun fleda ar cúaillib cell* 'you remains of a feast on the stakes of churches' no. 8 and *a chú chlechtas ar cnámaib* 'you hound who is accustomed to bones' no. 35. In no. 48, the subject is described as a vagrant who scrounges around bags and bottles in search of food and drink: *A*

in *MV* I §49: *Trúagán trúag, / nocha tabair do neoch lúag; / do-beir a n-as chumang dó: / bó.* 'Pitiful wretch, he does not give anybody payment (i.e. for a poem); he gives what he can: a cow!' (Ó hAodha 1991, 240 no. 37).

[47] Binchy (1979, 88–9) notes that while the term *Féni* is used in *Críth Gablach* to describe freemen of all ranks, in later tracts it is used specifically of freemen of common rather than noble rank.

phítig phaitig phíanánaig! / A thíagánaig étig aitig úarlámaig! 'You starving fellow, scrounging around bottles and bags! You ugly, case-carrying, cold-handed bag-carrier!' The insulting nature of metaphors and descriptions such as these can be understood in the context of the legal and social status of certain individuals and occupations as outlined in the laws and other sources. The law tract on status, *Uraicecht Becc*, classifies musicians alongside entertainers such as jugglers and jesters, subordinate occupations which had no honour-price in their own right: *Aes ciuil ⁊ airfite olceana monaig ⁊ araidh ⁊ luamain ⁊ comail*[48] *⁊ damai*[49] *⁊ creacoire*[50] *⁊ cleasamnaig ⁊ fuirseoire ⁊ braigeatoire ⁊ fodana olcena is a hinchaib caich oca mbiat no beta hae is as direnaiter nista saire ceana fo leith* 'Musicians and minstrels besides, acrobats and charioteers and steersmen and magicians and [animal] tamers (?) and raconteurs and jugglers and jesters and farters and subordinate professions besides, it is according to the honour of whoever employs them or who owns them that compensation is paid. They do not have separate independent legal status without him' (*CIH* vi 2281.30–7).[51] References to such entertainers in our poems include: *fetánach* 'piper' no. 50; *cornaire* 'horn-player' nos. 50, 52, 63, 78;[52] *crossán* 'jester' nos. 62, 68; *drúth* 'fool' nos. 8, 19, 23, 37, 53, 59, 72, 73, 82, 84, 85; *scélaige* 'storyteller' no. 50.

Drúth 'fool, buffoon' is one of the most common insults, occurring fourteen times as a substantive and once as an adjective. This term is used in the laws in relation to two categories of individuals: a mentally incapacitated person who is held to be legally incompetent and a type of professional entertainer.[53] In the former sense, the introduction to the *Senchas Már* includes the *drúth* among classes of individuals who do not

[48] In a diagram of the *Tech Midchúarda* in the Yellow Book of Lecan (YBL 418a 29), *comail* are placed alongside *faithi* 'seers' and *druide* 'magicians'. In *Uraicecht Becc*, the term is glossed *doniat in cerd comaind* 'who practise magic' (*UR* 140 s.v. *comail*). In *O'Dav.* §457, *Cerd cumainn* glosses *corrguinecht* 'sorcery', for which see p. 36 below. The plural form *certa commain* occurs in *Fled Bricrenn* (LU l. 9007), where it is one of the magic arts attributed to Uath mac Imomain, the other two being the ability to change form and druidry.

[49] *Damai* may contain the agent suffix *-e* (for which see L. Breatnach 1983, 194) attached to the root of 2 *damnaid* 'ties, subdues', in the sense of '[animal] tamer'.

[50] This word has been discussed by Kelly (1986, 185–6; 1988, 64 note 200).

[51] This passage is also found at *CIH* v 1617.11–20. It has also been translated by Mac Neill (1923, 280 §55).

[52] A gloss on the word *daernemid* 'dependent professionals', which is a citation from *Uraicecht Becc*, ranks horn-players alongside *na pipairedha ⁊ na clesamnaigh … ⁊ na cuislennaig* 'the pipers and the jugglers … and the pipers' (*CIH* iii 1108.23–4).

[53] See Smith (1932, 68–72) and Kelly (1988, 65, 92).

have independent legal capacity, such as dependent sons and women,[54] while in the *Triads* §205 and §235 he is grouped together with other legally incompetent people such as the *dásachtach* 'madman'. It is stated in heptad 6 that he is not held directly responsible for causing an injury or offence when someone else incites him: *Fuil fearus druth for cach slan dia laim 7 dia tenga is cach dotanurgair isitren* '[In the case of] a wound which a fool inflicts on someone, there is immunity for his hand and for his tongue. Whoever incites him pays the penalty for it' (*CIH* i 7.11–12).[55] In the sense of professional entertainer, *Miadṡlechta* associates him with the *réim* 'contortionist', one of nine landless grades who have no legal capacity: *Reimm dono .i. fuirseoir no druth; nach fer dobeir remmad fo corp 7 a enech ni dligh dire, uair teit asa richt ar beluib sluagh 7 sochaidhe* 'A contortionist, moreover, i.e. a jester or a fool; any man who brings distortion about his body and his face is not entitled to honour-price, because he goes out of his form before hosts and crowds' (*CIH* ii 585.25). It is often difficult to determine in which sense *drúth* is used in our poems. When the subject of no. 23 is addressed as *A drúith, cid taí dom airbire?* 'You fool, what is wrong with you that you are reproaching me?' it would appear that the poet is accusing him of stupidity. On the other hand, the epithet *drúth uí Domnaill* 'úa Domnaill's fool' no. 84 suggests a professional entertainer, and the subject of this poem is also referred to as *drúth Cille Cerbaill.* In the context of satire, however, the question is hardly of any great relevance, since both meanings would have been found equally insulting. The formula *drúth* qualified by a placename in the genitive occurs five times, while there are three instances of *drúth* qualified by the name of a population group. This would therefore appear to be a stock insult. *Drúth* can also be used as an adjective meaning 'wanton' or 'promiscuous' and occurs three times in this sense in the Early Irish metrical tracts, in all cases referring to women.[56] Other examples in literary and legal contexts suggest that this use of *drúth* generally applied

[54] See Thurneysen (1927, 177 §12). The text is found at *CIH* ii 351.26.

[55] In another version of the text, the phrase *dia tengaid* is glossed *.i. umin aeracus, uair is gnim diaithgina hí* 'i.e. concerning the satirising, for it is a deed of non-restitution' (*CIH* v 1885.26–7). A similar gloss is found in Middle Irish commentary on satire: *se 'ca rada isin ninadh .ii. corob gnim diaithgina in air.* See p. 83 below.

[56] The first example is found in *MV* II §103: *Dub Dúanach / dub drúth chongbálach chúanach* 'Dark[-haired] is Dúanach, dark[-haired], wanton, tenacious, surrounded by companies'. This stanza is also cited in *Bretha Nemed Dédenach* (*CIH* iii 1112.19–23) as an example of *molad co ndath aíre* 'praise with the colour of satire'; see p. 8 above. The other two examples are found in *MV* III: *Ingen drúth borrdúalach* 'a wanton, luxuriant-tressed girl' *MV* III §159; *a ben drúth i ndabaig* 'you wanton woman in a vat', no. 56 below.

to women.[57] *Bretha Nemed Toísech*, for example, warns against accepting the son of a wanton woman (*mac mná drúithe*) into the *íarfine* (*CIH* vi 2230.3–4; see Kelly 1997, 310). The term *báeth* 'foolish' has a similar semantic range.

The *crossán*, who features twice in our poems, is described in *Bretha Nemed Toísech* as engaging in activities similar to those attributed in *Miadślechta* to the *réim* 'contortionist' (Kelly 1988, 64–5). His lack of respectability is reflected in *Uraicecht na Ríar*, which states that seven *cumal*s are due as compensation to an *ollam* whose reciter has been led astray into bad practices (*for drochbésu*), explained in a gloss as *i crosanact no a ngaeid no a mbraeid* 'into buffoonery or stealing or plundering' (*UR* 102 §3 gloss 9). A distinguishing feature of the *crossán* may have been long, shaggy hair, since *Bretha Étgid* states that compensation is to be paid for shaving his head: *eiric giunta co lomad a ciabaib na crosan 7 na scoloc 7 na ningen mael 7 i cathair a ruisc 7 a findfad a malach* 'a fine for clipping with shaving for the locks of the jesters and the scholars and the crop-headed virgins and for their eyelashes and their eyebrows' (*CIH* i 304.11).[58] The tale *Séanadh Saighre* (Harrison 1984, 142) also contains a description of *nónbhar crosán ciabhach círdhubh* 'nine shaggy, jet-black *crosáin*' singing at a grave-side.[59] A reference to the *crossán*'s head-dress is found in a Middle Irish poem on the joints of meat appropriate for specific grades: *A cruachait do crosanaibh / ma cennaib coirigtir* 'Its rump to jesters, they are got up with head-dress(?)' (O'Sullivan 1968, 120 q. 3). This could also be translated as 'around whose heads it (i.e. hair) is arranged'. It is interesting to note that the subject of no. 62 below is described as a *crossán líath* 'a grey-haired jester'.

As regards the other occupations referred to, the subject of no. 2 is described as being incompetent at doorkeeping, a task which was normally carried out by a servant (Kelly 1988, 66 note 215).[60] Similarly, in describing the subject of no. 25 as *fer ara tabar / tírad ocus bró ocus críathar*

[57] For a discussion of the relationship between foolishness and lust see Clancy (1993, 106 ff.).

[58] This passage has also been translated and discussed by Mac Cana (2002, 221).

[59] For other references to the *crossán* see Harrison (1989, 104 ff.) Harrison (1984, 138; 1989, 61) states that *scurra* is the Latin word used most frequently to gloss *crossán*. This observation, however, appears to be based on a single instance of *crossán* glossing *scurra* (*hic scurra .i. crosan*), not vice versa (Stokes 1860, 4.14; 1893, 65). I have found no instances of *scurra* glossing *drúth*, *pace* Harrison (1989, 26).

[60] The doorkeeper (*dorsaid*) sometimes performs an important role in sagas, however. In *Cath Maige Tuired*, for example, the doorkeeper Camall mac Ríagail has the authority to question Lug about his various arts and skills (Gray 1982, 38 §53 ff.).

/ *ocus fuine ocus imḟuine* 'a man to whom is assigned drying and a quern and a riddle and baking and cooking' the poet associates him with menial tasks, some of which were performed by female slaves (Kelly 1997, 439). The simile *mesce chírmaire* 'as drunk as a comb-maker' no. 62 can be understood in terms of the low status of the comb-maker, who is classified in *Uraicecht Becc* along with the *tornaire* 'turner', *nascaire* 'ring-maker' and *cairem* 'leather-worker' as having the same legal status as a *fer midboth* (*CIH* vi 2281.1–3).[61] There are two references in our poems to the *gobae* 'blacksmith', who was of relatively high status. According to *Uraicecht Becc* (*CIH* vi 2277.40) and *Bretha Nemed Toísech* (L. Breatnach 1989b, 19 §18 and note), his honour-price was seven *séts*, which was the same as that of the *aire désa*, the lowest of the noble grades. Kelly (1988, 62–3) notes that the esteem in which he was held may be due to the importance of his trade in manufacturing weapons and agricultural implements. All references to the blacksmith in the Early Irish metrical tracts occur in satires, however, and allude to various aspects of his appearance. *MV* II §120 describes a blacksmith's daughter as *gnūis roglasse is rodergga* (Meyer 1919, no. 70): 'face of great paleness and of great redness'. In no. 74 below, the victim is described as *mac don gabainn glasléith* 'a son of the wan, grey smith', while in no. 33, the subject is addressed as *a ḟolt gobann gatbéimnig* 'you hair of a withe-striking smith'.

Poets

As outlined earlier, the work of the professional poet was expected to be of a high standard both in terms of metrical form and content. Given the hierarchical nature of the poetic establishment, one might expect critical exchanges between poets in much the same way as between members of modern-day professions and it is not inconceivable that some of the satires in *MV* III may have been composed in the context of such exchanges.[62] Some allusions to poets, poetry and learning are: *A Éirennaig / do drochrannaib is lomnán dorn* 'O Irishman whose fist is full of bad verses' no. 4; *Nochon ḟuil a maín co demin / amail do-gní dúana* 'His worth does not exist, indeed, in the way that he composes poems'

[61] For the low status of the *fer midboth* see Kelly (1988, 82). The *círmaire* is also described in an unflattering light in the *Triads* (Kelly *ibid.*, 63). Note also the curse *Nī raib uáid acht cairem 7 cirmaire nó nech bed fíu īad* 'May none spring from him but shoe-makers and comb-makers, or people of that kind!' (Meyer 1911, 66 §63).

[62] For an Early Modern Irish example of a poet criticizing another poet's work see Greene (1968).

no. 6; *a gerrfile* 'you stunted poet' no. 34; *a thenga thamain* 'you tongue of a *taman*' no. 42; *a drochfir dána* 'you bad poet' no. 47; *nír lessaigis in saíthe* 'you have not benefited learning' no. 49; *cáinte búaile* 'a satirist of the cowshed' no. 67; *felcháinte fir* 'an evil satirist' no. 80; *cáinte cam* 'a crooked satirist' no. 81.

It is significant that the two poetic grades mentioned above are the *cáinte* 'satirist' and the *taman*,[63] both of whom were of low status. *Bretha Nemed Toísech* states that a defining characteristic of the *cáinte* is his use of the threat of satire for extortion: *Aile bruth narmach, ailges do ceanduibh co nimderctar gruaide, combruth for bla nemtiger cainte* '"I demand the metal of armed men" — an instant demand so that cheeks are reddened, with a red glow [of shame] succeeding (i.e. replacing) renown — is what distinguishes a satirist' (*CIH* vi 2219.32–3).[64] *Uraicecht na Ríar* lists the three poetic sub-grades as *taman, drisiuc* and *oblaire*, stating of the *taman* that *canaid tres for cách* 'he assaults everyone with his recitations' and describing him in a gloss as *.i. creat chuaine ina filed in so* i.e. 'this is the dog's-body of the poets' (*UR* 112 §18). The *taman* was not universally condemned, however, as indicated by a passage in *Bretha Nemed Dédenach* which classifies him as a type of bard and states that he was capable of attaining noble status (that of an *aire tuíseo*) based on his compositions (*UR* 55 ll. 11–12). Clerical disapproval of the *cáinte*, as well as of the lower poetical grades and entertainers in general, has been discussed by McCone (1989, 127 ff.; 1990, 220–6), who draws attention to the propensity of grades such as the *taman* and *drisiuc* to use the threat of satire as a means of extortion. In the light of such clerical condemnation, it is interesting to note in religious sources the grouping together and denouncing of some of the categories of poets and entertainers mentioned in our poems. The Middle Irish poem *Ochtfoclach Choluim Chille* (Quin 1981) includes among those who will perish in hell *bancháinte* 'female satirists', *mná drútha* 'wanton women', *drúith* 'fools', *drochcáinte* 'bad satirists', *círmaire* 'comb-makers', *crossána* 'jesters', *clíara ciúil* 'musicians' and *cornaire* 'horn-players' (Quin 1981, qq. 41, 42, 44 and 46). The *drúth, cáinte* and *crossán* are also listed alongside harlots, heretics, gluttons and parricides as sinners who will be cast down to hell on Doomsday (Stokes 1907, 318 §30). Nagy (1999, 123–5) notes the occurrence of *cáinte, drúth* and *cléir áesa ceirdd/dána* 'bands of poets/craftsmen' among a number of Irish terms found as equivalents of Latin *preco* and portrayed in a negative light

63 *Taman* may, of course, be used here in the sense of 'blockhead'; see note on no. 42 below.

64 I am grateful to Liam Breatnach for this reference and translation.

in Irish lives of saints, while *gobae, drúth* and *cáinte* are also grouped together in a tract dealing with the observance of Sunday (O'Keeffe 1905, 208 §31).

Clerics

There are several references to clerics and churches. In no. 12, a priest's son is castigated for casting out his congregation, who are described as *sámud ara snáidther durthach* 'a congregation from which a church is protected'. Other examples include: *a scol chille cinn ar chinn ... a chorann maccléirig minn* 'you clerical school at odds ... you tonsure of a clerical student of relics' no. 33; *a thonn do cheólaib cléirig* 'you outpouring of melodies of a cleric' no. 35; *láir cháel chlérech ar cúairt chros* 'a clerics' scrawny mare on a circuit of crosses' no. 59; *athchaillech ic imthecht idraid otraig* 'an ex-nun going around cow-pats' no. 76; *sacairt ṡenóir ac súathad* 'an old priest kneading' no. 82. There are also references to meanness and inhospitality on the part of clerics and churches, as in no. 14, where the poet states that a church does not live up to its reputation for generosity.

The church was obliged to provide hospitality, as stated in heptad 1: *Tait .vii. cella la feine na dlegad dire na dicubus ceall o neitcither cach richt* ... 'There are seven churches in Irish law which are not entitled to penalty or penance-fine: a church from which every person is rejected ...' (L. Breatnach 1989b, 31 §6; see also Kelly 1988, 139–40). *Bretha Nemed Toísech* includes inhospitality among a list of circumstances which debase a church: *Coteat mífolad dóertho ecalso? Ní hansae: buith cen bathais, cen chomnai, cen oifrend, cen immon n-anmae ... esáin oíged úaidi* 'What are the disqualifications debasing a church? It is not difficult: being without baptism, without communion, without mass, without praying for the dead ... driving guests away from it ...' (L. Breatnach 1989b, 10 §6; see also Etchingham 1999, 75). The subject of no. 42 is satirised by being portrayed as relying on such charity: *cella do chobair* 'churches help you'. This may also be the intention behind the nickname *Cú na Cell* 'Hound of the Churches' no. 7. Also of interest in this regard are the examples of *dallbach tréntuinidi* and *tamall aíre* cited in the *Fodlai Aíre* tract on satire (§§7, 13), in which poets complain that they have not received hospitality at the churches of Clonard and Cell Aithcherda.

Women

Just as the use of insulting metaphors involving professions of low status reflects the aristocratic nature of Early Irish society, so the use of feminine imagery as part of the code of invective can be understood in the context of the patriarchial nature of that society. The law tracts provide us with information on the limited legal capacity of women, who are classified alongside children, lunatics and slaves as being *éconn* 'legally incompetent' (Kelly 1988, 68–79). An extended diatribe against women in *Tecosca Cormaic* §16 describes them as lewd, lazy, quarrelsome and crabbed, advising that *ferr a flescad a fóenblegon* 'it is better to whip them than to humour them'. The images of women in our poems are equally unflattering, emphasising characteristics such as wantonness and loquaciousness: *a bél mná uidre uime ibraide* 'you mouth of a sallow, crude, yew-like woman' no. 52; *a ben drúth i ndabaig* ' you wanton woman in a vat' no. 56; *ben chamlámach chomdálach* 'a crooked-handed, gregarious woman' no. 67; *ben ic coistecht ri toirm tuinne* 'a woman listening to the sound of a wave' no. 75.

Foreigners

A fear of 'otherness', often expressed as a form of racism, is reflected in the literature of many societies. In an analysis of Greek tragedy of the fifth century BC, for example, Hall (1989, 103) discusses the growth of Greek self-definition through the development of the concept of the barbarian and the portrayal of the other, inferior world beyond the Greek states. The literature of this period portrays Thracians as boors, Egyptians as charlatans and Phrygians as effeminate cowards. Hall argues that: 'in the case of ethnic stereotypes, the character traits imputed to other ethnic groups are usually a simple projection of those considered undesirable in the culture producing the stereotypes'.[65] In Irish literature, we find examples of stereotyping according to both social class and race in texts such as *Párliament na mBan* (Ó Cuív 1952) and *Pairlement Chloinne Tomáis* (Willliams 1981), which ridicules both the manners and appearance of settlers and of the Irish who copy them. In addressing

[65] I am grateful to Gráinne McLaughlin for this reference.

the subject of no. 73 as *Gúaire na ngallbróc, gáire gaill* 'Gúaire of the foreign shoes, a foreigner's laughter', the poet likewise mocks an attempt at imitating foreigners by adopting their custom of dress.[66]

The Early Irish metrical tracts contain references to foreigners in various contexts such as praise, satire and occasional poems, and the term *gall* in some of these instances may refer to Viking settlers. It is stated in *MV* II §128, for example, that: *rofersat Gaill grafainn fornn / atbath ar tonn indmais* 'the Norse have won the race on us, our wave of wealth has perished' (Meyer 1917, 43), while no. 44 below describes its subject as *a glas cam / fo gáir gall* 'you crooked bolt at the battle-cry of foreigners'.[67] Evidence from literary and annalistic sources suggests that the Vikings quickly became integrated into Irish society in both economic and military roles and the term *Gall-Goídil*, used to describe descendants of mixed Irish and Norse ancestry, indicates that there were marital as well as political and economic alliances between the two communities (Ó Cuív 1988, 85–6). On the other hand, a number of contemptuous references to the speech of the Vikings and the *Gall-Goídil* indicate that they continued to be viewed as a group apart from the rest of society. One such reference is found in the Middle Irish text *Airec Menman Uraird maic Coise*, which includes in a list of useless undertakings the phrase *gíc-goc Gallgaidhel* (Byrne 1908, 72. l. 6). This has been explained by Marstrander (1915–16, 383) as representing the stammering speech of the *Gall-Goídil*. The adjective *got* 'stammering, lisping' is also used contemptuously to describe the speech of foreigners in general, and particularly of Vikings.[68] This may be the intention behind a number of phrases in our poems which refer specifically to the speech or mouths of foreigners: *Mac ro boí oc gaillsig goit grúcbuirr* 'a son whom a stammering, surly, puffed-up foreign woman had' no. 5; *bél gaill gopluim* 'the mouth of a bare-mouthed foreigner' no. 69; *bérla in lomgaill* 'speech of the naked foreigner' and *mant in mergaill* 'jaw of the deranged foreigner' no. 84.

[66] For similar complaints in seventeenth and eighteenth century satires see Ó Briain (2006, 127–30).

[67] Meyer (1919, no. 61) translates *Gall* in this stanza as 'der Wikinger'.

[68] Cf. *a rí Gáedel is Gall ṅgot* 'O King of the Gaels and of the stammering foreigners' (Hayden 1912, 268 §43) and *coniuratar guit báin* 'Fair stammerers will be slain' (Stokes 1905, 46 §247). Stokes suggests, *ibid.* note 8, that this may refer to 'the fair-haired Norsemen'.

Animal Imagery

In descriptions of warriors and kings from the Old to the Classical Modern Irish periods, individuals are likened to real animals such as the bear, lion and serpent and mythological creatures such as the dragon and griffin. These creatures have connotations of strength and fierceness and are therefore suitable metaphors for describing heroes and warriors.[69] Some examples from verse are *leo níthach* (Meyer 1913, 17 q. 2): 'a warlike lion',[70] and *Eochu, art / are-chridethar cathroí* 'Eochu, a bear who hugs the battlefield' (Carney 1989, 51).[71] In her lament at their death, Deirdre describes the sons of Uisnech as *trí léomhain* 'three lions', *trí dreagain* 'three dragons', *trí seabhaic* 'three hawks' and *trí beithreacha beódha* 'three vigorous bears' (Mac Giolla Léith 1992, 134 ll. 772–85). Similar imagery is found in a number of praise poems in the Early Irish metrical tracts, for example: *drecon bruthmar brūithe elta* (Meyer 1919, no. 13): 'fierce dragon who crushes herds' *MV* 11 §4; *bēimm dobeir nathair do neoch* (Meyer 1919, no. 48): 'sting such as an adder imparts to all' *MV* III §48; *grīb gēratta* (Meyer 1919, no. 23): 'heroic griffin' *MV* III §29.

Animal imagery is a particularly striking feature of the satires in *MV* III. It will be seen, however, that common farmyard and wild animals and birds are employed here, in contrast to the more exotic creatures which feature in panegyric poetry. No. 58 is typical in its metaphorical use of domesticated animals: *Muiredach, mant capaill chróin, / cú dar céisib, / carpat bó bricce for benn, / bél daim dona Déssib* 'Muiredach, the jaw of a reddish-brown horse, a hound mounting piglets, the gum of a speckled cow on a prong, ox-mouth from the Dési.' Personal characteristics are sometimes described in terms of animal imagery: *gúaille cranda cailig* 'stiff shoulders of a cockerel' no. 22; *do gop gercaide* 'your grouse-like snout' no. 28; *a melṡrón mataid* 'you pug-nose of a dog' no. 38; *a ṡailchide ṡinnchaide ṡalachluim* 'you dirty one, fox-like, filthy and naked' no. 55; *gnúis ḟiaich* 'a raven's face' no. 59; *guth senchon ar slabraid* 'the voice of an old hound on a chain' no. 69; *gédglac* 'goose-handed' no. 70.

[69] For examples in Welsh and Irish poetry see Sims-Williams (1984, 190–2).

[70] Cf. also *leo Lorcc* (Meyer 1913, 28 q. 21); *leō Liphi* (Meyer 1919, no. 111). Examples of the subject being compared to a dragon (*draic, drecon*) are: *fri drauc Fīachaich* (Meyer 1914, 16 l. 7); *drauc Domplēn* (Meyer 1914, 18 q. 2); *Māir drecain dā Ēnna* (Meyer 1914, 19 l. 18).

[71] This verse has also been edited by Meyer (1914, 22 q. 1). Other references to bears are: *brīg bethri* (Meyer 1913, 42 q. 40); *bethir borb* (Meyer 1913, 18 q. 17); *tond mairnech mathrúamdae* (*LU* 8684, *rosc* passage in *Fled Bricrenn*); *bruth matho* (*LU* 8689, *rosc* passage in *Fled Bricrenn*).

Leach (1964, 28–9) identifies three categories of obscenities: (1) vulgar words, usually referring to sex[72] and excretion; (2) blasphemy and profanity; (3) animal abuse, in which a human being is equated with an animal of another species. While the first two categories are easily understood, Leach observes that animal abuse is much less easily accounted for and poses the question: 'Why should expressions like "you son of a bitch" or "you swine" carry the connotations that they do, when "you son of a kangaroo" and "you polar bear" have no meaning whatever?' He concludes that various categories of animals are used metaphorically to describe human characteristics, or as obscene euphemisms in invective, according to their relationship to man in terms of physical proximity, social value and edibility. He also notes (*ibid.* 47 ff.) that familiar animals such as bitch, cat, pig, swine, ass, goat and cur are often used in an insulting sense to describe human characteristics. Among the animals which feature in our poems are *cú* 'hound, wolf', *láir* 'mare', *bó* 'cow', *clíabach* 'deer' (?), *gabar/boc* 'goat', *broc* 'badger', *dam* 'ox', *orc/céis* 'piglet', *airech* 'pack-horse', *catt* 'cat' and *cáera* 'sheep'. In a discussion of the code of invective employed by the bards of the Clan Donald of Scotland and the *filí* of south-east Ulster during the seventeenth and eighteenth centuries, McCaughey (1989, 110) observes that satires from this period make frequent use of animal invective, occasionally with overtones of sex and excrement. It is noteworthy in this respect that animal invective in our poems is also sometimes combined with similar imagery: *a reithi folta fásaig dar fíad* 'you moulting desert ram mounting deer' no. 36; *a chacc cuirre uidre ittige* 'you shit of a brown wingy heron' no. 43; *cú dar céisib* 'a hound mounting piglets' no. 58; *Goll Mena mún cromgabair* 'Goll of Men, piss of a crooked goat' no. 67; *sceith bruic ar beraib* 'a badger's vomit on spears' no. 72.

The law tracts provide information on the value of certain animals which can help the modern reader to interpret some of the insults involving animal imagery. In no. 31, for example, the subject is addressed as *a cholpthach i cennach ndaim* 'you heifer for the price of an ox'. Middle Irish commentary on animal values (Kelly 1997, 62) states that a *colpthach* 'two-year-old heifer' is worth 8 scruples, while it is stated in *Sanas Cormaic* that

[72] It is difficult to establish the extent of sexual imagery in our poems as a full survey of this topic has yet to be carried out and the modern reader may see obscenity and *double entendre* where none was originally intended. For examples of sexual imagery in the Early Modern Irish tale *Ceasacht Inghine Guile* see C. Breatnach (2000). For examples of sexual imagery in 18th century Scottish Gaelic verse see Black (2001, nos. 30, 36, 48) and for a discussion of poems in praise of sexual organs see Arbuthnot (2002).

an ox which pulled the plough could reach the same value as a milch cow, which had a maximum value of 24 scruples (*Corm.* Y §209; Kelly 1997, 64–5).[73] In view of this, we might interpret the phrase 'you heifer for the price of an ox' as being used in the sense of an unequal bargain, since the ox was potentially much more valuable than the heifer. A similar idea is expressed by metaphors such as *a chuing ar argat* 'you yoke in exchange for silver' no. 34, *a dúan ar airech n-ellaig* 'you poem in exchange for a loaded pack-horse' no. 35 and *arcat ar lín* 'silver in exchange for linen' no. 75. In describing the victim of no. 62 as *screpall ar feóil n-aige* 'a scruple for the meat of a bullock', the poet equates him with the beast of lowest value, the *dartaid* in its first year of life, whose flesh was worth only one scruple (McLeod 1987, 99).

Cú 'hound' is a common laudatory epithet used of nobles and heroes and we have evidence from legal sources that hounds such as guard-dogs and hunting-dogs were highly trained and valued animals (Kelly 1997, 114–20). On the other hand, we find the hound's negative characteristics employed as insulting epithets in satire: *a chú chlechtas ar cnámaib* 'you hound who is accustomed to bones' no. 35, *a fíacla con ar cloich aílig* 'you hound's teeth on a dung-covered stone' no. 41 and *guth senchon ar slabraid* 'the voice of an old hound on a chain' no. 69.[74] In *Aislinge Meic Conglinne,* the monks of Cork are insulted in a similar fashion by being addressed as *a matadu ⁊ a latrannu ⁊ a c[h]onu cacca* (Jackson 1990, ll. 269–70): 'you curs and robbers and dung-hounds'.

There are many references to animals which were considered filthy or which were of relatively little worth, for example: *cáinte búaile ic brocairecht* 'a satirist of the cow-shed acting like a badger' no. 67; *mennán oc deól gabair gaite* 'a kid suckling a stolen goat' no. 77; *brénulcha buic* 'the stinking beard of a buck-goat' no. 86. Subjects are also described as being infested with lice: *A-táit sneda cona clainn / it chorainn. / A-táit na míla co mer ...* 'There are nits with their offspring in your tonsure. The lice are in a frenzy ... ' no. 15; *A brollach snedach srethfíar* 'you nitty, crooked-striped chest' no. 41; *ima agaid séolanart co snedaib* 'a nitty bed-cloth around his face' no. 72.

There are three references to fish: *a iuchra maigre a Mumain* 'you salmon spawn from Munster' no. 31; *a scatán demnaide* 'you devilish herring' no. 52; ... *ic teiched breccóice* '... fleeing from a little trout' no. 54. The category of birds is more numerous and includes farmyard birds

[73] For cattle prices and units of value see Kelly (1997, 587–99).

[74] Cf. also the nickname *Cú na Cell* no. 7 below.

such as *cailech* 'cockerel', *gaillín* 'capon', *cerc* 'hen', *géd* 'goose' and wild birds such as *fíach* 'raven', *corr* 'heron', *tragna* 'corncrake' and *crebar* 'woodcock'. The heron and corncrake often have negative associations in the literature and the triad of corncrake, nettles and elder is associated with barrenness in *Cáin Adamnáin*: ... *comad hē a comarbpa trom 7 nenaid 7 traghnae* ' ... so that his heirs are elder and nettle and the corncrake' (Meyer 1905b, §23; 13 note 3). These also appear as the three signs of an accursed site in the *Triads* §129: *Trí comartha láthraig mallachtan: tromm, tradna, nenaid* 'Three tokens of a cursed site: elder, a corncrake, nettles'. The heron is likewise portrayed in a negative or sinister light. There is evidence in legal sources that it was sometimes kept as a pet (Kelly 1997, 125–9) and its territorial nature suggests that it may have been vicious and prone to chase other farmyard animals and people. This characteristic may explain the description of the subject of no. 8 as being chased by a heron and a cat: *A chos dlochtáin ria catt, ocus corr dlúith ina díaid* 'You stem of a little bunch in front of a cat, with a heron close behind it'. The use of *corr* in the context of satire is particularly interesting in view of the heron's association with a type of magic known as *corrguinecht*.[75] Its solitary and unfriendly nature is portrayed in a Scottish Gaelic verse which contrasts the heron unfavourably with the friendly and gregarious wren: *Aon eun aig a' chorr / Is e gu doitheamh doirbh* 'the heron has a single chick which is surly and unpleasant' (Ó Cuív 1980–81, 63). A further negative aspect is reflected in its association with the satirist Athairne, who obtained the three herons of refusal and inhospitality (*corra diultada 7 doichle*) in order to drive guests away from his house (Thurneysen 1918, 398–9).[76]

Evidence from other sources indicates that animal imagery formed an important part of the code of invective at all periods of the language. A quatrain cited in *Bretha Nemed Dédenach* illustrates a type of satire known as *áer co ndath molta* 'satire with the colour of praise'. This is similar in form to the invectives classified in the present work as Type C[77] and

[75] Kelly (1997, 128) suggests that a description of the performance of a satire in *O'Dav.* §383 (*beith for leth-cois 7 for leth-laimh 7 for leth-suil* 'standing on one leg, with one arm outstretched and with one eye shut') refers to the imitation of the one-legged stance of the heron for magical purposes. *Corrguinecht* is listed as one of seven things which constitute a satire in *UR* (114 §24 and note). See also Borsje (2002, 92–6).

[76] The passage is translated by Koch and Carey (1997, 53). Three herons perform a similar function in the Early Modern Irish tale *Ceasacht Inghine Guile* (C. Breatnach 1996, 53 §7).

[77] The subject is named in the course of a series of abusive epithets in the nominative; see p. 3 above.

describes its victim as a periwinkle or sea-snail: *Caimper io(mgon)a im comhlaidh a thighe / imsging imbi conair cham. / faochain do ceil lermhuighe lind, / as goin do dhealg droighin Flann* 'A champion of battling at the door of his house, an enclosure in which there is a crooked road, a periwinkle who conceals the water of the sea-plain, a wound from the thorn of a blackthorn is Flann' (*CIH* iii 1112.14–17).[78] In the Middle Irish tale *Tromdám Guaire,* the poets Dallán Forgaill and Senchán Torpéist compose satires which resemble the invectives in *MV* III in both form and content. In the satire by Senchán, for example, the subject is described by a series of insulting epithets, including animal imagery, and his name is repeated, as is the case in several of our poems: *Hirusan atach n-ingne; fuighiull dhoibri; erball bo buach; ara fri haraidh; atach fria Hir[usan]* (Joynt 1941, l. 735): 'Hirusan, pleading of nails, remnant of a badger, tail of a cow in heat, charioteer against charioteer, pleading against Hirusan' (Carney 1955, 175).[79] It is noteworthy that Dallán and Senchán have to explain the meaning of their satires since they are unintelligible to their intended victims.[80]

As regards the later period, O'Sullivan (1987, xix) suggests that the poem beginning '*Truagh truagh an mhuc*' (Quin, 1965), which was interpreted by its editor as an unusual elegy on a dead pig, may have been composed at the beginning of the sixteenth century as a satire against a member of the Purcell family. She notes that the name Purcell is derived from *porcellus*, the Latin word for 'piglet', and that the family's coat of arms features a boar, sow and piglets. Commenting on the subject matter of the poem, Quin (*ibid.*, 27) draws attention to the 'identifications with smaller animals ... and the series of set phrases denoting worthless objects', while O' Sullivan (*ibid.*, xix) states that 'comparisons with smaller animals and worthless objects build up a picture of a miserable, slithery, slimy, loathsome, treacherous, dead pig'. Some examples of animal imagery in the poem include: *dairbín daol dubh* 'black beetles' grub' §6; *cerc arna creinn* 'a hen-pecked fowl' §9; *bainbhín na míol / seilche fliuch fúar*

[78] The first four words of the satire are also cited in *O'Dav.* §376. With *áer co ndath molta,* cf. *tár molta* 'outrage of praise', a type of satire illustrated in the *Fodlai Aíre* tract §12.

[79] Carney takes *fuighiull dhoibri* to mean 'remnant of a badger'. *DIL* cites the phrase *fuighiull doibhri* s.v. *dobre* 'otter'(?), where it is the only example, and suggests a translation 'remnant (food) of the otter'. *Fuighuill dhoibri* is explained in the text as a reference to the ancestor of cats, whose ears were torn off by an otter (Joynt 1941, ll. 741–4).

[80] Similarly, in the tale *Oidheadh Chlainne Tuirenn,* Uabhar explains the meaning of his poem to the king, following the latter's complaint that he cannot understand it: '*Is maith an dán soin ... acht nach tuigim aon fhocal de ná d'a chéill*' (Ua Ceallaigh 1927, 26): 'That is a good poem ... except that I don't understand a single word of it or its meaning'.

'louse-ridden bonham, cold slimy snail' §13; *cioróg na lúb / bleachtán na mbérg / certán* [*na*] *gcrúb* 'a wriggling maggot, harmful sow thistle, worm on trotters' §18; *Dreollán ar dhris . . . fideóg na bfidh* 'A wren on a briar . . . plover of woods' §30; *íarmar na muc* 'remnant of pigs' §37. Other creatures mentioned are the gadfly, horsefly, moth, maggot, worm, gnat, hare, cat, stoat, robin, blackbird, quail and jackdaw.

Animal imagery also features prominently in a satire against the noble families of Ireland composed by the sixteenth-century poet Aonghus Ó Dálaigh (O'Donovan 1852). Ó Dálaigh compares members of various families to hogs, curs, ducks and badgers and also describes them as being infested with lice. Mag Uidhir of Enniskillen, for example, is abused solely in terms of animal invective: *Broc ar ghairbhe a's ar ghlaise, Ap ar mhéid a's ar mhío-mhaise; Gliomach ar ghéire a dhá shúl — Sionnach ar bhréine an Barún!* 'A badger in roughness and in greyness, An ape in size and ugliness; A lobster for the sharpness of both his eyes, A fox for his stench is the Baron' (O'Donovan 1852, 52). Forbes (1905, 59–60) notes in relation to Scottish folklore concerning animals that 'the similarity between men and animals was used in various senses, generally unfavourable to the former . . . ' citing as an example of the use of animal invective a satire by the eighteenth century Scottish poet Alasdair mac Mhaighstir Alasdair. This is strikingly similar to the invectives in *MV* III in both structure and imagery: *Aodann gràineig, tàrr-aodann tuirc, / Com a' chnàimh-fhithich 's nàdar na muic', / Beul mhic-làmhaich 's fàileadh a' bhruic, / Spàga clàrach, sàilibh nan cusp, / Casa curra, uchd a'ghiomaich, / Sùile lionnach sgamalach fluich — / De dh'òirlichibh aoiridh bàrdail / Tomhaiseam o d'bhathais gu d'shàil thu, / 'S feannam do leathar, a thràill, dhiot / Chionn thu chàineadh a' Chaimbeulaich Dhuibh* 'You've a hedgehog's visage, a boar's belly-face, / The bone-raven's bosom and the nature of the pig, / The mouth of a catfish and the badger's stench, / Splay feet, heels full of kibes, / The legs of a heron, the lobster's breast, / Festering, scaly, watering eyes — / With inches of bardic satire / I measure you from your brow to your heel / And I flay your hide, you slave, off you / Because you have defamed Black Campbell' (Black 1986, 7). The animals employed by Alasdair mac Mhaighstir Alasdair in his satires are domestic creatures and vermin such as the dung beetle, pig and sheep,[81] while those used

[81] Some examples are: *Tuitidh tusa mar a bheisteag / 'Na t-ionad fein am buachair mart* 'Thou wilt fall like the dung-beetle (beastie) into thine own place, the cow's dung' (Forbes, *op. cit.*, 399); *'S cha b'ann leis a' phlàigh ud a thàrmaich o'n mhuic* 'And not with that vile herd, the offspring of swine!' (Campbell 1933, 52 l. 5); *Sgap agus sgaoil sibh mar chaoirich roimh mhàrtain* 'You scattered and fled like sheep from a marten' (Campbell, *op. cit.*, 60 l. 89);

in contemporary Scottish panegyric poetry include the lion, boar, viper and bull.[82]

Plants

There are several allusions to plants and plant by-products. Some of these, such as dock leaf and chaff, were of little economic importance, while others, such as wild oats, were considered a pest (Kelly 1997, 227, 242). Examples include: *a cháith lín i lladair fíaich* 'you chaff of flax in a raven's claw' no. 8; *píanán i mbí corca fásaig* 'a bag of wild oats' no. 30; *a barr feóir rossa / 'dar cossa cait* 'you head of woodland grass between the paws of a cat, no. 39; *a chos choppóice* 'you stem of a dock leaf' no. 54; *glacca remra i ros* 'fat hands in linseed' no. 59. There are also references to *ibar* 'yew' and *áth aba* 'hemlock', both of which are poisonous plants.[83] *Ibar* and the adjective *ibraide* 'yew-like' occur several times: *a airbe ibair* 'you fence of yew' no. 51; *a bél mná uidre uime ibraide* 'you mouth of a sallow, crude, yew-like woman' no. 52; *dabach ibarglic aithne* 'a skilfully wrought vat of yew as a deposit' no. 70; *cornaire isti ibraide* 'a ... yew-like hornplayer' no. 78. The law tract on farming, *Bretha Comaithchesa*, classifies the yew tree alongside the oak, hazel, holly, ash, Scots pine and wild apple as one of the *airig fedo*, 'nobles of the wood', and its wood was highly valued because its pliant quality made it suitable for the manufacture of domestic implements (Kelly 1976, 110; 1997, 383, 388).[84] In the light of this, the use of the adjective *ibraide* 'yew-like' and the metaphor *a airbe ibair* 'you fence of yew' as terms of abuse appears somewhat surprising. The branches and leaves of the yew tree are highly poisonous,

---

Tog dhinn a' mhuc 's a cuing, / 'S a h-àl breac, brothach, uirceineach, Le'n cuid chrom-shoc, thar tuinn 'Relieve us of our swinish yoke, And send the speckled, mangy brood Of snouted hogs o'erseas' (Campbell, *op. cit.*, 104 l. 5–7):

[82] Some examples are: *'Nam beathraichibh gu reubadh, / 'Nan leómhannaibh gu creuchdadh* 'Who are like bears for rending, Like lions too for wounding' (Campbell, *op. cit.*, 74 ll. 51–2); *'Nan nathraichibh grad-leumnach* 'Like serpents swiftly striking' (*ibid.*, 76 l. 53); *Mar choin air fasdadh éille* 'Like hounds their leashes straining' (*ibid.*, 76 l. 61); *'San leirg mar thairbh gun sgàth* 'In war like fearless bulls' (*ibid.*, 78 l. 86); *Mar sheochdain 's eòin fo 'n spàig* 'Like hawks that grip their prey' (*ibid.*, 78 l. 90). T. McCaughey (1989, 120 note 44) notes that exotic animals such as the ape, basilisk, crocodile and toad are also found as insulting epithets in 17th and 18th century Scottish and Irish poetry.

[83] For *áth aba* see note on no. 25 below.

[84] In a discussion of 'vegetal kennings' in 18th century Scottish Gaelic poetry, Black (2001, xxiii–iv) notes that the apple, ash, blackthorn, fir, hazel, oak, woodbine and yew are consistently portrayed as noble, while the alder, aspen, birch, briar, elder, elm, hawthorn, rowan and whitethorn are regarded as base trees.

however, a property which would render it unsuitable for the fencing-in of livestock.[85] A 'fence of yew' could therefore be taken as a metaphor for something useless or dangerous and a similar idea is expressed in the phrase *sonnach eidnén ós aill* 'an enclosure of ivy above a cliff' no. 61, since ivy is an unsuitable material for building an enclosure. The adjective *ibraide* 'yew-like' in the above examples may be used in the sense 'poison-tongued'. In no. 22, the poet asks *Cá rét ná teilciub cen terce / do sceirtiud a lecne líath lomda?* 'What thing will I not cast freely in order to peel away his bare, grey cheeks'? His answer that he will cast a *Delg scíad nó scían co n-eim chongna* 'A thorn of a thorn bush or a knife with a handle of horn' is of interest in view of the association of the blackthorn with the procedure for performing a *glám dícenn* satire.[86] Other references to thorns and thornbushes are *cocur daill dar draigne* 'the whispering of a blind man over blackthorns' no. 57 and *delg do delgaib draigin* 'one of the thorns of a blackthorn' no. 68.

Finally, we may note the use of metaphors involving the coupling of animals of different species or the mixing together of different species of plants: *crim muicce fíada ar áth n-aba* 'hart's tongue mixed with hemlock' (i.e. a medicinal herb mixed with a poisonous plant) no. 25; *glas cuilinn ar caschéith* 'a fetter of holly mixed in with a twisted thorn bush' no. 74; *a reithe folta fásaig dar fíad* 'you moulting desert ram mounting deer' no. 36; *cú dar céisib* 'a hound mounting piglets' no. 58; *cenn crúaid con ar caírig* 'a cruel head of a wolf on a sheep' no. 60.

[85] 'The branches and leaves of yews are exceedingly poisonous and have caused the death of many sheep and horses. The toxic principle appears to be particularly virulent when the leaves are partly withered; therefore, hedge trimmings should never be left within the reach of animals' (*Royal Horticultural Society Dictionary of Gardening* s.v. yew; see also Kelly 1997, 183).

[86] For *glám dícenn* see *Fodlai Aíre* tract §18. Note also the description *as goin do dhealg droighin Flann* 'a wound from the thorn of a blackthorn is Flann'; see p. 37 above.

2. An Old Irish Tract on Satire

The short tract on the classification of satire, beginning *Cis lir fodlai aíre?* 'How many divisions of satire are there?' was first published by Meroney (1950, 199–212), who also drew attention to its importance in relation to legal material dealing with penalties for the unjust composition of various types of satires.[1] Meroney's edition is based on the text of the Book of Ballymote (B), with variant readings from the Book of Uí Maine (M) and National Library of Scotland Gaelic MS 1 (Advocates MS 72.1.1) (E). The text of B is presented with minimal emendation and there is no detailed examination of the relationship between the manuscripts or the question of dating. The present edition is not based on any single manuscript witness, but attempts to reconstruct the Old Irish compilation (Y) from which the common exemplar of BME (X) is descended.

Manuscripts

The text is found in the following manuscripts:

B: The Book of Ballymote, RIA MS 23 P 12 (536), pp. 299a6–299b30 of the facsimile (Atkinson 1887). Late fourteenth century, vellum (Ó Concheanainn 1981, 19–20).[2]

M: The Book of Uí Maine, RIA MS D ii 1 (1225), fol. 138rb55–138va57 of the facsimile (modern foliation; 196rb55–196va57 old foliation)

[1] The tract has also been discussed by Mercier (1962, 108–113) and L. Breatnach (1988, 11–13).

[2] See *RIA Cat.* Fasc. 13, 1610 ff. A late copy of B is also found in TCD MS H 1. 15 (1289), pp. 594.8–595.28. Meroney (1950, 199) designates this T.

(Macalister 1941). Late fourteenth century, vellum (O'Sullivan 1989, 151–66).[3]

E: National Library of Scotland Gaelic MS 1 (Advocates MS 72.1.1), fol. 19ra58–19rb61. Fifteenth century, vellum (Mackinnon 1912, 180–1; Mackechnie 1973, Vol. 1, 111; 115 §24; Campbell 1963, 47–51; Ó Concheanainn 1975, 99–101). Ó Concheanainn (1975, 100) suggests a North Connacht origin for this manuscript and identifies the scribe as Ádhamh Ó Cuirnín, who also wrote sections of the Book of Lecan. He suggests that E may have been written c. 1425, after Ó Cuirnín's main contribution to the Book of Lecan was written.[4]

H: A shorter version of the text, with different definitions but without the illustrative examples, is found on the verso of a small vellum fragment in TCD MS H 3. 18 (1337) p. 870 (Abbott and Gwynn 1921, 157).[5] The fragment is in a poor state of preservation and much of the text is illegible.

Relationship of the Manuscripts

The text in BME is preceded by a copy of §§1–66 of the metrical tract *MV* I (Thurneysen 1891, 5–22; Ó hAodha 1991) and is followed in all three MSS by *In Lebor Ollaman.*[6] BME are very close and clearly derive from a common exemplar (X). A comparison of the MSS shows that BE often agree against M. In the table below (v) indicates that the reading occurs in verse:

	B	E	M
§2	im*morro*	im*morro*	quidem .i. im*morro*
	hai*n*simh	hainsim	tansem
	mainescert*er*	mainesceirter	masc*er*dt*er*
	coirt	coirt	guirt

[3] See *Catalogue of Irish Manuscripts in the Royal Irish Academy*, Fasc. 26 (Mulchrone 1943, 3314 ff.). Parts of M are illegible due to marginal staining.

[4] A section relating to the descendants of Míl of Spain (12vb6–20) is written in a different hand; see Mackecknie (1973, 114 §17).

[5] On the recto is a fragment of a text which lists nine types of *deach* 'syllable, foot' and eight grades of *dóerbaird* 'base bards' (Meyer 1898, 160; *UR* 51).

[6] Meroney (1950, 199 note 5) states that this text is 'merely an appendage to the *Auraicept na nÉces*, which Calder omitted from his edition'. It is, however, an entirely independent text which consists of a series of questions and answers, citations and etymologies relating to *Auraicept na nÉces* (Calder 1917).

§3	athais mbret*r*i	athais mbreitri	aithis
	cidh tri achuidbhius	cid triacuibdius	dius
	scailp	scailp	sclaip
	araile	araile	aile
§4	7 tamall aire	7 tarmall aire	*om.*
	7 tamall molta	7 tamall molta	*om.*
§8	an*n*so	andso	an*n*so sis
§9	nihabar	nihabar	noconabair (v)
§11	laidich	laidich	m*ac* laidich
	dobeith	dobeith	dobreith (v)
	ropaige	ropaige	ropaig
	fechtus	fechtus	fec (v)
§12	asamla	asamla	sa*m*la
§13	amal dorigni	amal dorigni	.i. dorigne
	airisin	airisin	iarsi*n*
§14	ceatra fathfer	ceatra fathfer	cect*ar* fathar (v)
§15	dofesid	dofeisid	dofessib (v)
§16	nidad rosu	nidad rosu	ni tathrosu (v)
	om.	*om.*	tirad (v)
	robmairg	robmairg	rotmairg (v)
§18	.i. mar leghthar i*n* i*n*ad eli	mar leghtar aninadh ele	.i. in*n*inu ele leghthar

There is no evidence to suggest that E (the later of the two MSS) is a copy of B, however. E agrees with M against B in reading *dogniter* against *digiter* B §5. In §7, E reads *bi* against *bith* BM, while in §12 it reads *suarach* against *ríarach* BM (rhyming with *ríabach*). Because large sections of M are illegible due to marginal staining, it is difficult to establish whether the text was superior to that of BE. M preserves a number of Latin phrases which are omitted or corrupt in BE and also has the reading *tirad* (v) §16 which is omitted in the other two MSS but is necessary for the syllable count. M also has the superior readings *dobreith* in §11 and *cectar fathar* in §14. On the other hand, there are serious omissions in §§3 and 4 (see above).

H differs from BME in varying degrees in its definition of each type of satire and omits the illustrative examples. It also inverts the order of §11 (*tár n-aíre*) and §12 (*tár molta*). Where sections of text correspond, H differs in reading *indessin* against *indisiu* BME §2, *bretri* against *mbretri* B, *mbreitri* E, om. M §3 and [*tamall*] *naire* against *aire* BE, om. M §4. In §2, HM read *tainsimadh* and *tansem* respectively against *hainsimh* B and *hainsim* E. It is impossible to establish the precise relationship between H and M, however, since only small sections of the texts correspond. H also contains some readings which are found in BE but omitted in M: *bretri* H, *mbretri* B, *mbreitri* E, om. M §3; *tamall naire 7 tamall molta* H, *tamall aire 7 tamall molta* B, *tarmall aire 7 tamall molta* E, om. M §4. H agrees closely with BME in §4.

Stemma

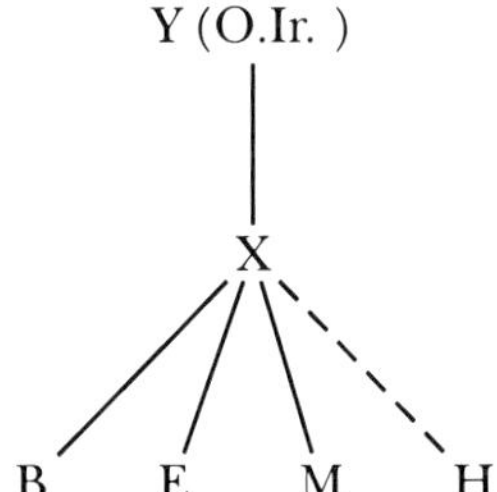

Orthography

The MSS show a number of later orthographical features, some examples of which are given below. The MS form is given first, followed by the form of the restored text in brackets. Length marks are rare in all MSS.

1. *ea* for *e* before a non-palatal consonant:

   B: theangaidh (thengaid) §2.

   M: neach (neuch) §3.

   E: leasanma (lesanmae) §3.

2. *g* and *d* for *c* and *t*:

   B: doradadh (do-ratad) §3.

   M: fagabair (fácabar) §10; rancadar (ráncatar) §3.

3. *gh, bh, dh, mh* for *g, b, d, m*:

   B: timtiridh (timthirthid) §2; maigh (Maig) §3; solamh (solam) §3; riabhach (ríabach) §12.

   M: amaigh (Maig) §3; gerraibh (gerraib) §3.

   E: taebhghil (tháebgil) §10; thengaidh (thengaid) §2; solamh (solam) §3.

4. Confusion of lenited *g* and lenited *d*:

   E: maighidh (maidid) §9.

Editorial Method

Normalised Text

c p t are restored where the manuscripts have *g b d* for post-vocalic voiced stops.

Lenition of consonants is silently normalised in accordance with Old Irish practice.

Final vowels are restored.

Accent marks are added silently.

Middle Irish forms occurring in all three MSS which are likely to have been introduced by the scribe of the common exemplar (X) have been restored to Old Irish. Where a Latin phrase is glossed in Middle Irish, only the Latin is given in the restored text.

The numbering in paragraphs 1–8 corresponds to that in Meroney's edition of the text. The illustration of *dallbach cen tuinide*, which is included along with *dallbach beccthuinidi* in §8 of Meroney's edition, is treated as a separate paragraph (§9) in the present edition, which thus affects the numbering of the subsequent paragraphs.

Manuscript Readings

The compendia *us, con, et/ed, er, acht, ar* and *air* are expanded silently. The abbreviations *dō, dā, im̄* and *l-* are expanded silently as *dono, dano,*[7] *immorro* and *no* respectively. The expansion of all other abbreviations is indicated by the use of italics.

Hairstrokes over *i* in the MSS are not indicated.

Where the text of a manuscript is illegible, this is indicated by a series of dots within brackets. Meroney's edition includes some readings which are now illegible and these are enclosed within braces.

[7] For *danó* ending in a long vowel in Old Irish see L. Breatnach 2003, 139.

A full transcription of the text of B is given in the variant readings, followed by significant readings from ME. Full readings from all MSS are given for §§16–17, however, since these stanzas present a number of textual difficulties. A full transcription of H is given on p. 64.

Note the following errors in transcription by Meroney: for *bréithre* H read *bretri*; for *gearaib* E read *gearraib*; for *clocha* E read *clotha* §3; for *frithshuidiu* B read *frithsuidiu*; for *frithuide* H read *frithuidi* §4; for *doduine* H read *dodune* §5; for *shamhla* H read *samla*; for *saill* E read *ṡall* §11; for *táir* H read *tar*; for *criiada criiada* E read *criiada criiadha* §12; for *ceadra* E read *ceatra* §14; for *g.dixit* M read *est dixit*; for *dofeisib* M read *dofessib* §15; for *brathair* E read *brathar*; for *nod* E read *not* §17.

Dating and Linguistic Analysis

Illustrative verses: Several of these contain features which point to a date of composition in the Old Irish period:

Deponent form: *ad-gládamar* (v. 1) §7.

Reduplicated preterite: *cechang-sa* (v. 2) §7.

Neuter article and nasalisation after a neuter noun: *a lín* (v. 1), *a leth n-áigi* (v. 2) §11.

Disyllabic *biäd* (v. 1) guaranteed by metre §11.[8]

The metre is restored by emending to Old Irish *cúlu* (*cul* BME) and *céne* (*cen* BE, *cein* M) §3.

Prose: The prose sections are brief and, aside from §§2, 3 and 13, consist mainly of an introductory statement naming the type of satire being illustrated, sometimes followed by a short explanation or attribution to a particular poet. An analysis of the prose also indicates a number of Old Irish features:

Distinction between deuterotonic and prototonic forms of compound verbs: *do-ratad, co tartad* §3; *do-gníther* §5; *dia ndéntar* §6.

[8] Contrast monosyllabic *do-chuaid* §7 (v. 2) and note that hiatus forms, including forms with hypercorrect hiatus, are found in Middle Irish verse (*SG* III §3.2).

Absence of independent pronouns as subject or object of verb.

Correct use of infixed pronouns: *ním thá* §2; *ros lil* §3.

Strong perfectives: *do-romaltar, ros lil* §3.

Nasalisation after neuter nouns: *tár n-aíre* §§4,11; *cét n-uinge* §14.[9]

The prose section cannot be earlier than the ninth century, however, since the example of *tár molta* (§12) is attributed to Cellach mac Cumascaig, whose *obit* is given in *AU s.a.* 867 (*recte* 868). Illustrative examples are attributed to Cormac (§3), Paitrén (§7), Fotacán Laídech (§11), Mac Dá Cherdae (§13), aue Derglega (§15) and Rechtgal aue Síadail (§17). The surviving stanzas attributed to Rechtgal aue Síadail indicate that he belonged to the late eighth or early ninth centuries (Ó hAodha 2000, 192). A wide range of literary and legal material is attributed to Cormac mac Cuilennáin, bishop and king of Cashel (died 908),[10] while the saint Mac Dá Cherdae is said to have possessed the characteristics of poet, sage and fool (O'Keeffe 1911, 18). I have not found any other references to poets named Paitrén, Fotacán Laídech and aue Derglega.

It seems likely, then, that the poems existed separately and were incorporated as illustrative examples in a tract which was compiled in the late Old Irish period. Aside from later orthographical features, Middle Irish forms occurring in both the verse and prose sections in all three MSS suggest that BME are derived from a Middle Irish exemplar of the text. Examples include:

ar dochuitidh B, *ardochuitig* M, *ardocuidigh* E (OIr. *for do chuit*) §2.

tri ceiniuil B, *tri ceniuil* ME (OIr. *trí chenél*) §6.

nihabar BE, *noconabair* M (OIr. *ní epur*) (v) §9.

do fesid B, *dofessib* M, *dofeisid* E (OIr. *ro-féssid*, rhyming with *Déssib*) (v) §15.

condearbairt B, *conebairt* M, *condebairt* E (OIr. *co n-érbart*) §17.

Of particular interest in this respect are several Latin words and phrases. In some instances, both Latin and a Middle Irish gloss are

[9] See note on *tamall aíre* p. 68 below.

[10] Cf. Mac Eoin (1981, 124 note 1).

preserved, while in others the Latin has dropped out leaving only the later gloss. The phrase *amail adubairt* (§2 BME), for example, may be a Middle Irish rendering of *ut dixit*, which is preserved in all MSS in §3 and §15 (corruptly in the latter case, where the MSS read *ut dicitur uaderglega* B, *ut est dixit hua derglega* M, *ut uadeirlega* E).[11] On two occasions, M has Latin readings, while BE have only the Middle Irish gloss: *aisneis quidem .i. immorro* M, *aisneis immorro* BE §2; *dixit iterum alius .i. adubairt fos neach eile* M, *adubairt fos neach aile* BE §3. In §18, BM gloss a Latin phrase which is omitted in E: *ut inalio legitur .i. mar leghthar in inad eli* (suprascript gloss) B, *ut* <...>{*gitur*} *.i. inninu ele leghthar* M, *marleghtar aninadh ele* E.

System of Classification

The tract classifies satire into three main types as *aisnéis* 'narration', *ail* 'reproach' and *airchetal* 'versification'. *Aisnéis* is a straightforward narration, while *ail* may take the form of either a nickname or a verbal insult (rhymed or unrhymed). The text illustrates two types of *ail* composed in response to a lack of hospitality on the part of a particular church: the nickname *Cell Chorrfesse* 'Church of the Wretched Meal' and a satirical stanza. *Airchetal* is further divided into ten types: *mac bronn* 'son of womb', *dallbach* 'innuendo', *focal i frithṡuidiu* 'word in opposition', *tár n-aíre* 'outrage of satire', *tár molta* 'outrage of praise', *tamall aíre* 'touch of satire', *tamall molta* 'touch of praise', *lánáer* 'full satire', *ainmed* 'lampooning, and *glám dícenn*. Three types of *dallbach* 'innuendo' are illustrated: *dallbach cen tuinide* 'unestablished *dallbach*',[12] *dallbach beccthuinidi* 'lightly established *dallbach*' and *dallbach tréntuinidi* 'firmly established *dallbach*'. Each type of *airchetal*, with the exception of *mac bronn* and *glám dícenn*, is illustrated by an example. The text also cites an illustration of *ró molta* 'excess of praise', although this is not included in the ten-fold classification of *airchetal* (§4). Note also that the illustration of *tamall aíre* (§13) is not in verse.

Evidence from legal sources indicates that there were other systems of classification. A seven-fold classification is outlined in the Old Irish heptad on satire, for which see p. 88 below. Aside from *lesainm lenas* and

[11] *Dicitur* is found elsewhere for *dixit* in later MSS; cf. *CIH* ii 583.30 = ii 677.10; ii 677.13; *ut dicitur CIH* ii 584.17 = *ut dixit* ii 677.27. I am grateful to Gerald Manning for these examples from *Míadṡlechta*.

[12] The stanza illustrating *dallbach cen tuinide* lacks an introductory heading in the MSS.

áer aicetail, the two systems differ considerably and the heptad contains types which are not found in the *Fodlai Aíre* tract. It distinguishes between satirising a person in their absence (*écndach n-écnairce*) and in their presence (*glámad gnúise*) and identifies two types of satire which entail taunting someone about their defects (*écoscnamat* and *noad ainme*).

A five-fold classification is found in the Old Irish glosses on the *Senchas Már*, where *áer* is glossed *.i. ata .u. cenela aire .i. tar nairi, tar molta, aucu ainmaith, glam dicend, no nech tamall* 'Satire, i.e. there are five types of satire, i.e. outrage of satire, outrage of praise, wishing evil, *glám dícenn* or any touch [of satire or praise]' (*CIH* iii 894.19).[13] This classification includes four of the types of *airchetal* mentioned in the *Fodlai Aíre* tract, namely *tár n-aíre, tár molta, tamall* and *glám dícenn*. Middle Irish glosses and commentary on a variety of legal texts also provide evidence that different types of satire were recognised. Some examples are: *.i. imini eim-coimsigter isan air, in eneclann, 7 ainfis ca cineol aire nosbeir co .u.thi* 'i.e. concerning the thing which is "promptly-arranged" for the satire, the honour-price, and lack of knowledge of the type of satire brings it to five days' (*CIH* ii 391.32; gloss on *Cethairṡlicht Athgabálae*);[14] *tincantain aire, cibe cinel aire* 'recitation of satire, whatever type of satire' (*CIH* i 47.32; heptad 52); *eric fo aicne in cineoil aire* 'body-fine according to the type of satire' (*CIH* i 47.36; heptad 52); *.i. in brath no in lanaer, no cipeth cinel aire .i. in glaim dicenn* 'i.e. the revealing [of a defect] or the *lánáer*, or whatever type of satire, i.e. the *glám dícenn*' (*CIH* ii 404.2–3; *Cethairṡlicht Athgábalae*); *Is amlaid icar fiach isin dallbach: fo aicned na haire bis and* 'It is thus that a penalty is paid for the *dallbach*: according to the type of satire it is' (*CIH* iii 972.4; commentary on *mac bronn* and *dallbach*); ... *obus inand cineal aoire* '... when it would be the same kind of satire' (*CIH* ii 733.19; commentary on *Córus Fine*).

As Meroney notes (1950, 200), citations from the *Fodlai Aíre* tract occur in legal glosses and commentary. The glossator of the heptad on satire cites material from §3 to illustrate *lesainm lenas* (gloss 2), *lesainm i mbí fírṡamail aíre* (gloss 13) and *ail ṡuthin* (gloss 14), while commentary on *Bretha Nemed Dédenach* (*CIH* v 1587.18–1588.4) cites the first lines of the verses illustrating *dallbach* (§6) and *focal i frithṡuidiu* (§10) to illustrate those types of satire. Line *c* of the stanza illustrating *focal i frithṡuidiu* is also cited in a Middle Irish glossary (*CIH* iii 949.39). Some of the terms

[13] The lemma *Aer* is from *Cethairṡlicht Athgabálae* (*CIH* ii 401.15).

[14] This refers to a delay of five days, as opposed to the normal three day period, before a person's property can be seized during the process of distraint (Binchy 1973, 43).

were known to lawyers, glossators and grammarians, as is clear from their occurrence in law texts, glossaries and metrical treatises, e.g.:

ail: *CIH* i 30.20 and 30.36 (heptad on satire).

lesainm: CIH i 29.17 (heptad on satire); *CIH* iii 927.29 (commentary on *Bretha Étgid*).

mac bronn: *CIH* iii 971.30 (citations and commentary on satire).

dallbach: *CIH* iii 950.20 (glossary); *CIH* iii 972.4 (commentary on satire); *CIH* v 1587.35 (citations and commentary on satire; see *Companion* 186); *O'Dav.* §603; *Auraic.* ll. 1930–1; *Trefocal* poem (Meroney 1953, 96).

focal i frithṡuidiu: *O'Dav.* §1547; *CIH* v 1587.31 (citations and commentary on satire); *Auraic.* ll. 1933.

tár/tamall: *O'Dav.* §1549; *CIH* iii 894.19 (Old Irish glosses on *Senchas Már*); *CIH* iii 964.23 (citations and commentary on offences covered by treaties); *CIH* vi 2122.3 (citations and commentary); *Auraic.* ll. 1932.

lánáer: *CIH* i 30.35 (heptad on satire); *CIH* ii 404.2 (gloss on *Cethairṡlicht Athgabálae*); *CIH* iii 927.31 (gloss on *Bretha Étgid*); *CIH* iii 1134.39 (gloss on *Bretha Nemed Toísech*); *CIH* vi 2218.4 (gloss on *ró* 'excess' in *Bretha Nemed Toísech*).

ainmed: *CIH* ii 386.21 and 403.18 (*Cethairṡlicht Athgabálae*); *CIH* vi 2199.23 (*Gúbretha Caratniad*); *CIH* vi 2113.29 = iii 1134.9 (commentary on *Bretha Nemed Toísech*).

ró molta: CIH vi 2113.30 (commentary on *Bretha Nemed Toísech*); *CIH* vi 2122.3 (citations and commentary).

glám dícenn: *CIH* i 30.35 (heptad on satire); *CIH* ii 404.3 (gloss on *Cethairṡlicht Athgabálae*); *CIH* iii 894.19 (Old Irish glosses on *Senchas Már*); *CIH* iii 927.31 (gloss on *Bretha Étgid*); *CIH* iii 1134.37 (glosses on *Bretha Nemed Toísech*); *CIH* v 1564.35 (Middle Irish commentary; procedure for performance); *CIH* v 1587.31 (citations and commentary on satire); *CIH* vi 2341.4,7 (glosses on *UR* §24); *MV* III §155 (procedure for performance); *O'Dav.* §32 (gloss on citation from *Bretha Nemed Dédenach*).

While the terms themselves are attested elsewhere, they are seldom illustrated by an example, so that it is impossible to establish to what extent they correspond to the types of satire illustrated in the *Fodlai Aíre* tract.

Text

§1 Cis lir fodlai aíre? Ní ansae, a trí .i. aisnéis 7 ail 7 airchetal.

§2 Aisnéis *quidem*: indisiu tri áinsem cen chuibdius, *ut dixit* in cáinte i tig alaili degduini — nírbo lour lais a chuit: 'In scerdfider salann duit for do chuit?' ar in timthirthid. 'Níthó,' ar sesom, 'ar ním thá ní fora scerter acht ma scerter for mo thengaid irecc. Nícon écen: is coirt cenae.'

§3 Ail danó .i. ail lesanmae lenas do neuch, nó aithis bréthre, cid tri chuibdius cid cen chuibdius, *ut dixit* Cormac:

Is do decraib in domain
búain mela a mecnaib ibair,
i scailp for conaib gerraib,
longud i scellaib scibair.

Lesainm danó, amail do-ratad for araili cill fil i Maig Ulad. Robo Les Mór a ainm ar thús, co ráncatar muinter Lis Móir Mo-Chutu danó don chill-sin, co tartad drochḟuirec mbecc dóib. Do-romaltar íarum co solam 7 do-cuatar do bailiu ailiu 7 do-ratad lesainm forsin cill ucut .i. Cell Chorrḟesse. Ros lil ind ail anmae sin do grés. *Dixit iterum alius*:

Mag Lacha —
nícon tráethfa mac flatha:
do-rat cúlu fri clotha
céne mbes úir im chlocha.

§4 Airchetal n-aíre danó: a-taat deich fodlai fair-side .i. mac bronn 7 dallbach 7 focal i frithṡuidiu 7 tár n-aíre 7 tár molta 7 tamall aíre 7 tamall molta 7 lánáer 7 ainmed 7 glám dícenn.

§5 Coté in mac bronn? Ní ansae: fo chlith do-gníther.

Translation

§1 How many divisions of satire are there? It is not difficult: three, i.e. narration and reproach and versification.

§2 Narration, then: a statement [made] in accusation, without rhyme, as the satirist said in the house of a certain nobleman — he did not deem his food sufficient: 'Will salt be sprinkled for you on your food?' said the servant. 'No', said he, 'for I have not anything on which it may be sprinkled, unless it is sprinkled directly on my tongue. It is not necessary: it's bark already'.

§3 Reproach then, i.e. the permanence of a nickname which sticks to someone, or verbal insult, whether rhymed or unrhymed, as Cormac said:

> Among the difficulties of the world are
> extracting honey from yew roots,
> being in a cleft above cur-dogs,
> dining on grains of pepper.

Nickname then, as was bestowed upon a certain church which is in Mag nUlad. Les Mór was its name at first, until the household of Les Mór Mo-Chutu came then to that church and a miserable, small meal was given to them. They ate quickly then and went to another place, and a nickname was bestowed upon that church, i.e. Church of the Wretched Meal. That nickname stuck to it always. Someone else said also:

> Mag Lacha —
> it will not overwhelm the son of a lord [with hospitality]:
> it has turned its back on generosity
> for as long as there may be clay around stones.

§4 Versified satire, then: there are ten divisions of it, i.e. son of womb and innuendo and word in opposition and outrage of satire and outrage of praise and touch of satire and touch of praise and full satire and lampooning and *glám dícenn.*

§5 What is the son of womb? It is not difficult: it is performed secretly.

§6 Dallbach danó. Ní fess cía dia ndéntar sainriud ⁊ a-taat trí chenél fair-side .i. dallbach tréntuinidi ⁊ dallbach beccthuinidi ⁊ dallbach cen tuinide.

§7 Dallbach tréntuinidi cétus, amail as-mbert Paitrén:

Sruithchlérech ad-gládamar
— ní chél i nach dú —
i Clúain Iraird oirdnidiu
asa caíniu clú.

Cechang-sa dia airlisi
— gním do-chúaid do ráith —
nícon bíth-si óbéle
do grés ar chiunn cháich.

§8 Dallbach beccthuinidi indso:

Ránac-sa a les
secha tét in glas
indid imdae grus
cenip imdae as.

§9 [Dallbach cen tuinide] :

Atá ben is' tír
ní epur a ainm:
maidid esse a deilm
amail chloich a tailm.

§10 Focal i frithṡuidiu .i. comarc molta ⁊ fácabar focal and for brú aíre, *ut dixit*:

Ro crechad anís co crissu,
crenaid claidbiu glassu;
tabairt mná dó — cid bad huissiu?
Ingen na mná massu.

A Thanaidi tháebgil Themra,
ní mé acht is tú:
a, be, ce, de, pe qú —
is sí bís i frithṡuidiu and sin qú.

§6 Innuendo, then, it is not known for whom exactly it is composed, and there are three types, i.e. firmly established innuendo, lightly established innuendo and unestablished innuendo.

§7 Firmly established innuendo first, as Paitrén said:

> It is a venerable cleric we address
> — I will not conceal it in any place —
> in eminent Clúain Iraird
> whose reputation is most fair.
>
> I stepped to his forecourt
> — a deed which was in vain —
> it was not always
> open to everyone.

§8 Lightly established innuendo here:

> I reached his farmyard
> past which the stream flows,
> in which cheese is plentiful
> although it does not come plentifully out of it.

§9 [Unestablished innuendo]:

> There is a woman in the land
> — I do not say her name —
> her noise breaks from her
> like a stone from a sling.

§10 Word in opposition, i.e. a quatrain of praise and a word is left there on the verge of satire, as he said:

> He has been tattooed from below to the waist,
> he buys blue swords;
> giving a woman to him, what would be more fitting?
> The woman's nail [would be] better.
>
> O fair-sided Tanaide of Tara,
> it is not I but you.
> A, b, c, d, p, q —
> it is 'q' which is in opposition there.

§11 Tár n-aíre, amail do-rigni Fotacán Laídech do ríg Laigen .i. áer fo ṡár cen ṡár a samlae:

> A lín fechtas do-breth dam
> biäd la Bran mballraid glain
> i flaithius Churrig co fib:
> roptar lir a blíadnai Brain.
>
> A leth n-áigi íarna rainn
> tuccad ó ríg Liphi luind;
> rop' áige n-óg dó-som tall
> ocus a ṡall fora druim.
>
> Teoir bairgena tuctha dún
> tre rúin a cúiltig ind ríg;
> bámmar-ni cethrur ḟer maith —
> ro-fitir in flaith ar lín.

A lín fechtas.

§12 Tár molta danó .i. molad fo thár cen ṡár a ṡamlae, amail do-rigni Cellach mac Cumascaig do ḟiur légind Chlúana mac Nóis:

> Alla, alla! Críada, críada!
> Bendic for mo dúana!
> Carais Rechtabrae a dinge
> co lár Cille Clúana.
>
> Mór a guth i ndurthaig clárach
> imbi senad ríarach;
> ro lég Rechtabrae mac Artrach
> trí chét spaltrach ríabach.

§13 Tamall aíre danó, amail do-rigni Mac Dá Cherdae. Do-cuaid-sium do Chill Aithcherdae i tír Ḟer Maige Féne. Ro híadad fris íarum indi 7 do-cuaid-sium íar sin do Chill Chomair. Do-ratad fáilte dó indi-sidi. Broccán mac Addi, is é rop' airchinnech indi, conid airi sin as-bert Mac Dá Cherdae: 'Comla nád tabarr frium i tig Broccáin maic Addi, ná tét i mudu i n-óenblíadnai: berar do Mac Aithcherdae'.

§11 Outrage of satire, as Fotacán Laídech composed for the king of Leinster, i.e. an excess of satire without appearing [to be] an excess:

As many times as food was given to me
by Bran of the fair limbs
in the lordship of excellent Currech,
so many were Bran's years.

Half a joint after it had been divided
was brought from the king of fierce Life;
there was a full joint for him yonder
and his salted meat in addition to it.

Three loaves had been given to us
in secret from the king's kitchen:
we were four good men —
the lord knew our number.

§12 Outrage of praise then, i.e. praise with insult, without appearing to be an insult, as Cellach son of Cumascach composed for the ecclesiastical scholar of Clonmacnoise:

Alleluia, alleluia! Credo, credo!
A blessing on my poems!
Rechtabrae loved being pressed
into the centre of the church of Clonmacnoise.

Great his voice in the wooden church
in which the clergy are submissive;
Rechtabrae son of Artri has read
three hundred ornamented psalters.

§13 Touch of satire then, as Mac Dá Cherdae composed. He went to Cell Aithcherdae in the territory of Fir Maige Féne. [The door] was closed before him there and he went afterwards to Cell Chomair. He was welcomed there. Broccán son of Adde was the superior there, so that it is for that reason that Mac Dá Cherdae said: 'The door which is not shut before me in the house of Broccán son of Adde, let it not go to waste for a single year — let it be taken to Mac Aithcherdae'.

§14 Tamall molta, amail ro ráid in fili:

A macu Gartnán, a degdías bráthar,
a ósair, a ṡinsir, a chechtar fáthar:
is fíu cét n-uinge in copchaille buide
fil im chenn for máthar.

§15 Lánáer .i. co roib ainm 7 us 7 domgnas indi, *ut dixit* aue Derglega:

Mu chara-sa a Cill Dá Chellóc
mad áil dúib ro-féssid:
píanán i mbí corca fásaig
Cíanán donaib Déssib.

§16 Ainmed danó, *ut dixit* in fer cétnae:

Nít adras-su (?) gíallai dam-sa
d'ingairiu mo cháerach;
a Chíarán cailg, carai tírad:
rot mairg mad dom áerad.

§17 Ró molta, amail do-rigni Rechtgal aue Síadail do Rígnaig, ingen bráthar maic Cinn Ḟáelad, do mnaí ríg Locha Léin, co n-érbart:

Má nod léna crécht for talmain
tre bunad céit buiden,
ba méite bad ríge folam
do neoch ná bad fuidel.

§18 Glám dícenn danó íar sin, *ut in alio legitur.*

§14 Touch of praise, as the poet said:

O sons of Gartnán! O worthy pair of brothers!
O younger! O elder! O each of you!
Worth one hundred ounces [of silver] is the yellow coif
which is about your mother's head.

§15 Full satire, i.e. so that there is name and lineage and abode in it, as aue Derglega said:

My friend from Cell Dá Chellóc,
if you wish you shall know:
a bag of wild oats
is Cíanán of the Déisi.

§16 Lampooning, moreover, as the same man said:

I have not respected (?) your service to me
for the herding of my sheep;
o stinging Cíarán, you love drying:
woe betide you if it is to satirise me.

§17 Excess of praise, as Rechtgal aue Síadail composed for Rígnach, the daughter of the brother of the son of Cenn Fáelad, the wife of the king of Loch Léin, when he said:

If a wound on the earth causes injury
through the stock of a hundred hosts,
it would be likely to be an empty kingship
for whoever would not remain.

§18 *Glám dícenn* then after that, as may be read in another place.

Manuscript Readings

A full transcription of H is given on p. 64.

§1 B: Cisl*ir* fodla aire ni*ansa* atri .i. aisnes 7 ail 7 aircetal.

§2 B: Aisneis immorro indisiu t*r*iahai*n*simh cen chuidhbus am*ail* adubhairt i*n*cai*n*ti itich alaile deghdhui*n*e nirbolor lais acuit i*n*scerdfidhear sala*n*n duit ar dochuitidh ar i*n*ti*m*tiridh. Nito ar seisiu*m* arni*m*ta ni arascert*er* acht mainescert*er* armotheangaidh arecha nucunecean iscoirt cheana.

q*u*ide*m* .i. immorro M, immorro E; tansem M, hai*n*sim E; chuibdius M, cuibdius E; am*ail* adubairt ME; nibo M; sceirtfidear E; ardochuitig M, ardocuidigh E; aseso*m* M; f*or*a sc*er*dt*er* M, arasceirt*er* E; masc*er*dt*er* M, mai*n*escert*er* E; f*or*mothe*n*gaid M; arecha ME; guirt M, coirt E.

§3 B: Ail dano .i. ail leasa*n*ma lenas do neoch no athais mbret*r*i cidh tria chuidbhius cid cen cuidbius ut d*ixit* cor*ma*c (*suprascript* c *written over* m-*stroke*). Is dodeacraib indo*m*ain buai*n* mela ar*m*ecnaib ibair ascailp f*or*conaib gearraib loṅgad iceallaib scibair. Leasai*n*m dano am*al* doradadh f*or*araile cill fil i*m*aigh ul*ad* roboleas mor ahai*n*m artus corancadar mui*nter* lis mhoir mochutu d*ano* donchillsi*n* cotardad drochfurec bec doib doro*m*altar iar*um* cosolamh 7 dochuadar dobaile aile 7 doradad lesai*n*m f*or*si*n*cill ucut .i. ceall chorrfesi roslil i*n*ail a*n*ma sin dogres. Adubairt fos neach aile. Magh lacha noco t*r*athfa m*ac* flatha dorat cul f*r*i clotha cenbes uir i*m*clacha.

aithis (*omits* bréthre cid tre chuib) M, athais mbreit*r*i E; no cid cen cuibdus M; ut dx (*suspension stroke illeg.*) M, ut d*ixit* E; de M; doman E; sclaip M; <. . .>ellaib M, cellaibh E; aile M; fill i*n*maigh M; doramaltar M, doro*m*hlatar E; i*n*dail M, inail E; d*ixit* ite*rum* alius .i. adubairt fos neach eile M; nocho traefa M, Adubairt fos neach aile E; nochot*r*aethfea E; cul ME; cei*n* bes M, cenbhes E; clotha E.

§4 B: Aircetal aire dano ataait .x. fodla fairside .i. m*ac* bro*n*n 7 dallbach 7 foc*u*l if*r*ithshuidiu 7 tar naire 7 tar molta 7 tamall aire 7 tamall molta 7 lanair 7 ain*m*edh 7 glai*m* diceand.

frisuidiu M, frithsuighiudh E; tarnaire ME; tarrmolta M; tarmallaire E; M *omits* 7 tamall aire 7 tamall molta; lanaer M, lanair E; gla*m* M, glai*mh* E.

§5 B: Caidi in m*ac* b*r*ond ni*ansa* foclith digit*er*.

caide ME; dognit*er* ME.

§6 B: Dalbach dano nifeas cia diandentar sai*n*driud 7 atait t*r*i ceiniuil fu*r*ri side .i. dallbach trentui*n*di. 7 dalb*ach* becc thuindhe. 7 dallb*ach* cen tui*n*di.

nocon fes M; t*r*i ceniuil ME; fu*r*ri ME; .i. dalbach t*r*en tunidhe M, Dallbach trentuinidhi E; bec tunide M, becctuinide E; tuinidhi E.

§7 B: Dallb*ach* trentui*n*edhe cetus am*ail* adb*er*t paitren. Sruth clereach adgladamar nicel ingach du icluai*n* iraird oirdnide asacai*ne* clu. cechangsa dia airlisi gni*m* dochuaid doraith nocobithsi obhele dogres arcind caich.

t*r*en tui*n*de M, trentui*n*ide E; cetuus E; adubairt patre M, atb*er*t paitre*n* E; nichel E; in*n*ach M, i*n*gach E; assa M; cai*n*u M, cai*ne* E; nochobithsi M, nochobisi E; caith M.

§8 B: Dallb*ach* becthui*n*edhe an*n*so. Ranacsa ales seach ateit i*n*glas i*n*ati*m*da gruus gencobi*m*da ass.

bec tu*n*ide M, becctui*nide* E; a*n*nso sis M; inad M; grus M, gruss E; cencop M.

§9 B: Ata bean astir nihabar ahai*n*m mhaighidh esdi adelm am*ail* cloich atailm.

noconabair M, nihabar E; esse M, eisti E; deilm M.

§10 B: Foc*ul* ifrithsuidhiu dano .i. comharc molta 7 facabhair foc*ul* an*n* f*or*bru aire ut d*ixit*. Ro creachad anis coc*r*issu creanaidh claid*mi* glasu tabhairt m*n*a do cidh badhuissiu ingu na*m*na massu A tanaidhi taebhghil teamra ni me acht is tu .a. be. ce. de. pe. qu. isi bis ifrithsuidhi an*n* sin .q.

frisuidiu M; co*m*ruc M; molta 7 E, molta M; fagabair M, focabair E; ar M; ut d*icitu*r E; coa M; claidbiu M; ingu E, *illeg.* M; toebgel M, taebhghil E; frisuidhiu M.

§11 B: Tar naire am*ail* dorighni fotagan laidich dorigh laigi*n* .i. air fosar gensar asamla Alin feachtus dobeith dam biadh labran ballraidh glain iflaitus currigh cofeb ropoler abliadhna brain. Alethnaidhi iarna rai*n*d tucad ori liphi lui*n*d. ropaige og dosu*m* tall 7 ashall f*or*adhrui*m*. Teora bairgi*n* tuctha dui*n*d t*r*erun acul tigi inrig bamarni ceat*r*ar fear maith rofit*ir* inflaith arli*n* ali*n* fechtus.

m*ac* laidich M; aer M, air E; dobreith M, dobeith E; febh ME; leir M, ler E; naigi M, naidhi E; ropaig M; og ME; teora ME; bair<. . . > M, bairge*n* E; dui*n*d ME; ru*n* ME; .iiii. M, ceat*r*a E; arlin. Alin fec M, arlin fechtus E.

§12 B: Tar molta dono .i. molad fothar cen sar asamla am*ail* dorighni ceallach m*ac* cu*m*asgaigh dofir leigi*n*d cluana m*ac* nois. Alla alla c*r*iiada c*r*iada benedic f*or*muduana carais reachtabra adi*n*ge colar cilli cluana. Mor aguth i*n*durtaigh clarach i*m*bi seanadh riarach roleg reachtabra m*ac* art*r*ach tricet spalt*r*ach riabhach.

sa*m*la M, ṡamla E; <. . . > ada M, c*r*iiada c*r*iiadha E; b*en*dic M, benedic E; suarach E; t*r*icat M, t*r*i .c. E.

§13 B: Tamall naire dano am*ail* dorigni m*ac* dac*er*ta. Doc*h*uaidhsi*m* dochill aithchearda itir fear muighi feni rohiadhadh ris iar*um* inti 7 dochuaidsi*m* iarsi*n* docill co*m*air doradad failti do intiside b*r*ocan m*ac* addi ise ropairchindeac*h* i*n*ti conidh airisin adubhairt m*ac* dachearda. Comla natabair rem itigh brocai*n* m*ei*c addhi natiat a imudu anenbli*adn*a b*er*ar dom*ac* aithc*h*earda.

naire ME; .i. dorigne M; rohiad E, *illeg.* M; docuaidsiu*m* M, 7 dochuaidsimh E; rob M, rop E; conad iarsi*n* M; dacerda so E; natabair rem ME; brocan M; tiat ME.

§14 B: Tamall molta am*ail* roraid i*n*fili. Am*a*cu gartna*n* adheig dhias brathar ashosar asi*nn*s*ir* aceat*r*a fathfer isfiu .c. nui*n*gi i*n*copcaille buidi fuil i*m*cheand f*or*matar.

ro<. . .>d M, roraid E; gartnan ME; asosar E, *illeg.* M; <. . .> ear M, si*n*dsear E; cect*ar* fathar M, ceat*ra* fathf*er* E; ui*n*ge M.

§15 B: Lanaeir .i. corob ai*n*m 7 uss 7 do*m*gnas i*n*ti ut d*icitu*r uaderglega. Mucarasa acill dachhellog madail daib dofesid piana*n* imbi corca fasaigh ciana*n* donadesib.

aer M, air E; coraib M; aus M, us E; in*n*ti E; ut est d*i*x*it* hua derglega M, ut uadeirlega E; dofessib M, dofeisid E, dona ME.

§16 B: Ai*n*medh dano am*ail* adubairt i*n*fear *cét*na Nidad rosugi alla damsa dingaire mocaerach achiaran cailg carai robmairg masdomaerad.

dano .i. <. . .> M, dono adubairt E; Ni tathrosu gillai da*m*sa dingair <. . .> mocairach aciaran cailg carai tirad rotmairg mas <. . .> M, Nidad rosu gialla damsa dingaire mocaerach aciaran cailg carai robmairg masdomaeradh E.

§17 B: Romolta am*ail* dorigni reactgal osiadhail dorignaigh i*n*gen bratar m*ei*c ci*n*d faeladh domai rig locha len condearbairt. Madhnodleana nac*r*echt f*or*talmui*n* t*r*ebunadh cetbuiden bad mede bad righe folu*mh* doneoch nabudhfuidhel.

dano am*ail* M; am am*ail* E; *m*nai M, mnai E; lein E, *illeg.* M; conebairt M, condebairt E; Madnodh lena nac*r*echt f*or*talmai*n* <. . .>d cet mbuide*n* bad mete bad rigne folam <. . .>nabad fuidel M, Madnot leana nacrecht f*or*talmui*n* trebunadh cetbuidhean bad mede badrighe folumh doneoch nadbudh fuidel E.

§18 B: Glam dici*n*d dano iarsi*n* ut i*n*alio legitur .i. mar leghthar i*n* i*n*ad eli (*suprascript gloss*).

dige*n*d M; ut <. . .>{git*ur*} .i. inninu ele leghthar M, marleghtar aninadh ele E.

Text of H

Paragraph numbers correspond to paragraphs in the *Fodlai Aíre* tract.

§1 Ataat t*r*ifodla f*or*air .i. aisneiss ail arcital.

§2 Aisnes .i. indessin triatainsimadh cin chuib{d}<. . .>{s c}o {n}nimmd*er*ccad gru{ade}.

§3 Ail .i. lessanmad no athais br*et*ri f*r*i nech.

§4 Airchital aire <. . .> x. fodlai fair {.i. mac} brond 7 dallbach foc*ul* i f*r*ithuidi 7 tair naire 7 tar molta {7 ta}mall naire 7 t{amall} molta 7 lanoer 7 anmed 7 glam dicend.

§5 Mac brond .i. {duine}doni aor 7 gabus i rrun do dune.

§6 Dallbach can ai*nn*m ind fhir diandentar ind {aer}.

§10 {Focu}l i f*r*ithsuide .i. mol*ad* huile acht in foc*ul* dedenach. Mad fo chuidbiud doneith*er* is leth <. . .> {l*ann*}(?) maniped immorro is dilsi loige aisti nuad nama.

§12 Tar molta .i. molad fo cuidb{*iud*} <. . .>.

§11 <. . .> re .i. aor cant*ar* can samla.

§§13,14 Tamall naire 7 molta .i. cin ainm cin lomnair.

§16 <. . .>r 7 ainmed.

§17 Glam di{c}end .i. f*or*bera cen{d} saegail nech co llua{dh is} telca.

Notes

§2 **Aisnéis.** As Meroney notes (1950, 206), *aisnéis aíre* is implied here. *Aisnéis* differs from *ail* and *airchetal* in lacking the fixed form of a nickname or verse. H adds {*c*}*o* {*n*}*nimmderccad gru*{*ade*} 'with reddening of cheek'.

ut dixit. *amail adubhairt* B, *amail adubairt* ME. For restoration of the Latin phrase *ut dixit* see p. 48 above.

for do chuit. *ar dochuitidh* B, *ardochuitig* M, *ardocuidigh* E. The MSS show Middle Irish confusion of the prepositions *for* and *ar* and the change of *i*-stem to velar inflection.

acht ma scerter. *acht mainescerter* BE, *acht mascerdter* M. The phrases *acht ma* 'except if, unless' and *acht mani* 'except if . . . not' are distinct in early sources but later can be used interchangeably.

irecc. *arecha* BME. *DIL* s.v. equates *arecha* with the phrase *ar aí* 'however', although there are no other examples to support this. I follow

Meroney in taking *arecha* as a corruption of the adverbial phrase *irec* 'absolutely, outright'; see *DIL* s.v. *rec(c)*.

is coirt cenae. *coirt* BE, *guirt* M. Here the poet complains that his tongue has dried up like bark for want of food and drink. A similar image is found in no. 26 below (p. 142), in which a household is described as having flesh shrivelled up like bark because of a paltry diet of salt on dry bread. Note that M differs from BE in reading the adjective *goirt* 'bitter', which would also make sense in the context. *DIL* cites the readings of BM s.v. 1 *sceirtid*, suggesting that B's reading *coirt* is for *goirt*, and also cites the reading of B s.v. *goirt*.

§3 **ail.** Marstrander (1962, 207) suggests that *ail* 'reproach' may be the same word as *ail* 'rock' and notes that *sten* 'stone' in Norwegian is used figuratively in a similar sense. The distinguishing feature of this type of satire is its permanent nature and the text states that it may take the form of either a nickname which sticks to the victim or a verbal reproach which may be rhymed or unrhymed. A rhymed satire would, of course, be more lasting than an unrhymed one, and this is reflected in a statement in *Bretha Nemed Dédenach*: *Cuin as ail? .i. ail suthain i rund* 'When is it a reproach? i.e. a lasting reproach in verse form' (*CIH* iii 1127.12, 36). *Ail suthain i rund* is listed as a type of satire in commentary on the heptad on satire; see p. 101 below. In *Cethairṡlicht Athgabálae*, the glossator makes a distinction between satire which is rhymed (*tria cubus*) and unrhymed (*cin cubdus*). The Old Irish text states that there is *athgabail treisi* ... *imm ainme im ecndach* ... 'distraint of three days' stay ... for blemishing [leg. *ainmed*], for satirising'. The phrase *imm ainme* is glossed *.i. cin cubdus .i. lesainm no aerad ⁊ ineclann uil ann ar treise* 'i.e. without rhyme, i.e. nickname or satirising, and honour-price is due for it after three days', while *im ecndach* is glossed *.i. athcantain aire .i. eneclann .i. tria cubus* 'i.e. repetition of a satire, i.e. honour-price, i.e. rhymed' (*CIH* ii 386.20, 33–4). Our text illustrates a nickname (*Cell Chorrfesse*) and a satirical verse, both of which criticise a church for inhospitality. A second stanza illustrating *ail* takes the form of a list of useless undertakings, probably also alluding to vain requests for food and hospitality.

lesainm. *Lesainm lenas* 'a nickname which sticks' is one of the seven types of satire listed in the heptad on satire (p. 88 below). The gloss on this (gloss 3) states that the amount of honour-price paid to the victim increases according to the length of time that the nickname sticks to him: one third is paid for a single utterance, one-half if it sticks to the victim for a year and full honour-price if it sticks to him permanently.

The fact that a nickname could stick to a person is indicated in a gloss in *Cethairṡlicht Athgabálae*, where the phrase *im on lesanma* 'for the blemish of a nickname' is explained as *.i. inni ata isin ainm is len no lista lenus he .i. ni fes in lile itir int ainm* 'i.e. the thing which is in the name which is an "injury" or which is wearisome [and] which follows him, i.e. it is not known if the name will stick to him at all' (*CIH* ii 391.28, 33–4). Similar etymological glosses are found in the heptad on satire (glosses 2 and 13).

According to commentary on the heptad, compensation is paid to the victim's kinsmen in the case of an *ail ṡuthin* 'lasting reproach' and a *lesainm i mbí fírṡamail aíre* 'nickname in which there is the true appearance of satire'. Gloss no. 3 on *lesainm lenas* in the heptad also states that honour-price is paid to the descendants of a victim of a *lánáer* and a *glám dícenn*, both of which are classified as types of *airchetal* in the *Fodlai Aíre* text. The belief that a nickname could cling to and shame not only the original victim but also his relatives is expressed in a passage in *Scéla Muicce Meic Dathó*, where Cet mac Mágach repulses a challenge by Mend mac Sálchada on the grounds that he had previously disfigured and shamed Mend's father: '*Cid ane' ol Cet 'meic na mbachlach cusna lesanmannaib do chomram cucum? Ar ba mese ba sacart oc baistiud ind anmasin for a athair, messe t<h>all a sáil de co claidiub conna ruc acht oínchois úaim'* (Thurneysen 1935, §12): 'What then', said Cet, 'the sons of churls with nicknames contending with me? For I was the priest at the baptism of that name upon his father. It was I who cut off his heel with a sword so that he had only one leg when he left me'. The patronym *mac Sálchada* refers to this disfigurement, the first element of *sálchada* being *sál* 'heel' (McCone 2007, 157).

aithis bréthre. *athais mbretri* B, *athais mbreitri* E, *aithis* M, *athais bretri* H. According to *DIL* s.v., *aithis* is a feminine noun (see *GOI* §294 (b)), while Marstrander (1962, 214) derives it from *fis* 'knowledge', which is masculine (*GOI* §307). There are no examples of nasalisation after *aithis* in the glosses and the nasalisation of *mbréthre* in BE is hardly sufficient evidence to suggest that it may originally have been neuter. *Aithis* is also used of a physical blemish believed to be caused by satire and occurs in the triad *ail 7 anim 7 aithis* 'reproach and blemish and reviling'. This triad is found in a variety of forms and is sometimes associated with *glám dícenn* (Meroney 1950, 218–9).

Is do decraib in domain etc. The metre of this stanza is *rannaigecht becc* (7^2 7^2 7^2 7^2). The phrases *ba deól mela a mecnaib ibair* and *ba longad i scellaib scibair* are found in a list of futile undertakings in *Aislinge Meic Conglinne* (Jackson 1990, ll. 857–9). *Nirbu buain mhela a mecnaib iobhuir* occurs in a similar list in *Airec Menman Uraird meic Cosse* (Byrne 1908, 72). For examples of similar phrases in Middle Irish satires see p. 225 below. T. F. O'Rahilly (1922, 128 ff.) notes the common formula of grouping together a series of such phrases. The glossator of the heptad on satire cites *is do decraib in domain* as an example of *ail ṡuthin* (gloss 14).

scellaib. *ceallaib* B, *<. . .>ellaib* M, *cellaibh* E. *Scellaib* has been restored on the basis of *ba longad i scellaib scibair* in *Aislinge Meic Conglinne.* This phrase is discussed by Kelly (1997, 342), who observes that *scell* can refer to the husk of ripe pepper as well as to the strong-flavoured seed, both of which would be unpleasant to eat.

do-romaltar. *doromaltar* B, *doramaltar* M, *doromhlatar* E. I follow the manuscripts in reading *do-romaltar,* which shows the syncopated form of the third plural *t*-preterite ending; cf. *-bertar, -bertatar* (*GOI* §684; *EIV* 76). The non-syncopated ending *-tatar* was the usual form in Middle Irish (*SG* III §12.49).

Cell Chorrḟesse. This nickname is found in the form *cella corrfeisi* in a Middle Irish glossary, where it is glossed *.i. cell a nebhar feis co corrach .i. englas* 'i.e. a church in which a feast is drunk restlessly, i.e. watery milk' (*CIH* v 1566.36–7). *Englas* is written as an interlinear gloss. I follow Meroney (1950, 204) in taking the first element as the adjective *corr,* which has a wide range of meanings and seems to be used here in the sense of 'wretched' or 'meagre'. An alternative interpretation is to take the first element as *corr* 'heron', since the heron is associated with satire in other sources; see p. 36 above. The intention then might be to suggest that guests have to wait a long time for their meal, just as a heron waits patiently for fish. The nickname is also cited in the forms *cell coire sin* and *cella coire isin* by the glossator of the heptad on satire (glosses 2 and 13) to illustrate *lesainm lenas* and *lesainm i mbí fírṡamail aíre* respectively.

Mag Lacha etc. As it stands in the MSS, the syllabic structure is 3^2 7^2 6^2 6^2. Emending *cul* BME and *cen* BE, *cein* M to OIr. *cúlu* and *céne* respectively gives a shortened form (*gairit*) of *deibide nguilbnech* 3^2 7^2 7^2 7^2.

Mag Lacha. Hogan (1910, 522–3) mentions several such places, one of which, Moylagh in Co. Meath, is the location of the church of Ros Dela. This church is referred to in notes on *Félire Óengusso* (Stokes 1905b, 188) and in glosses on St Fiacc's Hymn in the *Liber Hymnorum* (Atkinson 1898, vol. 1, 103). This may be the church in question here.

clotha. Meroney translates 'he has turned his back on famous places (?)'. *DIL* lists several meanings for *cloth,* including 'reputation' and, by extension, 'generosity', which would suit the context here. I take the subject of *do-rat* to be the church rather than *mac flatha* and translate 'it has turned its back on generosity'.

§4 **tamall aíre.** (*tamall aire* B, *tarmallaire* E, {*ta*}*mall naire* H). H shows nasalisation after *tamall*, while in §13 below all four MSS read *tamall naire.* I have found no evidence to suggest that it was originally a neuter noun, however, and the nasalisation may have arisen due to the influence of *tár n-aíre* in the preceding phrase. Such influence would also explain *tarmall* in E. Note also that nasalisation has been restored in *airchetal n-aíre,* although it is omitted in all four MSS.

§5 **Mac bronn**. According to BME, the main characteristic of a *mac bronn* satire is that it is composed secretly. H differs from this in defining it as a satire which is recited to another person in secret: {*duine*} *doni aor 7 gabus i rrun do dune* 'a person who composes a satire and recites it secretly to another'. *Mac bronn* is recognised as a specific type of satire in a bardic poem in the Book of the Dean of Lismore, where it is described in terms of a pregnancy: *Trí ráithe torrach a-tám / táinig m'ionbhaidh go h-iomlán; / trom taobh ón fhoilcheas fhaladh / toircheas aor an ollamhan.* 'I am nine months pregnant, my time for childbearing has come; (my) side is heavy from the concealed spite, the satire of the ollamh is a pregnancy' (Greene, 1945–47, 232 q. 4).

A passage of Middle Irish commentary states that the penalty paid by the poet for composing a *mac bronn* increases according to the number of people to whom he recites the satire:

> *Caide mac bronn 7 rl–. letheneclann isin mac brond forsin filid o bias ainm 7 ús 7 domnas and, 7 leth forsin fer diar gabad, uair rofogair in filidh do cen a hurdurcudh; a nécuibdius and sin. mad cuibdhe immorro, is letheneclann foraib a ndis 7 icaid fo chudruma.*
>
> *Dia naisnéighi in fili do neoch eile, is .iiii.raimthe letheneclainni la taeb a letheneclainni fein, 7 letheneclann o gach fir dia naisneighend do gres a necuibdius, 7 icaid in fili imarcraid; cid a cuibduis beide, is fon fiach is mo thecait a necuibdius .i. fo fiach in filed; 7 amail forbres indliged in filed ima indisin do-sum, forbridh a feich gu roa lanfiach na haire air .i. isin .u.id fir, is and rosoich fair, uair leth 7 .iiii.raimthe lethe ara indisin do dhís.*
>
> *Mas e indfethem robai aigi i nuair a denma a gabail do gach aenduine, gingo gaba acht d'aenduine, is laneneclann uadh.*

> *Ma roindis in fili d'aenduine i rún, 7 doroindis in fer sin d'fir eile, 7 ni hé a gabáil dorinde acht a hindisin, islan dó. uair islan gach mairne* [leg. *mairnes*] *mignima 7 rl-. 7 eneclann forsin filid.*
>
> 'What is the *mac bronn* etc.? Half honour-price for the *mac bronn* is due from the poet when name and lineage and abode are mentioned in it, and half is due from the man to whom it was recited, for the poet ordered him not to publish it abroad; that is for a non-versified satire. If there is versification, however, half honour-price is due from them both and they pay equally.
>
> If the poet tells it to someone else, one-eighth honour-price is due in addition to his own half honour-price and half honour-price is always due from every man to whom he tells it in non-versified form and the poet pays an additional amount (i.e. the poet pays extra for every person to whom he tells it). Even if they are versified, payment is according to the greatest penalty which they reach in the case of non-versification, i.e. according to the penalty of the poet. And as the illegality of the poet increases by telling it to him, his (the poet's) penalties increase until the full penalty of the satire extends to him, i.e. at the fifth man, it is then that it extends to him, because a half and one-eighth [honour-price] is due for telling it to two people.
>
> If the intention he had at the time of its composition was to recite it to every single person, even if he only recites it to one person, it is full honour-price that is due from him.
>
> If the poet told it to a single person in secret and that man told another man, and he did not recite it but told it, he is free from liability, for "anyone who reveals evil deeds is free from liability" etc. And honour-price is due from the poet' (*CIH* iii 971.30–972.3).

According to this text, the amount of honour-price paid by the poet increases by one-eighth for each additional person to whom he recites the satire. Half honour-price is due for the first recitation, half plus one-eighth for the second, half plus one quarter for the third, half plus three-eighths for the fourth and full honour-price for the fifth. The passage shows some confusion over the nature of a *mac bronn* satire, however, in stating that it includes the victim's *ainm 7 us 7 domnas* 'name and lineage and abode'. According to §15 of our tract, these are characteristics of *lánáer* 'full satire', while gloss 4 in the heptad attributes them to *áer aicetail* 'a recited satire'.

The extract *Caide mac bronn 7 rl.* may be a citation from our text. The citation *islan gach mairne mignima 7 rl-* is derived from *Cáin Ḟuithirbe*, a text which is preserved only in the form of glossed extracts (see *Companion* 212 ff.). It is also cited in *O'Dav.* §1272 among a number of extracts from *Cáin Ḟuithirbe*: *Mairned .i. faisneis nó brath, ut est slán cach mairnes mignímu .i. bi slán dontí dogni faisneis in drochmerlig no in drochgnima* '*mairned* i.e. a telling or betrayal, *ut est* "anyone who informs on evil deeds is free from liability", i.e. let every one who tells of the evil thief or the evil deed be exempt'. In Version A of *Cáin Ḟuithirbe*, the words *Slan cach* are glossed *.i. fer mairnis gadaige no luingsech no sechip drochduine, islan do* 'i.e. a man who informs on a thief or a pirate or any bad person is free from liability' (*CIH* iii 775.34–5). A further citation is found among a series of extracts from the heptads: *Slan cach mairne mignimu .i. islan donti dogni aisneis, ce beth in fer fora ndera aisneis aca agra* 'Anyone who informs on [*leg. mairnes*] evil deeds is free from liability, i.e. there is immunity for the person who gives information even though the man about whom he informs is suing him' (*CIH* iii 1049.17). According to Binchy, *CIH* iii 1049 note 1, this refers to a pledge for informing against a thief (*gell fri himaisneis tathat*; *CIH* iii 1049.24). See also Kelly (1988, 156).

§6 **dallbach.** The main characteristic of a *dallbach* is the anonymity of the victim, as stated in H: *can ainm ind fhir dia ndentar ind* {*aer*} 'without the name of the man for whom the satire is composed'. Three types of *dallbach* are distinguished, based on the amount of information given about the victim. A *dallbach tréntuinidi*, for example, contains more information than a *dallbach beccthuinidi* or *dallbach cen tuinide.*

DIL s.v. 2 *dallbach* suggests that this is the same word as 1 *dallbach* 'blindness, stupidity'. The first element is taken as the adjective *dall* 'blind, dark' in *Corm.* Y §489: *dallbach .i. dallfúach* 'i.e. dark word'. In Middle Irish commentary on satire (*CIH* v 1587.35), *dallbach* is also described as *in dallfocal* 'the dark word'. The glossary *Duil Dromma Ceta* defines it as *.i. airbire tre cuibhdius, 7 ni fes cia da ndéntar .i. dall-fuach* 'i.e. a rhymed reproach and it is not known for whom it is composed, i.e. a dark word' (*CIH* ii 613.6). The second element may be *-bach* 'breaking', which is found in compounds such as *murbach* (*muirbech*) 'breakwater', *bélbach* 'horse's bit' and *fótbach* 'cutting sods' (Uhlich 2002, 414). Cf.

also the gloss *bach .i. brisead* in a Middle Irish glossary (*CIH* iii 951.35). The term *dallbach* also occurs in a tract on metrical faults: *Trefocul . . . Cen dallbhach dona dallbaigib* '*Trefocul* . . . without one of the *dallbachs*' (*Auraic.* ll. 1930–1; see L. Breatnach 2004, 25).

A passage of Middle Irish commentary states that the oaths of at least three people are required in order to deny the composition of a *dallbach.* It also states that the compensation for a *dallbach cen tuinide* is less than that for a *dallbach tréntuinidi* or a *dallbach beccthuinidi.* This passage is part of a longer section of commentary on satire (*CIH* v 1587.18–1588.8), which is likely to be derived from *Bretha Nemed Dédenach* (*Companion* 186):

> *Dia ndentar* [leg. *Do-indedar*] *dallbach do triur .i. aisneiter in dallfocal; co toingter he do triur, 7 triur rucastar amarus foran filid and; a luigi doib a triur; 7 cid lín as lia doberadh amarus and, combeth a luighi doib uili, no cona beth acht a triur; no as triur ina deaghaidh do sena in dallbaidh trentuidhine, 7 cona triur ata in rith.*
>
> *Cid fodera cutrumus neneclainne isin dallbach bectuidine 7 isin dallbach trentuidhine, 7 cona triur atá .i. trian neneclainne 7 saine fira? is e in fath: saine in tuarustail fodera .i. sesedh neneclainne isin dallbach cen tuidhine, 7 deismirecht air: ata ben os tir . . .*
>
> 'A *dallbach* is denied by oath by three people, i.e. the dark word is related so that it is sworn by three people, and three people cast suspicion on the poet concerning it. The three people are to swear and if a greater number would cast suspicion concerning it, they would all swear, or there would be only three. Or three people are to swear on his behalf for denying the strongly established *dallbach* and it is as far as three people that the procedure extends.
>
> Why is it that there is an equal amount of honour-price for the lightly established *dallbach* and for the firmly established *dallbach* and that it extends to three people, i.e. there is one third honour-price and a difference of proof? This is the reason why: the difference of the description causes it, i.e. there is one sixth honour-price for the unestablished *dallbach,* and an example of it is: "There is a woman in the land" . . . ' (*CIH* v 1587.35–1588.4.)

This passage has also been translated by Meroney (1950, 208). The amount of honour-price seems to depend on the information contained in the satire. Although *dallbach tréntuinidi* and *dallbach beccthuinidi* contain different amounts of information about the subject, both provide at least some clues as to his identity and therefore entail the payment of compensation. *Dallbach cen tuinide*, on the other hand, contains no information about the victim. Binchy suggests, note u, reading *do-indedar* for *dia ndentar.* The extract *dia ndentar dallbach do triur* is also found in *O'Dav.* §603 among citations derived from *Bretha Nemed Dédenach*: *Do indedar .i. dínnis, ut est do indedar dallbach do triar* '*do-indedar*, i.e. denial by oath, *ut est* "a *dallbach* is denied by oath by three people"' (reading the verbal noun of *do-indet* for *d'ínnis* in Stokes' and Binchy's editions, as suggested in *Companion* 126 note 88). *Dallbach* is also associated with *dindís* 'denial by oath' in a Middle Irish glossary: *Dinnis .i. luighi, ut est dalbach trén tuidhin fiach* ... 'Denial by oath, i.e. swearing, *ut est dallbach tréntuinidi* of penalties ... ' (*CIH* iii 950.20). Kelly (1988, 200 note 68) notes that *dindís*, the verbal noun of *do-indet*, is the term used for denying guilt in a case of secret murder.

The section of commentary on *mac bronn* discussed above (§5) also contains information on the means of establishing compensation for a *dallbach*:

> *Is amlaid icar fiach isin dallbach: fo aicned na haire bis and iarna mes do filid choitchend; no is fon fiach doberar luigi and .i. nech diambi logh enech ina dhegaid in filed; no is fir fo thuarustal arra, no fir testa ma teist in filidh*
>
> 'It is thus that a penalty is paid for the *dallbach*: according to the type of satire it is, having been judged by an impartial poet; or it is according to the penalty that an oath is made concerning it, i.e. someone who has an honour-price swears on behalf of the poet; or it is an oath according to the evidence of oath-helpers, or the oath of a trustworthy witness if the poet be such' (*CIH* iii 972.4–6).

Fo aicned na haire may refer to the three types of *dallbach*, the highest penalty presumably being incurred by a *dallbach tréntuinidi.* The poet may rely on oath-helpers or may adduce evidence himself to prove that the satire is justified. The *Trefocal* poem refers to a *dallbach* which incurs no penalty: *Fa ma dalbach dina-tobngar díre n-ainech?* 'Or be cryptic allusion incurring no honor-appeasement?' (Meroney 1953, 96 §7).

fair. The MSS read the feminine singular form *furri.* I have not found any evidence to suggest that *dallbach* was feminine, however, and it is treated as a masculine *o*-stem in Middle Irish commentary: ... *do sena in dallbaidh trentuidhine* '... for denying the strongly established *dallbach*' (*CIH* v 1587.38).

§7 **Paitrén.** *paitren* BE, *patre* M. The name *Paitrén* occurs in a list of Laigin genealogies in the Book of Lecan (86 Vc 9) and a variant form is *Petrán ó Chill Lainni*, found in a Litany of Irish saints (*Corp. Gen.* 120 b 30 and *LL* 52192). I have not found any other attestations.

The metre is *cró cummaisc etir casbairdni ocus lethrannaigecht móir* (7^3 5^1 7^3 5^1), for which see Murphy (1961, [96]).

caíniu. *caine* BE, *cainu* M. I translate *caíniu* as 'most fair'. The comparative began to replace the superlative during the Old Irish period (*GOI* §366.3; *SG* III §6.15).

do-chúaid do ráith. Lit. 'which went [away] completely', i.e. which was in vain. Note that *cúaid*, which is disyllabic in Old Irish, must be read here as monosyllabic for metrical purposes.

§8 Versions of this stanza are cited in *Auraic.* ll. 1064–7 and ll. 4020–3 to illustrate the word *grus* 'cheese'. Meroney translates the second couplet as 'Where cheeses are plentiful though milk is scarce', reading *as* 'milk' rather than the preposition *a* 'out of'. The stanza has been translated into Modern Irish by L. Breatnach (1988, 12).

The metre is *lethrannaigecht mór* (5^1 5^1 5^1 5^1).

grus. Binchy (1941, 2 l. 27) reads *grús* but as Kelly notes (1997, 326 note 66) a short vowel is established by the metre of our poem.

§9 This stanza lacks the introductory heading which precedes every other example in the MSS. It is clearly an illustration of *dallbach cen tuinide*, however, and the first line is cited as an example of this type of satire in Middle Irish legal commentary, for which see note on §6 above. The stanza is also cited in a gloss on the word *deilm* 'loud noise' in *Amrae Choluimb Chille* (Stokes 1899, 158.11). It has been edited by Meyer (1919, no. 77) and translated by Greene and O'Connor (1967, 111–13).

The metre is *lethrannaigecht mór* (5^1 5^1 5^1 5^1).

§10 **Focal i frithṡuidiu.** H defines *focal i frithṡuidiu* as *molad huile acht in focul dedenach* 'everything is praise except for the last word', while BME describe it as a quatrain of praise containing one word of satire. As Meroney suggests (1950, 209), *frithṡuide* appears to be used here in the sense of opposition rather than equivalent (see *DIL* s.v. *fris-suidigedar*).

The term also occurs in the *Treḟocal* tract on metrical faults: *Trefocul ... Cen a focul frisin n-aprait filid frisuithi* '*Treḟocul* ... without their word which poets call *frisuithi*' (*Auraic.* l. 1933).

Middle Irish commentary on satire states that *focal i frithṡuidiu* is one of only two types which entail restitution, the other type being *glám dícenn.* Note that the citation *a chreachad anís aina cris* is taken from our text:

> ... *7 comadh he in dara hinad i fuil aithgin isan air, isin focul friaiche 7 isin ngloim ndicind; is ed doni focal frithaithe ann comrac aíre 7 molta .i. eric amail budh aír hi uịli. desmirecht er: a chreachad anís aina cris. ameiric faigeadh gin cuibdes ann no co neach a cuibdeas rann; o rachas, is laneneclann ind*
>
> '... and so that it is one of the two instances in which there is restitution for satire, for the *focal i frithṡuidiu* and for the *glám dícenn.* This is what constitutes a *focal i frithṡuidiu*: a coming together of satire and praise, i.e. compensation is as though it were all satire. An example of it is "*a chreachad anís aina cris*". Not liable to compensation is an unrhymed *faicet* until it goes into stanzaic versification. When it goes (i.e. when it is rhymed), there is full honour-price for it' (*CIH* v 1587.30–4).

The beginning of this passage has been translated by Thurneysen (1927, 215). For *faicet* see note on §13 below.

H adds *Mad fo chuidbiud doneither is leth* <...>*{lann}* (?) *maniped immorro is dilsi loige aisti nuad* [leg. *úad*] *nama* 'If it is composed in mockery, it is half [honour-price]; if it is not, however, there is only forfeiture from him of the reward for the metre'. This is similar to a gloss in *Gúbretha Caratniad* on the penalty for false praise; see p. 7 above. The term *focal i frithṡuidiu* is also found in a citation from *Bretha Nemed Dédenach* in *O'Dav.* §1547 (*Companion* 154): ... *Nó tenn .i. canamain, ut est isin focul frithṡaige. Inti fodnacuib fo inti nodteinn .i. canus fa dheoidh* 'Or *tenn,* i.e. recital, *ut est* in the word of opposition. He who leaves it or he who declares it, i.e. who repeats it at the end'.

The third line of the stanza illustrating *focal i frithṡuidiu* in our text is cited in a Middle Irish glossary: *Usa .i. coir, ut est tabairt mna do gemad usa* '*Usa,* i.e. "proper" *ut est* "*tabairt mna do gemad usa*"' (*CIH* iii 949.39).

The metre is *dechnad mór* (8^2 6^2 8^2 6^2).

ro crechad. Meroney translates 'he has been despoiled'. *Crechaid* is also used in the sense 'marks, sears', while the adjective *glas* 'light green, blue' is used to describe the colour of skin tattooed with woad (Kelly 1997, 267).

ingen. *ingu* BE. The definition of *focal i frithṡuidiu* suggests that the stanza should praise the subject while at the same time containing one word of satire. I have emended the MSS to read *ingen* 'nail', which may be the *focul for brú aíre,* the implication being that a sharp nail as an instrument for tattooing is of more interest to the subject than a woman. Accepting the restoration of the Old Irish form, there would also seem to be word play between *ingen* 'nail' and *ingen* 'daughter'.

A Thanaidi etc. Meroney prints this passage in prose form and notes that it illustrates the principle of contraries, i.e. *mé* versus *tú,* *a* versus *b* etc. It could equally be taken as a syllabically irregular verse, reading *qú* with a long vowel for rhyme with *tú.* I follow Meroney in taking the adjective *tanaide* 'thin' as a personal name. For other examples see O'Brien (1973, 219 §7(a)).

§11 **tár.** As *DIL* suggests s.v. 2 *tár,* this is probably the same word as 1 *tár* 'insult'. It is followed by nasalisation in all four MSS and also in the Old Irish glosses on the *Senchas Már* (*CIH* iii 894.19), which suggests that it was originally a neuter noun. The definitions of *tár n-aíre* and *tár molta* in BME as *áer/molad fo ṡár cen ṡár a samla* are similar to types of satire known as *áer co ndath molta* and *molad co ndath aíre* 'satire with the colour of praise' and 'praise with the colour of satire', illustrations of which are cited in *Bretha Nemed Dédenach* (*CIH* iii 1112. 13–23); see p. 8 above. H reads *.i. aor cantar can samla* 'i.e. a satire which is recited without [the] likeness [of a satire]'.

The contrast between *tár* and *tamall* is one of over- and understatement respectively and the examples of *tár molta* and *tamall molta* cited in our text illustrate this quite clearly. In §12, the poet is excessive in praising the very qualities which portray Rechtabrae as an arrogant and unlearned bibliophile. In §14, the satire lies in the fact that there is nothing to praise about the sons of Gartnán other than the fact that their mother's head-dress is worth one hundred ounces of silver. *Tár n-aíre, tár molta* and *tamall* are listed among five types of satire in the Old Irish glosses on the *Senchas Már*; see p. 49 above.

Fotacán Laídech. M reads *mac laidich,* which suggests that the scribe interpreted *laídich* as a personal name rather than as the epithet *laídech* 'celebrated in lays, songful'. In the tale *Airec Menman Uraird Maic Coisse* (Byrne 1908, 53.5), *Lanlaphrad*[*h*] *Laidhich* occurs in a list alongside *Ecna n-an Aithirne, Briatharchath Goburchind* and *Glandintlecht n-Etaine.* This pattern of common noun plus name indicates that *Laidhich* is also to be taken as a name in *Lanlaphrad[h] Laidhich. Laídech* is used as an epithet in *mac do Lugaid laidech lantrait* (*LL* 6476) and *As mé Laitheócc láidhech lán* (Meyer 1912b, 110 q. 13).

A lín fechtas etc. The metre is *rannaigecht mór* (7^1 7^1 7^1 7^1).

do-breth. *dobeith* BE, *dobreith* M. Meroney follows BE and reads *do beith.*

biäd. This is to be read as disyllabic in order to give a heptasyllabic line.

fib ... roptar lir. *feb* B, *febh* ME; *ropo ler* BE, *ropo leir* M. Meroney reads *feb*, rhyming with *ler*, and translates: 'In the barony of excellent Currech; plentiful were Bran's years (?)', stating in a note on *ler* that this interpretation is doubtful. I have emended the MSS to read *fib*, dative singular of *feb* (L. Breatnach 1997, 51 §2.1), and *lir*, equative of *il* 'many', with the meaning 'as many times as ... so many were ...' . The MSS have also been emended to read OIr. third plural perfect indicative of the copula.

teoir bairgena. *teora* BME, *bairgin* B, *bair<...>* M, *bairgen* E. The numeral *trí* (masc.), *teoir/teora* (fem.) is followed by the plural form of the noun in Old Irish. All three MSS read *teora* followed by a singular form, which is a Middle Irish development (*SG* III 8.7). Emending to the plural form *bairgena* and reading *teoir* still gives a heptasyllabic line.

dún ... rúin. *duind ... run* BME. The MSS read the later form *dúind* with palatal *-n* (*SG* III §13.8) and a non-palatal form of *rún* in accusative singular. The latter may have arisen as a result of confusion between nominative and accusative singular of *ā*-stems, although this feature is normally only found when the noun is the direct object of a verb (*SG* III §5.6). Alternatively, it may be an example of the treatment of *rún* as a masculine *o*-stem, for examples of which see *DIL* s.v. col. 120, l. 53. *Aicill* rhyme is not obligatory in this position

ar lín. This forms a *dúnad* with the opening words.

§12 **tár molta.** The distinction between *tár molta* and *ró molta* §17 is unclear, although the latter was recognised as a separate type of satire as shown by its occurrence in Middle Irish commentary: *leth isin romolad* (?) *trian isin tamain aire* 'half [honour-price] for the excess of praise and one third for the touch of satire' (*CIH* vi 2122.3). Binchy expands *romol–* and *tam–* as *romolad* (?) and *tamain* respectively, but it is likely that *ró molta* and *tamall* are the intended forms. *Tár molta, tamall molta* and *ró molta* are types of false praise; see p. 7 above. H reads *tar molta .i. molad fo cuidb{iud}* 'excess of praise, i.e. praise in mockery'.

Cellach mac Cumascaig. For his *obit* see *AU s.a.* 867 (*recte* 868), where he is described as *abbas Fobair, iuuenis sapiens et ingeniosissimus* 'abbot of Fobhar, a learned and most ingenious young man'. He is also named as the author of a poem about Feidlimid mac Crimthainn, king of Munster, in *FM s.a.* 839, for which see Ó hAodha (1991, 239 no. 34).

Alla alla etc. The metre is *dechnad mór* (8^2 6^2 8^2 6^2). This verse has been edited and translated by L. Breatnach (2006, 66).

alla. Meroney takes *alla* as representing a mispronunciation of *halleluliah*. The form *alle* is, however, attested as a variant of *aille* 'act of praising, giving thanks; hymn of praise'. *DIL* s.v. *aille* suggests that this may be a loan word from Latin *alleluia.*

críada, bendic. *criiada criada*; *benedic* B, <. . .>*ada*; *bendic* M, *criiada criiadha*; *benedic* E. M's reading *bendic* gives the required number of syllables. Meroney states (1950, 210) that these spellings represent Rechtabrae's mispronunciation of Latin. Anthony Harvey has suggested (personal comment) that since the spellings accurately reflect Irish pronunciation of Latin, the satire lies rather in portraying Rechtabrae as a pompous show-off who peppers his speech with Latin.

ríarach. E reads *suarach* 'mean' against *riarach* BM. *Ríarach* is the correct reading, since it rhymes with *ríabach* in line *d.*

§13 **tamall.** Note that the example illustrating *tamall aíre* is not in verse form, even though it is stated in §4 that it is one of the ten divisions of *airchetal n-aíre* 'versified satire'. All four MSS have nasalisation after *tamall*, for which see note on §4 above. H reads *tamall naire ⁊ molta .i. cin ainm cin lomnair*. . . 'a touch of satire and praise, i.e. without name without . . . (?)'.

Tamall aíre and *tamall molta* are recognised as specific types of satire in Middle Irish commentary on offences which are covered by treaties. This states that honour-price is paid *fo aicned in cheneil aire* 'according to the type of the satire': *bo isin tamall i cairde, cid tamall aire cidh tamall molta* 'a cow for a *tamall* in a treaty, whether it be a *tamall* of satire or a *tamall* of praise' (*CIH* iii 964.23). In *O'Dav.* §1549, *tamall* is glossed *.i. tadhall .i. tamall aire ⁊ tamall molta .i. tadall do faicet a molad* 'i.e. a touch, i.e. a *tamall* of satire and a *tamall* of praise, i.e. a touch as a *faicet* in praise'.

A passage in the *Trefocul* tract on metrical faults suggests that *faicet* was a type of satire which could be rhymed or unrhymed: *Trefocal* . . . *Cen tar. Cen tamall. Cen faicit co cuibdius. Cen faicit cen chuibdius* (*Auraic.* ll. 1932–3): '*Trefocal* . . . without *tár*, without *tamall*, without a rhymed *faicet* without an unrhymed *faicet*'. Calder translates '. . . without disgrace, without pause, without rhyming accident, without unrhyming accident', but *tar* and *tamall* are more likely to be used here in the technical sense of sub-divisions of satire. The term is also found in *Bretha Nemed Toísech*, which states: *sechtmadh eneclainne righ túath sin isin faigett gan chuibhdhes* 'that is one-seventh of the honour-price of a *rí túath* for the unrhymed *faicet*' (*CIH* iii 1135.23–4). Commentary on the heptad on satire also refers to an unrhymed *faicet*; see p. 99 below.

Mac Dá Cherdae. BME read *da*, although an alternation between *mo* and *do/da* is common (O'Brien 1973, 220 §10(b); cf. *Cill Dá Chellóc* §15 below). The saint Mac Dá Cherdae, also known as Comgan, is portrayed as both a sage and a fool in the literature (Kenney 1929, 420; O'Keeffe 1911).

do Chill Aithcherdae. The only example of Cell Aithcherdae in Hogan (1910, 175) is taken from our text.

rop'. *rop* BE, *rob* M. The final vowel (*ropo/ropu*) has dropped out before a word beginning with a vowel.

tét. *tiat a* B, *tiat* ME. ME read the Middle Irish form *tiat.* B's reading *tiat a* may have arisen through dittography as a result of the immediately following vowel in the phrase *imudu.* Meroney reads *tiata,* which he describes as 'corrupt', while *DIL* cites the stanza s.v. *tíata,* preceded by a query.

§14 The syllabic structure is irregular (10^2 11^2 10^2 6^2). Mercier's interpretation of this stanza (1962, 111) is particularly apt: 'The MacGartnan brothers are fine fellows: their mother buys her hats from Lilly Daché'. It has also been translated into Modern Irish by L. Breatnach (1988, 12).

fáthar. Thurneysen, *GOI* §443, takes this to be a later adaptation of OIr. *sethar,* second plural genitive personal pronoun. Aside from the form in our text, there are only two other examples cited in *DIL* s.v. *fathar.* The length of the vowel is established by rhyme with *máthar.*

cét n-uinge. Values are often expressed in terms of a particular weight of precious metal, normally silver (Kelly 1997, 593).

§15 **lánáer.** The metre is *dechnad mór* (8^2 6^2 8^2 6^2). A slightly different version of this quatrain is cited in *MV* III §210 as an illustration of the metre *trírech*; see no. 30 below.

It is clear from references in legal material that this was recognised as a specific type of satire. In *Cethairślicht Athgabálae*, for example, *áer* is described as a *cin tengad* 'an offence of tongue' and this is glossed *.i. in brath no in lanaer, no cipeth cinel aire .i. in glaim dicenn* 'i.e. the treachery or the *lánáer*, or whatever kind of satire, i.e. the *glám dícenn*' (*CIH* ii 404.2–3). It is also associated with *glám dícenn* in *Bretha Étgid*: *.E. mbreac: trefocal focra: 'gromfa gromfa, glamfa glamfa, aerfa aerfa' .i. gromfa iman nglasgabail, glamfa iman nglaim ndigind, aerfa iman lanair* 'Speckled negligence: *trefocal fócrai*: "I will mock I will mock, I will revile I will revile, I will satirise I will satirise" i.e. I will mock by means of the *glasgabáil*, I will revile by means of the *glám dícenn*, I will satirise by means of the *lánáer*' (*CIH* iii 927.30–1). The citation *gromfa gromfa* etc. is from the *Trefocul* poem (Meroney 1953, 99 §47; see p. 7 above). For *glasgabáil* see p. 96 below. A gloss in *Bretha Nemed Toísech* associates *lánáer* with excessive praise: *ni moltur nach ro .i. lanaoir* 'you are not to praise in any way excessively, i.e. *lánáer*' (*CIH* vi 2218.4). The phrase *ni moltur nach ro* also occurs in *Bretha Nemed Dédenach* (*CIH* iii 1114.15) in a passage dealing with the role of the poet in praise and satire (L. Breatnach 2006, 68). In gloss 3 on the heptad on satire, *lánáer* is listed as one of four types which entail the payment of honour-price to a person's descendants; see p. 88 below.

ainm 7 us 7 domgnas. *Cíanán* is *ainm* 'name', *dona Déssib* is *us* 'lineage' and *Cell Dá Chellóc* is *domgnas* 'abode'. This triad, which is also applied to the version of the stanza in *MV* III §210, occurs elsewhere and has been discussed by Meroney (1949). In gloss 4 on the heptad on satire, the phrase *ainm 7 us 7 domgnas* glosses *áer aicetail*. Legal commentary associates it with *mac bronn* 'son of womb', although it is clearly a more suitable description of *lánáer*, since secrecy is the main characteristic of the former type of satire; see p. 70. It occurs in a section of *Bretha Nemed Dédenach* which consists of a series of questions and answers on poetic art (*tuarustal núadh* 'a description of poetry'): *Cis lir a drecha?* 'How many are its forms?' (*CIH* iii 1128.35) *.i. ainm, ús 7 domhnus* 'i.e. name, lineage and abode' (*CIH* iii 1129.8). In an introductory passage to *MV* II in the Book of Ballymote, the triad is found as an explanation of *ord sluinte* 'order of naming', one of the sixteen divisions of *filidecht* (Thurneysen 1891, 30 (k)).

ut dixit. *ut dicitur* B, *ut est dixit* M, *ut* E. The Latin phrase *ut dixit* is corrupt or incomplete in the MSS. Meroney (1950, 210, §14) states that 'Something is wrong here ... but I cannot resolve the sign in M printed as "g;" it looks like a figure eight'. This is a standard abbreviation for Latin *est.*

aue Derglega. I have found no other references to this poet, who is also credited with the composition of the quatrain cited in §16. He is included in a list of poets by Meyer (1909, 57).

Cell Dá Chellóc. Hogan (1910, 187) identifies this as Kilmallock, County Limerick.

ro-féssid. The vowel length is confirmed by rhyme with *Déssib* (*GOI* §615).

píanán. This word is unattested elsewhere. In his edition of MV III §210, Meyer (1919, no. 164) translates 'ein kleiner Quälgeist (?)' 'a little pest', while Gwynn (1931, 13) suggests *locc péne* 'place of suffering'. I follow Meroney (1950, 206) in taking *píanán* as a variant of *bíanán* 'satchel'. In a Middle Irish satire (no. 48 below) the adjectives *píanánach* and *tíagánach* (from *tíag* 'satchel') refer to the subject's habit of scrounging around bags and other types of containers.

corca fásaig. Hogan (1910, 294) mistakenly takes this as a placename '*Corcu fásaig* in the Deisi', citing the example from *MV* III §210. Wild oats (*avena fatua*) are found growing in corn-fields to the present day and Kelly notes (1997, 227) that the reference in our text indicates that it was considered to be a worthless plant.

donaib. *dona* BME. The MSS show the loss of the dative plural ending (*SG* III §7.5.)

§16 **ainmed.** Meroney translates *ainmed* as 'sarcasm'. Glosses and commentary on *Cóic Conara Fugill* and *Cethairṡlicht Athgabálae* suggest that *ainmed* was a type of satire which entailed drawing attention to a person's blemish. This could be either a physical defect or an undesirable social condition; see p. 15 above. On the other hand, the stanza illustrating *ainmed* in our text, although difficult to interpret, does not seem to ridicule the physical appearance of its subject. The general sense may be that he is lazy in the performance of his duties as a shepherd.

The metre is *dechnad mór* (8^2 6^2 8^2 6^2).

Nít adras-su (?) gíallai dam-sa. *nidad rosugi alla damsa* B, *Ni tathrosu gillai damsa* M, *Nidad rosu gialla damsa* E. The meaning of this line is uncertain. Meroney reads *Nídad rosu gíalla dam-sa* 'There are no woods as surety (?) to me'. I have tentatively emended to first singular preterite of *adraid* 'adheres to, follows; respects' with second singular infixed pronoun used in a genitival function, for which see O'Brien (1938, 371–2).

a Chíarán cailg, carai tírad. *achiaran cailg carai* B, *aciaran cailg carai tirad* M, *aciaran cailg carai* E. BE omit *tirad*, which is necessary for the metre. Meroney reads *A Chíarán cailg carai* [ ] 'O Cíarán deceitful...'. *DIL* s.v. 2 *cailg* gives only one example with the meaning 'deceitful' and the reader is referred to *colg*. The couplet is cited s.v. *colg* (b) 'sting; stab, thrust' (col. 325 ll. 49-50), a meaning which seems suitable in view of the reference to satire in the final line. I take *cailg* as genitive singular of *colg* (declined as a masculine *o*-stem) used adjectively and *carai* as second singular present indicative of *caraid* 'loves'. The sense may be that Cíarán prefers to stay indoors, rather than to be outside herding sheep. A similar complaint is made of the subject of a Middle Irish satire (no. 19 below).

rot mairg mad dom áerad. *robmairg masdomaerad* B, *rotmairg mas*<...> M, *robmairg masdomaeradh* E. I follow M and read *rot mairg*; see *DIL* s.v. *mairg* (f) for other examples of this idiom. I have emended the MSS to read *ma* plus present subjunctive of the copula (*mad*) as opposed to Middle Irish third singular present indicative *mas* (OIr. *masu*).

§17 **ró molta.** Although this is not included among the list of versified satires in §4, it is recognised as a specific type in commentary on *Bretha Nemed Toísech*: *cia dire doberar i nainmedh ⁊ i nnair cen cinta ⁊ hi rro molta* 'what compensation is paid for lampooning and for satire without guilt and for excess of praise' (*CIH* vi 2113.29–30; see Meyer 1910, 300 and Dillon 1932, 45, 53). *Ró molta* also occurs alongside *tamall aíre* in a citation in legal material (*CIH* vi 2122.3); see p. 76 above.

The metre is *dechnad mór* (8^2 6^2 8^2 6^2).

This stanza is difficult to interpret and I can only offer a very tentative translation. It is also unclear why it is classified as excessive praise. Meroney translates 'If a wound be doing injury upon earth through stock of the first folk, There would be a neck-stump, a bare forearm to whatever was not a [mere] remnant'. It has also been translated by Ó hAodha (2000, 197): 'If a wound do injury upon earth through the original stock of a hundred groups, it would be a neck-stump, it would be a barren sovereignty for that which would not be a remnant'.

Rechtgal aue Síadail. Ó hAodha (2000) notes that the surviving stanzas attributed to this poet (which are all in the metre *dechnad mór*) suggest that he belonged to the late eighth or early ninth centuries.

má nod léna crécht. *Madhnodleana nacrecht* B, *Madnodh lena nacrecht* M, *Madnot leana nacrecht* E. As Meroney notes, the second *na* in all three MSS gives one extra syllable. He suggests that *crécht* 'wound', *méde* 'lower part of the neck' and *rig* 'forearm' may be used here in a transferred sense of features of the earth's surface. Cf. *créachta an tailimh* 'the ravines of the earth' (Dinneen s.v. *créachta*). The description of a ravine or wound on the earth's surface causing injury may be an allusion to the magical effects of satire. According to a Middle Irish text outlining the procedure for performing a *glám dícenn*, the earth swallows up the victim and his family if the satire is justified or the poet who composed it if it is unjustified (L. Breatnach 1988, 13). This motif has been discussed by Meroney (1950, 215).

ba méite etc. *bad mede* BE, *bad mete* M. I follow the reading of M and take this as the phrase *ba méite* 'it would be desirable, fitting, natural', which Meroney suggests as an alternative interpretation.

ríge. *righe* BE, *rigne* M. M differs from BE in reading *rigne* 'tenacity, toughness'. I follow Ó hAodha in reading *ríge* 'sovereignty'. Meyer reads *rige* 'forearm', although a nominative form *rig* would be expected here.

§18 **glám dícenn.** The first element is *glám* 'satire'. The meaning of the second element is less certain, although T. F. O'Rahilly suggests (1942, 140 note 3) that it is a compound of the negative prefix *dí-* and *cenn* 'head; end', used in this context as an adjective. He notes that in Middle Irish compounds of *-cenn*, the *c-* is sometimes nasalised rather than lenited.

The definition in H is difficult to interpret but seems to suggest that this type of satire could result in the death of the victim: *Glam di{c}end .i. forbera cen{d} saegail nech co llua{dh is}telca* '*Glám dícenn* i.e. it will surpass the end of someone's lifespan with ... throwing (?)'. An entry in a glossary explaining citations from *Bretha Nemed Dédenach* also conveys the evil effects of a *glám dícenn*: *Ni .i. olc, ut est arsaidh ní dicenn .i. astar olc do neoch an glam dicend* '*Ni* i.e. "evil", *ut est* "a [*glám*] *dícenn* incurs evil", i.e. a *glám dícenn* is an evil labour for someone' (*CIH* ii 603.32). Part of this citation is also found in *O'Dav.* §32. There are also many literary references to the power of the *glám dícenn* to cause physical harm and death (Borsje 2002, 92–6). A description of the elaborate procedure involved in its performance is found in *MV* III §155 (L. Breatnach 1988, 13 and *UR* 140). *Glám dícenn* is also discussed by Meroney (1950, 212 ff.).

Unlike the other types of satire mentioned in our text, there is no illustration of a *glám dícenn*, but it is stated that an example may be found elsewhere (*ut in alio legitur* 'as may be read in another place'). A well-known example is the satire against Caíar, the king of Connacht, which is cited in a corrupt form in *Uraicecht na Ríar* and is described in a gloss on that text as a *glám dícenn* (*UR* 114 §23). The same verse is also cited in a corrupt form in *MV* III §155, following the description of the performance of a *glám dícenn,* to illustrate the metre *laíd* (no. 21 below). It is also referred to in legal commentary which derives from *Bretha Nemed Dédenach,* and it may have originally formed part of that text (*Companion* 186):

> *Saeth lium bas caiar ri cruachna / 7 neide fer co neim / iman sgin narbo fiu scripul / conach eagar ina heim*
>
> *Gradh tuc ben chaiar do neide, 7 isi rourail eir glaim diceand do denam dó imin sgin tucad o rig alban dó*
>
> *Tri himfaebair na glaime diginn: imfaebar a denam im foichliche .s. .i. iss ed is foichlidhi .s. ann a luighi do tabairt do cona tibradh do neoch .ii. in .s.; imfaebur a denam um ní is luga na .uii. cumala gia dobera apad 7 trefocul; 7 umfaebar a denam gemadh .uii. cumala gen apad gen trefocal; 7 cumad he fatha a himfaebair-sin uair nach targaid caiar log .ii. do neide tar eisi na sgin; 7 is iat imfaebair na gláime .d.*
>
> *& coirpdire 7 eineclann 7 aithgin isin nglaim ndigind. cinnus sin, 7 se 'ca rada isin ninadh .ii. corob gnim diaithgina in air? is e fath a aithgina, uair roebleastar caiar rig conacht di, 7 comadh he in dara hinad i fuil aithgin isan air, isin focul friaiche 7 isin ngloim ndicind.*

> '"Grievous to me is the death of Caíar, king of Cruachu, and Néde, a man with venomous power, concerning the knife which was not worth a scruple, since there is no inlay in its handle".
>
> Caíar's wife loved Néde, and it was she who urged him to perform a *glám dícenn* for him concerning the knife which had been given to him by the king of Scotland.
>
> The three "double-edges" of the *glám dícenn* are (i.e. it entails both advantages and disadvantages): double-edged is its performance concerning the guarding of chattels, i.e. this is the guarding of chattels: to put him on oath in order that he might not give the chattel to someone else; double-edged is its performance regarding a thing which is less [in value] than seven *cumals,* even though notice and *trefocal* are given; double-edged is its performance even though [the chattels

> are worth] seven *cumals*, without notice and *trefocal* being given. So that this is the reason why that was double-edged: because Caíar did not offer another reward to Néde in place of the knife. And those are the double-edges of the *glám dícenn*.
>
> And body-fine and honour-price and restitution [are due] for the *glám dícenn*. How is that, when it is said in the other place that satire is a deed of non-restitution? The cause of the restitution is because Caíar, the king of Connacht, died from it, and so that it is one of the two places in which there is restitution for the satire, in the *focal i frithsuidiu* and in the *glám dícenn*' (*CIH* v 1587.18–31).

This passage has also been translated by Meroney (1950, 212–13). The phrase beginning *Tri himfaebair na glaime diginn* is found in a glossary explaining citations from *Bretha Nemed Dédenach* (Gwynn 1942, 55 §21; *CIH* ii 604.13). For other examples of *imfáebair* used in a legal context see Thurneysen (1931, 82) and Binchy (1979, 33). It is also stated in a Middle Irish gloss on heptad 6 that satire is a deed of non-restitution; see p. 26 (note 55) above.

3. The Old Irish Heptad on Satire

The Old Irish heptad on satire (no. 33 in the *Senchas Már* tract *Sechtae*)[1] begins by listing seven types of satire and then outlines the penalty for reciting a satire and for calling someone by a nickname. Additional information on the penalties for the unlawful use of satire is found in the accompanying Middle Irish glosses and commentaries. The *Fodlai Aíre* tract on the classification of satire was used as a source by a glossator of the heptad for his illustrations of *lesainm* 'nickname', *ail ṡuthin* 'lasting reproach' and *lánáer* 'full satire'.[2]

Manuscripts

There are two complete copies of the Old Irish text:

R: *CIH* i 29.17–31.5 = Rawlinson B 487 f. 58c. This manuscript contains a continuous copy of the entire *Sechtae* tract (*CIH* i 1.1–64.5) accompanied by Middle Irish glosses and extensive commentary. There is no indication of the date of the vellum section containing the heptads (Ó Cuív 2001, 134–41).

A: *CIH* iii 1050.28–1051.8 = TCD MS H 3. 18 (1337) p. 500 ll. 11–27. This manuscript contains a continuous copy of heptads 16, 34, 15, 27–9, 6–13, 17, 18, 25, 26, 30–3, 36 and 37 (*CIH* iii 1044.31–1053.2). The section containing the heptads may date from the sixteenth century (Abbot and Gwynn 1921, 358). The main text of the heptad on satire is followed by a section of commentary on

[1] See L. Breatnach 1996b, 23 and *Companion* 291. The text has been translated in *AL* v 229-35.

[2] Compare *Cell Chorrḟesse* and *is do decraib in domain* in §3 of the former with glosses 2, 13 and 14 on the heptad.

ail ṡuthin 'lasting reproach'. The Old Irish text of A differs significantly from R in reading *aer aicetail* against *aeraicetal, iar feib* against *feib, aire* against *air* and *ferthair* against *feartar.*

An abbreviated version of the heptad is found in TCD MS H 3. 17 (1336) col. 281 l. 8–282 l. 31 (*CIH* v 1840.21–1841.32). H 3. 17 is a composite manuscript which may date from the sixteenth century (Abbot and Gwynn 1921, 355). This version is designated B in the present edition. It consists of citations from the main text, glosses on *lesainm* and commentary on *tibre dá leithe, áer ó bard benar bís i céin canar* and *lesainm i mbí fírṡamail aíre.* Aside from some additional material which is discussed in the notes, the glosses and commentary in B are similar to RA.

An isolated citation from the main text (*sloindi de dire co .7.mad fer fertar*) and a fragment of commentary on *ail ṡuthin* are found in Middle Irish commentary on an extract from *Bretha Nemed Dédenach* dealing with the payment of honour-price to relatives (*CIH* iii 765.33–8). The commentary is similar to commentary in R (765.35–7 = 30.27 ff.) and A (765.34–5 = 1051.2–3).

Note the following errors in transcription in *CIH*: for *diceind* read *diccind* 29.23; for *i runaib* (?) (MS *irun–*) read *i runn* 29.23; for *airaicetal* read *aeraicetal* 29.24; for *trianeneclann* read *laneneclann* 30.2; after *filid* read *fein* 30.5; for *tubad* (MS *tub–*) read *tuba* 30.36; for *is leth* read *isi leth* 31.1; for *gnuis* read *gnuisi* 1050.29; for *is e* read *se* 1840.28; for *ma* read *mad* 1840.33; for *slan* read *ṡlan* 1840.38; for *ndernudh* read *nderrnudh* 1841.5; for *fris* read *friss* 1841.6; for *laneneclunn* read *laneclunn* 1841.25; for *dicinn* read *diciunn* 1841.25.

The restored Old Irish text is based on RA. This is followed by the diplomatic text and translation of the glosses and commentary in R as printed in *CIH.* The abbreviations *dō/ dā, im̄, lā, l-, .d.* and [*marcach*] *.d.* in *CIH* have been expanded silently as *dano, immorro, la Féniu, no, duais* and [*marcach*] *duaine.* Instances where the glosses and commentary in AB differ significantly from R are discussed in the notes.

The passage beginning *áer ó bard benar* consists of two four-line sections and is written in a *rosc* style (L. Breatnach 1984b, 452-3), with three stressed words in lines *a, b, c, d, g* and *h.* There is linking alliteration (*fidrad freccomail*) between lines *ab* (*benar* and *bís*), *bc* (*canar* and the unstressed preverb *con-*),[3] *cd* (*éirce* and unstressed *íar*), *de* (*áerthar* and the

[3] See Carney 1980-1, 253 §2.

second element of the compound *lesainm*[4] and *ef* (*aíre* and *ail*). There is also internal alliteration in lines *a*, *b*, *d*, *g* and *h*.

[4] See Carney *ibid.*, 255 §7.

Heptad 33

A-táat secht cenéla aíre la Féniu asa midither díre:[1] lesainm lenas,[2,3] áer aicetail, [4] écndach n-écnairce, [5] glámad gnúise, [6] tibre dá leithe, [7] écoscnamat ,[8] noad ainme. [9]

Áer ó bard benar
bís i céin canar[10]
con-la díabul n-éirce
íar feib aigthe áerthar.[11, 12]
Lesainm i mbí fírṡamail aíre,[13]
ail ṡuthin,[14]
sloinde de díre
co sechtmad fer ferthar.[15]

R: tait .uii. cinela aire la féniu asa miditer dire lesainm lenus aeraicetal ecnach negnairce glama gnuisi tibri da leithe. eccosc namat. noad ainme. aer o bard benar bis a cein canar conla diabul neirce feib aighthe aertar lesainm a mbi fir amail air ail suthuin sloinde de dire co sechtmad fear feartar.
A: Atait .uii. cenele aire asa midedar dire la féniu: leasain*m* lenas, aer aicetail, ecnach necnairce, glama gnuisi, tibre da leithe, ecosc namat, noud ainme, aer o bard benas bis i cen canar co*n*la diabul a nerce iar feib aithche aerthair; leasainm i mbi fir samail aire, ail suthain slui*n*de de dire co .uii.mad fer ferthair.

Glosses and Commentary

[1].i. atait .uii. ceinela aire da naisneiden*n* in fenechus asa meise*mn*aight*er* enecl*ann* am*ail* dlighis.

[2] .i. inni is len no is lista leis do radha ris conas lenand, am*ail* ata 'cell coire sin'.

[3].i. trian 7 lan 7 leth .i. t*r*ian fecht. 7 leth dia lenu fri bliaduin, 7 lan dia lenu do gres. lan ina .c.cantuin 7 leth ina hathchantuin. Cethardha i tabuir enecl*ann* do thiarmorthaib sun*n* .i. leasainm lenas 7 lanair 7 glam diccind 7 ail tsuthain i run*n*.

[4].i. aicetal na haoire a dta ain*m* 7 us 7 do*m*nus. lan mad .c.cantain.

[5] .i. athcantain a lanaoire, a ta leth.

[6].i. in glasgabail, a ta lan 7 .uii.m*ad* 7 .uii.m*ad* in .uii.m*aid.*

Translation

There are seven kinds of satire in Irish law for which compensation is estimated: a nickname which sticks; a recited satire; defaming in one's absence; satirising to the face; laughter on both sides; appearance-mockery; making known a blemish.

A satire which is composed by a bard who is far away and which is recited binds double compensation according to the status of the person (lit. 'face') who is satirised. A nickname in which there is the true appearance of satire, a lasting reproach: you are to declare compensation for it; it is supplied as far as the seventh man.

Glosses and Commentary

[1]There are seven kinds of satire which Irish law tells of for which honour-price is estimated as is due.

[2] i.e. to say to him that which is an injury to him or which is wearisome to him, so that it sticks to him, for example *Cell Chorrḟesse* 'Church of the Wretched Meal'.

[3] i.e. a third and full and a half [honour-price], i.e. a third for a single occasion and a half if it sticks to him for a year and full if it sticks to him always. Full [honour-price] for its first recitation and half for repeating it. There are four things for which honour-price is granted to descendants in this case, i.e. *lesainm lenas* and *lánáer* and *glám dícenn* and *ail ṡuthin* in verse form.

[4] i.e. recitation of the satire in which there is name and lineage and abode. Full [honour-price] if it is the first recitation.

[5] i.e. repetition of his full satire for which there is half [honour-price].

[6] i.e. the *glasgabáil* for which which there is full [honour-price] and a seventh and a seventh of the seventh.

[7].i. gaire uime e do cach leth. IN gaire im aisneis narg: mas i fiadnaise in rig dorigne iman duain, no cid ina ecmais manar diult roime na*c*h ceindeoch*ad* hi, enecl*ann* d'ic risin righ an*n*, 7 duas 7 frithduas do ic t*ara* cen*n* risin fili, 7 enecl*ann* do ic risin fil*id* 7 einecl*ann* d'ic risin marcach nduaine. Ma ro diult in ri roime immorro nach ceindeoch*ad* hi, ein*eclann* do ic risin fil*id* an*n* 7 ein*eclann* don marcach duaine 7 nocon ict*ar* ni risi*n* ri Mas iarna cendach don ri dorigned an gaire iman duain and, enecl*ann* do icc risi*n* rig, 7 is .c.f*aid* combeth duais 7 en*eclann* do ic risi*n* righ ar cach nduain, 7 nocon ict*ar* ni risin fil*id*; 7 tainig tairmesg na duaine de sin, 7 muna thisa rob*ad* slan.

IN tan bis in fil*i* 7 na marcaig duaine 7 in fer dia ngaba*r* ant airchetal a naenmaighin, dia mbuaidhirtar imna marca*ch*aib duaine, is duais 7 f*r*ithduais do ic tar cen*n* in fir dia ndent*ar* Mad in fil*i* 7 na marcaig duaine bet and, is laneneclann don fil*id* 7 frithduais dona marc*achaib* duaine Mad in fer dia ndent*ar* bes and 7 na marc*aig* duaine, is duais do ic dia cind muna roich 7 frithduais dona marc*achaib* duaine Einecl*ann* do*n* fil*id* mad he nosgab*a*, leth ma na marc*aig* duaine; re luagh an dana and so uile Mad iarna luagh, is leth do*n* fil*id* fein mad e gabus 7 cethraime ma na marc*aig* duaine, 7 duais do ic do cin*n* in fir isa dan mu*n*a ro deirgle; mad doruaicle, is a ic ris fein.

[8] .i. namuitt uma ecosc .i. ni suil, ni srub; .uii.m*ad* neneclainni in*n* .i. ro cet cen chuibdus.

[9] .i. urdracug*ud* na hainme, a ta lan no leth.

[10].i. in aor cin*n*es in bard bis a cei*n* 7 cantar-sideicc i foccus.

[11] .i. cai*n*-indlith*er* diabl*ad* neirce an*n* fo feabus na haighte ro haerad and .i. lan on file 7 leth o fir athchantana, is he diab*lad* adb*eir* sund.

[7] i.e. laughter around him from every side. The laughter at an *aisnéis narg*: if it is in the presence of the king that it was done concerning the poem, or even if it is in his absence, unless he had previously refused to buy it, honour-price is to be paid to the king in that case, and reward and counter-reward are to be paid for it to the poet, and honour-price is to be paid to the poet and honour-price is to be paid to the reciter. If, however, the king had previously refused to buy it, honour-price is to be paid to the poet in that case, and honour-price [is to be paid] to the reciter, and nothing is paid to the king. If it is after it had been bought by the king that the poem was laughed at, honour-price is to be paid to the king, and there is an opinion that reward and honour-price are to be paid to the king for every poem, and nothing is paid to the poet. And the hindering [of the recitation] of the poem came about as a result of that, and if it were not to come about there would be immunity from liability.

When the poet and the reciters and the man for whom the poem is recited are in one place, if the reciters are interrupted, reward and counter-reward are to be paid on behalf of the man for whom it is composed. If it is the poet and the reciters who are present, it is full honour-price [which is paid] to the poet and counter-reward to the reciters. If it is the man for whom it is composed and the reciters who are present, reward is to be paid on his behalf if he has not paid, and counter-reward is to be paid to the reciters. Honour-price [is to be paid] to the poet if it is he who recites it, half if it is the reciters. All this is before payment for the poem. If it is after payment, half [honour-price is paid] to the poet if it is he who recites it, and a quarter if it is the reciters. And reward is to be paid on behalf of the man whose poem it is if he does not purchase it; if he does purchase it, it is to be paid to himself.

[8] i.e. jeering at his appearance, i.e. 'it is not an eye, it is not a snout'; a seventh of honour-price for it, i.e. it has been recited without rhyme. [9] i.e. making known the blemish for which there is full or half [honour-price]. [10] i.e. the satire which the bard who is far away completes and it is recited nearby. [11] i.e. double compensation is 'fairly arranged' in that case according to the worth of the face which was satirised there, i.e. full [honour-price] from the poet and half from the man who repeats it: that is the doubling which he speaks of in this case.

[12] .i. Aer ro gabust*ar* fil*i* and sin 7 aimairis rucadh air comadh he fein doneith hi, 7 letheinecl*ann* uaidh 7 fir fon letheinecl*ainn* .ii. na*ch* he fein dorigne i, 7 coma ed-sin bu diabl*ad* and; no dono cena in fil*i* dorigne i is e ro gabust*ar* i, 7 ar fi*lid* .ii. isin crich ro cuiristar i, 7 eiric derbf*or*.g. [= derbforgill] uaidh don fili*d* arar cuirist*ar* i 7 einecl*ann* donti da ndern*a* an aer, 7 comu hed-sin bu diabl*ad* an*n*.

[13] .i. ain*m* is len no is lista leis a mbi samuil na haoiri iar fir, am*ail* ata 'cella coire isin' am*ail* adubru*m*air romuind.

[14] .i. am*ail* ata 'is do deacr*aib* in domhuin'. no dono is lan 7 leath 7 trian 7 cethr*aimthe* 7 .u.id 7 .ui.id 7 .uii.m*ad*.

[15] .i. is e airet dob*e*rar fog*al* einecl*ainn*i isin air, coruigi a .uii.m*ad* fer dona tiarmorthaib 7 coruigi an .x.m*ad* fer i fiad*nai*si, uair is cu*m*adh is air doib uili. in marbtha immorro coruigi in .x.m*ad* fer a fiad*nai*si, 7 ni fil ni do*n*a thiarmorth*aib* Ant ainmrainde do einecl*ainn* ata don coibdhealach ata f*or* aird isi*n* air, a leth do tiarmorth*aib* a comaici*n*ta cona cantain f*r*ia re, 7 mu*n*a cantar fria re nochon fuil nach ni ; 7 is cutru*m*a ata sin do*n*a tiarmor*taib* o fili 7 o fir a cantana, 7 is e airet reithis sin coruice mor.ui.er do tiarmort*aib* 7 coruice .x.neba*r* do neoch fuil ar aird; 7 ni fuil ni do tiarmorth*aib* isin lanair 7 a nail suthai*n* 7 an lesain*m* lenas 7 in .g.d. [= glam dicinn].

gne .ii. IS e airet ata in rith coruice .x.neba*r* da fuil ar aird 7 coruici mor.ui.er dona tiarmorth*aib* .U. earnaile a ta laneinecl*ann*: lanaer 7 glam diccind 7 ail tsuthain 7 tub*a* nainme 7 lesainm; 7 an cutruma ata o fil*id* cona mbeth ar aird isi leth doib cona mbeth ina tiarmorth*aib*; an cutrum*a* ata o fir a cantana doib cona mbeth ar aird curob in cutru*ma*-sin bes doib cona mbeth in tiarmorthaibh, uair is cutru*m*a doni fear athcantana fogal re re araoen. Nocha re re na tiarmorth*aide* immorro doni an fil*i* a air; cona cantain doib araoen sin re re na tiarmorth*aide*, 7 mana cantar nochon fuil nach ni.

[12] i.e. a poet recited a satire in that case, and suspicion was cast upon him that it was he himself who might have composed it, and half honour-price is due from him, and an ordeal for the other half honour-price that it was not he who composed it, and that would be the doubling in question. Alternatively, the poet who composed it recited it, and he attributed it to another poet in the territory. The compensation of false witness is due from him to the poet to whom he attributed it, and honour-price is due to the person about whom he composed the satire, and that would be the doubling in question. [13] i.e. a name which is an injury or which is wearisome to him in which there is truly the likeness of the satire, for example *Cell Chorrḟesse* 'Church of the Wretched Meal' as we said above. [14] i.e. for example, 'among the difficulties of the world'. Or alternatively, it is full and a half and a third and a quarter and a fifth and a sixth and a seventh [honour-price].

[15] This is the extent to which a share of honour-price is given for the satire: to the seventh man of the descendants and to the tenth man present, for it is equally that it is satire to them all. [In the case of] killing, however, [it extends] to the tenth man present and there is nothing for the descendants. The proportion of honour-price which is due to the kinsman who is present as compensation for the satire, half of it goes to the descendants of his own kin when it is recited during their lifetime, and if it is not recited during their lifetime there is nothing [due to them]. And it is equally that that is [paid] to the descendants by the poet and by the reciter, and this is how long that extends: to the seven men of the descendants and to ten men of those who are present. And there is nothing for the descendants [except] for the *lánáer* and for *ail ṡuthin* and for *lesainm lenas* and for *glám dícenn*.

[Here is] an alternative version. This is how far it extends: to ten men of those present and to seven men of the descendants. There are five divisions [of satire] for which there is full honour-price: *lánáer* and *glám dícenn* and *ail ṡuthin* and *tuba n-ainme* and *lesainm*. And the proportion which is due from the poet when they are present, half is due when they are descendants. The proportion which is due to them from the man who repeats it when they are present is the proportion which is due to them when they are descendants, for it is equally that the man who repeats it causes injury in the time of both. It is not during the lifetime of the descendants that the poet composes his satire, however; that applies when both of them recite it during the lifetime of the descendants, and if it is not recited, there is nothing due.

Notes

Main Text

lesainm. This is classified as a type of *ail* 'reproach' in the *Fodlai Aíre* tract §3.

áer aicetail. *aeraicetal* R, *aer aicetail* A. I follow A in reading genitive singular *aicetail*, qualifying *áer*. R reads a compound *áeraicetal*. *Aicetal* is defined in *O'Dav.* §33 as *.i. cuidhbius, ut est áer aicetail .i. aor co cuidhbius* 'i.e. rhyme, *ut est* a recited satire, i.e. a satire with rhyme'. *Áer aicetail* is glossed *ainm 7 us 7 domnus* in R. This triad is applied to *lánáer* 'full satire' in the *Fodlai Aíre* tract (§15). Middle Irish commentary (*CIH* iii 971.30–1) associates it with a type of satire known as *mac bronn* 'son of womb', for which see p. 68 above.

écndach n-écnairce. *Écndach* is listed among types of satire in *Cethairṡlicht Athgabálae*, where it is glossed *.i. athcantain aire* 'i.e. repetition of a satire'; see p. 65. An entry in *O'Dav.* §1430 also draws a distinction between satirising someone to their face (*glámad gnúise*) and in their absence: *Sinn .i. cuitbuidh .i. triar cin cuib[d]ius. Rinn .i. co cuib[di]us ina agaid. Glam gér .i. ainmedh i t'agaid 7 ecnairc* '*Sinn* i.e. mockery, i.e. three things without rhyme. *Rinn* i.e. with rhyme to his face. *Glám gér* i.e. satirising to your face and [in your] absence'. The same definition of *rinn* is also found in *O'Dav.* §1342. Note that the glossator of the heptad interprets *écndach n-écnairce* as a type of *lánáer* 'full satire'.

tibre dá leithe. The commentary suggests that this type of satire entailed interrupting the presentation of a praise poem by mocking or ridiculing it, thus causing the audience to laugh. In the Old Irish glosses on the *Senchas Már* the phrase *de lleith*, which Binchy takes to be a citation from our text, is glossed *.i. hi lleth na airechtae sin 7 ina lleth tall* 'i.e. on one side of that assembly and on its other side' (*CIH* iii 905.37–8). Another example of this type of ridicule is *búaidriud scél* 'interrupting stories', which is given alongside *abucht co n-imdergad* 'jesting so as to raise a blush' as one of the signs of a trickster in the *Triads* §90. A further possible reference may be found in *Bretha Nemed Toísech*. Binchy (1979–80, 45) suggests, albeit 'somewhat doubtfully', that the phrase *coscrad uad aenaig* 'disturbance by him of an assembly' may be a reference to the practice of disturbing the recitation of a poem. A Middle Irish gloss on this phrase gives examples of some of the types of disturbances that could take place at an assembly, but does not specifically mention disturbing the recitation of a poem: *.i. iomghuin, no deabhaidh, no dérad* 'i.e. slaying or fighting or refusing' (*CIH* iii 1136.35–6). Commentary on the phrase suggests that *dérad* may refer to the refusal of clients to attend an assembly: *Smacht ar daercele graid fene a nemdul ind 7 i tiachtain as* ... 'A fine on base clients of the *grád Ḟéne* for not going into it and for coming out of it ...' (*CIH* vi 2156.18).

écoscnamat. The gloss illustrating this type of satire (*.i. ni suil, ni srub* 'i.e. it is not an eye, it is not a snout') is a citation from *Bretha Nemed Toísech* (L. Breatnach 1988, 11; see p. 15 above). This gloss is also cited in *O'Dav.* §1297: *Namat .i. fanamad, ut est ecosc-namat .i. fanamad ima ecosc, ut est ní suil, ní* [*srub*] '*namat*, i.e. mockery, *ut est* "appearance-mockery", i.e. mockery about his appearance, *ut est* "it is not an eye, it is not a snout"'.

bís i céin canar. A Middle Irish gloss in *Gúbretha Caratniad* suggests that *molad gó* 'false praise' could be repeated as a form of mockery; see p. 7 above. A literary example of a satire being repeated in another place is found in *Aislinge Meic Conglinne.* Here it is stated that Manchín feared that a satire which Mac Conglinne had composed against him on account of his inhospitality would be repeated by children, thus causing him even further shame: *Gébdait me*[*i*]*cc beca na runda-sin* ... (Jackson 1990, l. 195): 'Little boys will sing those verses ...'.

íar feib. *feib* R, *iar feib* A. I follow A against R on the grounds that linking alliteration (in this case between stressed *éirce* and unstressed *íar*) is a feature of this section of text. *Feib* is found with the preposition *íar* in the phrase *a*[*s*] *a midetar fír iar febaib* 'out of which they measure truth according to excellences' (Stokes 1905, 18 §26).

aigthe. *DIL* s.v. *agad* states incorrectly that this word is 'not found in Old Irish glosses or in text of Laws'. For other examples in legal texts see Binchy (1966, 56).

sloinde. The verb *sluindid* is commonly used in law tracts in the context of declaring compensation, e.g. : *sloinn a coic* 'proclaim five [*séoit*] (Binchy 1966, 42 §33); *sluinn ind ala fichit set* 'Declare a further score of *séoit*' (Binchy *ibid.*, 44 §35).

co sechtmad fer. This refers to the degree of relationship to the victim of the satire. Cf. *Nech marbus a brathair no a fiẹr nó a fiẹr a mathar nó a athar nó a brathair a athar nó a mathar pendid .x. bliadna 7 lentar sin com-morfeiser etir maithre 7 aithri co hua 7 iarmu 7 indau 7 maccu anua co ingin ar meraib* ... 'Anyone who kills his brother or sister or the sister of his mother or father, or the brother of his father or mother, does penance ten years: and this rule is followed to seven degrees both of the mother's and father's kin — to the grandson and great-grandson and great-great-grandson, and the sons of the great-great-grandson as far as the finger-nails . . . ' (Gwynn 1913–14, 166 §2). This passage has also been translated by Binchy (see Bieler 1963, 271 §20) and is discussed by McLeod (2000, 19).

ferthar. The use of the conjunct form of the verb is an example of Bergin's law (Bergin 1938, 197).

Glosses and Commentary

[2] **is len no is lista.** This etymological gloss is cited in two other contexts. In gloss 13 on the heptad it explains *lesainm i mbí fírṡamail aíre,* while in *Cethairṡlicht Athgabálae* it explains the phrase *im on lesanma* 'for the blemish of a nickname'; see p. 66 above.

cell coire sin. Binchy suggests (*CIH* i 29 note *a*) that this may be an error for *celgaire* 'deceiver'. As noted by Meroney (1950, 207), it is probably a corruption of *Cell Chorrḟesse* 'Church of the Wretched Meal', a nickname which is cited to illustrate *lesainm* in the *Fodlai Aíre* tract §3.

[3] **eneclann do thiarmorthaib.** A person's descendants were also entitled to compensation if he was satirised after death (Kelly 1988, 137–8) and a citation from an Old Irish tract outlines the penalty for this offence: *aera cach fir mairb direnar(?) landiriu .l. eneclainn amail bid ina bethu* 'Satirising any dead man is paid for by full penalty [and] full honour-price as if he were alive' (*CIH* vi 2124.23–4). I follow Binchy, note j, in reading *.l.* as *lán.*

leasainm lenas ⁊ lanair ⁊ glam diccind ⁊ ail tsuthain i runn. *Lesainm, ail, lánáer* and *glám dícenn* are types of satire listed in the *Fodlai Aíre* tract §§3, 15 and 18 respectively.

[6] **glasgabail.** Meroney (1950, 224) translates this term as 'blue-grabbing', suggesting that it may have been a satirical onslaught which was believed to cause a dark bruise. There is insufficient evidence to establish precisely what it entailed, however. It is associated with the verb *glámaid* 'satirises, reviles' and with *glám dícenn,* which suggests that it was a considered to be a particularly powerful type of satire. In *Bretha Nemed Toísech,* the phrase *ná gláimhe ngrúaidhe* 'you are not to satirise cheeks' is glossed *.i. an glasghabháil,* while *ni gonae gruaidhe goaibh anṡoís ná súil na srúbh ná smech smiotghno* 'You are not to wound cheeks with

spears of satire nor eye nor snout nor chin with mimicry' is glossed *.i. glasgabhail ann so .i. ni rá* (about 8 letters lost) *gruaidhe o ghaeibh na ndroichsés na háoire* 'i.e. this is a *glasgabáil*, i.e. . . . cheeks by spears of the bad meanings of the satire' (*CIH* iii 1134.29–34, 40 and 1135.16–17; see p. 15 above). A text deriving from *Uraicecht Becc* lists *glasgabáil* and *glám dícenn* among the rights of an *ollam*: *Tri ruighlis ollaman filed .i. glamh díginn 7 glasbabail 7 tobach do tuathaib* 'Three things which are the peculiar right of the *ollam* of poetry, i.e. *glám dícinn* and *glasgabáil* and enforcing claims for the members of a *túath*' (L. Breatnach 1984, 189). *Glasgabáil* is also associated with *glám dícenn* and *lánáer* in glosses on *Bretha Étgid*; see p. 79 above.

A further instance of the term is found in glosses on heptad 26, which deals with invalid payments. Here the Old Irish text *gell mna d'inchaib* 'a woman's pledge for her honour' is glossed *.i. ini gellus in ben tar cenn a heinig .i. in ailges indligtech mad mo na .uii.mad loighi einech. .i. glasgabail gabur di* 'i.e. the thing which the woman pledges for the sake of her honour, i.e. the unlawful request if it is greater than a seventh of honour-price, i.e. it is a *glasgabáil* with which she is threatened (lit. 'which is taken to her')' (*CIH* i 25.14–20).

[7] **uime e.** As Binchy suggests, *CIH* i 29 note c, the second *e* is probably due to dittography.

im aisneis narg. The version in B (*CIH* v 1840.29) reads *im faisneis narg*. This type of satire is also mentioned in *Bretha Nemed Dédenach*: *Aithirne asbert ann so do mharbhadh an fir ro molustar resiu ad-cobrad a duas. Do aisneis narg do righneadh sunn.* 'Athairne said this concerning the killing of the man whom he had praised before he could pay (?) his [Athairne's] reward. This was done by means of an *aisnéis narg*' (*CIH* iii 1113.28–9). *Ad-cobrad* may be for *ad-comrad* < *as-comrad*, third singular past subjunctive of *as-ren* with perfective *-com-*. The examples of *aisneis narg* from our text and from *Bretha Nemed Dédenach* are cited in *DIL* s.v. 2 *arg* 'noble, great; (subst.) prominent person, champion', col. 396, ll. 48–9, and are preceded by a question mark. If the form is *arg* rather than *narg*, nasalisation in the phrase *im aisneis n-arg* would be regular after a noun in the accusative singular. In the example from *Bretha Nemed Dédenach*, however, nasalisation would not be expected after a dative singular noun, suggesting that the word may be *narg*.

As in the case of *glasgabáil* , there is scarcely enough evidence to establish what this type of satire entailed, although it does seem to have involved interrupting the recitation of a poem in some way. In the commentary on *tibre dá leithe* in our text it is described as causing laughter, which would certainly have ruined the effect of the recitation and shamed the person being praised.

dorigne. Read *do-rigned.*

manar diult roime. Here the glossator draws a distinction between whether or not the king had refused to purchase the poem, stating that if he had refused to purchase it he is not entitled to be compensated for the interruption.

frithduas. According to *DIL* s.v., this term only occurs in our text. In other compounds the prefix *frith-* is used in a reciprocal sense, e.g.: *frithḟolud* 'counter-benefit'; *frithgell* 'counter-pledge'; *frithgnam* 'reciprocal services by a client to a lord'; *frithguin* 'counter-wounding, killing in self-defence'; *frithnoíll* 'counter-oath'; *frithṡuide* 'opposition'. Neil McLeod has suggested (personal comment) that *frithdúas* 'counter-payment' may refer here to the payment made to the reciter. The procedure may have been for the reciter to receive the full reward for the poem, pass this on to the poet and in turn receive a portion back from the poet as his fee (this would be a payment going back in the opposite direction, hence 'counter-payment'). The commentary states that even though the interruption has spoiled the recitation, the poet and reciter must still be paid.

marcach duaine. To the citations in *DIL* s.v. 1 *marcach* may be added an example from *UR* 102 §3, where the phrase *ar dídin a ḟir meschétlaig muintire for drochbésu* 'for leading the member of his household who is competent to recite into bad practices' is glossed *.i. ara gabail dhe in ḟir muintire midheas a cedla, .i. a marcaid duaine, i crosanact no a ngaeid no a mbraeid* 'i.e. for taking from him the member of his household who "estimates his songs", that is, the reciter of his compositions, into buffoonery or stealing or plundering'.

7 is .c.faid etc. The version in B (*CIH* v 1840.36–8) differs slightly here in stating that the reciter is to be compensated for the interruption: *7 is .c.faid co mbeth duais 7 frithduais 7 eneclunn d'ic re marcuch duaine, 7 nochan ictar ni risin filid; 7 tainic toirmisc ann sin, 7 munu thisadh rop slan* 'and there is an opinion that reward and counter-reward and honour-price are to be paid to the reciter, and nothing is paid to the poet. And hindering [of the recitation] came about in that case, and if it were not to come about there would be immunity from liability'. R and B both state that the poet is not to be compensated if the disturbance takes place after his poem has been purchased from him.

IN tan bis in fili etc. A passage dealing with the penalties for interrupting the recitation of a praise poem is found on a small slip of vellum inserted between cols. 672 and 673 of TCD MS H 3. 17 (1337). This is important in that it stipulates in a gloss, which Binchy suggests was inserted later between the lines, that the value of the *frithdúas* 'counter-reward' payable to the reciter is one-seventh of the poet's reward:

> *Laneneclann don filid 7 duas 7 frithduas tar cenn in fir da ndernad ara buaidreth imun marcach nduaine, 7 atat i naeninad ann sin in fili 7 in fer da ndernad 7 in marcach duaine.*
>
> *Mad e in fili 7 in marcach duaine bes and, laneneclann don filid ann 7 frithduais don marcach duaine, 7 dar linn is coibeis .uii.maid loige aiste in filed iseig.*
>
> *Mad e in marcach 7 in fer dia ndentar bet ann, duais 7 frithduais d'ic tar cenn in fir dia ndentar, no a ic ris ma roic ni amach.*
>
> *Mad in marcach nama, is frithduais d'ic ris ar buaidred in aircetail uime Tanic tairmesc na duaine de-sein; 7 mani tised, conabad mo na faicet gin cuidbes e.*
>
> 'Full honour-price [is paid] to the poet and reward and counter-reward [are paid] on behalf of the man for whom it was composed on account of interrupting the reciter while reciting it; and the poet and the man for whom it was composed and the reciter are in the same place in that case.
>
> If it is the poet and the reciter who are there, full honour-price [is paid] to the poet in that case and counter-reward [is paid] to the reciter, and in our opinion that is the equivalent of one seventh of the reward for the poet's metre.
>
> If it is the reciter and the man for whom it is composed who are there, a reward and a counter-reward are to be paid on behalf of the man for whom it is composed, or it is to be paid to him if he has paid anything out.
>
> If it is only the reciter [who is present], a counter-reward is to be paid to him for interrupting him while reciting it. The hindering [of the recitation] of the poem came about as a result of that; and if it were not to come about, so that it [compensation] might not be more than [for] an unrhymed *faicet*' (*CIH* vi 2118.22–32).

For *faicet* see p. 77 above.

dia mbuaidhirtar etc. The version in B adds an additional phrase here: ... *dia mbuaiderthur imnu marcachuip duaine, is slan secunndum qosdum Eineclann ann don filid, 7 duas 7 frithduais d'icc do cinn in fir dia ndernudh* '... if the reciters are interrupted, there is immunity from liability according to some. Honour-price [is to be paid] in that case to the poet and reward and counter-reward are to be paid on behalf of the man for whom it was composed' (*CIH* v 1840.40–1841.1).

muna roich. Read *ro icc*, as suggested by Binchy (*CIH* i 30 note c).

[10] **in aor cinnes.** Thurneysen (1925, 310) suggests reading *caines*, third singular present indicative relative of *canaid* 'sings'. A form with palatal *-n-* would be unusual and, in any case, the text as it stands makes sense.

[11] **cain-indlither.** *Con* is frequently glossed by *cain* in etymological glosses: *confodlaither .i. is cain fodeiligtir* 'are apportioned (pl.), i.e. it is fairly they are divided' *CIH* ii 497.15 (*Cáin Aicillne*); *consla .i. ... cain luadhus* 'who departs, i.e. ... who fairly moves' *CIH* ii 420.5 (*Cethairṡlicht Athgabálae*); *ni conaraig dia .i. inni ro-chain-airgustar dia* 'That which God has joined together, i.e. the thing which God has fairly bound' *CIH* i 47.18 (heptad 51). I am grateful to Liam Breatnach for these references.

[14, 15] **is lan 7 leath 7 trian 7 cethraimthe 7 .u.id 7 .ui.id 7 .uii.mad; uair is cumadh is air doib uili.** This is similar to the following passage of commentary in A: *laneneclann cach fir co morseser, uair is cuma is aer doib uile; no dono is lan 7 leth 7 trian 7 cethraimthe 7 .u.id 7 .ui.id 7 .uii.mad* 'Full honour-price of every man to the seventh man, for it is equally that it is satire to them all. Or, alternatively, it is full and a half and a third and a quarter and a fifth and a sixth and a seventh [honour-price]' (*CIH* iii 1050.32–3). The text of A then diverges from R by incorporating a citation from *Immacallam in dá Thuarad*: *a dualgus aisi athbir (?) conid inic cach dib-so diaraile, ar is e i tiarmortacht iar tain* (*CIH* iii 1050.33–4). A fuller version is found in B: *A dualgus aoisi atbeir cona mac cach dib-so araili, ar is e int athair lais inti bis i remtechtus 7 is e in mac inti bis a tiarmorthuiph iar tain* (*CIH* v 1840. 27–8). The text of *Immacallam in dá Thuarad* reads: *a dualus aese atbeir Nede conid mac cech diib seo diarale, ar is he in t-athair lais inti bís i remthechtas, 7 is he in mac inti bís i tiarmórthecht iartain* (Stokes 1905, 30 gloss 8): 'on account of age Néde says that each of these is a son

of the other, for he takes the one who precedes to be the father and the one who follows to be the son'.

in marbtha. A genitive singular form would not be expected here and Binchy, *CIH* i 30 note j, notes that this appears to be an error for *marbad.* He refers to the corresponding version in B (*CIH* v 1841.16), where the manuscript reads *marb–*. Alternatively, he suggests adding *fogal* 'offence' before *marbtha.*

coruigi an .x.mad fer i fiadnaisi etc. According to the glossator, compensation for satire is paid to the victim's descendants as well as to those relatives present at the time of recitation. He also draws a contrast between killing and satire, stating that compensation is paid to the descendants in the case of satire but not in the case of killing. A tenfold gradation in the payment of honour-price for the relatives of a victim is also outlined in *Bretha Nemed Dédenach*: *Eochaid Dallan do deich mesruib ro-midair, ara-roich do coibdelachuib asa hua* (l. *n-ua*?) *eneclann* ... 'Eochaid Dallān hat über "zehn Maße" geurteilt, weshalb den Verwandten für ihren Enkel ein Ehrenpreis zukommt ...' (Thurneysen 1931, 44 = *CIH* iii 765.32–3).[5] This citation from *Bretha Nemed Dédenach* occurs in a text dealing with compensation for offences against kinsmen (*Companion* 33), where it is followed by a citation from the main text of the heptad on satire and a fragment of commentary on *ail ṡuthin*:[6]

> ... *cona cantain re re budéin, 7 manu cantar, nochan fuil ní doib. IS as gabhur-sin: sloindi de dire co .7.mad fer fertar; 7 int ainm-ruinde ita don lucht ata for aird gurub e a leth-sin bes dia comainm lenas 7 ail suthain a rrunn 7 d-a a glaim dicinn 7 a croli bais don lucht ata for aird, 7 ni aicinta ní don tiarmortachaib inndtib-seic.*

> '... with recitation of it during their own lifetime, and if it is not recited, there is nothing due to them. It is on account of it that that is said: "you are to declare compensation for it, it is granted as far as the seventh man". And the proportion which is due to the people who are present, it is half of it which is due for his additional name which sticks and lasting reproạch in verse and *glám dícenn*, then, and fatal injury to the people who are present, and nothing is expected for the descendants for those' (*CIH* iii 765.34–8).

[5] 'Eochaid Dallán has estimated with respect to ten measures on what basis the relatives receive an honour-price for their grandson'.

[6] For the text of *Bretha Nemed Dédenach* see *CIH* iii 1113.4–5.

Binchy suggests, *CIH* iii 765 note q, that the text following *comainm* is corrupt and that several words are omitted. It is more likely, however, that *comainm lenas* is synonymous with *lesainm lenas,* since *lesainm, ail ṡuthin* and *glám dícenn* occur together elsewhere in the heptad (*CIH* i 29.22–3, 30.32–3, 30.35–6). I take *d-a* as *dna,* a syncopated form of *danó.*

The text on compensation for offences against kinsmen also outlines a nine-fold system:

> *Laneneclann do neoch a fogail lain re athair; letheneclann do a brathair a athar Trian eneclainne do asa mac-seic; .iiii.aime eneclainne do asa uadh; eneclann otha sin coria na naoe fogla eneclainne.*
>
> 'Full honour-price for a person for a full offence against [his] father; half honour-price to him for his father's brother. A third honour-price to him for the latter's son; a quarter honour-price to him for his grandson; honour-price from then on as far as the nine divisions of honour-price' (*CIH* iii 765.20).

Ant ainm rainde. Binchy transcribes this as one word, although it is written as two separate words in R. It is written as a single word *ainmroinne* in B (*CIH* v 1841.18). It is transcribed as a single word in *CIH* iii 765.36, although it is written as two words in the manuscript (*ainm ruinde*). *DIL* s.v. *ainmm* col. 156, l. 53 ff. cites a number of examples, taking the first element as *ainmm* 'name' but stating that the meaning is 'uncertain in phrase *a. rainde*'. The dative plural form *anmannaibh rainne,* which occurs in a Middle Irish text dealing with the payment for building a *dam liac* 'stone church', shows that we have to do with two words, the second being the genitive singular of *rann* 'part, share': *int ainmrainne gabus in crann ina cloich gurub e int ainmrainne-sin do lethlogh bes fair, ⁊ is e rainn rachus arna anmannaibh rainne-sin in roinn teit ogun durthach* 'the proportion which wood[work] bears to stone[work] is the proportion of half-price that shall be paid for it; and these proportions will be distributed according to the rule applied to the *durthach*' (*CIH* vi 2100.3–5). The passage is also translated in Petrie (1845, 364–5).

Ainmrainde is translated as 'proportion' in *AL,* e.g. v 34.17, 72.10, 235.1. Neil McLeod has suggested (personal comment) that in legal texts the term is sometimes used in a more specific sense than 'proportion' and seems to refer to a specified/fixed amount or 'designated fraction'.

He notes that other examples are found at *CIH* i 130.13 and 139.4, iii 1023.35 and vi 2077.39–40.

ni fuil ni do tiarmorthaib isin lanair etc. *Acht* is to be supplied here on the basis of B, which reads *ni fuil dona tiarmorthaib sin acht a lanaoir* ... (*CIH* v 1841.22).

o fir a cantana. Binchy suggests (*CIH* i 30 note l and 31 note a) that *a cantana* is probably to be read as *athchantana.* Cf. *o ḟir athchantana* (*CIH* v 1841.28) and *fer athchantana* (*CIH* v 1841.29–30).

.U. earnaile a ta laneineclann etc. The version in B (*CIH* v 1841.25) omits *tuba n-ainme.* A five-fold classification of satire is also outlined in the Old-Irish glosses on the *Senchas Már*; see p. 49 above.

tuba nainme. The verb *do-ben* (verbal noun *tuba*) is used in the tale *Echtra Fergusa maic Léti* in the sense of taunting a person about a blemish; see p. 18 above.

cona mbeth in tiarmorthaib. Binchy suggests (*CIH* i 31 note b) reading *in(n)a.* A adds the following gloss: *.i. is comaicenta riu cona cantain fria re, ⁊ mana cantar re re nochan uil nac ní* 'i.e. it is of the same nature to them as if it were recited during their lifetime, and if it is not recited during their lifetime, they receive nothing' (*CIH* iii 1051.2).

4. A Miscellany of Mediaeval Irish Satires

The satires edited below are cited as illustrations in a Middle Irish metrical tract which has been edited in diplomatic form by Thurneysen (1891, 67–105) as *Mittelirische Verslehren* III. The tract illustrates a wide range of metres, classifying them into four sections as *gnáthaisti* 'common metres' (§§2–127), *gnátha medónda* 'moderately well-known' (§§128–47), *anaichinti* 'unfamiliar' (§§148–66) and *écoitchenna* 'uncommon' (§§167–210).[1] Panegyric, satiric, religious, topographical and occasional poems are cited as examples. Although it is stated at the beginning of the tract that there are 365 types of metres, the text ends with *finit* after citing 209 metrical illustrations. The satires are dispersed throughout the tract and illustrate many different metres, from varieties of *deibide, dían, rannaigecht* and other well-established forms to more unusual and often syllabically irregular metres.

Thurneysen's edition of *MV* III is based on the Book of Ballymote (which contains two copies of the text) and TCD MS H 2. 12 and includes notes and a description of the metres. He subsequently published (1912, 60–72) readings from the Book of Uí Maine and TCD MS H 1. 15. Two important manuscripts, National Library of Scotland Gaelic MS 1 (Advocates MS 72.1.1) and National Library of Ireland G 3 (of which TCD MS H 1. 15 is a copy), were not available to Thurneysen. Satires from *MV* III have been published without translation as illustrations in reference works on metrics by Meyer (1909) and Murphy (1961). Meyer does not

[1] I follow Thurneysen (1891, 99 note 2) in emending to *écoitchenna* against the MSS (*donacoitchennaib* Book of Ballymote and *donacoitchiund* Book of Uí Maine), as this gives a system of classification going from common to uncommon in decreasing order of frequency.

provide manuscript readings, while Murphy does so only on a few occasions and neither editor consulted National Library of Scotland Gaelic MS 1 or National Library of Ireland G 3. Meyer also published (1919, 27–37) a number of satires with selected variant readings and translation into German under the heading *Spott- und Schmähliede*r. Forty-two satires in the present work are previously unedited, apart from Thurneysen's diplomatic text. It should be noted in this regard that Thurneysen sometimes prints stanzas as continuous prose or in a form which obscures the metre.[2]

Manuscripts

Two complete and four incomplete copies of *MV* III survive: [3]

Complete copies

B: The Book of Ballymote, RIA MS 23 P 12 (536). Late fourteenth century, vellum (Ó Concheanainn 1981, 19–20).[4] Complete copies of *MV* I, II and III are contained in this manuscript. *MV* I is found on pp. $296^{b}15$–$299^{a}5$ and pp. $306^{b}11$–$308^{a}40$ (Thurneysen designates the copy on p. $306^{b}11$ ff. as B^{a}); *MV* II is found on pp. $301^{b}24$–$305^{b}3$. The text of *MV* III is found on pp. 289a1–296b1 of the facsimile (Atkinson 1887). According to Ó Concheanainn (*ibid.*, 18), pp. 289–90 were written by Robeartus Mac Síthigh and p. 291 ff. by Solamh Ó Droma. The text of B has many omissions, as will be seen below. On the other hand, B preserves the important reading *demhain* no. 49 against *dem* M and *du* E.

M: The Book of Uí Maine, RIA MS D ii 1 (1225). Late fourteenth century, vellum.[5] Parts of M are illegible due to marginal staining. The complete version of *MV* III is found on folios 133rb20–134vb60 and 136ra1–137rb62 (modern foliation; 191rb20–192vb60 and 194ra1–195rb62 old foliation) of the facsimile (Macalister 1941).[6] M also contains a copy of *MV* I

[2] Nos. 22, 34, 63, 77 below.
[3] See Thurneysen (1891, 2–4; 1912, 59–60) for a brief discussion of the MSS.
[4] See *RIA Cat.* Fasc. 13, 1610 ff.
[5] See *RIA Cat.* Fasc. 26, 3314. For a description of hands see O'Sullivan (1989, 151–66).
[6] Folio 135 is unrelated to *MV* III and contains part of *Auraicept na nÉces*.

(195va10–196rb54 = §§1–67 of Thurneysen's edition). There are quite a few instances of dittography in M, for example: *rochuidhi roich uidhi* no. 19; *etrananach* no. 28; *reharam* no. 38; *hucucuind* no. 42; *agob ingob* no. 47; *cera cera* no. 71; *sacairt sacairt* no. 82.

Incomplete copies

E: National Library of Scotland Gaelic MS 1 (Advocates MS 72.1.1). Fifteenth century, vellum (Mackinnon 1912, 180–1; Mackechnie 1973, Vol. 1, 114; Campbell 1963, 47–51; Ó Concheanainn 1975, 99–101). *MV* III is found on folios 16va1–18rb3 and E also contains a copy of *MV* I (folios 18rb16–19ra57). The copy of *MV* III is incomplete due to the loss of the folio corresponding to §§128–92.[7] E also omits §82 (no. 11 of the present edition). It preserves the following important readings which are omitted in the other MSS: *oros* no. 12; *arargad* no. 34; *no ferrmar* no. 77; *corp* no. 86.

B^b: The Book of Ballymote, RIA MS 23 P 12 (536). An incomplete copy of *MV* III is found on p. 288a28–288b51, immediately preceding the complete version. This consists of *MV* III §§29–59 and includes nos. 5–8, 33, 57–8 and 80 of the present edition. I follow Thurneysen in designating this copy as B^b. According to Ó Concheanainn (1981, 18), this section was written by Maghnus Ó Duibhgeannáin.

H: TCD MS H 2. 12 (1308). No date is given in the *Catalogue* (Abbott and Gwynn 1921, 86). Murphy (1956, 173) assigns H to the fifteenth century, but does not offer any evidence in support of this date.[8] This copy, which comprises *MV* III §§1–9 and §§22–76, is found on pp. 15b12–19b33.[9] A blank space of approximately one and a half columns in size has been left between §9 and §22 and the text breaks off after the first three words of §76 due to the loss of a folio. This manuscript also contains a copy of the complete text of *MV* I (pp. 10b13–15b10).

[7] The following satires are missing in E due to the loss of this folio: nos. 19–25, 26 (the beginning is missing), 39–45, 52–6, 69–76, 83–4 of the present edition.

[8] Ó hAodha (2002, 233 note 3) states that Anne O'Sullivan was of the opinion that H is to be dated to the early fifteenth century but no supporting evidence is provided.

[9] This contains nos. 1–10, 33, 57–62 and 80–1 of the present edition.

G: National Library of Ireland G 3. Fourteenth century, vellum.[10] This is the earliest extant Irish manuscript containing didactic material relating to the training of poets. The scribe has been identified as Ádhamh Ó Cianáin, who died in 1373 (Carney 1969, 123; Ó Cuív 1973b, 118; Ó Macháin 1991, 274).[11] An abridged version of *MV* III, comprising the following thirty-five quatrains, is found on folios 14ra1–15rb21: *MV* III §§2, 3, 5, 8, 16, 18, 19, 21, 25, 28, 31, 33, 36–8, 43, 48, 51, 58–60, 62, 68, 100, 105, 108, 115, 117, 119, 120, 124, 132, 135–6, 151. This includes nos. 1, 2, 5, 10, 17, 37, 50, 52, 66–7 and 80 of the present edition. G illustrates only 35 types of metre and does not include any of those classified in BME as *écoitchenna.* It also omits the prose sections contained in BMEH, citing only the name of the metre and the illustration. G occasionally gives a different metrical name, for example: *comtrom* BME, *cenntrom* G no. 50; *int anaichnid dona druimnib suíthib* BM, *druimni saitheadh* G no. 52; *ochtchasbairdne chorránach* BME, *don casbairdni corranaigh aichillich* G no. 67.[12] There is evidence to suggest that the compiler extracted his metrical illustrations from a longer version of the text which was similar to that found in BME. The metrical name of *MV* III §135 is stated in G to be *slat brectad corránach* which is, however, the name of the metre illustrated in §134 as found in BM.[13] Similarly, G gives the metrical name of *MV* III §108 (no. 66 below) as *sednaidh gairid bhacach,* while BME omit the adjective *gairit.* MV III §107, which is not found in G, illustrates *sétrad gairit* and *gairid* may have been mistakenly copied from this.

Three copies of *MV* III are not independent:

TCD MS H 1. 15 (1289) contains copies of B and G by the eighteenth-century scribe Tadhg Ó Neachtain (Abbott and Gwynn 1912, 54–5). The copy of B is found on pp. 571.18–588.11 and the copy of G on pp. 625–8. Thurneysen (1912, 60–9) designates the latter as T.

[10] See *Catalogue of Irish Manuscripts in the National Library of Ireland,* Fasc. 1 (Ní Shéaghdha 1967, 23).

[11] See also *Catalogue,* Fasc. 1, 13.

[12] These stanzas are not found in H.

[13] The relevant folio is missing in E.

British Museum MS Egerton 153 pp. 79–85 is a copy of B. The text has many omissions and breaks off at the end of *MV* III §78. This manuscript was written in 1818 by Edward O'Reilly.[14]

National Library of Ireland G 138 pp. 97–104 is an eighteenth century copy of B containing sections of *MV* III.[15]

Thurneysen's Transcription of *MV* III

Note the following (mostly minor) errors and omissions by Thurneysen: for *acait* H read *acaith* no. 8; for *dob– ... an* B read *dober modan* no. 13; for *mocair... blethe* B read *mochaire... .u. blethe* no. 13; for *... conbuide* B read *uaconbuide* no. 13; for *fer* B read *for* no. 13; for *braíse* M read *braisse* no. 17; for *ardidhs–* M read *ardidhecht* no. 22; for *dotacradh* M read *datacradh* no. 22; for *dalbaig* M read *dabbaig* no. 22; for *ineithle* B read *meithle* no. 22; for *conbungile* M read *combungile* no. 23; for *mhuintiri* B read *mhuindtiri* no. 26; for *caemríge* B read *caenrige* no. 29; for *caemhraighe* M read *caenraighe* no. 29; for *dochleamna* B read *dochleamhna* no. 31; for *afiacla* B read *afiachla* no. 41; for *atadhgain* B read *atadgain* no. 41; for *fir* B read *fir* no. 41; for *digradaibh* M read *digradibh* no. 48; for *ageuim* M read *agemm* no. 49; for *deamhnaidhe* B read *demnaidhe* no. 52; for *icrossaib* M read *icossaib* (suprascript *o* without insertion marks) no. 53; for *indleacaile* B read *indlecaile* no. 55; for *nibalbduine* B read *mbalbduine* no. 56; for *mad* H read *inad* no. 61; for *níall* H read *máll* no. 62; for *crodh* B read *crod* no. 63; for *longaire* M read *longhaire* no. 63; for *sebche* B read *selche* no. 64; for *acli* B read *ach* no. 64; for *lini* M read *lim* no. 67; for *suithe* B read *suite* no. 69; for *icrandghail* B read *icrandhghail* no. 69; for *comdme* B read *coindme* no. 70; for *tenm* B read *temn* no. 71; for *tuille* om. M read *tuinde* om. no. 75; for *cossaibh* B read *cossaib* no. 77; for *nacroithet* M read *nachroithet* no. 78; for *dinmolaim* B read *dimolaim* no. 83; for *chellmíll* M read *chellinill* no. 83; for *gerinill* M read *gerrinill* no. 83; for *nglasfuarote* B read *nglasfuarrote* no. 83; for *lomraim* B read *lomraimh* no. 84; for *niuirbrind* B read *inuirbrind* no. 84.

[14] See *Catalogue of Irish MSS in the British Library* [*formerly British Museum*] vol. 1 (O'Grady 1926, 148).

[15] See *Catalogue of Irish Manuscripts in the National Library of Ireland*, Fasc. 4 (Ní Shéaghdha 1977, 85 ff.).

Relationship of the Manuscripts

Relationship of BME

BME are clearly derived from a common exemplar (here designated X).[16] Not only are the copies of *MV* III very close, but they are followed by the same set of texts in all three manuscripts: a short passage on the grades of ecclesiastics and poets and the appropriate colours to be worn by various categories of individuals;[17] the metrical tract *MV* I;[18] the *Fodlai Aíre* tract on the divisions of satire (Chapter 2 above); *In Lebor Ollaman*.[19] As regards the relationship between the manuscripts, Ó Concheanainn's suggestion (1975, 100–1) that E was written *c.* 1425 means, of course, that BM could not have been copied from E and this is supported by the textual evidence outlined below. A detailed examination of the text indicates that each copy is derived independently from a common exemplar:

ME contain readings which are omitted in B:

et*ir* dasc*r*in M, et*ir* dasg*r*in E, no. 34.

amias ME, no. 35.

iarngabail M, iarnagabail E, no. 49.

naighe M, naige E, no. 62.

cna*m*, indairib, der M, cnai*m*, i*n*dairib, der E, no. 68.

taebh M, taeb E, no. 82.

ME cite a second example of *ardchasbairdne* (*MV* III §116a) which is not found in B.[20]

[16] The following analysis is based mainly on the satirical quatrains in *MV* III but it has sometimes been necessary to supplement the evidence by drawing on the remainder of the text.

[17] This section, beginning *Septem sunt gradus ordinis*, consists of four statements in Latin, each of which is translated into Irish and followed by an illustrative stanza. Two of the stanzas dealing with grades of ecclesiastics are from a longer poem (Meyer 1905, 499 §3 and §1).

[18] The stanzas follow the same order in BME against H, e.g.: *MV* I §§36, 41, 39, 37, 43, (38, 40, 42 omitted) BME against §§36, 37, 38, 39, 40, 41, 42, 43 H. Ó hAodha (2002, 233) states of BME that 'It is clear these three copies all have the same origin'. Note that Mackechnie (1973, Vol. I, 115 §23) is mistaken in stating that E omits *MV* I §§37 and 39.

[19] See p. 42 above.

[20] See Thurneysen (1912, 66) for readings from M. E reads: Ardcasbairne an*n*so Huacorm*aic* oncarragmuaide risar comhraig c*r*andṡecaire niropian copellecmeru corṡen deg*r*ian gaillfeda*n*u.

BM contain readings which are omitted in E:

so im*morro* anas dian aireng ina cirt B, so im*morro* anas dia*n*aireng i*n*acirt M, *MV* III §21.

E omits no. 11.

BE contain readings which are omitted in M:

abair BE, no. 64.

ua B, h*ua* E, no. 65.

M omits *MV* III §14.

No two manuscripts agree consistently against the other, which suggests that there may have been a number of intervening copies between BME and the common exemplar.

BM agree against E, e.g.:

duthaig B, duthaigh M, dual E, no. 1.[21]

orcomai*n* B, orchomai*n* M, oros comai*n* E, no. 12.

cailus B, chailius M, cainis E, no. 13.

airgetlaib BM, argadlaim E, no. 31.

ageam B, agem*m* M, ageid E, no. 49.

suathadh B, suathadh M, fatath E, no. 82.

BE agree against M, e.g.:

amhai*ne* B, amai*ne* E, ume M, no. 17.

amu*main* B, a mu*mh* ai*n* E, amutai*n* M, no. 31.

amhucṡuil B, amucṡuil E, i*m*muchail M, no. 38.

Adomhunghoirt B, Adomango<.>t E, Adoma M, no. 49.

iarnitaidh B, iarnitaid E, iarnitai*n* M, no. 51.

uachuan B, ua cua*n* E, hua conchuan M, no. 60.

mallramhach B, mall ramach E, mallaranach M, no. 67.

cen indtliucht B, cini*n*dtlecht E, ce*n*inthucht M, no. 82.

ME agree against B, e.g.:

fochois caich M, focois caich E, acos chaech B, no. 8.

acht ME, f*or* B, no. 17.[22]

armona M, ar*m*ona E, aro*m*na B, no. 77.

[21] H also reads *dual*.

[22] The scribe of B (or of his exemplar) has read the *-acht* compendium as *f–* (*for*).

Glosses and Corrections in BME

All three manuscripts contain glosses and corrections, some of which are written above the line. Readings such as *deartan .i. sneachta* B, *derta .i. snechta* M, *dertan .i. snechta* E (all suprascript) *MV* III §1 and *donadesibh .i. uss and sin* B, *donaidesib .i. us insin* M, *dona deisibh .i. us annsin* E, no. 30, indicate that BME are copying from a glossed copy of the text:

bruigh B, b*r*on*n*aigh E, brui*n*d .i. b*r*ondaigh (*suprascript*) M, no. 35.

salachluim B, salachdui*n*d no salachluim M, no. 55.

lega M, leadha E, gela no lega (*suprascript*) B, no. 59.

damhaibh B, damaib E, danaibh no damaibh M, no. 68.

fer mara M, fear mara B, fear no ferrmar(*suprascript*) mara E, no. 77.

E sometimes combines readings found in B and M, citing one as a correction. This indicates that the scribe of E had access to at least two sources or a glossed copy:[23]

itcorai*n*d M, idcholai*n*d B, itcolai*n*d no itcorai*n*d (*suprascript*) E, no. 15.

ingalur felgabur M, ingalar fealghalar B, ingalar no feoil gabar fealgalar E, no. 27.

Esce feris inso .i. bricht nadrach M, Eisce feris .i. firesca (*suprascript*) B, Eisce feris .i. far esca (*suprascript*) .i. bricht natrach E, no. 47.

tarb M, damh B, dam no tarb (*suprascript*) E, no. 68.

Gair gaill B, Gair guill M, Gair gaill no guill (*suprascript*) E, no. 85.

corranchi M, corraighi B, corraigi no corranaichi (*suprascript*) E, no. 86.

Relationship of B to B^b

B^b is very similar to B and both often agree against ME. On the other hand, B sometimes agrees with one or more of the other MSS against B^b and *vice versa*, which indicates that neither can be a copy of the other.

[23] Other examples are: *gab rim* M, *gab rind* B, *gab ruim no rind* (suprascript) E, *MV* III §79; *sciathanbras* M, *sciathanglas* B, *sciathanglas no bras* (suprascript) E, *MV* III §100.

BB^{b} agree against ME:[24]

cnaplui*ng* BB^{b}, capluing ME; nadail BB^{b}, madail ME; ṡloig BB^{b}, gloir ME, no. 5.
bus BB^{b}, is M, as E, no. 7.
acos chaech BB^{b}, fochois caich M, focois caich E, no. 8.

B or B^{b}agree with one or more MSS:

i*n* crand BM, c*r*and B^{b}, *illeg.* E, no. 7.
Auscreitlin B, Auscrelli*n* B^{b}, Ahuscrelin M, no. 33.
dui*ne* B, fine B^{b}ME, *MV* III §49.

There are also several omissions in B or B^{b}, for example:

amui*n* anall BM, amai*n* anall E, anall B^{b}, no. 7.
buaidh ḟear fail brian broga inbuair BME, *om.* B^{b}, *MV* III §50.
slog B^{b}, slogh ME, *om.* B, *MV* III §52.

Relationship of H to BB^{b}ME

H generally stands apart from BB^{b}ME and it preserves an important reading (*ednen* no. 61) which is omitted in the other MSS. There are also instances, however, where it agrees with one or more of the MSS against the others.

H goes against BB^{b}ME:[25]

cornd H, crand BB^{b}M, *illeg.* E, no. 7.
olc H, lag BB^{b}E, lach M, no. 8.

H agrees with one or more manuscripts:

dual HE, duthaig B, duthaigh M, no. 1.
dochur HE, adochu*r* B, adocur B^{b}, adocha*r* M, no. 6.

[24] Other examples are: *buidi* BB^{b}, *baite* M, *baiti* E, *MV* III §30; *indealb* BB^{b}, *indaebh* M, *indeb* E, *MV* III §41; *nanaem* BB^{b}, *dancaem* M, *dan coem* E, *MV* III §47.

[25] Other independent readings in H are: *merge acore* H, *erge choire* B, *erge coire* M, *ergi coire* E, MV III §29; *corrigdath* H, *corighrath* B, *gorrigrath* M, *corigrath* E, MV III §41; *caidhi* H, *cruaide* B, *cruadhi* M, *cruaide* E, MV III §46; *slataib* H, *sladait* BE, *slatait* M, MV III §46; *brecht* H, *reacht* B, *recht* M, *racht* E, MV III §52; *cein* H, *chaimh* B, *caem* M, *caem* E, MV III §55; *botha* H, *afotha* BME, MV III §72. H omits a number of readings, e.g: *dáilus* B, *dail as* M, *dailis* E, *om.* H, MV III §28; *ceitri buille* BM, *cetri buille* E, *om.* H, MV III §38; *geib dhuain mbriain* B, *geib duain mbriain* M, *geib duain mbrian* E, *om.* H, MV III §50; *idu aiss* B, *idhuais* M, *iduais* E, *om.* H, MV III §58.

.h. concua*n* H, hua conchuan M, ua cua*n* E, uachuan B, no. 60.

i*m*moin H, imoin B, imonaig ME, *MV* III §2.

stat HME, smot B, *MV* III §4.

Relationship of G to BB^{b}MEH

G contains a number of independent readings, including an important reading (*aingaire* no. 52) which is omitted in BM.[26] It also shares some readings with H against BME, which suggests that it belongs to the same line of transmission as H.

G goes against BB^{b}MEH:

caeblui*n*g G, cnaplui*n*g BB^b, capluing MEH, no. 5.

illoi*m* G, loi*m* BMEH, no. 10.

abhruiti*n* G, i*n*bruitin BME, inbrutin H no. 10.

mhaise G, amaise B, amaisse M, amaisi E, no. 17.

at*r*oid G, adruith BME, no. 37.

lughe G, lui*n*de B, lui*n*di M, no. 52.

fidh G, doḟid B, dofird M, doḟidh E, no. 67.

athbr*a*ighi leathair G, leathbraici laithir B, lethbraigi laithir B^b, lethbraice laithir M, lethbraigi <. . .> hair E, letbroici lathir H, no. 80.

GH agree against BB^{b}ME:[27]

GH cite a different stanza to illustrate *deibide fo-cheil a cubaid* (no. 2 below).

maighni G, maigni H, mhuighi B, muighi M muigi E, no. 10.

cuil G, chuil H, *om.* BB^{b}ME, no. 80.

tairbh G, tuirb H, *om.* BB^{b}E, fola M, *MV* III §48.

icanesbius H, eca nesbus G, icaneabus B, icanebas M, icaneibiss E, *MV* III §28.

[26] The folio is missing in E and the stanza is not found in H.

[27] Nineteen stanzas are common to both GH: *MV* III §§2–3, 5, 8, 25, 28, 31, 33, 36–8, 43, 48, 51, 58–60, 62, 68. This includes nos. 1, 2, 5, 10 and 80 of the present edition.

Relationship of G to H

H cannot be a copy of G, the earlier of the two manuscripts, as it contains many metrical illustrations which are found in BME but not in G. H also occasionally agrees with one or more of the other MSS against G and *vice versa*:

> anii isdual H, ani isdual E, in*n*i isduthaigh G, i*n*di isduthaig B, ini is duthaigh M, no. 1.
>
> letbroici H, leathbraici B, lethbraice M, lethbraigi B^bE, athb*r*aighi G, no. 80.
>
> domidh BME, demidh H, dhorn G (rhymes with *bir*) *MV* III §28.
>
> tair H, tathair BB^b, thathair MEG (rhymes with *chath*air H, catair B, cathair B^bMEG, *MV*III §36).

Stemma

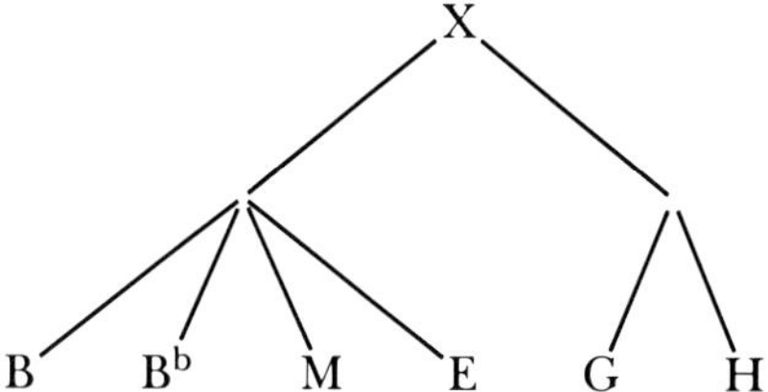

Orthography

All MSS show a number of late orthographical features, some examples of which are given below. The orthography of H is more conservative than that of the other MSS in that it exhibits only two later features, namely the writing of *gh, bh, dh* for *g, b, d* and the confusion of lenited *g* and lenited *d*. M, by contrast, shows the greatest variety of later features. Also noteworthy is the consistent use in G of the *spiritus asper* to indicate lenition of *c, p, t* and *g* and the use of the *punctum delens* to indicate lenition of *b, d, m* and *f*. Length marks are rare in all MSS. The form of the MS is given first, followed by the restored form in brackets.

1. *ea* for *e* before a non-palatal consonant:

   B: gearr (gerr) no. 31; bean (ben), chleachtus (chlechtas) no. 35; ḟeadanaig (ḟetánaig) no. 50.

M: ceall (cell) no. 8; sneachta (snechta) no. 12; ceallog (Chellóc) no. 30; gearr (gerr) no. 31.

E: ceall (cell) no. 8; bealltaine (Belltaine) no. 28; ceallog (Chellóc) no. 30; dealb (delb) no. 51.

G: Aireamh (Airem) no. 10; meana (Mena) no. 66; cearc (cerc) no. 67.

2. *g*, *b*, *d* for *c*, *p*, *t*:

B: ḟeadanaig (ḟetánaig) no. 50; scadan (scatán) no. 52; cogur (cocur) no. 57; maidi (maite) no. 60; gobluim (gopluim) no. 69.

M: edrom (éttrom) no. 10; ṡagairt (ṡacairt) no. 12; gob (gop) no. 28; coigleann (choiclenn) no. 31; seagail (secail) 38; feadanaigh (ḟetánaig) no. 50.

E: lag (lac) no. 8; sagairt (ṡacairt) no. 12; liathroide (líathróite) no. 31; gragain (Grácáin) no. 66.

G: clogthaigh (clocthaig) no. 37; ḟeadanaigh (ḟetánaig) no. 50; sgadan (scatán) no. 52.

3. *gh*, *bh*, *dh*, *mh* for *g*, *b*, *d*, *m*:

B: ceolaibh clerigh (cheólaib cléirig) no. 35; fiadh (fíad) no. 36; uidhir (uidir) no. 51; aibhne (aibne) no. 57; deisibh (Déisib) no. 58; cliabaigh (clíabaig) no. 61; mhallacht (mallacht) no. 71.

M: inadiaidh (ina díaid), fleadha arcuaillibh (fleda ar cúaillib) no. 8; diultadh (díultad) no. 28; acertaigh ochorcaigh (a chertaig ó Chorcaig) no. 37; indemhain (in demain) no. 51.

E: odhur (odor) no. 12; dubh (dub) no. 28; fasaigh (fásaig) no. 30; clemhna (chlemna) no. 31; bregaigh (brécaig) no. 46; cnamha (chnáma) no. 47; dobhurtanaig (dobarthanaig), crinlamhaigh (chrínlámaig) no. 48.

G: tabhair (tabair), duthaigh (dúthaig) no. 1; criathradh (críathrad) no. 2; damh (dam) no. 5; corrmhil (corrmíl) no. 80 .

H: There are no examples of *mh* for *m*; demidh (de mid) *MV* III §28; faidhbi (faidbe) *MV* III §37; indaebh (ind áeb) *MV* III §41; brogha (broga) *MV* III §50; slogh (slóg) *MV* III §52; tnuidh (tnúid) *MV* III §55; ategh (a teg) *MV* III §62; inatigh (ina tig) *MV* III §65.

4. Confusion of lenited *g* and lenited *d*:

   B: drolmuide (dromlaige) no. 52; flegha (ḟleda), stuaide (stúaige) no. 67; othraidh (otraig) no. 76; fosaigh (fossaid), tradhna (tragna) no. 77.

   M: lecaidh (leccaig) no. 36; madaigh (mataid) no. 38; rebaidh (rebaig) no. 39; fossaigh (fossaid) no. 53; gamnaidhe (gamnaige) no. 56; deodhanacht (d'Éoganacht) no. 72.

   E: laghar (ladair) no. 8; diultagaid (díultadaig) no. 28; geoigh (geóid) no. 49; fosaigh (fossaid) no. 77.

   G: There are no examples.

   H: inadiaig (ina díaid) no. 8; ainglighe (ainglide) *MV* III §62.

5. Final, lenited *d* not written:

   M: armerugu : gelugu (merugud : gelugud) no. 16; diultu (díltad) no. 65.

6. Confusion of lenited *g* and lenited *b*: [28]

   B: chossaigh (chossaib) no. 53; snedhaigh (snedaib) no. 72.

7. Lenited *b* for lenited *m*:

   BM: airgetlaib (argatlaim) no. 31.

8. Confusion of lenited *c* and lenited *t*:

   M: crethe (chreche) no. 63; roithet (roichet) no. 78.

[28]Cf. also *crandaigh* (*crannaib*) M, *MV* III §91 and *dairbrib* (*dairbrig*) M, *MV* III §124. For other examples see *SG* III §3.19.

Editorial Method

There is no single superior manuscript witness of the text of *MV* III, as is clear from the evidence cited above. BME are very close, containing a longer version of the tract and consequently a greater number of satires than B^{b}GH. The text in B has many omissions, however, while parts of M are illegible due to marginal staining. In the case of E, a folio is missing and large sections of the manuscript are illegible as a result of the application of chemicals during the nineteenth century. The other manuscripts contain only a small selection of satires.[29] In view of this, all six manuscripts witnesses (BB^{b}MEGH) have been drawn upon when establishing a normalised text.

The vocabulary of these satires is often difficult and obscure, and many words and compounds are otherwise unattested. Some words are cited under the wrong head-words in *DIL*, where the readings given are often those of B as published in *Irische Texte*. Examples include: *galluirge* 'of a foreign club' (rhyming with *cambuirbe*) s.v. *uirge* 'testicle' no. 16; *chongna* 'of horn' (rhyming with *lomda*) s.v. *con-cnaí* 'gnaws' no. 22; *tairnge* 'point' (rhyming with *aibne*) s.v. *tragna* 'corncrake' based on B's reading *traigne* no. 57; *cenn* 'scum' s.v. *cenn* 'head' no. 64; *bladach* 'splendid' (rhyming with *dabach*) s.v. *bluch, blach* 'salt meat' based on B's reading *blach* no. 70; *úa Scuirre* s.v. 1 *corr* 'projecting part, end, corner', based on B's reading *Uas cuirri* no. 72; *scéith* 'thorn bush' (in compound *ar cascéith*, rhyming with *glasléith*) s.v. *géith* (no meaning given) based on B's reading *arcass geith* no. 74. In other instances, the same word is interpreted differently when cited under two different head-words in *DIL*. For example, *ardáin* no. 41 is cited s.v. 1 *ardán* 'drinking vessel' but is taken as a placename s.v. 1 *bí* 'pitch', based on Meyer's edition (1919, no. 62). Some words are not given as head-words in *DIL*, e.g.: *clocaile, ocaile* no. 9; *drenntaide* no. 28; *-métlánaig, detbudánaig* no. 40; *dígrádaig* no. 48. On account of the many textual difficulties, therefore, complete variant readings are provided.

Normalised Text

c p t are restored where the manuscripts have *g b d* for post-vocalic voiced stops.

[29] B^{b}: 9 satires; G: 13 satires; H: 19 satires.

Lenition of consonants is silently normalised in accordance with Old and Middle Irish orthographical practice.

Accent marks are added silently. Hairstrokes over *i* in the MSS are not indicated.

Metres which are syllabically irregular are divided into lines on the basis of end-rhyme and internal rhyme, as this is often the only means of determining the metrical structure.

Manuscript Readings

The compendia for *-us, con, et, er, acht, ar, air* and *ur* are expanded silently. The abbreviations *dō, dā, im̄* and *l-* are expanded silently as *dono, dano, immorro* and *no* respectively. The expansion of all other abbreviations is indicated by the use of italics.

Where the text of a particular manuscript is illegible this is indicated by a series of dots within brackets. Some readings which are now illegible are taken from Thurneysen's edition (1891; 1912, 59–72) and these are enclosed within braces.

Dating and Linguistic Analysis

Thurneysen (1912, 86–9) has suggested that the text was compiled *c.* 1060, based on the identification of a number of individuals mentioned in the metrical illustrations. He suggested that Flannacán úa Cellaig, the subject of no. 32 below, may be the *rí Breg* whose pilgrimage to Rome and death are recorded in *AU s.a.* 1028 and 1060 respectively. Máel Inmain, the grandfather of Dúngal, no. 76, may be the anchorite of Glendalough whose death is recorded in *FM s.a.* 953, while Gilla Cellaig, the subject of no. 64, may be the *rí Hua Fiachrach Aidne* whose death is recorded in *AU s.a.* 1003. In most instances, however, it is impossible to identify the subjects of our poems with any degree of certainty because of the compilatory nature of the tract and the fact that the stanzas are cited out of context.

Additional evidence for dating has been adduced by Mulchrone, who suggests (1954, 15) that *MV* III §142 refers to the plundering of Clonmacnoise in 1050. Byrne (1973, 153) has identified the subject of *MV* III §19 as Domnall mac Murchada, who was king of Leinster from 1072–5. According to Kelleher (1988), *MV* III §2 may be a description of a battle fought at Móin Mór, Co. Cork, in 1152. If Kelleher is correct, this would indicate a date of compilation considerably later than 1060.

As regards linguistic criteria for dating, it should be noted that *MV* III is not a homogeneous text but consists rather of a collection of isolated metrical illustrations. The *Irish Grammatical Tracts* are similar in structure, in that they contain metrical examples from all periods of Classical Irish. Some of the illustrations, such as *MV* III §§66, 100, 118 and 210, have been taken from existing sources and modified by the compiler, while other metres and metrical names appear to have been created specifically for inclusion in the tract (McLaughlin, 2005b). The absence of finite verbal forms, particularly in many of the invectives, sometimes makes it difficult to establish a date on linguistic grounds alone.[30] The following features, however, suggest that the tract was compiled during the Middle Irish period. Readings of the restored text are given:

Phonology

The confusion of final unstressed vowels is indicated by rhyming examples such as: *maisse* : *braisse* (OIr. *maisse, braissi*; end-rhyme lines *bd*) no. 17; *balbduine* : *Charnmaige* (OIr. *balbduini, Charnmaige*; end-rhyme lines *ac*) no. 56; *chornaire* : *longaire* (OIr. *cornairi, longairiu*; internal rhyme) no. 63; *anma* : *gamna* (OIr. *anmae, gamno*; internal rhyme) no. 76 etc.

Hiatus forms are contracted in: *-ró* no. 6; *díaid* : *ḟiaich* no. 8; *lór* no. 16; *do-chuaid* no. 19; *ól* nos. 31, 51; *óil* no. 24; *scín* no. 50; *úa* nos. 57, 75 etc.; *uí* nos. 37, 44, 52 etc.; *Uíb* no. 35.

Note the analogical spread of palatalisation in: *cambuirbe* (: *galluirge*) no. 16; *uige, tuige* no. 19; *uime* ... *luime* no. 52.

[30] In his edition of no. 51 below, for example, Meyer restores final unstressed vowels while I have normalised in accordance with Middle Irish standards. The contracted form *ól*, fixed by the metre, suggests a Middle Irish date of composition for this stanza.

Morphology

Article

There are no examples of the earlier disyllabic form of the article. Note the accusative plural masculine form *na saithe* no. 12 and the genitive plural masculine forms *na ngallbróc* no. 73 and *na ndrúth* no. 85. *Na* has replaced *in(d)* in nominative plural masculine *na míla* no. 15. Final *-ib* is lost in the dative plural form of the article plus preposition in *ocna búaib* no. 19.

Noun

1. Loss of neuter gender: *in crann* no. 7.

2. Dative plural for accusative plural: *sech lecnaib* (: *chertaig*) no. 37; *dar céisib* (: *Déisib*) no. 58; *etir dá dámaib* (: *chnámaib*) no. 68.

3. Accusative plural for nominative plural: *serthe* no. 22 (*SG* III §5.11).

4. Middle Irish dative singular of *n*-stem: *don arbur* (OIr. *arbaimm*) no. 23 (in *aicill* rhyme with *adbul*).

5. Dental stem declined as *ā*-stem: *-scéith* no. 74.

6. Confusion between nominative and accusative singular of feminine *ā*-stem: *cen glám* no. 47 (*SG* III §5.6).

Adjective

1. Loss of dative plural ending: *co cossaib clama* (rhyming with *mara*) no. 77.

2. Replacement of the superlative by the comparative: *én is ettchu d'énaib* no. 68. This development began during the OIr. period (*SG* III §6.15; *GOI* §366).

Adverb

Co is used to form an adverb in *co demin* no. 6 (*SG* III §9.1).

Numerals

Loss of the feminine form (*dí*) of the numeral *dá* 'two': *dá blíadain* no. 27; *ar dá charaid* no. 68 (*SG* III §8.3).

Prepositions

1. Middle Irish *amlaid* (OIr. *samlaid*) fixed by alliteration in the phrase *ní hamlaid ro-ḟúaramar* no. 14.
2. *For* 'on': OIr. *for* > *ar* nos. 8 (confirmed by elision), 33, 59, 60 etc.
3. *Fri* 'towards, against': OIr. *fri* > *ri*: *rit* no. 8; *ri* no. 60. OIr. *fri* preserved in no. 11.
4. *Íar* 'after': except for *ar* no. 22, OIr. *íar* is preserved in nos. 19, 46, 51.
5. *Oc* 'at': Middle Irish *acaib* is established by rhyme with *apair* no. 64.
6. *Re* 'before': *reime* (: *bleide*) (OIr. *riam*) no. 13; *remum* (: *ferunn*) (OIr. *rium*) no. 18.

Conjunctions

1. *nach* (*can*) no. 49 (OIr. *nád*).
2. *mar* nos. 14, 26 (OIr. *immar*).

Verb

1. Analytic form: *ísaid tú* no. 23 (Greene 1958, 1973; *EIV*, 193; *SG* III §10.19).
2. Loss of deponent inflexion: *nír lessaigis* no. 49; *dimmolaim* no. 83; *chronaigim* (?) no. 83 (*EIV*, 236 ff.; *SG* III §12.4).
3. Simplification of compound verbs: *ḟúarus* no. 29; *nít choiclenn* no. 31.
4. Addition of third plural personal ending to the impersonal form *fil*: *ní fuilet* no. 17 (*SG* III §12.191, 12.194; O'Daly 1946, 88).
5. Third singular conjunct present indicative ending *-enn/-ann*: *nít choiclenn* no. 31 (*SG* III §12.12).

6. Spread of the first singular conjunct present subjunctive deponent ending to non-deponent verbs: *coro benur* no. 9; *dá tucur* no. 23 (*SG* III §12.79). Note also *dá* for earlier *día* and the subjunctive of *benaid* formed from the present stem (*SG* III §12.77).

7. Spread of the *s*-preterite: *tánacas, do-cúadas* no. 16; *ḟúarus* no. 29; *ro ben* no. 29; *ro chorrmaid* no. 69 (O'Daly 1946, 61–6; Quiggin 1910, 197–202; *SG* III §12.53).

8. Copula form: *isat* no. 8 (*vs. at* nos. 28, 53) (*SG* III §12.194).

9. The form *dernsat* no. 11, showing the use of the historical passive stem as active (*SG* III §12.66).

10. Confusion of preverbs: *ro-ḟúaramar* no. 14 (OIr. *fo-*).

11. Short *e* future *-geba* (rhyming with *fleda*) no. 8 (Greene 1978, 61 ff.).

12. *Apair*, rhyming with *acaib* (OIr. *epir*) no. 64.

13. *Raga* (OIr. *-riga/rega*) no. 18 (*SG* III §3.12).

14. *Gebid* no. 7 (*SG* III §12.198).

Verbal System

The reading of the restored text is given, with significant MS variations in brackets.

Present Indicative Active

1sg.:	Abs.:	*foclaim* no. 13.
		dimmolaim no. 83.
		chronaigim (*tronaigim* B, *cro andoghaimh* M) no. 83.
		lomraim no. 84.
	Prot.:	*ní cuinchim* no. 84.
3sg.:	Conj.:	*nít choiclenn* (*nicoitgleann* B, *nit coigleann* M, *nicoiglenn* E) no. 31.
		nach can no. 49.
		asa maid (*isamhuigh* B, *isamaig* M) no. 79.
	Deut.:	*do-beir* nos. 1, 28.
		do-gní no. 6.

	Prot.:	*ní tabair* no. 1.
		nocho déna no. 2; *nocho déine* no. 17.
		nocho thaille no. 18.
	Rel.:	*ṡeccas* no. 26.
		chlechtas no. 35.
		ibes no. 47.
3pl.:	Prot.:	*nach roichet* no. 78.

Present Indicative Passive

3sg.:	*ara snáidther* (*snaiter* BM, *snaidthir* E) no. 12.
	ara tabar no. 25.

Imperative Active

2sg.:	*imthig* no. 19.
	ith no. 19.
	roich no. 19.
	apair no. 64.
2pl.:	*íarraid* no. 5.
	tibid no. 7.
	gebid no. 7.

Present Subjunctive Active

1sg.:	Abs.:	*ḟócraim* no. 5.
	Conj.:	*coro benur* no. 9.
	Prot.:	*dá tucur* no. 23.
3sg.:	Conj.:	*ro mela* no. 71.
	Prot.:	*muna ró* no. 7.
2pl.:	Prot.:	*ara féssid* (*conrofesedh* B, *arafesed* M, *arrofessadh* E) no. 30.

Present Subjunctive Passive

3sg.:	Prot.:	*mani déntar* no. 26.

Future Active

1sg.:	Deut.:	*do-bér* no. 13 (*ter*).
	Prot.:	*ná teilciub* no. 22.
2sg.:	Abs.:	*ísaid tú* no. 23 (3 sg. with independent pronoun).
	Conj.:	*ní geba* (: *fleda*) no. 8.

3sg.:	Conj.:	*nocon ain* no. 9.
		raga (*bis*) no. 18.
	Prot.:	*ní ró* no. 6.

Preterite Indicative Active

1sg.:	Conj.:	*má ro cháinius* (*marcailus* B, *marochailius* M, *marocainis* E) no. 13.
		náro áerus no. 13.
	Deut.:	*ro-cúala* no. 1.
		do-cúadas no. 16.
	Prot.:	*nochon acca* no. 3.
		tánacas (contracted deut.) no. 16.
		nochon ḟúarus no. 29.
2sg.:	Conj.:	*nír lessaigis* (*nira* ME) no. 49.
3sg.:	Abs.:	*gabais* no. 3.
	Conj.:	*ro chuir* no. 12.
		ro gab no. 20.
		ro ḟírchrap no. 22.
		ro ṡecc no. 26.
		ro ben no. 29.
		ro memaid no. 39.
		ro chorrmaid (*rochomraidh* B, *rocorrmaidh* M) no. 69.
	Deut.:	*do-chuaid* no. 19.
		do-rala no. 25.
		as-bert no. 26.
	Prot.:	*nocon ḟuair* no. 78.
1pl.:	Deut.:	*ro-chúalamar* no. 14.
		ro-ḟúaramar (*rofuaramar* B, *fotuaramar* M, *ro fuaramar* E) no. 14.
3pl.:	Prot.:	*'na ndernsat* no. 11.

Preterite Indicative Passive

3sg.:	*do-acrad* (*dohacradh* B, *datacradh* M) no. 22.
3pl.:	*tucait* (?) no. 64.

The Substantive Verb

Present Indicative

2sg.: *cid taí* no. 23.
3sg.: *a-tá* nos. 11, 14, 17, 20.
oca tá no. 35.
nochon ḟuil nos. 6, 7 (*ter*), 79.
3pl.: *a-táit* (*bis*) no. 15.
ní ḟuilet no. 17.

Consuetudinal Present

3sg.: *i mbí* nos. 30, 66, 73, 79.
Rel.: *bís* nos. 28, 74.
3pl.: Rel.: *i mbít* no. 57.

Future

2sg.: *ní bia* no. 19.

Preterite

3sg.: Rel.: *ro boí* no. 5.

The Copula

Present Indicative

2sg.: *isat* no. 8.
at nos. 28, 53.
3sg.: *is* nos. 10, 13, 22, 35.
nocho nos. 17 (*ter*), 18, 19 (*bis*), 20, 29 (*bis*), 64 (*quater*).
ní no. 60, 80.
masa no. 13.
Rel.: *is* nos. 1, 8.
is (genitive rel.) no. 4.
i nach no. 82.
3pl.: *at* no. 53.

Present Subjunctive

3sg.: *mad* no. 5.
cencop no. 5.
cid no. 9.
Rel.: *bas* no. 7.
anbas no. 22.

Preterite

1sg: *óbsa* no. 3.
3sg.: *robo* no. 16.
dárbu no. 25.
Neg.: *nírob* no. 11.
nír no. 22.
nochorbo no. 24.

Other Linguistic Features

The satires in *MV* III contain a large number of words and compounds which are unattested elsewhere and some of these may have been coined specifically for metrical purposes. In nos. 40 and 48, for example, the language appears artificial due to a large number of compound adjectives. No. 40 is particularly striking in that it contains many adjectives ending in *-ánach,* some of which are formed from nouns ending in *-án.* In other cases, however, *-ánach* appears to be a new suffix, replacing the normal adjectival suffix *-ach* for metrical purposes. Examples include *-métlánaig* from *métal* 'a paunch', *-gréchánaig* from *gréch* 'a scream' (cf. *gréchach* 'screaming') and *-líacánaig* from *líacán* 'stone pillar' no. 40; *thíagánaig* from *tíag* 'bag' and *phíanánaig* from *píanán* 'bag' no. 48; *breccánaig* from *breccán* 'speckled thing' no. 53.

Otherwise Unattested Words

Nouns: *gipáin* (: *Britáin*) no. 46; *phítig* no. 48; *breccánaig* (: *senáraig*) no. 53; *breccóice* from *brecc* (: *fetóice*) no. 54; *cenn* (nom. sg. in the sense 'scum') no. 64; *garlaig* (*slabraid : tragnaib : cranngail*) no. 69; *gablóc* (: *anfót*) no. 73; *idraid* no. 76; *casbúaróte* (: *glasḟúaróte*) no. 83. Note also a number of nouns ending in *-aile*: *ocaile, clocaile* no. 9; *gataile, cetaile, lataile, lecaile* no. 55 (cf. also *brethaile MV* III §130 and *imsergaile MV* III §149).

Verbal nouns: *gelugud* (: *merugud*) nos. 16, 29; *senugud* (: *merugud*) no. 20; *brocairecht* (: *stocairecht*) no. 67; *bechairecht* no. 86.

Adjectives: *dretránach* (or *dretnánach*): *etránach* no. 28; *drenntaide* : *gercaide* (: *Belltaine* : *eltaide*) no. 28; *aicedphellaig* : (*taicedbennaig*) no. 32; *scuitemail* no. 33; *phaitig* : *aitig* no. 48; *cúaránaig* (: *úarlámaig*) no. 48; *deidblénach* (: *eidnénach*) no. 67.

Nominative for vocative of o-stems

There are several examples of the use of nominative for vocative of masculine *o*-stems (Bergin 1921–23, 92–4): *a ḟolt* no. 33; *a charpat* no. 34; *a barr* no. 39; *a glas* no. 44. The fact that these words are used metaphorically is significant, since in Bardic poetry the nominative was normally used for the vocative of *o*-stem nouns in this context (*SG* IV §4.12).

Absence of finite verbal forms

A particularly noteworthy feature is the absence of finite verbal forms in many of the invectives. Thirty-six of the fifty-six invectives (64%) do not contain a finite verb. This can be further broken down as follows: 74% of type A (nos. 32–4, 36–8, 40–6, 48); 86% of type B (nos. 50–2, 54–6); 56% of type C (nos. 58–9, 61–3, 65, 67–8, 70, 72, 75–7); 43% of type D (nos. 81, 85–6).[31]

[31]This feature has been observed by Mercier (1962, 114), based on a smaller sample of poems.

Metres

Based on an analysis of the metrical tracts, Thurneysen (1891, 139–61) has identified four main groups:[32]

1. Stanzas with rhyming couplets in which both lines and end-words are homosyllabic, e.g. *rannaigecht becc scaílte* (7^2 7^2 7^2 7^2), no. 11; *rinnard aiclech* (6^2 6^2 6^2 6^2), no. 17, *aí idan* (9^2 9^2 9^2 9^2), no. 42.

2. *Deibide* stanzas, e.g. *deibide imrinn chenntromm* (8^2 8^4 ; 8^2 8^4), no. 32; *deibide baisse fri tóin* (3^2 7^2 ; 7^1 1^1), no. 1.

3. Stanzas with rhyming couplets containing:

   (a) heterosyllabic lines and homosyllabic end-words, e.g. *dechnad mór scaílte* (8^2 6^2 8^2 6^2), no. 6.

   (b) homosyllabic lines and heterosyllabic end-words, e.g. *cró cummaisc etir rannaigecht móir ocus casbairdne* ($7^3 7^1 7^3 7^1$), no. 33.

   (c) heterosyllabic lines and heterosyllabic end-words, e.g. *dían airseng impóid* (4^3 8^1 4^3 8^1), no. 4.

4. Stanzas of a different structure. This includes many of the metres classified as *écoitchenna*, such as *meisce Rómáin* (8^3 $9^3 4^2$ $8^2 9^3$), no. 23 and *bánrothán* (8^2 7^2 7^2 8^2 8^2 8^2 ; 8^2 10^2 8^2 8^2 8^2), no. 75. Some metres in this section are so irregular that it is questionable if syllabic count is at all relevant.[33] Examples are *int anaichnid dona druimnib suíthe* (8^3 11^3 10^3 12^3 10^3 15^3), no. 52 and *deilm laíde la díchetal* (10^3 6^2 5^3 9^2), no. 56. In such cases (e.g. nos. 42–4, 47–9, 52, 56, 84) it may be more appropriate to analyse the stanzas in terms of the number of stresses per line, rather than the number of syllables. Carney (1971, 53–4) notes that although stressed metres are found primarily in archaic poetry they were not entirely replaced by the later syllabic forms and are preserved in modern forms such as *caoineadh*. It may also be significant that the majority of these irregular metres are found in the final section of the tract, which contains the highest percentage of satires and invectives.

[32]This classification is followed by Meyer (1909, 13–26). For a review of the standard reference works on metrics see L. Breatnach (1996, 67–70).

[33]A detailed analysis of the metres illustrated in *MV* III is outside the scope of the present work and I intend to discuss these in an edition of the complete text.

Distribution of Satires

The satires in *MV* III are distributed throughout the tract as follows:

Gnáthaisti

This section contains the largest number of metrical illustrations and 43 of the 127 illustrative examples (34%) are satirical. The metres dealt with here are varieties of *deibide* (*MV* III §§2–17), *dían* (*MV* III §§18–29), *dechnad* (*MV* III §§30–46), *rannaigecht* (*MV* III §§47–95), *aí freisligi* (*MV* III §§96–9), *laíd lúascach* (*MV* III §§100–2), *sétrad* (*MV* III §§103–8), *casbairdne* (*MV* III §§109–18) and *rinnard* (*MV* III §§119–27). Satirical quatrains are cited among the illustrations for each of the above types. Twenty-one of the forty-three satires in this section illustrate types of *rannaigecht*,[34] while there are six examples of *rinnard*,[35] five of *deibide*,[36] three of *dechnad*[37] and two each of *dían*[38] and *sétrad*.[39] There are eight satires illustrating composite metrical forms, all of which consist of a mixture of *rannaigecht* with one or more other metres.[40] No. 62, for example, illustrates a mixture of three different metres: *cummasc slaite brechte ocus rinnairde ocus lethrannaigechta móire* 'a mixture of *slat brecht* and *rinnard* and *lethrannaigecht mór*'. The syllabic structure is $5^3 5^3$, 5^1; 6^2 5^1, 5^1, comprising two lines of *slat brecht* (5^3), one line of *rinnard* (6^2) and three lines of *lethrannaigecht mór* (5^1).

Gnátha medónda

The *gnátha medónda* section (*MV* III §§128–47) illustrates five types of metre: *rathnuaill bairdne*; *slat brecht*; *ochtfoclach*; *laíd luibenchosach* and *laíd trebraid*. Four of the twenty illustrations are satirical (20%).

Anaichinti

The *anaichinti* section (*MV* III §§148–66) illustrates varieties of *sretha deich*, *druimne suíthe*, *anamain* and *bricht*. Eight of the eighteen illustrations cited in this section are satirical (44%), including both types of

[34] Nos. 7–13, 33–5, 58–65, 80–2.
[35] Nos. 17–18, 37–8, 51, 68.
[36] Nos. 1–3, 31–2.
[37] Nos. 5–6, 57.
[38] Nos. 4, 50.
[39] Nos. 36, 66.
[40] Nos. 9, 10, 33, 58, 60, 62, 64.

druimne suíthe (*imgarb* and *anaichnid*) and five of the nine varieties of *bricht*.[41]

Écoitchenna

It is noteworthy that satires predominate in the final section of the tract (*MV* III §§167–210), which illustrates uncommon metres. Thirty-one of the forty-four metrical illustrations are satirical (70%). This section also contains the highest proportion of invectives.[42] Many of the satires in the *écoitchenna* section are metrically complex, often having more than four lines and an irregular number of syllables in the lines and in the end-words. Some stanzas also have obscure metrical names which give no indication of the syllabic structure, such as *imthecht daill isin chepaig* 'wandering of a blind man in the plot' no. 25, *menmarc Mongán* 'Mongán's desire' no. 71 and *bánrothán* 'little white wheel' no. 75. The names may even, in some instances, reflect an association with literary sources and satires known to the compiler of the tract (McLaughlin 2005b, 121–31). This section also contains satires illustrating varieties of *deibide* (*deibide airenn chorránach* no. 27) and *anair* (*anair imrinn scaílte* no. 74).

As can be seen from the table below, the highest proportion of satires and invectives is found in the *anaichinti* and *écoitchenna* sections of the tract:

[41] Nos. 22, 40–1, 53, 70.

[42] Tranter (1997, 89) offers no evidence in support of his claim that the *écoitchenna* section 'contains texts of poems apparently used for occult purposes'.

Section	No. of metrical illustrations	Satires/ invectives	%	Invectives	%
Gnáthaisti	127	43[43]	34%	25[44]	20%
Gnátha med.	20	4[45]	20%	2[46]	10%
Anaichinti	18	8[47]	44%	6[48]	33 %
Écoitchenna	44	31[49]	70%	23[50]	52%

Table 4.2: Percentage of satires and invectives in each section of *MV* III

These statistics suggest that there may have been a correlation between metre and subject-matter and that irregular or unusual metres may have been considered more suitable for the composition of satire than for praise poetry. Thurneysen (1912, 86) has observed in relation to the metres of *MV* III that the satiric poet is more likely to use non-standard metres than the panegyric poet. As regards the Old Irish period, Ó hAodha (1991, 222) notes that almost 50% of the forty-four original stanzas in *MV* I are eulogies.[51] The metres dealt with in this tract are varieties of *dechnad, ollbairdne, casbairdne, dúan, bairdne, rannaigecht* and *deibide* and it is noteworthy that *MV* I allocates varieties of *deibide* and *rannaigecht*, metres which are common in *dán díreach*, to the two lowest grades of bard (*bóbard* and *túathbard*).

A Middle Irish poem on different types of metre by the eleventh century poet Cellach úa Rúanada (Thurneysen 1891, 106; 1912, 74–7; 1913, 22–4) also suggests that certain metres were deemed appropriate for particular subjects. *Rannaigecht mór* is described as *cāem do dēnam na ndūan* 'fair for making the praise poems' (§4), *debide scaílte* is described as *ind aiste blāith brass / i ṅgnāthaigther in senchass* 'the powerful, smooth metre in which historical narrative is practised' (§9), while it is stated of *rannaigecht becc* that *ní gláma sund* 'you are not to satirise here (i.e. in

[43] Nos. 1–18, 31–8, 50–1, 57–9, 60–8, 80–2.

[44] Nos. 31–8, 50–1, 57–68, 80–2.

[45] Nos. 19–20, 39, 83.

[46] Nos. 39, 83.

[47] Nos. 21–2, 40–1, 52–3. 69–70.

[48] Nos. 40–1, 52–3, 69–70.

[49] Nos. 23–30, 42–9, 54–6, 71–9, 84–6.

[50] Nos. 42–9, 54–6, 71–9, 84–6.

[51] Four stanzas in *MV* I are satirical; see Ó hAodha (1991) nos. 36, 37, 40, 44 and p. 10 above.

this metre)' (§5) (Thurneysen 1912, 75–6).[52] P. A. Breatnach (1997, 52) notes that *rannaigheacht mhór* and *deibhidhe* are the most common metres in a corpus of thirty elegies composed in the fifteenth century. A further possible connection between metre and subject matter is highlighted by Mackinnon (1909, 116 note 1), who notes that while *casbairdne* in the earlier period is used of a specific metrical form, *casbhardacht* in modern Scottish Gaelic is generally restricted to satire or invective.

[52] For the reading *ní gláma* see Thurneysen (1913, 23).

Texts

Satires and Curses

1. Ro-cúala
ní tabair eochu ar dúana;
do-beir a n-í is dúthaig dó —
bó.

2. Mac Con Aba,
nocho déna mada
acht críathrad mine do mac
Máenaig, ocus doirseóracht.

3. Óbsa becán gabais gleith
i tír cháich cen fíarfaigid;
nochon acca béolu eich
amail béolu in Líathainig.

4. A Éirennaig,
do drochrannaib is lomnán dorn,
a Albanaig,
a Lochlannaig, a goblán gorm.

5. Íarraid dam gall cas a cnápluing,
— mad áil duit — glas gécruinn.
Fó lim cencop ogmóir fócraim,
a rí in tromglóir thétmaill.
Mac ro boí oc gaillsig goit grúcbuirr
co pútraill óig étruimm.

Translations

1. I have heard
   he does not give horses in exchange for poems;
   he gives what is natural for him —
   a cow.

2. The son of Cú Aba
   does nothing ineffectual
   except sifting flour for the son of Máenach
   and door-keeping.

3. Since I was a child he set about grazing
   on everyone's land without asking;
   I have never seen a horse's mouth
   like the mouth of Líathainech.

4. O Irishman
   whose fist is full of bad verses,
   o Scotsman,
   o Norseman, o blue swift.

5. Let you seek for me a curly-headed foreigner from a hempen ship,
   if it please you: a fetter of a branching chain.
   I do not care if he is not a learned man I denounce,
   o king of the powerful, stately voice.
   A son whom a stammering, surly, puffed-up foreign woman had,
   with a full, frizzy fringe.

6. Nochon ḟuil a maín co demin
amail do-gní dúana;
ní ró a dochur i Maig Ḟemin
i tenid cen túaga.

7. Nochon ḟuil a maín immaig
nochon ḟuil a maín anonn
nochon ḟuil a maín anall.
Tibid uile im Choin na Cell:
muna ró sligid bas ḟerr
gebid ina chenn in crann.

8. Uch, a lorcáin, isat lac!
A chos dlochtáin ria catt,
Ní geba túaignim ri tenn,
a bun fleda ar cúaillib cell,
Ní mó is ráiti rit, a drúith!
ocus corr dlúith ina díaid.
a thamain chrín fo choiss cháich,
a cháith lín i lladair ḟíaich.

9. Cid malé a ocaile
dar lim nocon ain;
tele dam in clocaile
coro benur air.

10. Airem Maigne Muiccín,
is maith lais loim técht;
éttrom lais in bruitín,
rothrom lais in cécht.

11. Cindus a-tá úa Conaill,
ocus Conn mac Cinn Ḟáelad?
'Na ndernsat fri mac nDubáin
nírob uráil a n-áerad.

6. His worth does not exist, indeed,
in the way that he composes poems.
He will not cause his damage in Mag Femin,
without axes in fire (i.e. without sharpened axes).

7. His worth is not outside,
his worth is not thither,
his worth is not thence.
Let you all laugh at Cú na Cell:
if he does not attain to a better course,
let you assail him with the stick.

8. Alas, you little mite, you are weak! No more should be said to you, you fool! You stem of a little bunch in front of a cat, with a heron close behind it.
You will not reach vaulted heaven by force, you withered stump under everyone's feet, you remains of a feast on the stakes of churches, you chaff of flax in a raven's claw.

9. Though his ... be together,
I think it will not protect [him];
bring me hither the ...
so that I may strike [it] against him.

10. The ploughman of Maigen of Muiccín
likes a drink of thickened milk;
the little goad seems light to him,
too heavy seems the plough.

11. How is the grandson of Conall,
and Conn, son of Cenn Fáelad?
For what they did to the son of Dubán
it has not been excessive to satirise them.

12. Mac int ṡacairt ó Ros Comáin
ro chuir na saithe isin snechta:
sámud ara snáidther durthach,
tráill odor ulchach ar echtra.

13. Acht masa deired dom dúanaib, do-bér mo dán do neoch aile,
do-bér mo geimel ar chúalaib, do-bér mo chaire ar chúic bleide.
Foclaim rim cháin is rim chubus, má ro cháinius úa Con Buide
is fortail dom dáil cen dulus, náro áerus duine reime.

14. A chell cháem, ro-chúalamar
do chlár cen chrád, cen chréidim;
ní hamlaid ro-ḟúaramar,
mar a-tá a tásc fo Éirinn.

15. A-táit sneda cona clainn
it chorainn.
A-táit na míla co mer
do ḟuilled,
a Chonaill.

16. Tánacas a Cíarraigib —
robo lór a cambuirbe;
do-cúadas ar merugud
do gelugud galluirge.

17. Ní ḟuilet a maíne,
nocho mó a-tá a maisse,
nocho mór a géire:
nocho déine acht braisse.

12. The son of the priest from Ros Comáin
who cast the crowds into the snow:
a congregation from which a church is protected,
a sallow, bearded thrall on an expedition.

13. But if there is a refusal for my poems, I will bring my craft to someone else, I will give my fetter in exchange for bundles of firewood, I will give my cauldron in exchange for five drinking cups.
I affirm by my rule and conscience, if I have reviled the grandson of Cú Buide, that my argument is victorious without voraciousness (?) and that I have not satirised a person before him.

14. O beautiful church, we have heard
of your table being without misery, without decay:
we did not find it
the way it is described throughout Ireland.

15. There are nits with their offspring
in your tonsure.
The lice are in a frenzy
to increase,
o Conall.

16. I escaped from the Cíarraige —
their perverse boorishness was enough;
I went astray
as a result of having been brightened by a foreign club.

17. His riches are non-existent,
and his beauty is no greater,
not great is his acuteness:
he does nothing but boast.

18. Nocho mac fir threbair,
nocho thaille i ferunn,
nocho raga im degaid,
nocho raga remum.

19. A drúith na nDéise, a chloicenn chéise,
ní bia dár n-éise 'muig ocna búaib.
A druim re séise, nocho dom réir-se,
nocho fom chéill-se do-chuaid do chíall.
Imthig, a duine! Ith imm is uige,
roich uide íar n-uide adíu co Rúaim.
A lorcán luige, a bolgán buide,
for tolclár tuige ret tóin aníar.

20. A-tá ar merugud: nocho mebal.
Ro gab senugud sleman solam.
glaca gataige . . . imar
airem apaide, inar odar.

21. [Maile, baire, gaire Caíar,
cot-mbéotar celtrai catha Caíar,]
Caíar di-bá, Caíar di-rá — Caíar!
fo ró, fo mara, fo chara Caíar!

22. Lachtnán úa gormfíaclach Gadra,
gúaille cranda cailig, diad cen damna.
Is ed ro fírchrap a fine
ar tuidecht a thige tíartúaid cen tarba.
Do-acrad anbas dúthaig don athair;
d'apaid ná ríg nír adba.
Rosc fir methle, maise aitinn,
serthe capaill íarna chor, corr craplám.
Cá rét ná teilciub cen terce
do sceirtiud a lecne líath lomda?
Delg scíad nó scían co n-eim chongna,
ic lot ladra Lachtnán!

18. He is not the son of a prudent man,
 there is no room for him on a holding,
 he will not go after me,
 he will not go before me.

19. You fool of the Déise, you piglet's skull,
 you will not stay behind us outside with the cows.
 You [who turns your] back on reason, it is not to my will [and]
 it is not to my reason that your reason has submitted.
 Go away, man! Eat butter and eggs!
 Reach by degrees from here to Rome!
 You little mite in a bed, you yellow belly,
 your bed-board of straw behind your backside!

20. He is confused: it is no shame.
 He has begun to age calmly [and] quickly.
 The hands of a thief . . . ,
 a sallow ploughman, a dun-coloured tunic.

21. [Evil, death, short life to Caíar,
 spears of battle will have killed Caíar,]
 may Caíar die, may Caíar depart — Caíar!
 Caíar under earth, under enbankments, under stones!

22. Lachtnán, blue-toothed grandson of Gadra, stiff shoulders of a cockerel, smoke (?) without cause. It is the case that his kin has truly shrivelled up after coming to his house in the north-west without profit.
 That which is natural for the father was pleaded; it was not an abode for abbot or king. Eye of a reaper, beauty of a gorse bush, shanks of a horse after being thrown down, a pointed withered hand.
 What thing will I not cast freely in order to peel away his bare, grey cheeks? A thorn of a thorn bush or a knife with a handle of horn, wounding Lachtnán's fist!

23. A drúith, cid taí dom airbire?
Dá tucur duit mnaí co mbungile
isint ṡamrud,
ísaid tú do ṡáith don arbur
is do ḟeór adbul i n-Urbile.

24. Tallad a ulcha
dé is 'tig óil,
rim ḟer cumtha
nochorbo cóir.

25. Conchobar úa Cadla,
crim muicce fíada ar áth n-aba: cuin do-rala in cara i n-úathad?
Duine dárbu ró brígrad bríathar,
fer ara tabar tírad ocus bró ocus críathar
ocus fuine ocus imḟuine cen ithe do Ráith chlíathad Crúachar.

26. As-bert mani déntar icuib
cuilbir nó binn, siu ná thall,
salann ar arán cen imm,
co cnámaib cinn is men ann.
Ro ṡecc feóil ar muintire
mar ṡeccas a rúsc im chrann.

27. Allas dé isin ló thé!
Conaire!
Dá blíadain dó i ngalar,
felgabar
fonaide!

23. You fool, what is wrong with you that you are reproaching me?
    If I give you a woman of real beauty
    in the summer,
    you will eat your fill of the corn
    and of luxuriant grass in Urbile.

24. The removal of his beard
    from him in the alehouse,
    it was not fair
    to my companion.

25. Conchobar grandson of Cadla, hart's tongue mixed with hemlock:
    when was the friend alone?
    A man to whom the power of words was excessive, a man to whom is assigned drying and a quern and a riddle and baking and cooking, without eating, for Ráth Chrúachan of battles.

26. He said unless a . . . or a pleasing thing
    is done by you here or yonder [there will be]
    salt on bread without butter,
    with head bones and meal in it.
    The flesh of our people has shrivelled up
    as its bark shrivels up around a tree.

27. Sweat from him on the hot day!
    Conaire!
    May he be two years in sickness —
    an evil, roasted goat!

28. A Dergáin deirg díultadaig,
a díultad Día Belltaine,
dar Brigit, at becnárach!
It durn bís do gop gercaide,
ic gol tís it churn dub,
drenntaide, dretránach.
Teist do-beir Cú Arad ort
tú labar, olc,
eltaide, etránach!

29. Nocho gairit a merugud etir Múscraige is Cáenraige;
nochon ḟúarus a gelugud co n-arm cháembuide chírmaire;
nocho chosmail a chlothaige risna clíara i carn Chíarraige;
ro ben mór do ṡúaig ṡochaide re arm n-íarnaide n-ídlaide.

30. Cara dam a Cill Dá Chellóc,
ara féssid:
píanán i mbí corca fásaig
Cíanán dona Déssib.

28. O ruddy, stingy Dergán,
you refusal on May Day,
by Brigit you are shameless!
Your grouse-like snout is in your fist,
weeping below into your black drinking-horn,
quarrelsome and drunk(?).
The account which Cú Arad gives of you [is that]
you are boastful, wicked, pasty and interfering!

29. Not short is his straying between Múscraige and Cáenraige.
I did not find him brightened by the fair, yellow weapon of a combmaker.
His fame is not like the fame of the poetic bands in the mound of Cíarraige.
He took away a great amount from a fair fight of hosts by means of an iron, engraved weapon.

30. A friend of mine from Cell Dá Chellóc,
so that you may know:
a bag of wild oats
is Cíanán of the Dési.

Invectives (A)

31. A meic Con Lemna, a láir gerr,
ben do chlemna nít choiclenn,   a chorr líathróite lubain,
a cholpthach i cennach ndaim,
a ól ordlach d'argatlaim,   a iuchra maigre a Mumain.

32. A meic Ḟlannacáin uí Chellaig,
a rí in tíre taicedbennaig,
a gabáil ṡréin brainig bennaig
ós muing airig aicedphellaig.

33. A uí Scélín scuitemail,
a scol chille cinn ar chinn,
a ḟolt gobann gatbéimnig,
a chorann maccléirig minn.

34. A uí Chuinn, a charpat lenaim liúin,
a chuing ar argat i Medaib Siúil ṡirthe,
a gerrfile, a gait balláin etir dá scrín,
a chennide chrannáin chrín etir crithre.

35. A Gilla Duinn a Dermaig,   oca tá in ben donn deólaid,
a mías bruinn ar brut trebraid,   a thonn do cheólaib cléirig,
is tú in cailech d'Uíb Cellaig,   a chú chlechtas ar cnámaib,
a dúan ar airech n-ellaig,   a ḟertas áraid d'Éilib.

31. O son of Cú Lemna, you stunted mare, the wife of your in-law does not protect you, you end of a ball of a tassel,
you heifer for the price of an ox, you draught of inches of orpiment, you salmon spawn from Munster.

32. O son of Flannacán úa Cellaig,
o king of the prosperous-hilled land,
o holder of a pointed, horned bridle
above the mane of a pack-horse covered in implements.

33. O ridiculous grandson of Scélín,
you clerical school at odds,
you hair of a withe-striking smith,
you tonsure of a clerical student of relics.

34. O grandson of Conn, you gum of a pathetic child,
you yoke in exchange for silver in Meda Siúil of raiding parties,
you stunted poet, you withe of a goblet between two shrines,
you old wooden helmet among flames.

35. O Gilla Donn from Dermag, who has the swarthy, mean wife,
you dish of chaff on a woven cloth, you outpouring of melodies of a cleric,
you are the cock of the Uí Cellaig, you hound who is accustomed to bones, you poem in exchange for a loaded pack-horse, you rung of a ladder from Éile.

36. A Gilla leóchaill leccaig Mo Laise,
a lecca cuirre garbglaise grían,
a ṡeiche chorcra, a chacc ar másaib,
a reithe folta fásaig dar fíad.

37. A uí dínnim Dergáin,
a drúith chaíl ar clocthaig,
a rann lem sech lecnaib,
a chertaig ó Chorcaig.

38. A errmór athbruit fo lus, a mucṡúil,
a mellṡrón mataid;
a ithe imme re harán secail,
a Gille in Chataig.

39. A meic uí Gemaid, etronn ro memaid
is, a meic rebaig, a lenaim laic,
beca do bossa, cáela do chossa,
a barr feóir rossa 'dar cossa cait.

40. A Domnaill doburlúpánaig bodurgrúcánaig bodurmétlánaig,
ón chomrainn chomargrúcánaig comardídánaig
caratgréchánaig!
A uí airim brocṡalaig amarmíchánaig a'adlíacánaig!
A ulcha gaillín detbudánaig cúarlúpánaig caladgríantrágthaig
canatgréchánaig!

41. A brollach snedach srethḟíar,
a ḟíacla con ar cloich aílig,
a uí Thadcáin, a tholltimṗáin, a meic Alcáin,
a bí ar burd ardáin, a ṡaíbfir.

36. O miserly, stony Gilla Mo Laise,
you cheek of a rough grey heron of river bottoms,
you purple pelt, you shit on buttocks,
you moulting desert ram mounting deer.

37. O shabby grandson of Dergán,
you puny fool on a belfry,
you [body]-part softer than cheeks,
you ragamuffin from Cork.

38. You big-pointed part of a worn-out goad under a stem, you pig-eye,
you pug-nose of a dog,
you eating of butter with rye bread,
o Gille in Chataig.

39. O son of úa Gemaid, we have quarrelled
and, you playful youth, you weak child,
small are your hands, skinny your feet,
you head of woodland grass between the paws of a cat.

40. O Domnall, dark and crooked, harsh and wrinkled, harsh and pot-bellied, from the company which is equally wrinkled and equally unskilled, screaming at friends!
You grandson of a ploughman [who is] filthy like a badger, of unregulated wailing and blotchy like a stone pillar!
You comb of a capon, smoky-coloured, bent and crooked, hard and dried up like gravel, screaming like a whelp!

41. You nitty, crooked-striped chest,
you hound's teeth on a dung-covered stone,
o grandson of Tadgán, you pierced *timpán*, o son of Alcán,
you pitch on the rim of a goblet, you perverse man.

42. A meic uí Chuinn, cella do chobair,
a gleic im thuinn, a thenga thamain,
a meic uí Chuinn, a chrithre im chella,
a rigthe gerra glassa gadair.

43. A máelscolb do messair,
a eclas crainn, a chacc cuirre uidre ittige,
a eóin ré n-ossaib,
a ḟertas a braind bicire, a Bressail!

44. A uí Ḟlannáin,
a láir mall,
a lethchoss geóid,
a glas cam
fo gáir gall.

45. A uí Scandail,
a scían espa,
a cherc usce,
a choss escra.

46. A meic dúir daill iffirnn,
a thigaill ar graphainn
ar gairdi do gipáin,
a geóid íarna gabáil,
a ḟeóil tarra togáin,
a ithe i míl étaig,
a uí brécaig Britáin.

47. A uí Chuinn,
a chossa daim, a drochḟir dána,
a gop in gair cen glám cen gráda,
a díabail omda ibes in linn,
a chongna clíabaig i cinn do chnáma.

42. O son of úa Cuinn, churches help you,
you wrestling with a wave, you tongue of a *taman*,
o son of úa Cuinn, you sparks around churches,
you short grey forelegs of a hound.

43. You blunt splinter from a measuring vessel,
you wooden stomach, you shit of a brown wingy heron,
you bird fleeing from deer,
you shaft from . . . , o Bressal!

44. O grandson of Flannán,
you sluggish mare,
you one leg of a goose,
you crooked bolt
at the battle-cry of foreigners.

45. O grandson of Scandal,
you useless knife,
you water-hen,
you stem of a goblet.

46. You dour, ignorant son of hell,
you last bridle on a horse race
because of the shortness of your ragged tunic,
you captured goose,
you belly meat of a pine marten,
you eating of a clothes' louse,
o deceitful grandson of Britán.

47. O grandson of Conn,
you feet of an ox, you bad poet,
you snout of pus (?) without satire, without qualifications,
you rude devil who drinks the ale,
you deer's antler at the end of your bones.

48. A Dalláin dobarthanaig dígrádaig!
A chammáin chrínlámaig confathmannaig cúaránaig!
A phítig phaitig phíanánaig!
A thíagánaig étig aitig úarlámaig!

49. A Domangairt,
a dronn geóid íarna gabáil,
a gemm dubgorm demain,
a bachlaig báin im brait,
a bél chaillige caíche,
a chonadmairt chícaraig,
nach can ceól isin chamáir,
a chossa cromma crebair,
a chrúachaide lenaim laic:
nír lessaigis in saíthe.

48. O unlucky, degraded Dallán!
You gnarled-handed, dog-haired, sandal-wearing crooked fellow!
You starving fellow, scrounging around bottles and bags!
You ugly, case-carrying, cold-handed bag carrier!

49. O Domangart,
you hump of a captured goose,
you dark-blue jewel of the Devil,
you pale, thieving churl,
you mouth of a one-eyed hag,
you greedy voracious ox
who does not sing songs at daybreak,
you crooked feet of a woodcock,
you swollen stomach of a weak child:
you have not benefited learning.

Invectives (B)

50. A ḟetánaig,
a chornaire, a chléraige,
a ḟis fon tír,
a chris cen scín, a scélaige.

51. A mír do duine, a delb in demain,
a chír i cuile, a chrebair chuilig,
a athbró íchtair, a airbe ibair,
a ól íar n-ítaid, a inair uidir.

52. A uí chúic patán pellbuide,
a scatán demnaide for druim dromlaige,
a bél mná uidre uime ibraide,
a ingaire bó luime luinne longaire,
a maise taise tréise tibride,
a imlige baise céise caise coise cornaire.

53. A drúith na hAlla, at cranda i cossaib,
a drúith na hAlla, at fanda fossaid;
a breccánaig díuit, a dord im dronda,
a drúith na hAlla, senáraig corra, chromma, chama fot chossaib.

54. A diripi talman ic teiched breccóice,
a ben co n-aillsin duib eógainn,
a chos choppóice,
a luirgne fetóice ar feórainn.

50. You piper,
you horn-player, you wandering musician,
you enquiry throughout the land,
you belt without a knife, you storyteller.

51. You bit of a man, you form of the Devil,
you comb in a larder, you flea-ridden woodcock,
you worn-out lower quern, you fence of yew,
you drink after thirst, you dun-coloured tunic.

52. You descendant of five yellow-furred leverets,
you devilish herring on the top of a vat,
you mouth of a sallow, crude, yew-like woman,
you herding of a bare, fierce, screeching cow,
o splendour of weakness [and] of foolish guile,
o licking around the handle of a curved *céis* at the foot of a horn-player.

53. O fool of Alla, you are wooden around the feet,
o fool of Alla, they are weak [and] stiff;
you foolish, freckled fellow, you buzzing around crowds,
o fool of Alla, old, pointed, bent, crooked bindings around your feet.

54. You ... of the ground fleeing from a little trout,
you woman with a tumour, black and scurfy-topped,
you stem of a dock leaf,
you shins of a plover on a river bank.

55. A mairbthine mongthige minchuile,
a ṡailchide ṡinnchaide ṡalachluim,
a rith gataige im chlecaire
a brataire in becaige
in gataile in cetaile
ri gataile ni cetaile
in lataile ind lecaile
a apaide acaite anachluim.

56. A bennimle bruit dar broinn mbalbduine,
a ben drúth i ndabaig,
a daill Charnmaige,
a gerringne gamnaige galair.

55. You thick-maned ... of a little gnat,
you dirty one, fox-like, filthy and naked,
you flight of a thief around a ...
you robber of the small cow (?),
... , ... ,
... , ... ,
... , ... ,
you sallow ... bog-barren (?) one.

56. You pointed edges of a cloak across the breast of a dumb man,
you wanton woman in a vat,
you blind man of Carnmag,
you stunted hoofs of a sick stripper.

Invectives (C)

57. Úa Cuinn, cocur daill dar draigne,
focul i mbít rainn co rigne,
géim daim arathair tri aibne,
tairnge tarathair i tidle.

58. Muiredach, mant capaill chróin,
cú dar céisib,
carpat bó bricce for benn,
bél daim dona Déisib.

59. Gilla in Naím, gnúis ḟiaich, fíacla lega i lis,
dlochtán crema i cris, net is ela as;
drúth Lemna, láir cháel chlérech ar cúairt chros,
glacca remra i ros, bos fo gerrga nglas.

60. Adastar lára i lláim,
lecca phuint dar pundainn,
cenn crúaid con ar caírig,
maite odar aílig,
lúa ri lúag, lecca chúar,
úa Con Cúan, ní cundail.

61. Sonnach eidnén ós aill,
deidblén ac dul i lluing,
dán ina díamair daill,
cnám clíabaig caim úa Cuinn.

62. Methmac Muiredaig, mesce chírmaire,
crossán líath ic linn,
screpall ar ḟeóil n-aige, óinmit ar eoch mall,
breccar claime i cinn.

57. The grandson of Conn, the whispering of a blind man over blackthorns,
a phrase consisting of stiff verses,
the roar of a plough ox being whipped,
the point of an auger into bunches of corn stalks.

58. Muiredach, the jaw of a reddish-brown horse,
a hound mounting piglets,
the gum of a speckled cow on a prong,
ox-mouth from the Dési.

59. Gilla in Naím, a raven's face, teeth of a leech in an enclosure,
a little bunch of garlic in a belt, a nest abandoned by a swan;
the fool of Líamain, a clerics' scrawny mare on a circuit of crosses,
fat hands in linseed, a palm under a blue dart.

60. A mare's halter in a hand,
a side of a pound weight across a sheaf of corn,
a cruel head of a wolf on a sheep,
a brown midden stick,
a kick against reward, a curved cheek
is the grandson of Cú Chúan: he is not seemly.

61. An enclosure of ivy above a cliff,
a weakling going into a ship,
a craft which is a dark, obscure thing,
a bone of a crooked deer is the grandson of Conn.

62. The degenerate son of Muiredach, as drunk as a comb-maker,
a grey-haired jester at ale,
a scruple for the meat of a bullock, a fool on a slow horse,
mangy spots on a head.

63. Mac ríg na nDése, delb om, clíar chreche,
seche chon fo chom chlíabaig,
cornairecht chornaire ar chrod,
lon ic longaire i Líamain.

64. Gilla Cellaig, cenn for sallaib,
seilche co ndíb mbennaib,
finna ar gúaire cullaig allaid
challaig Gilla Cellaig.

Nocho Gilla Cellaig etir,
nocho cenn for sallaib, apair!
Nocho finna ar gúaire
cullaig allaid cucaib;
immar tucait a challaig
nocho Gilla Cellaig acaib.

65. Finn úa Buide
linn i mbleide,
díltad dona,
íchtar eime.

66. Goll Mena do muintir Grácáin,
gall ic cnúasach cnó,
ballán i mbí bainne lomma,
dallán Dromma Bó.

67. Goll Mena mún cromgabair,
bert ḟleda for lomgabail,
brissiud stúaige ic stocairecht,
cáinte búaile ic brocairecht,
cerc i cill, crann eidnénach,
linn deidblénach drolmánach,
stiúir d'ḟid lim long mallrámach,
ben chamlámach chomdálach.

63. The son of the king of the Dési, a rude form, a rapacious band,
a hound's hide under the breast of a deer,
the horn-playing of a horn-player for wealth,
a blackbird screeching in Líamain.

64. Gilla Cellaig, a scum on flitches of bacon,
a snail with two horns;
a hair on the bristles of a fat (?) wild boar
is Gilla Cellaig.

He is not Gilla Cellaig at all,
he is not a scum on flitches of bacon, let you declare [it]!
He is not a hair on the bristles
of a wild boar [coming] to you (?);
as his . . . were brought (?),
it is not Gilla Cellaig [who is] with you.

65. Finn, grandson of Buide,
ale left in a goblet,
wretched refusal,
the base of a handle.

66. Goll of Men of the family of Grácán,
a foreigner collecting nuts,
a goblet in which there is a drop of milk,
the little blind man of Druim Bó.

67. Goll of Men, piss of a crooked goat, a hen in a church, an ivy-covered tree, a load for a feast [carried] on a bare fork, weak ale on the handles of a vat,
breaking a handle [of a trumpet] while trumpeting, a softwood rudder of slow-rowing ships, a satirist of the cowshed acting like a badger, a crooked-handed gregarious woman.

68. Rí Connacht, cenn tamain, dám etir dá dámaib,
lommarc ar dá charaid, cnám do chnámaib clíabaig,
erp d'erpaib i ndairib, én is ettchu d'énaib,
delg do delgaib draigin, dér do déraib díabail.

69. Dall Bóruime,
bél gaill gopluim, guth senchon ar slabraid,
brú arna tromguin itir tragnaib,
fíacail cam órbuide,
a hol cumgucht ro gerrchod ngarlaig,
gáe ro chorrmaid tria chrú i cranngail.

70. Úa Mesen,
mac gobal líathglas coindme,
gort íchtair ḟaithche,
gédglac dronngerr gopdub,
gall bladach ar bilairlic,
dabach ibairglic aithne.

71. Rí Cera, Cú Chonnacht,
ro mela mo mallacht!
Teimnide, tais, deir Mide,
snáith glais ri gallat.

72. Úa Scuirre,
sceith bruic ar beraib,
ócdrúth odur d'Éoganacht,
ima agaid séolanart co snedaib.

68. The king of Connacht, a block-head, a company between two [other] companies, a bare piglet [standing] on two haunches, one of the bones of a deer,
one of the does in groves, the most winged bird of birds, one of the thorns of a blackthorn, one of the tears of a devil.

69. Dall Bóruime, the mouth of a bare-mouthed foreigner, the voice of an old hound on a chain, a belly after being heavily wounded among corncrakes;
a crooked yellow-gold tooth, his ... against the short ... of a brat, a spear-head which has broken sharply through his wound in a spear-shaft.

70. The grandson of Mesen,
a proper boy of grey-blue thighs,
a field of the lower part of a green,
goose-handed, short-humped, black-gobbed,
a splendid foreigner on a watercress-covered flag-stone,
a skilfully wrought vat of yew as a deposit.

71. The king of Cera, Cú Chonnacht,
may my curse grind him!
Swarthy, feeble, herpes from Meath,
blue threads attached to a foreign helmet.

72. The grandson of Scorr (?),
a badger's vomit on spears,
a sallow young fool from the Éoganacht,
a nitty bed-cloth around his face.

73. Dál re díbe drúth Durlais,
Gúaire na ngallbróc, gáire gaill,
fíacail círe, cleth i curchais,
dar anfót imthecht fostán,
gablóc i mbí crostál crainn.

74. Lachtnán mac Luchduinn uí Gadra,
glas cuilinn ar cascéith,
ubull buide bís for abaill,
mac don gabainn glasléith.

75. Úa Cléirig, carpat crín cuirre,
arcat ar lín, leth fairre
fainne finne, trost buille,
ben ic coistecht ri toirm tuinne,
timme súile lonna i luinne,
láech ic íarraid lomma is imme.

Gestul im géim drochbó duinne,
láir is láech ic léim íar n-escur uirre,
estud mochbró itir muille,
pistol cuinge cuirre cruimme
cruinne tuille truimme tinne!

76. Dúngal meta úa Maíl Inmain,
athchaillech ic imthecht idraid otraig.
Dúngal — duine i cnuc ac creic a anma ar achtaib,
úrad buide ar brat gamna,
glac duibgeltaig gortaig.

77. Goll Gabra, gréch muice mairbe ar omna,
mennán oc deól gabair gaite, gotán;
Goll Gabra, gort fossaid férmar mara,
tragna co cossaib clama ar cnocán.

73. A tryst with stinginess is the fool of Durlas,
Gúaire of the foreign shoes, a foreigner's laughter,
a tooth of a comb, a house post in a clump of reeds,
a steady course through negligence,
a little forked branch in which there is a wooden cross-adze.

74. Lachtnán son of Luchdonn úa Gadra,
a fetter of holly mixed in with a twisted thorn bush,
a yellow apple on an apple-tree,
a son of the wan, grey smith.

75. The grandson of Cléirech, the withered upper beak of a heron,
silver in exchange for linen, the side of a pliant, white post,
the sound of a blow,
a woman listening to the sound of a wave,
weakness of a fierce eye instead of fierceness,
a warrior asking for a sip of milk and butter.

An achievement involving the bellowing of a bad, brown cow,
a mare with a warrior jumping onto her after falling off,
a storehouse of speedy querns among mills,
a peg of a yoke — pointed, crooked,
round, hollow, heavy, hard!

76. Cowardly Dúngal, grandson of Máel Inmain,
an ex-nun going around cow-pats.
Dúngal — a man on a hill selling his soul for conditions,
a yellow patch on a calfskin cloak,
the grasp of a swarthy, starving lunatic.

77. Goll of Gabar, the scream of a dying pig on a spear,
a kid suckling a stolen goat, a little stammerer;
Goll of Gabar, a level grassy field by [lit. 'of'] the sea,
a corncrake with mangy feet on a mound.

78. Gilla Pátraic, plág mellgaile,
nocon ḟuair slántroit senmaire:
tlám do tharr ágmuilt ḟidnaige,
ciste nach roichet foglaide,
adarc bó rodraige,
cornaire isti ibraide.

79. Finn úa Ségda,
sút srón gaṁna ar guin i ngill
— nochon ḟuil maith ann anall —
asa maid carr i mbí fuil! Finn!

78. Gilla Pátraic, a plague of blind fury,
he did not escape unharmed from a fight with musicians:
a flake from the belly of a fierce wether in bedding,
a chest which robbers do not come to,
a horn of an infertile cow,
a ... yew-like hornplayer.

79. Finn grandson of Ségda,
there is a calf's nose as a pledge for wounding
— there is no good in him from of yore —
out of which bursts a bloody scab! Finn!

Invectives (D)

80. Ní mó iná corrmíl corr nó chuil,
bró tholl 'na thig,
íall lethbráice láithir do choin,
felcháinte fir.

81. Duine dall,
muine menn,
cáinte cam,
gall cen chenn.

82. Drúth Gailenga cen intliucht, sacairt ṡenóir ac súathad,
traigle i nach úathad uidre,
muccaid íar maidm a charann,
crossán machaire ic merle, upaid i salann suirge.

83. Senubull for slimabaill,
delb dimmolaim, selb chronaigim
cellinill cennḟolaim
do chamḟulang casbúaróte.
Fannadall i finnArainn —
rith rindogaim, slat sengḟuidill,
gat gerrinnill, cnap cammuilind,
fo gallṡeminn glac gallṡalainn
— tre gerrolainn nglasḟúaróte.

84. Ingen demain, drúth uí Domnaill ocon duiblinn;
tinme lenaim, luch i comrainn, cuingid chuibrinn;
gruth a Caimlinn.
Bérla in lomgaill, merga in mondaill lenga lomraim;
lúth in buirbrinn, mant in mergaill, drúth Cille Cerbaill:
ní cuinchim 'sin cairling.

80. He is no more than a crooked midge or a flea,
a hollow quern in his house,
a thong of a single shoe which is thrown to a dog,
an evil satirist.

81. A blind man,
a conspicuous hiding-place,
a crooked satirist,
a headless foreigner.

82. The fool of Gailenga without intelligence, an old priest kneading,
a very dun-coloured shoelace,
a swine-herd with a broken leg,
a wandering, thieving jester, a love potion in salt.

83. An old apple on a slender apple-tree,
a form which I disparage, property which I claim
...
for a crooked support ... (?).
A useless visit in fair Arran —
a course of *rindogam* (?), plundering of meagre leftovers,
a withe of a short trap, a knob of a crooked mill,
under a foreign rush a handful of foreign salt
— for the sake of of a cold, grey, short fleece.

84. A devil's claw, úa Domnaill's fool at the black pool;
hacking a child, a mouse in a portion of food, seeking a share of food; curds from Caimlinn.
Speech of the naked foreigner, a crazy spear of the blind trickster (?) ... which I cut off,
vigour of the rough, hasty one (?), jaw of the deranged foreigner,
the fool of Cell Cherbaill: I do not seek him in the ... .

85. Drúth Dala,
deired líathróite for lúth,
colptha saillige etir dá ṡáith,
cáith chaillige, cacc na ndrúth.

86. Corp cáerach corraige duibe,
térnuma muilt,
bechairecht bai buide,
brénulcha buic.

85. The fool of Dala,
the end of a ball on the move,
a shank of salted meat in between two meals,
a hag's chaff, the fools' shit.

86. The body of a restless black sheep
escaping from a wether,
... yellow bee-keeping,
the stinking beard of a buck-goat.

Manuscript Readings

1. *a.* rochuala BMG, Rocuala E, docuala H. *b.* nithobair eochu arduana B, nithabair eochu arduana M, nitabair eocho arduana E, nitabhair eocho ardhua*na* G, nitabair eocha araduana H. *c.* dober i*n*di isduthaig do B, dob*eir* ini is duthaigh do M, dob*eir* ani isdual do E, dob*eir* in*ni* isduthaigh dho G, dob*eir* anii isdual do H. *d.* bo BMEG, bó H.

2. *a.* m*ac* conaba H, mac conaba G. *b.* nocadeni mada H, nocho denan*n* mada G. *c.* acht c*r*iatrath mine dom*ac* H, acht c*r*iathradh me*ni* dom*ac* G. *d.* maenaig 7 dorseoracht H, maenaich 7 doirrseoracht G.

3. *a.* obsabecan gabus gleth B, osa bega*n* gabas glet .i. ingelt (.i. ingelt *suprascript*) M, obsa began gabus gleith E, obsa becan gabais gleith H. *b.* atir caich ganfiarfaighidh B, itir caich gen fiarfaigid M, itir caich genfiarfaibid E, atir caich ganfiarfuigthe H. *c.* noconaca beolu eich B, nogonacca beolu eich M, nocofaca beola eich E, niconacca beolu eich H. *d.* am*ail* beolu i*n*liathanaigh B, am*ail* beolu inliathanigh .i. cenain*n* (.i. cenain*n* *suprascript*) M, am*ail* beola i*n*liathanaigh E, am*ail* beolu inliathai*n*ig H.

4. *a.* Aeiri*n*naigh B, Aere*n*naigh M, Aer*en*aig E. *b.* dod*r*ochran*n*aibh islo*m*nan dornn B, dod*r*ochra*n*naibh islo*m*nan dorn M, dodroch ran*n*aib aslo*m*nan dorn E. *c.* aalbanaigh BM, aalbanaig E. *d.* alochlandaigh agoblan gorm B, alochlan*n*aigh agoblan gorm M, alochlan*n*aigh agoblan gorm E.

5. *a.* Iaraid dam gall cass acnaplui*n*g B, Iaraid dam gall cas acnaplui*n*g B[b], iarraidh damh gallcas acapluing M, IAraig dam gall casacaplui*n*g E, Iarraidamh gall cas acaeblui*n*g G, Iarraid dam gall cas acapluing H. *b.* nadail duit glass gegrui*n*d B, nadail duit glas gegruind B[b], madail duit glas gegrui*n*d M, madail duit glas gegrui*n*d E, mad ail duid gas gegrain*n* G, madail duit glas gecraind H. *c.* foli*m* gengubogmoir fog*r*aim B, folim gengubogmhoir fog*r*aim B[b], folimge*n* goboghmoir foc*r*aim M, fo lium gengubogmoir fogruim E, fo lim gengub ogmoir og*r*aim G, fo lim cen copógmoir foc*r*aim H. *d.* ari int*r*omsloig tedmaill B, ari intromṡloig tedmaill B[b], ari intromgloir thedmaill M, ari i*n*tormgloir tedmaill E, arai in tromghloir tedmhaill G, ari intormgloir tetmaill H. *e.* m*ac* robai aggaillsigh goit grudbairr

B, mac robai aggaillsig guit grudbairr B^{b}, Mac robi ic gaillsigh goit gruitbairr M, Mac roboi acgoillsig goit grudbair E, m*ac* robhi agaillsigh guid grudbairr G, mac roboi icgaillsig goit grucbuirr H. *f.* coputraill oig ed*r*uim B, coputraill oig etrui*m* B^{b}, cobutraill oig edrui*m* M, gopud*r*aill oig edruim E, gup udraill oig edruim G, coput*r*aill óic etruim H.

6. *a.* nochonḟail amai*n* codemi*n* B, Noconfuil amain code*min* B^{b}, Noconuil amain codemin M, Nocho fuil amai*n* (amai*n suprascript*) codemi*n* E, Noconfuil amain codemin H. *b.* am*ail* dogni duana B, am*ail* dogni duana B^{b}, am*ail* doni duana M, am*ail* doni duana E, amail doni duana H. *c.* niro adochu*r* amaigh femi*n* B, niroadocur amuigh fe*min* B^{b}, niro adocha*r* imuig emin M, nirodochur amuigh femi*n* E, nirodochur i*m*maig fem*in* H. *d.* tenidh centuaga B, tenid centuaga B^{b}, itenig centuara M, tenig centuara no gentuad (no gentuad *suprascript*) E, itenid centuara H.

7. *a.* noconḟuil amai*n* amuig B, nochonfuil amain amuig B^{b}, Noconuil amai*n* amuigh M, Nochofuil amai*n* amuigh E, nuchanfuil a*m*máin a*m*muich H. *b.* noconḟail amai*n* anu*n*d B, nochonfuil amai*n* anund B^{b}, noconuil a mui*n* anu*n*d M, nochofuil amai*n*e anu*n*d E, nuchanuil amái*n* i*n*nu*n*d H. *c.* nochonḟail amui*n* anall B, noconfail anall B^{b}, noconuil amui*n* anall M, nocho fuil amai*n* anall E, nuchanuil .a*main.* anall H. *d.* tibid uile i*m*choi*n* naceall B, tibid uili imcoi*n* naceall B^{b}, tibid uile i*m* choi*n* naceall M, tibid uili imcoi*n* na ceall E, tibid uli i*n*choi*n* nacell H. *e.* menero sligi busfearr B, mi*n*arosligi bus f*er*r B^{b}, menero sligi isferr M, mi*n*a rosligidh asferr E, munaró sligid asferr H. *f.* gebid i*n*acen*n* i*n* c*r*and B, gebid inaceand c*r*and B^{b}, gebid i*n*ace*n*d i*n*crand M, geibidh ia (n-*stroke illeg.*) <. . . > E, gebid inace*n*d incornd H.

8. *a.* Uch alorcai*n* isidlag nimo israiti rit ad*r*uith BB^{b}, Uch alorcan isatlach nimo israite rit adruith M, Uch alorccai*n* isat lag nimo asraiti rit ad*r*aith E, Uch alorcai*n* isatolc nimo israiti rittt adruith H. *b.* acoss dlochtai*n* riacat 7 corr dluith i*n*adiaidh B, acos dlochtain riacat 7 corr dluith inadiaid B^{b}, achos dlochtai*n* riacat 7 corr dluith i*n*adiaidh M, acos dlochtan riacat 7 corr dluith i*n*adiaid E, incosdhlochtain ricat 7 corrdlúith inadiaig H. *c.* nigeba tuaighnea*m* riten*n* athamai*n* cri*n* acos chaech B, nigeba tuaigneam ritend atamai*n* crin acos chaech B^{b}, nigeba tuaignei*m* ritend athamain c*r*in fochois caich M, nigeba tuagnem riaten*n* ataman c*r*in focois caich E, ni gebe tuágne*m* ritend ata*m*ain c*r*in focois caich H. *d.* abu*n* fleagha arcuaillibh cell achaith lin alagair fiaich B, abun

fledha arcuaillib cell acaithli*n* alaghar fiaich B[b], abu*n* fleadha arcuaillibh ceall achaithlin illathair fiaich M, abun fleda arcuaill ceall acaith lin alaghar fiaich E, abun fleda arcuaillib cell acaith lin illadair fiaich H.

9. *a.* Cid maile aoccule B, Cid male aoccule M, cid male Aocc uile E, Cid male ao cuile H. *b.* darli*m* nochonai*n* B, darlim noco nain (a *suprascript*) M, darliu*m* noco nain E, darlim noconain H. *c.* Tele damh i*n* chloch aile B, Tele da*m* i*n*clocale M, Tele da*m*h i*n* cloch ale E, dale dam incloc ale H. *d.* corob*en*or air B, corob*en*or air M, corb*en*ar air E, corro benur air H.

10. *a.* Aireamh mhuighi muicci*n* B, Aire*m* muighi muici*n* M, Airi*m* muigi muicin E, Aireamh maighni muici*n* G, Aire*m* maigni mucci*n* H. *b.* ismaith less loi*m* thecht B, is maith lis loi*m* thecht M, asmaith lais loi*m* techt E, maith les illoi*m* techt G, is*m*aith lais loi*m* técht H. *c.* etro*m* les i*n*bruiti*n* B, Edro*m* lais i*n*bruitin M, et*r*om lais i*n*bruiti*n* E, edrom leis abhruiti*n* G, éttro*m* lais inbrutin H. *d.* rotro*m* les i*n* cecht B, rot*r*om lais i*n*checht M, rot*r*o*m* lais i*n*cecht E, rat*r*omles icecht G, rot*r*om lais incecht H.

11. *a.* Cindus ata huaconaill B, Cin*n*as ata uaconaill M. *b.* 7 con*n*d m*a*c ci*n*n ḟaeladh B, 7 con*n* m*a*c cind faeladh M. *c.* i*n*and*er*nsat tri m*a*c dubain B, i*n*andersat f*r*i m*a*c ndubai*n* M. *d.* niroburail anaerad B, nirab*ur*ail anaerad M.

12. *a.* Mac intṡagairt orcomai*n* B, Am*eic* i*n*ṡagairt orchomai*n* M, M*a*c i*n*tsagairt oros comai*n* E. *b.* ro chuir na saithi isi*n* snechta B, rochuir nasaithi isi*n* sneachta M, rocuir nasaithe isi*n*tsnechta E. *c.* samadh arasnait*er* durthach B, samudh arasnait*er* duirthach M, samad ara snaidthir durthach E. *d.* traill odur ulchach areacht*r*a B, t*r*aill odhur ulcach arechtra M, t*r*aill odhur ulcach arect*r*a E.

13. *a.* Achd masaderd do*m*duanaibh dob*er* modan doneoch ele B, Achtma sadhereadh do*m*duanaibh dob*er* modha*n* doneoch eile M, Acht masaderedh do*m*duanaib dob*er* modan do neoch aili E. *b.* dob*er* moghemel archualaibh dob*er* mocaire <...> .u. blethe B, dob*er* mogemel archualaibh dob*er* mochaire ar .u. bleidhe M, dob*er* mogeimhil arcualib dob*er* mocaire ar .u. bleide E. *c.* foclai*m* ri*m*chain is ri*m*chubus marcailus uaconbuide B, Foclaim ri*m*chain isri*m* cubus marochailius ua conbuidhe M, Foclai*m* rimcai*n* isremcubus marocainis

h*ua* conbuide E. *d.* isf*or* taill do*m*dail cendulus naroaerus dui*ne* remhe B, is fortaill dodail ce*n* dulus naroerus dune reme M, isfortail domdail cendulus naroaerus dui*ne* reimhe E.

14. *a.* Acheall chae*m* rochualamar B, Achell chaem rotchualamar M, Aceall caemh rocualamar E. *b.* dochlar gan chradh gan credi*m* B, doclar ce*n* chradh ce*n* credhim M, doclar gan crad gan creidi*m* E. *c.* niham-laidh rofuaramar B, niha*m*laidh fotuaramar M, nihamlaidh ro fuaramar E. *d.* mar ata atasc fo eiri*n*d B, i*m*arta itasc foneiri*n*d M, mar ata atasc foeri*n*d E.

15. *a.* Atait nasnedha conaclai*n*d B, Atat sneadha conaclai*n*d M, Atait nasneda cona clai*n*d E. *b.* idcholai*n*d B, it corai*n*d M, itcolai*n*d no itcorai*n*d (no itcorai*n*d *suprascript*) E. *c.* atait na mila co*m*er B, Atait namila comer M, atait namila comer E. *d.* do fhuilet B, dafuilledh M, dofuiled E. *e.* achonaill BM, aco*n*aill E.

16. *a.* Tanagas aciaraighibh B, Tanagus aciarragi M, Tanagas acia-rraigib E. *b.* roboloor aca*m*buirbe B, robolor aca*m*mbuirbi M, robolor acambuirbi E. *c.* docuadhus ar*m*earughudh B, docuadas armerugu M, docuadus armerug*ud* E. *d.* dogelughudh galluirge B, dogelugu galluirgi M, dogelug*ud* galluirge E.

17. *a.* Nifuilet amhai*ne* B, Niuilet ume M, Nifuilet amai*ne* E, Nifuilead amhai*ne* G. *b.* nochomo ata amaise B, nocho mo ata amaisse M, nocho mo ta amaisi E, nocho mho ata mhaise G. *c.* noco*m*or agere B, nocho mor agere M, nocho mor agere E, nocho mhor ag*er*e G. *d.* nocdene f*or*braise B, nocho dene acht braisse M, noc dene acht b*r*aisi E, nocho de*n*a acht b*r*aise G.

18. *a.* Noco m*ac* fir trebair B, Nocho m*ac* fir trebair M, Nocho m*ac* fir trebair E. *b.* nocotaille ifearu*n*n B, nocho taille iferu*n*d M, nocotaille (co *suprascript*) iferu*n*d E. *c.* nocoragha i*m*degaid B, nochoracha i*m*deagaidh M, nocho raga idedaid E. *d.* noco ragha remu*m* B, nocho raga romu*m* M, nocho raga remum E.

19. *a.* Adruth nandeisi acloicceand ceisi B, adruith nandese aclogen*n* ceisi M. *b.* nibia darndeisi amuigh ognabuaibh B, nibia darneisi muigh ocnamaib M. *c.* adrui*m* re seise nochodu*m*reirsi B, adrui*m* risese nocon-darmese M. *d.* nochofomcheilsi dochuaidh dochial B, noconfo*m*cellse

docuaidh dociall M. *e.* imthigh adhuini ith im isuidhi B, imthigh aduini ith im is uighe M. *f.* roich uidhi iarnuidhi adiu coroi*mh* B, rochuidhi roich uidhi iarnuidhi adiu coroim M. *g.* alorcai*n* luighi abolcai*n* buidhi B, alorcan luigi abolcan buidhi M. *h.* f*or* tolclar tuighi rianoi*n* aniar B, for tolcar thughi re toi*n* aniar M.

20. *a.* ata armerughud nochomeabal B, Ata armerugudh nochomebul. M. *b.* rogabh seanughudh sle*m*an solamh B, rogab senugudh slemain solum M. *c.* glaca gadaide i*m*ar B, glacca gataige i*n*bar M. *d.* aire*m* abaidhe ai*n*arodhar B, airem abbuidhe i*n*arodur M.

21. Gaiar robha gaiar rata gaiar fomhuru gaiar B, ga<. . .>robo gaiar rata gaiar fomuru gaiar M.

22. *a.* Lachtnan uaghor*m*ḟiaclach gadra B, lachtan ua gor*m*fiaclach gadra M. *b.* guaile c*r*anda cailigh diadh gan da*m*na B, guaille crama caligh diad cendamna M. *c.* iss*ed* rofirc*r*ap afi*ne* B, is*ed* rofirchrap afine M. *d.* artigheacht athighi tiartuaidh cen tarba B, ardidhecht athighi tiar thuaidh ce*n* tarba M. *e.* dohac*r*adh anbas dutaid donathair B, datacradh anbas duthaigh donathir M. *f.* dabaidh narigh niradbha B, dabbaig narig nirfagba M. *g.* rosc fir meithle maissi aiti*n*d B, rosc fir meithle maise ataind M. *h.* serthi capaill iarna cor corr c*r*aplam B, serte capaill iarnachor corr c*r*aplam M. *i.* ca raet natelgiub centerce B, caeraet natelciubh cen terce M. *j.* do sgerded alecni liathlo*m*dai B, doscerdiut alecne liath lo*m*dai M. *k.* gealg sgiag no scian connem concnai B, delg sciadh no scian conei*m* concnai M. *l.* iclot ladra lachtnain B, iclot ladhra lachtnain M.

23. *a.* A druith cid tai do*m*airb*ir*e B, Adruith cid dai do*m*airb*ir*i M. *b.* datucar duit mnai combui*n*ghile B, datucur duit mnai co*m*bu*n*gile M. *c.* isintṡa*m*radh B, isi*n* tṡa*m*radh M. *d.* isaidh tu doṡaith donarbhor B, isaid tu dosaith donarb*ur* M. *e.* isdoḟeor adbhul inurbhuile B, is dofeor adbol i*n*durbile M.

24. *a.* Tallad aulcha B, Tallad aulchai M. *b.* de astigh oil B, de istigh oil M. *c.* ri*m*ḟear cumtha B, roimfer cu*m*tha M. *d.* nochorbochoir B, nochor bocoir M.

25. *a.* Conchobhar uacadla B, Conchob*ur* uadcadla M. *b.* c*r*im muici fiadha arath naba B, c*r*im muicce fiad*h*a arath naba M. *c.* cuin dorala

incara i*n* nuathad B, cui*n* darala i*n*cara i*n*uathadh M. *d.* duine darburo b*r*ighrád briathar B, dui*n*e darboro brigradh b*r*iathár M. *e.* fear aratabhar tirad 7 bro 7 c*r*iath*ar* B, fer aratabar tiradh 7 bro 7 c*r*ia M. *f.* 7 fui*n*e 7 i*m*fui*n*e B, (7 *om.*) fui*n*e 7 i*m*uine M. *g.* ce*n* ithe doraith cliathad c*r*uachadh B, cenithe doraith cliathban cruachan M.

26. *a.* Isbert mi*n* na dentar icuib B, ISbert mi*n* na ṅdentar icuib M. *b.* cuilbir nobi*n*dsiu nathall B, cuilbir nocobind siu nathall M. *c.* sala*n*n araran ganim B, saland araran cenim M, (*preceding folio missing*) ga*n*imh E. *d.* cocna*m*aibh cind ism*en*and B, cocnamaib ci*n*d ism*en*and M, cocnamaibh ci*n*d ism*enan*d E. *e.* rosec feoil ar mhui*n*dt*ir*i B, rosec feoil amuindtire M, rosecc feoil arm*uin*t*ir*i E. *f.* marṡeacas rusc imcrand B, marseccas arusc imcrand M, mar seacus arusc imc*r*and E.

27. *a.* Allus de isinlo the B, Allus de isin lo te M, Allus de isi*n*lo the E. *b.* conaire BME. *c.* dablia*dain* do ingalar B, d<.> bliadhain do ingalur M, dablia*dain* do ingalar no feoil gabar E. *d.* fealghalar B, felgabur M, fealgalar E. *e.* fonaidhe B, fonaide ME.

28. *a.* Adregai*n* d*eir*g diultadaig B, Adergai*n* dirg diultadhaig M, Adregai*n* d*eir*g diultagaid E. *b.* adiultadh diabealltai*n* B, adiultadh dia belltaine M, adiultad dia bealltai*n*e E. *c.* arbh*r*ighet adbecnaireach B, darbrigit adbecnarach M, darb*r*iget adbecnaireach E. *d.* idurr*n*n bhis doghob gercaide B, itur*n*d bis dogob gerrcai te M, iduirn*n* bis dogob ger caide E. *e.* igul tis idcurrnd dub B, igul tis it curnd dub M, icultis it<. . . .>uirn*n* dubh E. *f.* dreandtaide dreadanach B, drentai de dredranach M, dre<. . .> d<.>ednanach E. *g.* teist dob*eir* cu arad ort B, teist dob*eir* cuaradh ort M, teist dob*eir* cu aradhort E. *h.* tu labor olcc B, tulabar olc M, tu labor olc E. *i.* eltaide edranach B, eltaide et*r*ananach M, eltaide edranach E.

29. *a.* Nocogairet amherughudh iti*r* musg*r*aidhe iscae*n*rige B, Nocho gairit amerugudh et*ir* muscraighe iscaenraighe M, Noc<. . .>it*ir* musgraide is <. . .>aige E. *b.* nochonuarus agealughudh conar*m* cae*m*buide cir*m*u*r*e B, nogo*n*uarus agelugud conarm coembuide cirmaire M, <. . .> caembuide cirm*aire* E. *c.* nococosmail aclothaighe ris nacliara icarnciarraide B, nocho chosmail aclothaige risna cliara icarnd ciarraige M, nocho<. . .>ail aclo<. . .>acliara icarn ciarraide E. *d.* robhean robean mor do ṡuaidh sochaidhe rear*m* niarnaighi nidlaighe

B, roben mor dosuaidh socaide <...> arm niarnaidhe nidhlaidhe M, robean mor dosuaid sochaidhe rehar*m* niarnaigi nidlaige E.

30. *a.* Cara damh acill dacheallog B, Cara damh icill daceallog M, Cara damh icill daceallog E. *b.* conrofesedh B, arafesed M, arrofessadh E. *c.* pianan i*m*bi corca fasaigh B, pianan .i. rus (.i. rus *suprascript*) imbi corca fa<...>igh (*illeg. gloss written above* fa<...>igh) M, pianan imbi corcca fasaigh E. *d.* cianan donadesibh .i. uss and si*n* B, cianan donaidesib .i. us insin M, cianan dona deisibh .i. us an*n*sin E.

31. *a.* A m*eic* conlea*mh*na alair gearr B, am*eic* conle*n*na alair gearr M, am*eic* conlena alair gerr E. *b.* bea*n* dochlea*mh*na nicoitglean*n* B, ben doclea*m*na nit coigleann M, be*n* docle*mh*na nicoiglen*n* E. *c.* achorr liathroiti lubai*n* B, achorr liathroide lubai*n* M, acorr liathroide lubai*n* E. *d.* acolbthach acendach ndai*m* B, acholbthach icendach ndai*m* M, acolpach icean*n*acht ndaimh E. *e.* aol ordlach dairgetlaib B, aol ordlach doairgetlaib M, aol ordlac dargadlaim E. *f.* aiuchra maigri amu*m*ai*n* B, aiuchra maig*r*i amutai*n* M, aiuc*r*a maigre amu*mh* (a *suprascript*) ai*n* E.

32. *a.* am*eic* flan*n*acai*n* iceallaigh B, am*eic* la*n*dugai*n* iceallaigh M, Am*eic* flan*n*agai*n* h*ui*cell*aig* E. *b.* ari i*n*tiri taicedben*n*aigh B, ari i*n*tiri taigedh pe*n*daig M, ari i*n*tiri taiceda pen*n*aig E. *c.* agabail srenbruinigh ben*n*aig B, agabail sren b*r*ainigh bendaigh M, agabail srei*n* b*r*ainigh ben*n*aig E. *d.* osmui*n*g airig acetpellaig B, osmai*n*g airig acetpellaig M, osmoi*n*g airigh aicedpellaigh E.

33. *a.* Auscreitlin scuitemail B, Auscrelli*n* scuitemail B^{b}, Ahuscrelin scutemuil M, Auisclerig scuitemail E, Ahui scelin scutemail H. *b.* ascol cilli cind arcind B, ascol cilli cind arcind B^{b}, ascol cille ci*n*d air chi*n*d M, ascol cilli cind arci*n*d E, ascol cille cind archind H. *c.* afolt gaba*n*n gadbemnigh B, afolt goband gadbemnig B^{b}, afolt goband gatbemnigh M, afolt goband godbemnig E, afolt goband gatbeimnigh H. *d.* acoran*n* m*a*cclerig mi*n*d B, acorand m*a*cclerig mi*n*d B^{b}, achora*n*d m*a*c cleirigh mi*n*d M, acora*n*d m*a*ccleirig mi*n*d E, achora*n*d m*a*ccleirig mind H.

34. *a.* A .h. chui*n*d acharbat leanai*m* leoin B, Ahuchui*n*d acharbat lenaim leoin M, Ahuacuind acarbat lenai*m* leoi*n* E. *b.* acui*n*g amedaibh siuil sirthe B, achui*n*g amedaibh siuil sirthe M, acui*n*g arargad amedaib siuil sirthi E. *c.* agerfile icait ballain B, Agerrfile icait ballain et*ir* dasc*r*in M, Agerr file agaid ballai*n* et*ir* dasg*r*in E. *d.* acendide c*r*an cu*r*udaibh

crin etir crithre B, acendide crandain crin etir crithre M, acennaighi crandain crin etir crithre E.

35. *a.* agilla duind adearmuigh ocata in bean donn deolaig B, Agilla duind adermaigh occada inbean donn deolaid M, Agilla duind adermaigh (m *suprascript*) ocata inben donn deolaigh E. *b.* bruigh arbrat treabraidh atonn doceolaibh clerigh B, amias bruind .i. brondaigh (.i. brondaigh *suprascript*) arbrut treabraidh athonn do ceolail (*sic*) cleirigh M, amias bronnaigh arbrut trebraig atonn docheolaib cleirig E. *c.* istu incaileach dibcellaig achu chleachtus arcnamaibh B, istu incailech duib cellaigh achu clechtas arcnamaib M, istu in cailech doib cellaig acú (cú *represented by q with accent*) clechtas arcnamaib E. *d.* aduan araireach neallaigh afeartais araidh delibh B, aduan arairech nellaigh afeartas araidh delibh M, aduan arraireach nellaigh afertas araidh deilib E.

36. *a.* Agilla leochaille leacaigh molaise B, Agilli lecchuille lecaidh molaisse M, Agilla leochaille leccaig mo laisi E. *b.* aleca cuirre garbhghlaisi grian B, aleccu cuirre garbglaisse grian M, aleca cuirre garbglaisi (l written *suprascript*) grian E. *c.* asechi corcra achac armaslaidh B, aseche corcha achach armaslaid M, aseichi corcra achac armaslaidh E *d.* areithi folta fasaigh ar fiadh B, arethe folta fasaigh darfiadh M, areithi folta fesaig arfiadh E.

37. *a.* A dinnim deargain B, Ahu dinnim dergain M, Ahudinnimh dergain E, audindimh dergain G. *b.* adruith chail archlochtaigh B, adruith coil arclocthaigh M, adruith cail ar cloctaig E, atroid cael arclogthaigh G. *c.* arandlem seach lecnaib B, arand lem sechlecnaibh M, arandlem seach lecnaib (n *suprascript*) E, arand leamh seach leacnaibh G. *d.* acertaig acorcaig B, acertaigh ochorcaigh M, acertaigh acorcaig E, acertaigh acorcaigh G.

38. *a.* Aere mor aahbruit folus amhucsuil B, Ahermor athbruit folas immuchail M, Asearr mor aahbruit folus amucsuil E. *b.* amheallsron madaigh B, amellron madaigh M, ameallsron madaig E. *d.* a ithi ime reharan segail B, Aithe imme rehararn seagail M, aithi ime reharan secail E. *d.* agilli inchadaigh B, agilli incataig M, agilli incadaigh E.

39. *a.* Ameic higeamaid edrond romebaidh B, Ameic higemaidh edrond romebaidh M. *b.* ocus ameic rebaig a leanaib laic B, ocus ameic rebaidh alenaim laic M. *c.* beca dobossa caela darcosa B, beca dobassa

caela darcossa (o *suprascript*) M. *d.* abarr ḟeoir rossa dar cossa cait B, abarr eoir rosa darcossa cait M.

40. *a.* A domhnaill dobhurlubanigh bodhurghruganaigh bodhurmedlanaigh B, ado*m*naill dobor lupanaigh bodorgrucanaigh bodor metlanaigh M. *b.* onco*m*rai*n*d co*m*o*r*g*r*uganaigh co*m*ordidanaigh caradgrecanaigh B, oncho*m*rai*n*d comorgruanigh cho*m*ar ditanaigh caradg*r*eganaigh M. *c.* ahua airi*m* bhrocsalaigh amarmicanaigh aladliacanaigh B, ahua bairb b*r*oc sadhail amarmicanaigh aladliacanig M. *d.* aulcha gaill i*n*dedbudanaigh cuarlubanaigh caladg*r*iant*r*agthaigh canadg*r*ecanaigh B, uilcuagall indedbutanigh chuarlupanig caladg*r*iantragthanigh canadhgrecanaigh M.

41. *a.* A brollach sneadach sreathar B, Abrollach sneadach srathḟiar M. *b.* aḟiachla con ar cloich ailigh B, afiacla co*n* oclachailidh M. *c.* atadgai*n* athollti*m*pain am*eic* alcai*n* B, aahui tadhgai*n* atholl ti*m*pain am*eic* alcain M. *d.* abhi arburd ardai*n* aṡaibh f*ir* B, abi aburd ardan athibair M.

42. *a.* Am*eic* .h. cui*n*d cealla dochabair B, Am*eic* huchuind cella dochobair M. *b.* aghlec imthui*n*d ateanga tamhai*n* B, aclecc i*m*tui*n*d atea*n*ga thamhai*n* M. *c.* am*eic* i cui*n*d ac*r*ithri i*m*chealla B, am*eic* hucucui*n*d acrithri imcealla M. *d.* arighthi gearra glassa gadhair B, arigthe glassa gerra gadhair M.

43. *a.* A maelscolb domeasair B, Amoel scolp domesair M. *b.* aeglas c*r*aind achacc cuirre uidhri etighe B, aeclas craind acach cuirre uidhre ittighe M. *c.* a eoin rendossaibh B, aeoin renosaibh M. *d.* aḟeartais ab*r*aind bicire abreassail B, afertas abrai*n*d bicere abresail M.

44. *a.* Ailandai*n* B, Ahui ḟlandain M. *b.* alair mall BM. *c.* alethchoss geidh B, aleth chos geoidh M. *d.* aglais cham B, aglas cham M. *e.* fogair gall BM.

45. *a.* A hui scandail B, Ahui scandlain M. *b.* ascian espa BM. *c.* achearc us*ce* B, acerc uisci M. *d.* achosegr*a* B, acos escra M.

46. *a.* A m*eic* duir daill iffir*n*d B, A*m*e*ic* duir daill iffir*n*d M, Am*eic* duir daill iffirn*n* E. *b.* athigaill arg*r*apai*n*g B, athigaill argraphaind M, athigaill arg*r*apai*n*g E. *c.* argairdi dogibai*n* B, adgairde dogibbai*n* M, argairdi do

gibhai*n* E. *d.* agheoidh iarnaghabail B, ageoidh iarnagabail M, ageoid iarnagabail E. *e.* aḟeoil tarra toghain B, afeoil tarra thogain M, afeoil tairi togai*n* E. *f.* a ithi imil edaig B, a ithi imbil etaigh M, aithi i*n*mil etaig E. *g.* a ibhregaigh britain B, ahui bregaidh britain M, aibregaigh britai*n* E.

47. *a.* a ui cui*n*d acossa daimh adhrochḟir dana B, Ahuicui*n*d achossa daimh adrochfir dana M, Auicui*n*d acossa dai*mh* ad*r*ochfir dana E. *b.* aghob ingair ganglam gang*r*ada B, agob ingob i*n*gair cenglam ceng*r*ada M, agob i*n* gair ga*n*glam gang*r*ada E. *c.* adiabail omda ibis inli*n*d B, adiabuil omdha ibis inlind M, adiabail omhda ibis i*n*lind E. *d.* acongna cliabaigh achind dochnama B, acho*n*gna acliabaigh acind dochnama M, a con*n*gna cliabaigh acind docnamha E.

48. *a.* Adallain doburthanaig dig*r*aidhib B, Adallain dobartanaigh digradibh M, Adallai*n* dobhurtanaig dig*r*adib (*second* d *suprascript*) E. *b.* a camai*n* c*r*inlamaigh confacmandaigh cuaranaigh B, acamain crin lamaigh co*n*fachmandaigh cuaranaigh M, acamai*n* c*r*inlamhaigh confachmandaig cuaranaig E. *c.* a phitigh phaitigh phiananaigh B, afitigh paitigh phiananaigh M, aphitig paitigh piananaigh E. *d.* athiaghanaigh etigh aitigh uarlamhaigh B, atiganaigh etig aitigh uaṙlamaigh M, athiaganaigh eitig aitigh uarla*m*aig E.

49. *a.* Adomhunghoirt (*followed by space for 5 or 6 letters*) B, Adoma M, Adomango<. . .>t (*followed by space for 7 or 8 letters*) E. *b.* adrond geoid B, adrond geuidh iarngabail M, adrond geoigh iarnagabail E. *c.* ageam dubgor*m* demhain B, agem*m* dub gorin dem M, ageid dubgorm du E. *d.* abachlaigh bain i*m* mbrait B, bachlaic bai*m* imbrait M, bachlaig bai*n* i*m*mbrait E. *e.* a bhel cailligi caiche B, abel caillighe caiche M, abel cailligi caichi E. *f.* aconaḋhmairt cicaraigh B, aco*n*nadh mairt cicaraigh M, aconadhmairt cicaraig E. *g.* nach can ceol isi*n*camhair B, nacan ceol isi*n*camair M, nach can ceol isi*n*camair E. *h.* acossa c*r*oma creabhair B, acosa c*r*oma crebair M, acossa croma crebair E. *i.* ac*r*uachaidhi leanaim laic B, acruachaiti lenai*m* laic M, acruachaidi leanaim laicc E. *j.* nirleasaighis insaithi B, niralessaigis insaithi M, niraleasaigis insaithi E.

50. *a.* aḟeadanaig B, Afeadanaigh M, Afedanaig E, Aḟeadanaigh G. *b.* acor*n*aire acliaraige B, achorrnaire acleraige M, acornaire acliaraide E, acor*n*aire acliaraighe G. *c.* afis fa*n*tir B, afis fontir M, afis fontir E, afis fontir G. *d.* ac*r*is ganscin ascelaige B, acris gansgi*n* ascelaige M, ac*r*is ga*n* scin asgelaigi E, ac*r*is gansgin asgelaighe G.

51. *a.* A mhir dodhui*ne* adealbh i*n*deamai*n* B, Amir dodui*ne* adelb i*n*demhai*n* M, Amir dodui*ne* adealb i*n*demai*n* E. *b.* achir icuile achreabhair cuiligh B, achir icuili achrebair chuiligh M, achir icuile acrebair cuilig E. *c.* aathbro ichtair aairbhe ibair B, aathbro ichtair aairbi ibair M, aathbro ictair aairbe ibair E. *d.* aol iarnitaidh ainair uidhir B, aol iarnitai*n* amair uidhir M, aol iarnitaid ainair uidir E.

52. *a.* A uich chuicphatan peallbhuide B, Ahuichuichpatan pellbuidhe M, Auachaich phatan pheallbhuidhe G. *b.* ascadan de*m*naidhe f*or* drui*m* drolmuide B, ascadan de*m*naidhe f*or* druim d*r*omlaige M, asgadan deamh naidhe ard*r*uim d*r*omhlaighe G. *c.* abhel mna uidhre ib*r*aidhe B, abel mna uidre ibraide M, abhel mhna uidhri ui*mh*i ib*r*aidhe G. *d.* bo lui*m*ne lui*n*de longaire B, boluimi lui*n*di lo*n*gaire M, ai*n*gaire bho lui*m*e lughe lon*n*ghaire G. *e.* amaisse taisse t*r*esse thibhraide B, amasse thasse trese tibrige M, amhaise thaise t*r*ese thibhrighe G. *f.* ahi*m*lighe baisse cesse coisse cornaire B, ahimlige base cese case cose cornaire M, aimlighe baise cese caise coise cor*n*airne G.

53. *a.* Adruith nahalla adc*r*anda icossaib B, Adruith naalla at c*r*anda icossaib (o *suprascript*) M. *b.* adruith nahalla atfanda fossaid B, adruith nahalla rofanda fossaigh M. *c.* abrecanaigh diuit adord i*m* dronda B, abreacanaigh diuit adordim dronda M. *d.* a druith nahalla senaraigh corra c*r*oma cama fodchossaigh B, adruith nahalla senaraigh corra c*r*oma cama fotchassaib M.

54. *a.* A dhiripi talmhu*n* ic techidh brecoigi B, Aidrip bi talman icteched brecoige M. *b.* abean conaillsin duibeogai*n*g B, aben caillsi*n* duibeogai*n*g M. *c.* achoss copoigi B, acos copoice M. *d.* aluirgni feadoigi ar feorai*n*d B, aluirgne fetoige arfeorai*n*d M.

55. *a.* Amhairbhthene mongthighi mhi*n*chuile B, Amarbthene mongthige mi*n*cuile M. *b.* asalchide si*n*nchaidhe salachluim B, asailcidhe sindchaidhe salachdui*n*d no salachluim M. *c.* i*m*arith gadaidhe i*m*cleacaire B, arith gataighe i*m*clecaire M. *d.* abrataire i*n*becuidhi B, abrataire inbecuidhi M. *e.* i*n*gataile i*n*cetaile B, i*n*gataile M. *f.* rigataile nichetaile B, *om.* M. *g.* i*n*lataile i*n*dlecaile B, indlecaile M. *h.* apaidhe acaite anachlai*m* B, apudhi accaite anachlui*m* M.

56. *a.* A beand i*m*le bruit darbroi*n*d mbalbdui*n*e B, Abend imle bruit darbrai*n*d malbduini M. *b.* abean druth indabaig B, aben druth indabaigh M. *c.* adaill char*n*muighi B, adaill carnmaige M. *d* agerri*n*gni ga*mh*naighi galair B, agerri*n*gne ga*m*naidhe galair M.

57. *a.* Uacui*n*d cogur daill dar draigne B, Uacuind cogur daill dard*r*aigni B^b, Uacui*n*d cogu*r* daill dar draigni M, Uacui*n*d cocur daill dard*r*aigne E, Huacuind cocur daild dard*r*aigni H. *b.* focul imbidh ri*nn* coraigne B, focul imbid rind <...> igne B^b, focul i*m*bit rai*n*d coraighne M, focul am bidh ri*n*d coraigne E, foc*ul* imbit rui*n*d corrigni H. *c.* gem dai*m* arathair t*r*ia aibhne B, gem daim arathair t*r*ia aibhne B^b, gem damh arathair t*r*ia aibne M, geim daimh aratair t*r*iaibne E, geim daim arathair t*r*iaaibni H. *d.* traigne tarathair tidle B, t*r*ai <...> arathair tidle B^b, tairnge tarathair thaidle M, tairg*n*i tarathair atidle (a *suprascript*) E, tair*n*ge tarathair atidli H.

58. *a.* Muiredhach mant capaill croi*n* B, Muiridhach mant capaill croin B^b, Muiredach mantt capaill croi*n* M, Muiridac mant capall c*r*oin E, Muiredach mant capaill croi*n* H. *b.* cu darceisibh B, cu darceisib B^b, cu darcesib M, cudarceisib E, cu tarcessib H. *c.* carpat bo b*r*icce f*or*ben*n* B, carpat bobrice f*or*be*n*d B^b, carput bo bricce f*or* bend M, carbat bo bricce f*or* bend E, carbat bo bricci f*or*bei*n*d H. *d.* bel daimh donadeisibh B, bel daim dunadeisib B^b, bel daim donadeisibh M, bel daimh donadeisib E, bel dai*m* donadesib H.

59. *a.* Gilla na nae*m* gnuis fiaich fiacla gela no lega (no lega *suprascript*) illiss B, Gilla innai*m* gnuis fiaich fiacla lega iliss M, Gillananae*m* gnuis fiaich fiacla leadha alis E, Gilla innai*m* nús fiaich fiaclai lega hillis H. *b.* dlochtan cremha ac*r*iss ned is eala as B, dlochtain c*r*ema ic*r*is ndet iselaas M, dlochtan c*r*ema ac*r*is ned aseala as E, dlochtan <...>a (*small tear in MS*) ic*r*is net isel as H. *c.* druth le*m*na lairchael clerigh arcuairt cross B, druth lemhna lair coel clereach arcuair cros M, d*r*uth lemna lair cael cler*ech* ar cuairt cros E, druth lemna lair coel clerech arcuairt c*r*os H. *d.* glaca reamra aros bos fa gearrga nglas B, glacha ra*m*ra hiros bos fogerga nglas M, glacca remra hirros bos fogerrga glas E, glacca remra hirros bos fog*er*r ganglas H.

60. *a.* Adastar lara hilaim B, Adhastar lara ilai*m* M, Adastar lara bana ilaim E, Adastar lara illaim H. *b.* lecu phui*n*t dar pundai*n*d B, lecu pui*n*t darpundai*n*d M, leca puin*n*t dar pun*n*ai*n*d E, lecu phuit darp

(*sic*) pundai*nd* H. *c.* cean*n* cruaid con arcairig B, ce*nd* cruaidh co*n* archarig M, cen*n* cruaid co*n* ar caeirig E, cend c*r*uaid con arcairig H. *d.* maidi odur ailig B, maide odhur ailig M, maide od*ar* oilig E, mate odar óilig H. *e.* luige re luag leccu chuar B, lue .i. luac (.i. luac *suprascript*) riluag leccu cuar M, lu<. . . > luad leca cuar E, lue rilog leccu chuar H. *f.* uachuan nicundaill B, hua conchuan nicunaill M, ua cua*n* nicun*n*aill E, .h. concua*n* nicundaill H.

61. *a.* Sondach osaill BM, Son*n*ach osaill E, Sondach ednen ósaill H. *b.* dedblean ic dul alui*n*g B, deiblean icdul ilui*n*g M, deidble*n* agdul alui*n*g E, dedblen acdul illui*n*g H. *c.* da*n*ma diamair dhaill B, dan madiamair daill M, dan madiamair daill E, dán inadiamair daill H. *d.* cna*m* cliabaigh cai*m* uacui*n*d B, cna*m*h cliabaigh cai*m* uacui*n*d M, cnai*m* cliabaig caim h*ua* cui*n*d E, cna*m* cliab*aig* cai*m* .h. cuin*n* H.

62. *a.* Meth m*ac* muiredhaig meisgi chirmuire B, Methm*ac* mo*r*eadaigh mesci cirmaire M, Maeth m*ac* mu*r*idaig meisci cir*m*aire E, Methm*ac* mu*r*edaig mesci chirmairi H. *b.* c*r*ossan liath agli*n*d B, c*r*osan liath hiclind M, c*r*osan liath igli*n*d E, c*r*osan liath iclind H. *c.* screpall arfeoil eoi*n*mhet areoch mall B, sc*r*epol arfeoil naighe oi*n*mhit areochmall M, sgrepal arfeoil naige eoi*n*mit areoch mall E, sc*r*epul arfeoil naige ónmit areoch máll H. *d.* breccar claime aci*n*d B, breccor claimhe ici*n*d M, breacor claime aci*n*d E, brecór claime hicin*n* H.

63. *a.* Macc righ nandesi dealb omh cliar creche B, M*ac* righ na*n*dese delb omh cliar crethe M, M*ac* (*suspension stroke over* m *and suprascript* c) rig nandesi delb omh cliar cre chi E. *b.* sechi con fochu*m* cliabaigh B, seche con focom cliabaigh M, seichi co*n* no (no *suprascript*) fochom cli abaigh E. *d.* cor*n*airecht cornaire arcrod B, Cornairecht cornaire arcrodh M, Corn*n*airecht cornnaire (*several illeg. suprascript letters*) E. *e.* lon ic longairi aliamai*n* B, lon iclonghaire alliamain M, lo*n* aglongaire aliamai*n* E.

64. *a.* Gilla ceallaigh cean*n* f*or*saillib B, Gilla ceallaigh cen*n* f*or* saillibh M, Gilla cell*aig* cen*n* f*or* saillib E. *b* selche *con*dibmbea*n*naibh B, selche condibhen*n*aibh M, seilchi conib ben*n*aibh E. *c.* fi*n*n arguairi cullaigh allaidh B, fi*n*d arguaire chullaigh allaigh M, find arguaire cull*aig* all*aig* E. *d.* callaigh gilla ceallaigh B, callaigh gilla cellaigh M, call*aig* gilla cell*aig* E. *e.* Noco gilla ceallaigh et*ir* B, Nocho gilla cellaigh it*ir* M,

Nocho gilla ceallaig it*ir* E. *f.* noco cean*n* f*or*saillibh abair B, nocho cen*n* f*or* saillibh M, nococean*n* (co *suprascript*) forsaillib abair E. *g.* nocofi*nn*a aguairi B, noconfi*n*a aguaire M, nocho fi*n*da aguaire E. *h.* cullaigh allaig *cu*baidh B, cullaigh allaigh chugaib M, cull*aig* all*aig* cuccaib E. *i.* imartucait ach allaigh B, i*m*mar tugaid achallaigh M, i*m*martugait nacall*aig* E. *j.* nochoghilla ceallaig acaib B, nocho gilla ceallaigh accaibh M, nocho gilla cell*aig* agaib E.

65. *a.* Fi*n*d uabuidhe B, Find buidhe M, Find h*ua* buide E. *b.* li*n*d i*m*blede B, lind i*m*bleidhe M, lind imblede E. *c.* diultad dona B, diultu dona M, diultad (i *suprascript*) dona E. *d.* ichtar e*mh*e B, ichtur emhe M, ictar emhe E.

66. *a.* Goll mena domui*n*ti*r* gragai*n* B, Goll mena domuin*n*tir gragain M, Goll mena domui*n*dtir gragai*n* E, Goll meana domui*n*tir g*r*acai*n* G. *b.* gall acnuasach cno B, gall icnuasach cno M, gall achnuasach (n *suprascript*) cno E, gaill icnuasach cno G. *c.* ballan ambi bai*n*di loma B, ballan i*m*bi bai*n*ne loma M, ballan ambi bai*n*di loma E, bhallan i*m*bi banda loma G. *d.* dalla droma bo B, dalla dro*m*ma bo M, dallan droma bo E, dallan d*r*omabo G.

67. *a.* Goll mena mun c*r*omghabhair cearc icill c*r*and eidneanach B, Goll mena munc*r*omgabair cerc icill cra*n*d eidhneanach M, Goll mena mun cromgabair cearcc icill crand eidneanach E, Goll m*en*a mu*n* cromghobhair cearc icill c*r*and edhnenach G. *b.* beart flegha f*or* lo*m*gabail li*n*d dedblenach drolmhanach B, b*er*t fleadha f*or* lomgabail li*n*d deidbleanach d*r*olmanach M, b*er*t flega forlomgabail lind dedblenach d*r*olmanach E, b*er*t fleadha f*or*lo*m*ghabhail li*n*d dedhblenach d*r*omla*n*ach G. *c.* Brisidh stuaide icstocairecht sdiuir dofid li*m* long mallramhach B, Brissiudh stuaige ic stogar stiuir (*first* i *suprascript*) dofird lim lo*n*g mallaranach M, Brisead sduaide icstocairecht sdiuir dofidh limh long mall ramach E, brisiudh sduaighi igsdocairecht (g *suprascript*) sdiur fidh lim long mallra*mh*ach G. *d.* cai*n*te buaile icbrocairecht bean ca*m*lamhach co*m*hdhalach B, cai*n*te buaile icb*r*ocairecht bea*n* ca*m*la*m*ach cho*m*dalach M, cai*n*te buaile icbrocairecht bean camlamach comdalach E, cai*nte* buaile igb*r*ocairecht bean chamlamach co*mh*dalach G.

68. *a.* Righ connacht cea*n*n tamhai*n* damh et*ir* damhaibh B, Ri con*n*acht cen*n* tamai*n* tarb et*ir* danaibh no damaibh M, Righ

con*n*acht cen*n* tamai*n* dam no tarb (no tarb *suprascript*) et*i*r damaib E. *b.* lo*m*arc ardacaraid dochnamhaib cliab oig B, lo*m*arc dardacarit cna*m* docnamaibh cliabaigh M, lomarc ardha charaidh cnai*m* docnamaib cliabhaig E. *c.* erb dearbaibh en is edchu denaib B, erb dferbaibh indairib en isetchu denaib M, erb derbaib i*n*dairib en isedchu denaibh E. *d.* delg dodealgaibh draighin deraibh diabhail B, delg dodelgaibh indairib (indairib *crossed out*) draigi*n* der doderaibh diabuil M, delg dodelgaib draigi*n* der doderaib diabail E.

69. *a.* Dall borai*m*e B, Dall boroime M. *b.* bel gaill goblui*m* guth seanchon ar slabhradh B, bel gaill gobluim guth senchon arslab*r*aidh M. *c.* bru arnat*r*omghui*n* it*ir* tradnaibh B, bruar nat*r*omgui*n* etir t*r*adnaib M. *d.* fiacail cam orbuidhe B, fiacail cham orbuidhe M. *e.* aholchumgucht rogearrchod ngarrlaigh B, aholchu*m*gucht rogerr chod ngarlaigh M. *f.* gae rocho*m*raidh t*r*ia chru icrandhghail B, gae rocorrmaidh t*r*ia cru icrangail M.

70. *a.* Ua mesean BM. *b.* m*ac* gobal liathghlas coindme B, m*ac* gobol liathglas coi*n*dme M. *c.* gort icthair aichthe B, gort ichtair faiche M. *d.* gedglac d*r*oindghearr gobdhubh B, gedh glach d*r*ongerr gobdub M. *e.* gallblach ar bilarlic B, gallbladhach arbilar lic M. *f.* dabach ibharghlic aithne B, dabach ibair glic aithne M.

71. *a.* Rig ceara cu connacht B, Ricera cera cu connacht M. *b.* romeala momhallacht B, romela momallacht M. *c.* temn detais dernidhe B, temhnidhe tais deirmidhe M. *d.* snaith ghlais rigallat B, snaith glais rigallat M.

72. *a.* Uas cuirri B, Uascuirri M. *b.* sceith bruic arbearaib B, sceith bruic arberaib M. *c.* og druth odhur deoghanacht B, oc druth odur deodhanacht M. *d.* imaghaid seolanart co snedhaigh B. i*n*aigid seolanart cosnedhaibh M.

73. *a.* Dal re dibi druth durrlais B, Dalre debi druth durlais M. *b.* guaire na*n* gallbrocc gairi gaill B, guaire nangallbroch gairi gaill Ṁ. *c.* fiacla ciri cleth icurghais B, fiachail cire cleath icurgais M. *d.* daranfot i*m*teact fosdan B, dar anfot i*m*techt fostan M. *e.* gablog i*m*bi c*r*ostal craind B, gobloc i*m*bi crosdal crai*n*d M.

74. *a.* Lachtnan m*ac* luchdui*nd* igad*ra* B, Lachtnan m*ac* luchdui*nd* hugadhra M. *b.* glass cuili*nd* arcass geith B, glas cuili*nd* arcasceith M. *c.* uball buide bis arabaill B, ubull buidhe bis f*or*abaill M. *d.* m*ac* dongabhaind glaisleith B, m*ac* do*n*gabai*nd* glasleith M.

75. *a.* Uaclerigh carbat c*r*in cuirre B, Uaclerigh carbat c*r*in cuirre M. *b.* arcat ar lin leth fairre B, arcat arlin leth farre M. *c.* fainde fi*nd*e trostbuille B, fai*nd*e fi*nd*e trostbuille M. *d.* bean icoisteacht ritoir*m* tui*nd*e B, ben icoistecht retromtui*nd*e M. *e.* time suile londa illui*nd*i B, ti*mm*e suili londa ili*nd*i M. *f.* laech ic iarraidh lo*mm*a isimi B, laech iciarraidh loma isime M. *g.* gestal i*m*gem drochbho dui*nd*e B, gestul i*m*gem droch bo dui*nd*e M. *h.* lair islaech icle*m* iarnesgar uirre B, lair isloech icleim iarnescur fu*r*ri M. *i.* esdad mochbhro it*ir* muilli B, estudh mochbro it*ir* muille M. *j.* pistal cuinge cuirre crui*m*e B, pistul cui*n*ge cuirri crume M. *k.* c*r*uinde tui*nd*e tuille trui*m*e tinde B, crui*nd*e tuille tr*um*me tinde M.

76. *a.* Dunghal meta uamael i*n*mai*n* B, Dungal meta uamail i*n*mai*n* M. *b.* athchailleach ici*m*teacht id*r*aidh oth*r*aidh B, athcaillech icimthech id*r*aidh otraigh M. *c.* du*n*ghal dui*n*e icnuc icrec aan*ma* arechtaibh B, du*n*gal duine icnuc acreic aa*n*ma arachtraibh M. *d.* uradh buidhe arbrat ga*m*na B, uradh buidhe ar brat ga*m*na M. *e.* glac duibgealtaig gortaigh B, glac duibgeltaigh gortaigh M.

77. *a.* Goll gobra grech muice mairbe aro*m*na B, Gollgobra grech muice mairbe armona M, Goll gob*r*a grech muicci mairbe ar*m*ona E. *b.* mendan ac deol gabair gaide gotan B, m*e*nnan icdeul gabair gaite gottan M, mendan acdeol gabair gaide gota*n* E. *c.* goll gabr*ra* gort fosaigh fear mara B, gollgabrai gort fossaig fer mara M, goll gobra gort fosaigh fear no ferrmar (no ferrmar *suprascript*) mara E. *d.* tradhna cocossaib clamha ar cnocan B, tradhna co cossaib clama arcnocan M, tradna cocossaib clama arcnoca*n* E.

78. *a.* Gilla pad*r*aig plagh mellghaile B, Gilla padraic plag mellgaile M, Gilla padr*aic* plag meallgail<.> E. *b.* noconhuair slan troid seanmaire B, noco*n*uair slantroit se*n*maire M, <...> air slantroit se*n*maire E. *c.* tlam dotharr agmuilt ḟidhnaigi B, tlam dotar agmuilt idhnaidhe M, tlam dotair agmuilt <...> E. *d.* cisdi nach roichet foglaidi B, cisti nachroithet foglaidhe M, <...>oichet foghlaide E. *e.* adarc bó rodraide B, adarc bo rodraige M, adarc bo <...>od<...> E. *f.* cornaire isti ib*r*aighi B, cornaire isti ibraige M, <...>aide E.

79. *a.* Find ua segda B, Find uasegdha M, Find ua se<. . . >a E. *b.* sud sro*n* ga*mh*na argui*n* i*n*ghill B, sut so*n* gamna arguin i*n*gill M, <. . . > argui*n* i*n*gill E. *c.* noconfuil maith a*n*n anall B, noconfuil maith a*n*d anall M, noco*n*n fuil (f *suprascript*) maith and a<. . . >all E. *d.* isamhuigh carr i*m*bi fuil fi*n*d B, isamaig carr i*m*bi fuil find M, <. . . > find E.

80. *a.* Nimo inacorrmhil corr no B, Nimo inacorrmil corr no B^b, Ni mo i*n*dacorrmil corr no M, Nimo ida corrmil corr no E, Nimo i*n*acorrmhil corr na cuil G, Nimo anda corr mil corr (.c. *written above corr*) no chuil H. *b.* bro toll tall inathigh B, bro toll tall inatig B^b, bro coll tall i*n*athig M, bro toll tall i*n*atigh E, brotholl nathaigh G, broth (.d. *written above broth*) oll natigh H. *c.* iall•leathbraici laithir dochoin B, iall lethbraigi laithir docoi*n* B^b, iall lethbraice laithir do*n* choin M, iall lethbraigi<. . . >hair docoi*n* E, iall athb*r*aighi leathair duchoin G, iall letbroici lathir docoi*n* H. *d.* fealcainti fir B, felc (*ends here*) B^b, felchai*n*te fir M, felcainti fir E, fealcai*n*ti fir G, felchai*n*ti fir H.

81. *a.* Dui*n*e dall BME, Duine dall H. *b.* mune meand B, mui*n*e me*n*d M, mui*n*e men*n* E, mune m*en*d H. *c.* cai*n*ti ca*m* B, cai*n*ti cam M, cainti cam E, cante ca*m* H. *d.* gall ga*n* chen*n* B, gall gan ceand M, gall cen cend E, gall cen cendd H.

82. *a.* Druth gaileng cen indtliucht sacaird seanoir ac suathadh B, Druth gaile*n*g ce*n*inthucht sacairt sacairt senoir icsuathadh M, Druth gailing cini*n*dtlecht sagairt si*n*oir ic fatath E. *b.* traigle i*n*achuathadh fuidhre B, traigle taebh inachuathadh uidre M, t*r*aigle taeb inach uath*ad* uidre E. *c.* muccaidh iarmaidi achara*n*n B, mucaidh iarmaidhm achara*n*d M, mucaid iarmaid*m* acharand E. *d.* crosain machaire ic merle opaidh isala*n*n suirge B, crosan machaire ic merle aupaid isala*n*d suirghe M, c*r*osa*n* mach aire igmerle (er *symbol written over* g) aupait isalan*n* suirghi E.

83. *a.* Senubhull f*or* slim (*space for about 2 letters*) aibill B, Se*n*ubull f*or*slimabaill M. *b.* dealb dimolai*m* sealb tronaigi*m* B, delb dimolaim selb cro andoghaimh M. *c.* cheillinill ceandfolai*m* B, chellinill cendolaim M. *d.* doca*m*folang casbhuarote B, dochambolang casbuarote M. *e.* fandadhall ifindarai*n*d B, fa*n*dadall ifi*n*darai*n*d M. *f.* rith ri*n*dogai*m* slat senguigill B, rith ri*n*dogaim slat se*n*g fuighill M. *g.* gad geri*n*nill cnap camuilind B, gat gerrinill cnap ca*m*muili*n*d M. *h.* fogallsemind

glac gallsalai*n*d B, fogallsemi*n*d glac gallsalai*n*d M. *i.* tre gearrolaind nglasfuarrote B, tre gerrola ind nglasfuarothe M.

84. *a.* Ingean deamai*n* druth ido*m*naill oconduibhli*n*d B, Inge*n* demai*n* druth hui do*m*naill oconduibli*n*d M. *b.* ti*n*mhi leanai*m* luch ico*m*raind cui*n*dghidh cuibri*n*d B, ti*n*me lenai*m* luch ico*m*rai*n*d gu*n*gidh cuibri*n*d M. *c.* g*r*ath icai*m*lind B, gruth icamli*n*d M. *d.* berla inlo*m*ghaill merga i*n*mondaill lenga lo*m*raimh B, berla i*n*dlo*m*gaill merga i*n*mo*n*daill lenga lorai*m* M. *e.* luth inuirbri*n*d ma*n*t i*n*mearbaill druth cilli cearbaill B, luth i*n*buirbrind mantt i*n*mergaill druth cille cerbaill M. *f.* nicui*n*dhgi*m* sincairli*n*g B, nicui*n*chi*m* si*n* cairli*n*g M.

85. *a.* Druth dala BME. *b.* deredh liathroide f*or*luth B, deredh liath raite forlut M, dered liathroide f*or* luth E. *c.* colpa saillighi it*ir* dasaith B, colpdha saillighe et*ir* daṡaith M, colpa saillighi it*ir* dasaith E. *d.* caiṭh chaillighi cac na*n*druth B, caith caillige cac nandruth M, caith caillighi cac nandruth E.

86. *a.* (*space for 4 or 5 letters at beginning of stanza*) caerach corraighi duibhi B, Cairech corranchi duibhi M, Corp caerach corraigi no corranaichi (no corranaichi *suprascript*) duibhi E. *b.* ternumtha muilt B, ternamtha muilt M, ternumha muilt E. *c.* beacairecht (*space for several letters*) buide B, becharecht bai buidhe M, beachairecht bai buide E. *d.* brenulcha buic B, brenulcha buicc M, brenulca buicc E.

Notes

1. *MV* III §3.

Editions: Meyer (1917, 44; 1919, no. 72); Murphy (1956, 90: 1961, [128]).

The metre is *deibide baisse fri tóin* 'slap on the backside *deibide*' (3^2 7^2 ; 7^1 1^1), classified as *gnáthaiste*. The final line of *deibide* normally consists of seven syllables. A similar stanza is cited in *MV* I §49 and *MV* II §71 as an example of this metre (Murphy 1961, [127]; Ó hAodha 1991, 240 no. 37). The satire lies in the implication that the subject is a commoner (*bóaire*) of low social standing; see p. 23 above.

ní tabair eochu ar dúana. Payment for poems was not purely discretionary, as indicated by a passage in *Bretha Nemed Dédenach* which outlines the appropriate payment for specific types of metres; see p. 6 above. According to a passage in *MV* I §68, payment for *núachrutha* 'new forms' (metres associated with the bards) was not fixed but depended on factors such as the generosity of the patron and the excellence of the poem (Ó hAodha 1991, 218). H's reading *araduana* is unacceptable as it gives an extra syllable.

dúthaig. *duthaig* B, *duthaigh* MG, *dual* EH. The reading of EH, *dúal* 'natural, fitting', could also be followed here, in which case the vowel of *as* would not be elided. Note that E normally agrees with BM against HG.

2. *MV* III §5.

Edition: Murphy (1961, [120]).

The metre is *deibide fo-cheil a cubaid* '*deibide* which conceals its rhyme' (4^2 6^2 ; 7^1 7^3), classified as *gnáthaiste*. A slightly different version of this stanza is cited in *MV* I §56 and *MV* II §78 to illustrate this metre (Murphy 1961, [119]; Ó hAodha 1991, 242 no. 44). The concealment of rhyme lies in the fact that a line break occurs between the words *mac* and *Máenaig*, which form a syntactic unit and are normally uttered without a pause. BME omit this verse and cite a different stanza, which has a similar break in the syntactic unit in the first couplet: *A uí / Niallgusa nídat nemní. /Ní gand / do-rala duit dá scríbend* 'O son of Niallgus, you are not unimportant. It is not sparingly that you have happened to write it'.

mada. I follow Murphy (1961, 115) in taking this as a substantive use of the adjective *madae* 'vain, ineffectual'.

do mac. The version in *MV* I §56 reads *don maenaig*, while that in *MV* II §78 reads *la mac maenaig*. *MV* I §56 also adds *is innell corrgat* 'and arranging of pointed withes' before *ocus doirseóracht.* Note that Murphy and Ó hAodha omit this reading.

críathrad mine. The subjects of our poems are often depicted performing tasks associated with individuals of low status; see p. 24 above.

3. *MV* III §6.

Editions: Meyer (1917, 44; 1909, no. 25); Murphy (1961, [133]).

The metre is *deibide imrinn* '*deibide* with rhyme all around' (7^1 7^3 ; 7^1 7^3), classified as *gnáthaiste.* In *MV* III §7 the order of the lines is changed and the same verse illustrates *cró cummaisc etir rannaigecht móir 7 casbairdne* 'an enclosure composed of a mixture between *rannaigecht mór* and *casbairdne*' (7^3 7^1 ; 7^3 7^1). The stanza is cited as an illustration of *emain* in *MV* II §20 and also in a text on poets which derives from *Uraicecht Becc* and includes material from our text and *MV* II (*CIH* ii 556.18 ff.; see *UR* 11). *Deibide imrinn* and *emain* are similar in structure, and a Middle Irish poem on the birth of Áedán mac Gabrán (O'Brien 1952) is composed of a mixture of both metres.

Óbsa becán gabais. *obsabecan gabus* B, *osa began gabas* M, *obsa began gabus* E, *obsa becan gabais* H. The version of this stanza in *MV* II §20 reads a third singular preterite copula form: *obobegan gabus* (Book of Ballymote) and *obubecán gabais* (Laud 610) (Thurneysen 1891, 37). The MSS of *MV* III, however, clearly suggest a first singular form, which is the reading followed by Meyer (1909, no. 25): *Ōp-sa becān gabsus gleith.* Bergin (1916, 164) states that 'the variants *obu, obo, obsa* and *gabais, gabus* (IT. III 37 and 68) point to a reading *Ō bu becān gabais gleith* "since he was small he grazed"' and this is the reading followed by Murphy. Meyer's reading of first singular preterite of the copula is supported by the MSS of *MV* III, however, and it should also be noted in this regard that he gives the source of his later edition (1917, 44) as *MV* III §6 rather than *MV* II §20.

Líathainig. Murphy (1961, 129) takes *Líathainech* 'Grey-faced one' to be the name of a horse, but the satire here seems to lie rather in comparing the subject's appearance to that of a horse. M glosses *inliathanigh* with *.i. cenainn,* genitive singular of *cenann* 'white-headed, white-faced'. This adjective is normally applied to animals and *DIL* s.v. cites two examples of horses described as *cenann.* The version of this stanza cited in the text deriving from *Uraicecht Becc* (*CIH* ii 556.18 ff.) glosses *in liathánuig* with *.i. in liath macha,* which was the name of one of Cú Chulainn's horses. The stanza is attributed to Cú Chulainn in the version of *MV* II §20 in the Book of Ballymote (Thurneysen 1891, 37).

4. *MV* III §20.

Editions: Meyer (1909, 23 §61); Murphy (1961, [33]).

The metre is *dían airseng impóid* 'reversed *dían airseng*' (4^3 8^1 4^3 8^1), classified as *gnáthaiste.* *MV* III §21 cites a version of this stanza *ina cirt chóir cen impód* 'in its proper arrangement without reversal': *A Éirennaig, / a Albanaig, a Lochlannaig, / a goblán gorm / is lomnán dorn do drochrannaib* (Murphy 1961, [33a]).

do drochrannaib is lomnán dorn. This phrase suggests that the subject is being criticised for the composition of faulty verse. For similar allusions see p. 28.

is. For *as/asa,* a relative form of the copula used with a genitival function see L. Breatnach (1980b, 1-2) and cf. *asa caíniu clú* 'whose reputation is most fair', *Fodlai Aíre* tract §7.

goblán gorm. *DIL* s.v. 2 *gablán* gives the meaning 'name of a bird'. Since *gablán* is a diminutive form of *gabul* 'a fork' it must refer to a bird with a forked tail. *Goblán* is sometimes qualified by a word in the genitive, e.g. *gabhlán gainmhe* 'sand-martin' and *gabhlán gaoithe* 'swift' (Dinneen). In the present context *goblán gorm* may allude to a bird such as the swift, which is black/blue in colour and is known for its persistent cry. The intention may be to suggest that the subject of this satire has a loud voice and the poet may also be ridiculing his speech by addressing him as an Irishman, Scotsman and Norseman. For other allusions to the babbling speech of foreigners see p. 32. Note that the victim of no. 63 is described as *lon ic longaire i Líamain* 'a blackbird screeching in Líamain', which seems to be a description of his high-pitched voice.

5. *MV* III §31.

The metre is *dechnad fota fordálach* 'prolonged *dechnad fota*' (8^2 6^2 8^2 6^2 8^2 6^2), classified as *gnáthaiste.* The adjective *fordálach* 'delaying, prolonged' refers to the addition of an extra couplet. Murphy (1961, [41]) follows Meyer (1909, 19 §32) in citing an example of this metre from a source other than *MV* III on the grounds that the present verse is 'hard to understand'. Although the metrical structure is straightforward, there are quite a few textual difficulties. In general, however, the poem seems to describe a foreigner being brought in chains from a ship (possibly as a slave). The description of the *gaillsech* 'foreign woman' as 'stammering' and 'puffed up' is in keeping with other derogatory descriptions of the speech and appearance of foreigners both in the satires in our text and in other literary sources;

see p. 32 above. It is also interesting to note that both foreigners mentioned in the poem are said to have curly or frizzy hair.

íarraid dam ... mad áil duit. Note the use of the singular prepositional pronoun with the plural imperative form. Cf. also no. 64 below, where a singular form of the imperative (*apair*) is used with plural prepositional pronouns (*cucaib, acaib*).

cnápluing. *cnapluing* BB^b^, *capluing* MEH, *caebluing* G. This line is cited in *DIL* s.v. *cnaplong* 'studded ship' and Marstrander (1915, 133) takes the first element to be Old Norse **knapp* 'lump, knob', referring to a type of ornament. It is clear from the metrical structure, however, that a long vowel is required for consonance with the other end-words. G reads *cáep* 'lump, mass', while the reading of BB^b^ points to a compound with *cnáip* 'hemp'. The reading of MEH could have arisen as a result of the loss of an *n*-stroke. I follow BB^b^ and read *cnáplong* lit. 'hemp-ship'. Archaeological evidence from a Viking site in Waterford suggests that hemp (*Cannabis sativa*) may have been used in the manufacture of rope for ships (Wincott Heckett 1997, 755; see also McGrail 1993, 75 and Crumlin-Pedersen 1997, 190). Vendryes (1959–) s.v. *cnaplong* takes the form in our text as nominative plural, but it is dative singular of a feminine *ā*-stem after the preposition *a*.

mad áil duit. BB^b^ read *'na dáil* 'together with him' against the other MSS.

glas. *glass* B, *glas* B^b^MEH, *gas* G. H agrees with BB^b^ME in reading *glas* 'lock, fetter', while G reads *gas* 'spring, shoot; stripling'. Binchy (1962, 71-2) notes that in the earliest stratum of the law tracts *glas* refers to a shackle for the feet in contrast to *slabrad*, which is used of a chain around the neck. This distinction was lost in the later period.

gécruinn. *gegruind* BB^b^ME *gegrainn* G, *gecraind* H. I tentatively take this to be genitive singular of a compound of *géc* 'branch' and *rond* 'a woven chain' *Glas gécruinn* 'a fetter of a branching chain' may be an allusion to the foreigner being shackled.

Fó lim. The idiom *is fó limm* 'I deem good, am satisfied with' is discussed by Binchy (1972, 35 note 1). The phrase can also be used in the sense of 'I care not'; see *DIL* s.v. *fó* col. 175, l. 56.

ogmóir. Rhymes with *tormglóir.* The basic meaning is 'ogham-writer' and Murphy (1961, 118) suggests 'one skilled in *ogam* writing, a man of learning'. *DIL* s.v. suggests that the term is used here in the later sense of 'an orthographist, a correct writer'. It is difficult to construe the meaning of this line. Is it describing the foreigner referred to in line *a* as an unlearned person?

ḟócraim. *fograim* BB[b], *focraim* MH, *fogruim* E, *ograim* G. I take this as first person present indicative of *fúacair* 'proclaims, denounces'. A lenited form (as reflected in G) is required for alliteration, which indicates that the form is relative (*SG* III §11.35).

tromglóir. *tromsloig* B, *tromṡloig* B[b], *tromgloir* M, *tromghloir* G, *tormgloir* EH. Rhymes with *ogmóir.* The evidence of the MSS (MEGH) is strongly in favour of reading *-glóir* against the reading of BB[b] (genitive singular of *slóg* 'host'). The first element in BB[b]MG is the adjective *trom* 'heavy', which seems to be used here with the meaning 'powerful'. EH differ from the other MSS in reading the noun *toirm, torm* 'noise, tumult' as the first element.

thétmaill. The adjective *tét-* is found in compounds with *balc* 'strong', *béim* 'act of striking', *buillech* 'striking blows' and *ag n-allaid* 'stag', all of which suggest a meaning such as 'mighty' or 'powerful'. Murphy (1956b) notes that in its primary sense *tét-* is equivalent to Latin *luxuria. DIL* s.v. 6 *tét-* col. 161, l. 8 suggests that the first element in *tétmaill* may be the noun *tét* 'rope, string of a stringed instrument', which is unlikely in the present context. I take the second element as genitive singular of the adjective *mall* 'slow', which can also be used in the sense of 'dignified'; see *DIL* s.v. *mall* (d) and (e).

grúcbuirr. *grudbairr* BB[b], *gruitbairr* M, *grudbair* E, *grudbairr* G, *grucbuirr* H. The MSS show variation between *grud* BB[b]EG, *gruit* M and *gruc* H. M's reading is unsuitable metrically, since this word rhymes with *pútraill.* Although the evidence of the MSS (BB[b]EG) points to *grúd* as the first element of this compound, I have found no other examples of such a word. On this basis, I tentatively follow H and take the first element to be *grúc* 'anger, grudge'. I take the second element as dative singular of the adjective *borr* 'swollen'.

pútraill. *Pútrall* is used specifically of hair below the crown of the head. With *co pútraill étruimm* cf. *folt n-etrom* 'fluffy (?) hair' (*TBC* l. 5259).

6. *MV* III §44.

The metre is *dechnad mór scaílte* 'scattered *dechnad mór*' ($8^2\ 6^2\ 8^2\ 6^2$), classified as *gnáthaiste. Scaílte* indicates the lack of consonance. The subject of this verse is ridiculed for his lack of skill in composing poetry. For similar types of satires consisting of a series of negative statements see p. 10 above.

i Maig Ḟemin. According to Hogan (1910, 408), this encompasses an area extending from Cashel to Clonmel, Co. Tipperary. Ó Corráin

(1971) notes the existence of another Femen in Brega which is mentioned in annalistic entries and is associated with the Uí Néill.

i tenid cen túaga. *centuaga* BB^{b}, *centuara* MH, *centuara no gentuad* E. *DIL* cites this line s.v. 1 *túag* 'arch, curve' col. 332, l. 54, based on the reading of B. Although the evidence of the MSS (MEH) supports the reading *túara* 'signs', this seems to make little sense. BB^{b} read *túaga* 'axes', a reading which is also suggested by E's correction *no gentuad* (showing confusion of final lenited *-d* and *-g*). 'Axes [in fire]' may refer to tempering a blade (Kelly 1997, 487), possibly used here in a metaphorical sense of the skill of satire. For similar imagery of forging and tempering skills in poetry see McManus (2004, 100, note 9). An anecdote in *LL* l. 13582 which recounts how Aithirne sent his servant Greth to the blacksmith Eccet Salach *do chor béla i tenid* 'for putting an axe in fire' may also have a double meaning and be intended metaphorically as a threat of satire.

7. *MV* III §53.

The metre is *rannaigecht brecht mór* 'varied *rannaigecht mór*' (7^1 7^1 7^1 7^1 7^1 7^1), classified as *gnáthaiste.* For similar types of satires incorporating a series of negative statements see p. 10 above.

im Choin na Cell. As suggested by Thurneysen (1912, 86), Cú na Cell is probably a nickname. The subject is described as being destitute and the name may be an allusion to the fact that he relies on the charity provided by churches; see p. 30.

Tibid. *tibid* BB^{b}MEH. This must be either third singular present indicative or second plural imperative for rhyme with *sligid. Uile* indicates that a plural verbal form is intended.

muna ró sligid bas ḟerr. *menero sligi busfearr* B, *minarosligi bus ferr* B^{b}, *menero sligi isferr* M, *mina rosligidh asferr* E, *munaró sligid asferr* H. I take *ró* as Middle Irish third singular present subjunctive of *ro-saig* and *sligid* as accusative singular of *slige* 'road, way', verbal noun of *sligid* 'cuts'. The readings *sligi/sligid/sligidh* show the Middle Irish alternation of long and short forms in accusative and dative singular of dental stems (*SG* III §5.11). *Slige* can also be declined as an *-ia* stem. *Sligi* BB^{b}M is unsuitable metrically, as this word rhymes with *tibid* in the preceding line. I follow BB^{b} in reading third singular present subjunctive relative of the copula.

8. *MV* III §54.

Edition: Meyer (1919, no. 67).

The metre is *ochtrannaigecht mór* 'eight-fold *rannaigecht mór*' (4 x [7^1 7^1]), classified as *gnáthaiste.* The prefix *ocht-* is used in *MV* III of varieties of *rannaigecht, rinnard* and *casbairdne* which consist of eight lines instead of four; cf. *ochtrannaigecht becc mór* no. 13 and *ochtrinnard becc* no. 51 in the present edition. As well as describing the subject as weak and insignificant, the poet also appears to be ridiculing him for being overly zealous in his religious observance: *Ní geba túaignim ri tenn* 'you will not reach vaulted heaven by force'. The description of the victim as a small bunch of straw being chased by a cat and a heron in turn may be a humourous allusion to the fact that he cannot escape death, in spite of his piety (i.e. if the cat does not catch him, the heron will).

lorcáin. *lorcain* BB^{b}H, *lorcan* M, *lorccain* E. Rhymes with *dlochtáin*. In no. 19 below *lorcán* is used as a term of contempt in the phrase *a lorcán luige* 'you little mite in a bed' (rhyming with *tolclár*). This word also occurs in an Early Modern Irish satire, where it rhymes with *bochtán* 'wretch' (Quin 1965, 33 q. 43; see p. 37 above). Here it occurs among a series of phrases such as *dubhóg na sar* 'black offspring of nits' and *banbh tana trúagh* 'thin spare bonham', which indicates that it has negative connotations. Quin (*op. cit.*, 37 note 43) takes it as a derivative of *lorc*, a word 'of uncertain status and meaning', and tentatively suggests 'mite', while *DIL* cites both examples from *MV* III s.v. *lorgán* and suggests 'straggler (?); sluggard (?)'. Meyer in his edition takes it as the personal name Lorcán.

dlochtáin. *DIL* cites this line s.v. ?4 *dlochtán* where it is the only example and no meaning is given. I take it as 1 *dlochtán* 'small bunch', a diminutive form of *dlocht* 'bunch, wisp'. Cf. *dlochtán crema i cris* 'a little bunch of garlic in a belt' no. 59 and note the similar metaphor *a chos choppóice* 'you stem of a dock-leaf' no. 54.

ria. *ria* BB^{b}ME, *ri* H. Meyer does not translate this word but suggests reading a disyllabic form in order to give a line of seven syllables. *Ria catt* is followed by the phrase *ocus corr dlúith ina díaid* 'with a heron close behind it', a context which suggests that it is a disyllabic form of the preposition *ré* 'before, in front of'. For examples of disyllabic forms of prepositions in Old Irish verse see Carney (1964, xxviii).

geba. I take this as an example of the short *e*-future for rhyme with *fleda* (Greene 1978, 61–2).

túaignim. *tuaighneam* B, *tuaigneam* B^{b}, *tuaigneim* M, *tuagnem* E, *tuágnem* H. Rhymes with *cúaillib.* I follow Meyer in taking this as a compound of 1 *túag* 'vault' and *nem* 'heaven'. The form *nim*, which is required here for metrical purposes, is attested in Middle Irish and shows a shift from neuter to feminine declension; see *DIL* s.v. *nem.*

fleda. *fleagha* B, *fledha* B[b], *fleadha* M, *fleda* EH. Rhymes with *geba.* The genitive singular form is normally *flede* but cf. *bert fleda* (rhyming with *Mena*) no. 67.

9. *MV* III §67.

Edition: Murphy (1961, [97]).

The metre is *cró cummaisc etir casbairdne ocus lethrannaigecht* 'an enclosure composed of a mixture between *casbairdne* and *lethrannaigecht*' (7^3 5^1 7^3 5^1), classified as *gnáthaiste.* This stanza is difficult to interpret on account of a number of textual problems, although the general sense does seem to be a threat to harm the subject in some way.

a ocaile. *aoccule* BM, *Aocc uile* E, *ao cuile* H. Rhymes with *clocaile.* Since the text states that this metre is a mixture of *casbairdne* (7^3) and *lethrannaigecht* (5^1), lines *a* and *c* must end in trisyllables. I have found no other examples of the words *ocaile* or *clocaile,* however. Murphy emends to a palatal form *óic* ('warriors') in line *a* and adds nasalisation after *cloc* in line *c*: *Cid 'ma-le a óic uile / dar lim nocon ain; / taile dam in cloc n-aile / coro benar fair* 'Although his warriors are together, I do not think that it will protect [him]. Give me the other bell so that I may ring [it] against him' (my translation). This gives a metrical structure of 7^2 5^1 7^2 5^1 and he suggests that the stanza might be more properly described as *cró cummaisc etir rannaigecht mbic ocus lethrannaigecht móir* 'an enclosure composed of a mixture between *rannaigecht becc* and *lethrannaigecht*'. There is no reason to assume that the metrical name given in the text is incorrect simply because the words *ocaile* and *clocaile* are otherwise unattested, however. *MV* III contains a considerable number of such words, several of which end in *-aile*; see, for example, no. 55 below.

in clocaile. *in chloch aile* B, *inclocale* M, *in cloch ale* E, *incloc ale* H. Rhymes with *ocaile.* This is written as two separate words in BEH. Murphy's emendation to *in cloc n-aile* 'the other bell', although impossible metrically, would nevertheless make sense in the context of satire or cursing, since the ringing of a bell by a saint or cleric against a person in order to curse or excommunicate him is well documented in the lives of saints and other sources (Meyer 1905b, 10 §§18, 20, 21; Mulchrone 1939, l. 1303; O'Neill 1981, 41). *Cloc* 'bell' may well be the first element in *clocaile,* but I cannot explain the suffix *-aile.*

air. Murphy emends to *fair* against the MSS.

10. *MV* III §68.

Edition: Murphy (1961, [113]).

The metre is *cró cummaisc etir rinnaird ocus lethrannaigecht* 'an enclosure composed of a mixture between *rinnard* and *lethrannaigecht*' (6^2 5^1 6^2 5^1), classified as *gnáthaiste*. Note the rhyme between voiced and voiceless stops in *Muiccín* : *bruitín*. Although this would not be permitted in *dán díreach*, there are several other examples in *MV* III: *gatbéimnig* : *maccléirig* no. 33; *laic* : *cait* no. 39; *gipáin* : *Britáin* no. 46; *focul* : *cocur* no. 57; *muccaid* : *upaid* no. 82. As Kelly notes (1997, 495), the ploughman who is the subject of this satire 'evidently had the reputation for overuse of the goad on his oxen, and laziness in his manipulation of the plough'.

Maigne Muiccín. *mhuighi muiccin* B, *muighi muicin* M, *muigi muicin* E, *maighni muicin* G, *maigni muccin* H. The MSS show confusion between *maigen* 'place' (GH) and *mag* 'a plain' (BME). I follow GH and take *Maigne Muiccín* as genitive singular of the placename Maigen, qualified by the personal name Muiccín. Muiccín of Maigen (also known as Óengas Láimidan) is associated with Saint Moling, who entrusted him with keeping his manuscripts safe during a raid (Stokes 1908, 36–8; Dobbs 1950, 229–30). Moling's saintliness is demonstrated by the fact that he forgave Muiccín for the destruction of some of these manuscripts after the latter had hidden them in a damp cave. Dobbs has identified Maigen as Moyne in North Kilkenny and also notes the existence of a cave (Derc Ferna) in an adjoining townland. This may have been the cave in which Muiccín is said to have hidden Moling's manuscripts. Murphy takes *Maige Muiccín* as genitive singular of an unidentified placename *Mag Muiccín*, which is the interpretation followed by Kelly (1997, 495).

loim técht. *loim thecht* BM, *loim techt* EG, *loim técht* H. Murphy reads *loim thécht*. The lack of lenition in EGH points to the preservation of the neuter gender. I take this as referring to a drink of thickened milk (*as técht*), which was made by adding rennet from the stomach of a calf to fresh milk (Kelly 1997, 324).

in bruitín. *inbruitin* BME, *abhruitin* G, *inbrutin* H. Rhymes with *Muiccín*. As Murphy states (1961, 65), this can be taken as a diminutive form of either *brot* 'goad' or *brat* 'cloak', although the former would lead to rhyme between voiced and voiceless stops. The context suggests that *bruitín* 'little goad' is the intended reading and, as noted above, there are other examples in the tract of this type of rhyme. Note that G reads *abhruitin* 'his little goad'.

11. *MV* III §82.

Editions: Meyer (1919, no. 87); Murphy (1961, [51]).

The metre is *rannaigecht becc scaílte* 'scattered *rannaigecht becc*' (7^2 7^2 7^2 7^2), classified as *gnáthaiste*. This stanza is omitted in E. By enquiring after the well-being of the grandson of Conall and the son of Cenn Fáelad, the poet indicates that both have suffered the ill-effects of having been justifiably satirised.

Conn mac Cinn Ḟáelad. Thurneysen has suggested (1912, 88) that an approximate date can be established for Conn mac Cinn Ḟáelad on the basis of the deaths of Manchán (*Tig. s.a.* 1045) and Mael-Sechlainn mac Cinn Ḟáelad (*AU s.a.* 1050), whom he takes to be his nephew and brother respectively. It is impossible to establish whether the subject of the present stanza is related to these individuals, however.

'Na ndernsat. *inandernsat* B *inandersat* M. I follow Murphy in emending *ina* of the MSS to *'na*. Meyer reads *Ina ndernsat*, which gives an octosyllabic line. Note Middle Irish *dernsat*, showing the use of the historical passive stem as active (*SG* III §12.66) and the Middle Irish form of the relative particle a^n (*SG* III §10.25).

12. *MV* III §88.

The metre is *rannaigecht becc mór scaílte* 'scattered *rannaigecht becc mór*' (8^2 8^2 8^2 8^2), classified as *gnáthaiste*. The son of a priest is satirised here for casting his congregation into the snow. This would have been considered a serious offence, since the church was legally obliged to provide hospitality; see p. 30 above.

Mac int ṡacairt ó Ros Comáin. *Mac intṡagairt orcomain* B, *Ameic inṡagairt orchomain* M, *mac intsagairt oros comain* E. I follow BE and read *mac* against *ameic* M on the grounds that the final line of the poem refers to the subject in the nominative case. The satires in our text do not switch between the second and third persons, thereby avoiding the fault *écnairc fri frecnairc* as illustrated in the *Trefocul* tract on metrical faults (*Auraic.* ll. 5171–5). E's reading *oros comain* gives the required number of syllables and the addition of the vocative particle in M may simply be an attempt to add an extra syllable.

13. *MV* III §89.

The metre is *ochtrannaigecht becc mór* 'eight-fold *rannaigecht mór*' (4 x [8^2 8^2]), classified as *gnáthaiste.* The stanzas illustrating *ochtrannaigecht mór* no. 8 and *ochtrinnard becc* no. 51 are similar in structure. Here the poet states that if his poems are rejected he will employ his craft of poetry on someone else's behalf and that this would be similar to exchanging a fetter for bundles of sticks or a cauldron for five drinking cups. This may be an allusion to a bad or unequal bargain, with *geimel* and *caire* being used metaphorically of the poem which is given in exchange for payment. For a similar sentiment see Best (1905b, 168 ll. 85–88). The statements *is fortail dom dáil cen dulus* 'that my argument is victorious without voraciousness (?)' and *náro áerus duine reime* 'that I have not satirised a person before him' suggest that the intention may be to deny an accusation of having unjustly satirised the grandson of Cú Buide. This may have originally formed part of a longer composition, since it would be unusual for a poem to begin with the words *acht masa.*

deired. *derd* B, *dhereadh* M, *deredh* E. Rhymes with *geimel.* There are only two other examples of this spelling cited in *DIL* s.v. *derad* 'refusing'.

dán. *Dán* seems to be used here in the sense of 'skill, craft', in opposition to *dúan*, the actual composition.

Foclaim rim cháin is rim chubus. *Cáin* is normally used of promulgated legislation and may refer here to the regulations governing the use of satire by poets. In *Bretha Nemed Dédenach* this is referred to as *cáin n-enech* 'the regulation of honour'; see p. 5 above. *Cubus,* on the other hand, appears to refer here to natural law or personal morality.

má ro cháinius. *marcailus* B, *marochailius* M, *marocainis* E. I have emended to first singular preterite of *cáinid* 'reviles'. The form in E is second singular preterite of this verb. I am uncertain as to the form *cailus/chailius* in BM, which may be from the verb *coillid* 'damages, violates' with *-l-* for *-ll-*.

fortail. Thurneysen expands *isf–* B as *isfer.* ME have a *plene* reading here, however, and *fortail* is established by rhyme with *foclaim.*

dulus. This word is not well attested and the meaning is uncertain. Only four examples are given in *DIL* s.v. *dulas,* including the citation from our text. An examination of the various contexts in which it occurs may help in establishing a possible meaning. The first example is found in a metrical rule of Echtgus húa Cuanáin which warns against the dangers of partaking of holy communion while not believing in the sacrament: *Cib ē noscaithea co cair / cen a c[h]reitim in chuirp sin / is mōr a* *dulus in trōigh / ōn turus tēid don altōir* 'Whoever consumes it sinfully without believing in that body, great is the *dulus* of the wretch on account of the journey he makes to the altar' (van Hamel 1917–19, 349 §81). The second example, a genitive singular form *dulais*, suggests that the word is an *o*-stem. This is found in the *Liber Flavus Fergusiorum* (Section II folio 39r[a]21) in an unpublished tract dealing with the seven daughters of humility: *IN aíne ⁊ da hingeanuibh .i. dicur an craeis ⁊ díl in dulais ⁊ na hanab aisi ⁊ iaraid na haenda ...* 'Concerning fasting and its daughters, i.e. banishing of gluttony and destruction of *dulus* and *hanab aisi* (?) and seeking of unity ...'. The citation from this text in *DIL* s.v. *dulas* is inaccurate as a *ceann fá eite* symbol has been overlooked and several words are omitted. This MS is also wrongly identified in the list of Abbreviations in *DIL* (the shelf number is RIA 23 O 48, rather than RIA 23 P 3). Versions of this text in two later MSS suggest that *dulus* may have been misunderstood by the scribes. The phrase *dil in dulais* is omitted in TCD F 5. 3 (667) p. 177b, while Egerton 136 folio 79[b] substitutes *an dolaigh* 'of the burden'. The third example given in *DIL* occurs in *Aislinge Meic Conglinne*: '... *airm i n-airlím[fa] thar do déta ó na biadu immda inganta ilerda it-chótamar; i n-indraithfither do dulas ...* (Jackson 1990, 29 ll. 896–8): 'a place in which your teeth will be polished by the many, wonderful, varied foods we have told of; in which your *dulas* will be destroyed ...'. Jackson (*ibid.*, 165 s.v. *dulas*) states 'meaning uncertain, perh. "depression" or "hunger"'. In all three examples *dulus* is associated with eating and appetite and Liam Breatnach has suggested to me (personal comment) that it may be an abstract formation from *dul* 'satirist'; cf. *dulsaine* 'mockery, satire'. If this is the case, *dulus* in the above examples and in our text could be taken to mean 'voraciousness'. McCone (1989, 129–30) observes that satirists are often portrayed as voracious characters who use the threat of satire for extortion rather than as a legitimate sanction. One such example is Cridenbél in the saga *Cath Maige Tuired* (Gray 1982, §§26–9).

14. *MV* III §96.
Edition: Murphy (1961, [101]).
The metre is *aí freisligi* (7^3 7^2 7^3 7^2), classified as *gnáthaiste*.

ro-chúalamar. *rochualamar* B, *rotchualamar* M, *rocualamar* E. M reads a Middle Irish third singular masculine (originally neuter) infixed pronoun (*SG* III §10.6).

do chlár. Murphy (1961, 99 s.v. *clár*) translates 'board, board-work'. I take *clár* to mean 'table', the sense being that the poet has found the church's reputation for hospitality to be unfounded. This would have been a justifiable reason for satire, since the church was bound to provide hospitality to guests; see p. 30 above.

ní hamlaid. The Middle Irish form *amlaid* (Old Irish *samlaid*) is fixed by alliteration with *ro-ḟúaramar.*

ro-ḟúaramar. *rofuaramar* B, *fotuaramar* M, *ro fuaramar* E. As in the case of *rot-chúalamar* in line *a*, M reads a Middle Irish infixed pronoun here. It also preserves the original preverb *fo,* while BE read *ro.* Middle Irish lenition is confirmed by alliteration with *amlaid.*

15. *MV* III §102.

The metre is *in laíd lúascach is lugu* 'the smallest rocking poem' (7^1 3^2 7^1 3^2 3^2), classified as *gnáthaiste.* Meyer (1909, 24 §69) describes *laíd lúascach* as an extension of *deibide scaílte* by the addition of a fifth line which rhymes with the second line (*chorainn* : *Chonaill* in the present example). This stanza is cited as an example of *breccad* or 'multiple' rhyme by Ó Máille (1973, 83–4). The allusion to the subject's lice-infested tonsure indicates that he is a cleric and it is noteworthy that several satires in *MV* III are directed against churchmen and churches; see p. 30 above.

sneda. *nasnedha* B, *sneadha* M, *nasneda* E. I follow M and omit the definite article for metrical purposes. For other references to lice in satires see p. 35.

chorainn. *idcholaind* B, *it coraind* M, *itcolaind no itcoraind* E. B reads *cholaind* 'body', M reads *coraind* 'tonsure', while E corrects *cholaind* to *no itcoraind* 'rather "in your tonsure"' in a *suprascript* addition. I have followed M and the correction in E. Both readings are suitable metrically, however, as they form *rinn/airdrinn* rhyme with *clainn* (line *a*) and full rhyme with *Chonaill* (line *e*).

A-táit ... co mer. Note the Middle Irish use of the preposition *co* to form an adverb (*SG* III §9.1) and the use of substantive verb with adverbialized adjective.

do ḟuilled. *do fhuilet* B, *dafuilledh* M, *dofuiled* E. Rhyme with *mer* (line *c*) indicates that this word ends in a lenited *-d,* which is the reading of ME. The form in B could be taken as Middle Irish *do-fuilet* 'they are at hand', but this would give imperfect rhyme.

16. *MV* III §111.

Edition: Murphy (1961, [84]).

The metre is *casbairdne scaílte* 'scattered *casbairdne*' (7^3 7^3 7^3 7^3), classified as *gnáthaiste.* The resemblance between this verse and no. 29 below is striking and both stanzas may have originally been connected in some manner. Note, for example, the reference to *Cíarraige* and the otherwise unattested form *gelugud* 'brightening', which in both instances rhymes with *merugud.*

tánacas. I follow Murphy (1961, 104) in taking this as Middle Irish first singular preterite of *do-icc* 'comes'. *DIL* s.v. *do-icc* col. 298, l. 10 takes it as a preterite passive form.

ar merugud. Murphy emends to *for* against *ar* of the MSS. These prepositions were confused during the Middle Irish period (*SG* III §13.4). Cf. *a-tá ar merugud* 'he is confused' no. 20 and *nocho gairit a merugud* 'not short is his straying' no. 29.

gelugud. There are only two attestations of this word in *DIL* and no meaning is given. Both occur in *MV* III and in each case *gelugud* rhymes with *merugud.* Murphy (1961, 110) suggests the meaning 'making white, whitening', presumably taking *gelugud* as verbal noun of the denominative verb *gelaigid* 'grows white'; cf. *senugud* (also rhyming with *merugud*), verbal noun of *senaigid* 'grows old' no. 20. In the present stanza, the whitening is said to have been caused by a foreign club, while in no. 29 below it is caused by the 'weapon' of a combmaker (i.e. a comb). In both instances this may refer to a change in the colour of the skin as a result of having been beaten and it is interesting to note in this regard that the term *bánbéim* 'white wound' is used in legal sources to describe a wound which does not draw blood (Thurneysen 1925, 41 §60). Although it is impossible to establish for certain if the two verses are connected, it is tempting to speculate that the 'foreign club' complained of here is to be equated with the comb described sarcastically as a weapon in no. 29.

galluirge. Rhymes with *cambuirbe.* I follow Murphy (1961, 109 s.v. 1 *Gall*) in taking this as a compound of *gall* 'foreign' and *lorg* 'club'. Cf. the compounds *gallat* 'foreign helmet' no. 71 and *na gallbróc* 'of the foreign shoes' no. 73. *DIL* cites this line s.v. *uirge* 'testicle', suggesting that this may be the second element. *Lorg* 'stick' makes better sense in the present context and is also preferable on metrical grounds, since the *-g-* of *uirge* is lenited.

17. *MV* III §120.

Editions: Meyer (1919, no. 85); Murphy (1961, [109]).

The metre is *rinnard aiclech* '*rinnard* with *aicill*' (6^2 6^2 6^2 6^2), classified as *gnáthaiste. Aicill* rhyme is between *géire* : *déine.* For other satires which contain a series of negative statements about the subject see p. 10 above.

Ní ḟuilet. *Nifuilet* BE, *Niuilet* M, *Niḟuilead* G. MG show Middle Irish lenition after *ní* (*SG* III §11.1). The Middle Irish form *-fuilet*, which shows the addition of a third plural personal ending to *fil* (*SG* III 12.191), is fixed by the syllable count.

déine. *dene* BME, *dena* G. Rhymes with *géire.* I follow Meyer and Murphy in taking this as third singular prototonic present indicative of *do-gní*, although a palatal form of this verb is unusual in Middle Irish (OIr. *-dénai* > *déna*). A second example occurs in *MV* III §175, where *déine* (which Murphy takes as second singular prototonic present indicative) rhymes with *réide* (Murphy 1961 [74]).

acht. B reads *f* plus a suspension stroke, which has probably arisen as a result of the *-acht* compendium having been misread as *for.*

18. *MV* III §121.

Edition: Murphy (1961, [110]).

The metre is *rinnard scaílte cen aicill* 'scattered *rinnard* without *aicill*' (6^2 6^2 6^2 6^2), classified as *gnáthaiste.* Charles-Edwards (2000, 137) notes that early Irish society placed a strong value on the *aithech* 'commoner' being a *fer trebar* 'prudent man'. By stating that the subject of this satire is not the son of such a man, the poet indicates that he does not stand to inherit anything and can have no prospects or status in society. The meaning of the final couplet is less clear but may simply be intended to portray him as an untrustworthy person, i.e. someone whom the poet would neither follow nor trust to have following him.

nocho thaille i ferunn. For other examples of a palatal form *taille* see *DIL* s.v. 2 *do-alla. Ferann* is generally used of a specific territory or holding, which was sometimes attached to a particular office such as poet or physician (Kelly 1988, 101). The sense here may be that the subject will neither inherit land (since his father is imprudent) nor acquire it on account of holding a particular office through his own merit or skill. The verb *do-alla* is also used in heptad 50 in the sense of finding room on a holding. Here it is stated that the son of a living father is entitled to rent land without his father's permission when there is no room for him to farm on his father's land: *focreic tire. in tan na talla i tir la athuir .i. in tan na tuillend i fearand in athar 'maraon risin athair* 'Renting of land when there is no room for him on land with his father, i.e. when there is no room for him on the father's land along with the father' (*CIH* i 45.34–46.1). This passage has been translated and discussed by McLeod (1992, 70).

raga. Murphy emends to *rega* against the MSS. *Raga* is a regular Middle Irish development of OIr. *-rega* (*SG* III §3.12).

19. *MV* III §141.

Edition: O'Curry (1873, 393).

The metre is *ochtḟoclach corránach becc* 'hooked [extended] *ochtḟoclach becc*' (5^2 5^2, 5^2 4^1, 5^2 5^2, 5^2 4^1 ; 5^2 5^2, 5^2 4^1, 5^2 5^2, 5^2 4^1), classified as *gnáth medónda.* As Murphy states (1961, 85), the adjective *corránach* 'hooked' 'indicates that extra lines have been added to the normal form of a stanza'. For an example of *ochtḟoclach becc* see no. 39 below. Note also that *lethrannaigecht mór chorránach* 'hooked [extended] *lethrannaigecht mór*' (4 x [5^1 5^1]), no. 59 below, is an extended form of *lethrannaigecht mór* (5^1 5^1 5^1 5^1). The rhyming of *chéill-se* : *réir-se* with *séise* : *éise* : *chéise* : *Déise* would not be acceptable in *dán díreach.*

The main point of this satire appears to be that the subject has not heeded the advice of the poet (*nocho fom chéill-se do-chuaid do chíall* 'it is not to my reason that your reason has submitted'), although it is impossible to establish further details due to the lack of context. He is portrayed as a layabout (*a lorcán luige* 'you little mite in a bed' and *for tolclár tuige ret tóin aníar* 'your bed-board of straw behind your backside') who is more interested in lying in bed than in staying outside to herd cattle.

'muig ocna búaib. *amuigh ognabuaibh* B, *muigh ocnamaib* M. M reads a variant form *'muigh*, which is necessary for the syllable count. Cf. *gus 'niogh mar dho-níodh Mairghrég* (Carney 1945, 17 l. 378 and note p. 111), "*táit 'mach ar áis nó ar écin*" (*Met. Dind.* III, 80 l. 44) and *Caille Nathfráich ó ṡin 'mach* (*Met. Dind.* III, 308 l. 67). I am grateful to Gordon Ó Riain and Liam Breatnach for these references. I follow B's reading *ognabuaibh* and take the phrase to mean 'outside with the cows' against O'Curry's translation 'After us the cows shall not enjoy their plains'.

séise. Watkins (1963, 215) differentiates between *séis* 'musical art' from *seinnid* 'plays a musical instrument' and *séis* 'meaning' from Latin *sensus.* Both words are given s.v. *séis* in *DIL.*

nocho dom réir-se. *nochodumreirsi* B, *nocondarmese* M. I follow B for rhyme with the endwords *Déise* : *chéise* : *éise* : *séise* : *chéill-se.*

nocho fom chéill-se do-chuaid do chíall. Lit. 'it is not under my reason that your reason has gone'. *Téit* is used with the preposition *fo* in the sense 'submits'.

Ith imm is uige. Cf. *a ithe imme re harán secail* 'you eating of butter with rye bread' no. 38. References to butter are significant in the context of satire because it was a luxury food which was the entitlement of individuals of high status (Kelly 1997, 326). The exhortation to 'eat butter and eggs' may be ridiculing the fact that the subject of this poem is of low status yet has delusions of grandure. A similar implication may lie behind the description of the subject of no. 75 as *láech ic íarraid lomma is imme* 'a warrior asking for a sip of milk and butter' (i.e. food to which he is not legally entitled). For an explanation of the phrase *a ithe imme re harán secail* see note on no. 38.

roich uide íar n-uide. *uidhi* BM. *DIL* s.v. *uide* col. 59, l. 52 cites two examples of the phrase *uide íar n-uide* with the meaning 'gradually, by degrees'. O'Curry translates 'Seek tutor after tutor, pursue [thy way] to Rome', taking *uide* as a variant of *aite.* Rhyme with *luige, buide* etc. indicates that a lenited *-d* is intended. Note also the elision of a stressed vowel in *uide íar.*

co Rúaim. *coroimh* B, *coroim* M. I have emended the reading of the MSS, since the metrical structure suggests that this word should rhyme with *búaib.* In the illustration of *ochtfoclach mór chorranach* cited in *MV* III §143 there is rhyme between the end-words of the corresponding lines. *Roich uide íar n-uide / adíu co Rúaim* is probably intended simply as an exhortation to go away.

lorcán. *lorcain* B, *lorcan* M. Rhymes with *tolclár.* This word is also found in no. 8 above, where the poet states *Uch, a lorcáin, isat lac,* 'Alas, you little mite, you are weak'. O'Curry takes *lorcán* as a personal name and reads *A Lorcan luigi, a Bolcain buidhi* 'O Lorcan of the vows, O yellow *Bulcan*'.

a bolgán buide. This line is cited in *DIL* s.v. *Bolcán* 'Vulcan'. For the significance of the colours dun and yellow in satire see p. 23 above.

tolclár. *tolclar* B, *tolcar* M. Rhymes with *lorcán.* I follow *DIL* s.v. 1 *tolg* in taking this as a compound of *tolg* 'cubicle; bed' and *clár* 'board'. This is the reading of B. O'Curry, *op. cit.*, takes the first element as the adjective *toll* 'hollow' and translates 'upon the bare board'. A meaning such as 'hollow board of straw' would be appropriate in the sense of an uncomfortable bed, although *tollchlár* would be the expected form.

ret tóin. *rianoin* B, *re toin* M. Note that B differs from M here in reading *ria nóin* 'before evening'.

20. *MV* III §146.

The metre is *laíd trebraid becc* ($5^3\ 4^2$, $5^3\ 4^2$; $5^3\ 2^2$[?], $5^3\ 4^2$), classified as *gnáth medónda.* The pattern of internal rhyme helps to establish the metrical structure. There is rhyme between *merugud* (a) : *senugud* (b) and *gataige* (c) : *apaide* (d) and *aicill* rhyme between *mebal* (a) : *sleman*

(b) and *imar* (c) : *inar* (d). The subject is described as having become old and confused and the phrase 'hands of a thief' also suggests that he has begun stealing. The epithet *inar odar* 'a dun-coloured tunic' may be an allusion to his low status, which would also accord with the description of him as 'a sallow ploughman'; see p. 23.

senugud. Rhymes with *merugud.* Only this example is cited in *DIL*, where it is given as the verbal noun of *senaigid* 'grows old'.

sleman solam. I take these as attributive adjectives qualifying *senugud.*

imar. *imar* B, *inbar* M. In addition to disagreement between the two MSS, a further problem exists in that this line is two syllables shorter than the other three lines. Metres classified as *gnátha medónda*, unlike those in the *écoitchenna* section of the tract, tend to be syllabically regular, which suggests that some letters have been lost. The pattern of alliteration indicates that the line should contain a word beginning with *g*, but I have been unable to establish what this might have been. Taking *imar* as the end-word (or part thereof) gives *aicill* rhyme in both couplets.

airem. Describing the victim as belonging to a low social class is a common form of insult; see p. 23 and cf. *a uí airim brocsalaig* 'you grandson of a ploughman [who is] filthy like a badger' no. 40.

21. *MV* III §155.

Only the last two lines of this stanza are cited in a corrupt form in *MV* III to illustrate the metre *laíd*, which is classified as *anaichnid.* The full verse is cited as an example of a 'satire with a spell' in *UR* 114 §23, from which the text and translation in the present work are taken. The syllabic structure is 8^2 9^2 10^2 10^2. The verse takes the form of a curse woven around the name of the victim, which is repeated six times. For examples of other satires where the name is repeated see p. 14 above. It is set in a literary context in an anecdote in *Corm.* Y §698, which tells how the wife of Caíar, the king of Connacht, fell in love with her husband's nephew, Néide, and encouraged him to compose a *glám dícenn* satire against his uncle, stating that a man with a blemish caused by satire could not be king; see p. 83 above. In *MV* III it follows a description of the performance of a *glám dícenn* satire, while in *UR* it is described in a Middle Irish gloss as a *glám dícenn.*

22. *MV* III §164.

The metre is *trébricht* 'threefold *bricht* (8^2 10^2 8^2 11^2 ; 10^2 7^2 8^2 10^2 ; 8^2 9^2 8^2 6^2)', classified as *anaichind. DIL* defines *bricht* as 'an octosyllable, (a group of eight syllables) as a metrical unit'; see Thurneysen (1891, 130) and Murphy (1961, 27). *MV* III cites examples of nine types of *bricht* metres in descending order from *noíbricht* 'ninefold *bricht*' to *bricht fén*, five of which are satirical (22, 40, 41, 53, 70 of the present edition). These stanzas do not conform to any regular syllabic pattern, however, which indicates that the term *bricht* is not used in *MV* III to mean an octosyllabic metrical unit. Cf. also *bricht nathrach Néde* no. 46, where *bricht* means 'incantation, charm'.

This satire is irregular both in the syllabic structure and in the number of stresses per line and Thurneysen (1891, 99) prints it as continuous prose. It is one of the longest satires in *MV* III and it has been divided into three four-line sections on the basis of end-rhyme and internal rhyme. The first section, for example, is linked to the second by end-rhyme between *Gadra* (a) : *damna* (b) : *tarba* (d) : *adba* (f), while sections two and three are connected by end-rhyme between *craplám* (h) : *Lachtnán* (l). The repetition of *Lachtnán* at the end of the poem forms a *dúnad* 'closure' of the type classifed as *saigid* (Murphy 1961, 44).

Lachtnán is criticised for his lack of hospitality towards his visitors, who are described as having 'shrivelled up' after visiting his house. A similar sentiment is expressed in no. 26 below: *Ro ṡecc feóil ar muintire / mar ṡeccas a rúsc im chrann* 'the flesh of our people has shrivelled up as its bark shrivels up around a tree'. This is one of four satires in *MV* III in which the poet states his desire to harm his victim, in this case by wounding him with a thorn or a knife; see p. 11.

Lachtnán úa gormḟíaclach Gadra. This may be the same person as *Lachtnán mac Luchduinn uí Gadra* no. 74. Meyer (1920, 7–8) discusses both occurrences of this name in *MV* III and also notes a reference to a *Lachtnán mac Taidc huí Gadra* in a poem attributed to Cúán úa Lothcháin.

diad. *DIL* cites this line s.v. 5 *diad*, preceded by a query. No meaning is given. I take it as a nominative form of *dé* 'smoke'; cf. *DIL* s.v. 1 *dé* col. 166, l. 1, where it is stated that a nominative form *diad* is 'modelled on the *ā*-stems'. Mac Eoin (1974, 60–1) cites a number of examples of consonantal stems which take the form of the genitive singular as nominative singular and switch to *o/ā*-inflexion.

ro ḟírchrap. The adjective *fír* may be prefixed to verbs in poetry, often with an intensive force; see *DIL* s.v. *fír* col. 149, ll. 20–1. Note the similar use of an adjective in the verbal form *ro chorrmaid* no. 69.

do-acrad. *dohacradh* B, *datacradh* M. This line is difficult to interpret. I tentatively take the verbal form as third singular passive preterite of *do-accair* 'pleads, sues'.

anbas. I take this as *an*, a Middle Irish form of the relative particle plus third singular present subjunctive of the copula (*SG* III §10.25).

aitinn. *aitind* B, *ataind* M. *DIL* cites the line containing this word s.v. *aittenn* 'furze' col. 279, l. 55, based on the reading of B. Although the reading of M rhymes with *capaill* in the following line, there are no other examples of this spelling cited in *DIL*. *Aicill* may not be necessary in this position, since it is not present in the final couplet and the rhyme between *athair* (e) : *apaid* (f) is imperfect.

serthe. This is an example of the Middle Irish replacement of nominative plural by accusative plural in dental stems (*SG* III §5.11).

chongna. *concnai* BM. *DIL* cites this line s.v. *con-cnaí* 'gnaws'. I have emended to *chongna* (rhyming with *lomda*) on the grounds that all the other lines end in a disyllable.

Lachtnán. *lachtnain* BM. I have emended the reading of the MSS to a non-palatal form (*GOI* §280.1) for rhyme with *craplám*.

23. *MV* III §170.

Edition: Meyer (1919, no. 68).

The metre is *meisce Rómáin* 'drunkenness of Rómán' (8^3 9^3 4^2 8^2 9^3), classified as *écoitchenn*. For the use of personal names in the metrical names of satires in *MV* III see McLaughlin (2005, 128–30). Vowel length in *Rómán* is established by rhyme with *mórgráin* in *Saltair na Rann* (Stokes 1883, l. 7250; Knott 1952, 119) and also by rhyme with *Crónán* and *mórán* in *Félire Húi Gormáin* (Stokes 1895, 90 §4e).

Here the poet ridicules the subject's stupidity by stating that even if he were to give him a wife, he would still eat grass and corn in the summer. Liam Breatnach has suggested to me that the implication may be that he would not appreciate the economic advantages of having a wife, whose duties would include the production of dairy foods (known as *saimbiad* 'summer food') (Kelly 1997, 318, 450).

cid taí. When the substantive verb is used in nasalising relative clauses with the meaning 'to be angry, vexed', the particle *no* is normally found with second person singular forms, e.g. *cid no taí* (*GOI* §779.2).

Dá tucur / do ḟeór. Meyer emends to *dia tuc* and *d'ḟeór*, which gives two octosyllabic lines. The name of the metre gives no indication of its syllabic structure, however, and many of the metres illustrated in the final section of the tract are irregular.

co mbungile. *combuinghile* B, *combungile* M. Rhymes with *Urbile.* Meyer translates 'mit weißem Gesäß' 'with a white backside'. As far as I am aware, however, *bun* is not used with the meaning 'backside' in Irish. It may be used here in an abstract sense with the meaning 'real'; see *DIL* s.v. *bun* col 241, l. 61.

arbur. Note the Middle Irish short form of the dative of an *n*-stem (OIr. *arbaimm*).

Urbile. *urbhuile* B, *urbile* M. I follow Meyer in taking this as a variant of the placename Airbile or Ard Bile in Kerry; see Hogan (1910, 21). For the variant spelling *air-* and *ur-* see *SG* III §3.3. *DIL* cites the reading of B s.v. *airbuile* (preceded by a question mark) and suggests the meaning 'frenzy', taking the first element as the intensive prefix *air-* and the second as 2 *baile.*

24. *MV* III §176.

Editions: Meyer (1917, 49); Murphy (1961, [73]).

The metre is *ábacht chummaisc* 'mixed humour' (5^2 4^1 4^2 4^1), classified as *écoitchenn.* The example of *ábacht scaílte* 'scattered humour' cited in *MV* III §175 (Murphy 1961, [74]) has a similar syllabic structure (5^2 4^2 4^2 4^2). An example of *ábacht ḟata* 'long humour' is illustrated in *MV* III §173; see no. 72 below.

This stanza describes a practical joke which entailed shaving off someone's beard while he was drunk. *Abucht co n-imdergad* 'jesting so as to raise a blush' is given as one of the signs of a trickster in the *Triads* §90. The subject of our poem was also the victim of a crime, since shaving a person's hair without his consent was treated as an offence. *Bretha Étgid* states that a fine was to be paid for shaving the hair, eyelashes and eyebrows of various classes of individuals; see p. 27 above. A fourteenth century legal text attributed to Giolla na Naomh mac Duinn Shléibhe Mhic Aodhagáin also states that two cows are to be paid in compensation for shaving a person's hair: *da ba isin cnocbeim ⁊ isin giunadh gan lomad* 'two cows for the wound which causes a lump and for the shaving without making bare' (*CIH* ii 694.24).

tallad a ulcha. I follow Murphy in taking *tallad* as the verbal noun of *do-alla* 'takes away', while Meyer reads third singular preterite passive of the same verb and translates 'His beard was taken off him'. Either way, the sense is the same.

25. *MV* III §178.

Edition: Meyer (1919, no. 167).

The metre is *imthecht daill isin chepaig* 'wandering of a blind man in the plot' (6^2, 9^2 9^2, 9^2, 5^2 9^2, 9^2 9^2), classified as *écoitchenn.* Meyer interprets this stanza as a praise poem and classifies it under the heading 'Aus Liedern der Freundschaft' 'From poems of friendship'. The imagery, however, suggests that it is satirical in that the subject is described as preparing food for the people of Ráth Chrúachan while not partaking of it himself. The tasks assigned to him are also menial ones which would not befit a man of high social standing. Winnowing and grinding, for example, were lowly occupations associated with women and female slaves (Kelly 1997, 439, 450).

crim muicce fíada ar áth n-aba. *Crim muicce fíada* 'hart's tongue' (*Phyllitis scolopendrium*) is a type of fern which was used to cure burns. The literal meaning 'garlic of wild pig' may indicate that it is also an edible plant. The significance of the metaphor 'hart's tongue (or wild garlic) mixed with hemlock' is that a poisonous plant (hemlock) has been mixed with an edible and medicinal herb. A similar metaphor is found in *Bretha Nemed Toísech*, where the phrase *áth i fochlucht* 'brooklime mixed with hemlock' describes the *fine*'s acceptance of the son of a promiscuous woman in terms of the mixing of edible and poisonous plants (*CIH* vi 2230.3; Kelly 1997, 310 note 284). The nasalisation of *aba* can be taken as an instance of the confusion of accusative and dative after prepositions in Middle Irish (*SG* III §5.1) and confirms that *áth aba* is to be read as two separate words. This is also indicated by rhyme with *Cadla* in line *a* and by the syllabic structure (each line ends in a disyllable). It is cited as a single word in *DIL* s.v. *athaba.* Kelly (1997, 184 note 10) takes it as two words (*áth aba*) and suggests, *ibid.* 310 note 285, that the second element is genitive singular of *ab* 'river'. He notes that *áth aba* has also been equated with the poisonous plants deadly nightshade and hellebore. Meyer translates 'Zungenfarn an der Furt des Flusses' 'fern's tongue on the ford of the river', taking the first element as *áth* 'ford'.

brígrad. *DIL* s.v. *bríg* col. 189, l. 28 takes this as a compound of *bríg* 'power' and *-rád* 'speech', although rhyme with *tírad* indicates that the vowel of the second element is short. I follow Meyer in taking the second element as the collective suffix *-rad,* as found in *macrad* 'boys', *damrad* 'oxen' etc. The form *brígrad* is also found in *Met. Dind.* IV, 200 64–5: *mar cach linn cen líg-blad / nísbaí brígrad búadach* 'like a pool void of lustre: she lost her victorious powers'.

do Ráith chlíathad Crúachan. *doraith cliathad cruachadh* B, *doraith cliathban cruachan* M. *Chlíathad* is inserted between the elements of the placename Ráth Chrúachan, the royal site of Rathcroghan in Co. Roscommon. I have followed the reading of B for rhyme with *bríathar* and *críathar.* Meyer follows M and reads *do Ráith chlíathbán Crúachan,* taking *clíathbán* as a compound of *clíath* 'woven fence' and *bán* 'white' in the sense 'with white wattles'.

26. *MV* III §192.

A slightly different version of this poem is cited in *MV* I §69 and *MV* II §89 to illustrate the metre *lethmimasc* (Meyer 1909, 25 §73; 1917, 42; 1919, no. 75; Murphy 1961, [61]). Ó hAodha (2002, 238–9) suggests that it is a later addition to the tracts. Note that the readings *co cnámaib cinn* in Murphy's edition are taken from our text.

The metre of the version in *MV* III is classified as *écoitchenn* and it is introduced by the phrase *Arosc rere so* B, *Arosc rere inso* M. Thurneysen interprets this as *a rosc rere* in his diplomatic editon of the text (1891, 102 §192) but as *rosc rere Seastain* in the index of metres (1891, 176). The word division in *a rosc rere* indicates that he took *a* to be the possessive pronoun, referring to *seastain* in the name of the preceding stanza, *toirrcheas seastain* (*MV* III §191). Murphy (1961, 76) suggests that *árosc réire* may mean 'utterance in accordance with demand'. An alternative explanation suggested by *DIL*, s.v. *ríar* col. 59, ll. 45, 56, is that the name of the metre has dropped out and the metrical illustration is introduced simply by the common phrase *árosc rére* 'for instance'.

The syllabic structure is 8^2 7^1 7^1 7^1 7^3 7^1 and the lines have been divided on the basis of end-rhyme between *thall* : *ann* : *chrann* and *aicill* rhyme between *imm* : *cinn.* The first couplet, which is not found in the version in *MV* I §69, is difficult to interpret but the verse seems to be a complaint that the poet's household has been given an unappetising diet of salt on dry bread with bones, with the result that their skin has shrivelled up like bark.

cuilbir. This is the only example cited in *DIL* and no meaning is given.

nó binn, siu ná thall. *nobindsiu nathall* B, *nocobindsiu nathall* M. B's reading gives a syllabic count of 7^1 against M's 8^1. The context suggests that *binn* is a noun and I tentatively take it to be a substantive use of the adjective *binn* 'melodious; pleasing'. *Siu* 'here' can also be used of this world as opposed to *thall* 'the next world'; see *DIL* s.v. 1 *siu.*

salann ar arán. A similar image is found in the *Fodlai Aíre* tract §2, where a satirist complains that he does not want salt sprinkled on his paltry serving of food since his tongue has already dried up like bark.

is men ann. In his editions of version of this poem in *MV* I and II, Meyer reads *is menann* (1909, 25 §73, 1917, 42) and *is menand* (1919, no. 75) 'it is clear'. Murphy reads *is men ann* 'with meal in it'.

27. *MV* III §196.

The metre is *deibide airenn chorránach* 'hooked [extended] *deibide airenn*' (7^1 3^3 ; 7^2 3^3 3^3), classified as *écoitchenn.* The pattern of rhyme is similar to no. 15 above (*in laíd lúascach is lugu*) in that there is *rinn/airdrinn* rhyme between the endwords of lines *ab* and *cd* (*thé* : *Conaire* and *galar* : *felgabar*) and rhyme between the endwords of lines *be* (*Conaire* : *fonaide*). This is a curse against the victim, rather than a satire ridiculing specific vices or personal characteristics.

thé. *DIL* s.v. *te, té* states that the vowel is 'both long and short in (syllabic) verse'. L. Breatnach (2003, 137 §6) has shown that rhymes such as *immallē* : *tē* and *tē* : *nglē* indicate that the vowel of *té* is long in Early Irish. This is also the case in *dé* (line *a*).

Conaire. *DIL* cites the first two lines s.v. *conar* 'way, road', col. 425, l. 44. It is difficult to see how a genitive singular form of *conar* would make sense here and I therefore take *Conaire* as a personal name, rhyming with *fonaide.* An alternative is to read *co n-aire* 'with a burden', which would give *deibide* rhyme between *té* and *aire* but would lead to the loss of rhyme between lines *b* and *e.*

dá. *da* BE, *d*<.> M. BE show the loss of the OIr. feminine dual form *dí.* Only the first letter is legible in M.

felgabar. *fealgalar* B, *felgabur* M, *fealgalar no feoil gabar* E. BE read *galar* 'disease' as the second element of this compound. M reads *gabur* 'goat', while E corrects *galar* to *no feoil gabar* 'rather "flesh of goats"'. This suggests that the second element is *gabar*, rather than *galar.* A trisyllabic word is required for metrical purposes. For *fel* instead of *fell* in compounds see *DIL* s.v. *fell* col. 72, l. 54 ff.

28. *MV* III §202.

The metre is *dúthracht Moga Ruith do Ṡimón* 'Mug Ruith's prayer to Simon' (7^3 7^3 7^3; 8^3 6^1 6^3; 7^1 4^1 6^3), classified as *écoitchenn.* Mug Ruith was said to have studied druidism under Simon Magus in Italy and he is portrayed in Irish apocryphal tradition as the executioner of John the Baptist (O'Leary 2001). A Middle Irish poem (Ó Cuív 1973, 102–13) on the beheading of John the Baptist states that John asked God to curse the Irish because of Mug Ruith's act, and this may account for his association with the metrical name of a satire.

Dergáin. *dregain* BE, *dergain* M. Both *Dergán* and *Dregin* (genitive) are attested as personal names; see *DIL* s.v. I follow M's reading against BE on the grounds that the first element of the name is echoed in the following adjective *derg.* Cf. also *A uí dínnim Dergáin* 'O shabby grandson of Dergán' no. 37.

a díultad Día Belltaine. The description 'you refusal on May Day' suggests that the subject is being criticised for failing to honour his contractual obligations; see p. 11 above.

becnárach. *becnaireach* BE, *becnarach* M. I follow M against BE for rhyme with *dretránach* and *etránach.*

gercaide. This is the only example in *DIL*, where it is suggested that it is an adjective from *gercc* 'grouse'; cf. *sinnchaide* 'fox-like' from *sinnach* 'fox' no. 55.

drenntaide. This word is not cited in *DIL*. I take it as an adjective from *drennad* 'quarrel' plus the suffix *-aide. Drenntaide* and *gercaide*, both of which are otherwise unattested, may have been coined for *breccad* rhyme with *Belltaine* and *eltaide.*

dretránach. *dreadanach* B, *dredranach* M, *d<.>ednanach* E. Rhymes with *becnárach* and *etránach.* The MSS reflect three different forms, none of which is attested elsewhere: *dretánach* B, *dretránach* M and *dretnánach* E. The reading of B is unsuitable metrically. *DIL* cites lines *ef* s.v. ?*dredánach* (based on B) but does not give a translation, although the context suggests that this adjective is pejorative. With B's *dreadanach* cf. Modern Irish *dradán* 'a (drunken) gabbler' (Ó Donaill) and *dradánacht* 'lingering about a tavern in a state of intoxication' (Dinneen). Some such meaning would suit the present context in the light of the description of the subject as *ic gol tís it churn dub* 'weeping below into your black drinking-horn'.

etránach. This is the only example cited in *DIL*, where the meaning 'meddlesome' is suggested.

29. *MV* III §205.

The metre is *cúanairt chorránach Chon Roí* 'Cú Roí's hooked [extended] pack of hounds' (8^3 8^3, 8^3 8^3, 8^3 8^3, 8^3 8^3), classified as *écoitchenn.* The reference here may be to Cú Roí mac Dáire, who was betrayed and killed by Cú Chulainn in the tale *Aided Con Roí maic Dáire* (Best 1905). The personal names Cú Roí and Cú Chulainn both contain the element *cú* 'hound' and a Middle Irish poem (Meyer 1901, 41) describes the fight between the two warriors as *dā choin ac congail ferda* 'two hounds manfully fighting'. An association such as this may account for the use of *cúanairt* 'pack of hounds' as the metrical name of this satire.

The subject is described as being unskilled in poetry, as indicated by the unfavourable comparison with the poetic bands in the mound of Cíarraige, and it is also stated that his power lies in the use of a weapon rather than in his poetic craft. There may be a connection between this verse and no. 16 above, in which the poet complains that he has been badly treated by the Cíarraige.

nocho gairit ... nocho chosmail. For other satires which contain a series of negative statements see p. 10 above.

Cáenraige. *caenrige* B, *caenraighe* M, <. . .> *aige* E. Rhymes with *cháem-buide.* Thurneysen reads *caemríge* B (1891, 104) and *caemhraighe* M (1912, 71). The stroke over *-ae-* in B looks more like an *n*-stroke, however, while M has a *plene* reading. Several examples of Cáenraige are given in Hogan (1910, 136). All of these are located in Munster. One is in Co. Limerick, for example, while in another instance Cáenraige is used as a variant for Éoganacht Chaisil. To the examples in Hogan may be added *triúcha céad Caonraighe atá cois na Sionainne,* which the editor identifies as the barony of Kenry (Mac Piarais 1908, 7 §9).

gelugud. See note on *gelugud* no. 16.

ro ben mór do ṡuáig ṡochaide. *robhean robean mor do ṡuaidh sochaidhe* B, *roben mor dosuaidh socaide* M, *robean mor dosuaid sochaidhe* E. I take *mór* as a substantive use of the adjective and *suáig* as a compound of *so/su-* 'good' and *ág* 'fight'; cf. *DIL* s.v. *so-* col. 308, l. 74.

ídlaide. The basic meaning is 'heathen, pertaining to idols', from *idal* 'an idol'. *DIL* s.v. suggests an extended meaning 'engraved or adorned with images (of heathen deities)?' and this seems to be the sense in which it is used in our text. Note the parallelism in the phrases *co n-arm cháembuide chírmaire* and *re arm n-íarnaide n-ídlaide.*

30. *MV* III §210.

Edition: Meyer (1919, no. 164).

The metre is *trírech* 'threefold [metre]' (8^2 4^2 8^2 6^2), classified as *écoitchenn.* A slightly different version of this verse in the metre *dechnad mór* is cited in the *Fodlai Aíre* tract §15 (p. 58 above) as an example of *lánáer* 'full satire'. Meyer, *op. cit.*, classifies this verse under the heading *Aus Liedern der Freundschaft* 'From songs of friendship', although the description of Cíanán as 'a bag of wild oats' is clearly meant as an insult.

ara féssid. The version in the *Fodlai Aíre* tract reads *mad áil dúib ro-féssid* 'if you wish you shall know'.

píanán. For a discussion of this word see p. 80 above. M glosses *píanán* as *.i. rus.* Neither *rus* 'cheeks' nor *rús* 'knowledge' would make sense in the context and M's reading may be an error for *rúsc* 'bark', used here in the extended meaning of 'a receptacle made of bark'.

dona Déssib. This is glossed as *us* 'lineage' in all three MSS, while the first element of *trírech*, the name of the metre, is explained by the etymological gloss *trí áirigthe inti .i. ainm ⁊ uss .i. slondud ⁊ domnas* 'there are three specified things in it, i.e. name and lineage, i.e. family name and abode'. *Cíanán* is *ainm*, *Cell Do Chellóc* is *domgnas* and *dona Déssib* is *uss.* For the triad *ainm ⁊ us ⁊ domgnas* see p. 79 above.

31. *MV* III §12.

The metre is *deibide scaílte chorránach* 'hooked [extended] *deibide scaílte*' (7^1, 7^2 7^2 ; 7^1, 7^3 7^2), classified as *gnáthaiste.* The metrical structure of this stanza has been discussed by Ó Cuív (1989, 55), who notes that, although *corránach* forms did not come into general use, an example cited in *IGT* V provides evidence that experimentation in such extended forms continued into the later period.

Con Lemna. *conleamhna* B *conlenna* M, *conlena* E. I follow B in reading *Lemna*, genitive singular of the placename *Líamain*, rhyming with *chlemna. Cú* 'hound' qualified by a placename in the genitive (e.g. Cú Ulad) is a common formula in personal names (O'Brien 1973, 228). Cf. also *drúth Lemna* 'the fool of Líamain' no. 59 and *lon ic longaire i Líamain* 'a blackbird screeching in Líamain' no. 63.

nít choiclenn. *nicoitgleann B, nit coigleann M, nicoiglenn E.* I take this as Middle Irish third singular present indicative of *coiglid* 'conceals, spares, protects' (earlier *con-ceil*) plus second person singular infixed pronoun as found in M. B's *nicoitgleann* appears to be a corruption of the form with the infixed pronoun.

a chorr líathróite lubain. The subject is likened to the end of a tassel on a garment, possibly in the sense that it trails along the ground and becomes dirty and ragged. Note the similar description *deired líathróite for lúth* 'the end of a ball on the move' no. 85. Other allusions to a dirty appearance or ragged clothing are: *senáraig corra / chromma, chama fot chossaib* 'old, pointed, bent, crooked bindings around your feet' no. 53;

a ṡailchide ṡinnchaide ṡalachluim 'you dirty one, fox-like, filthy and naked' no. 55; *úrad buide ar brat gamna* 'a yellow patch on a calfskin cloak' no. 76.

a cholpthach i cennach ndaim. *a colbthach acendach ndaim* B, *acholbthach icendach ndaim* M, *acolpach iceannacht ndaimh* E. For an explanation of this phrase see p. 34. *DIL* suggests that *cennach* may be a neuter noun and cites B's reading *cendach ndaim* in support of this. The nasalisation of *daim* is caused by the fact that *cennach* is in the accusative after the preposition *i*, however. E differs from BM in reading *cennacht* 'leadership'.

d'argatlaim. Kelly (1997, 257–8) notes that although *Bretha Déin Chécht* lists *arcetluim* as one of three foreign herbs with healing properties, it is explained elsewhere as the mineral orpiment. It is likely to be used in the latter sense here, i.e. a draught of a poisonous substance.

32. *MV* III §15.

Editon: Murphy (1961, [131]).

The metre is *deibide imrinn chenntromm* 'heavy-headed *deibide imrinn*' (8^2 8^4 ; 8^2 8^4), classified as *gnáthaiste.* The adjective *imrinn* indicates that, in addition to *rinn/airdrinn* rhyme, there is also full rhyme between the couplets. Meyer (1909, 18, note 1) states that *cenntromm* indicates the extension of the end-rhyme from three to four syllables.

This satire resembles the example of *tamall molta* 'touch of praise' cited in the *Fodlai Aíre* tract §14 (p. 58 above) in that the insult becomes apparent only at the end. In the present instance the subject, despite being hailed as king of a prosperous land, is made to look ridiculous by being described as riding a pack-horse.

Flannacán úa Cellaig. For a suggestion as to his identity see p. 118.

taicedbennaig. *taicedbennaigh* B, *taigedh pendaig* M, *taiceda pennaig* E. Rhymes with *aicedphellaig.* The reading of E is hypersyllabic. *DIL* s.v. *tocad* 'good fortune, prosperity' takes this as a compound of the later form *taiced* and *bennach* 'peaked' and suggests the meaning 'of prosperous hills'. If, as suggested by Thurneysen (1912, 87), Flannacán úa Cellaig is a king of Brega, *bennach* probably means 'hilled' rather than 'peaked' or 'mountainous'.

a gabáil ṡréin brainig bennaig. *Bennach* 'pointed, peaked; horned' may be used here to mean ornamented with horn. *DIL* s.v. *bennach* col. 76, l. 52 suggests the meaning '(of a bridle) edged with points (?)'.

aicedphellaig. *acetpellaig* BM, *aicedpellaigh* E. *DIL* cites this line s.v. ?*acetpellach.* Murphy does not translate the term but suggests (1961, 94) that the simplex *pellach* would mean 'having a rug' or 'having rugs'. I take this as genitive singular of a compound of *aiced* 'materials, implements' and *pellach*, an adjective from *pell* 'skin, rug'. Murphy's emendation to *aicedphellaig* is supported by the reading of E.

33. *MV* III §56.

Editions: Meyer (1919, no. 81); Murphy (1961, [95]).

The metre is *cró cummaisc etir rannaigecht móir ocus casbairdne* 'an enclosure composed of a mixture between *rannaigecht mór* and *casbairdne*' (7^3 7^1 7^3 7^1), classified as *gnáthaiste.*

Scélín. *screitlin* B, *screllin* B^b, *screlin* M, *sclerig* E, *scelin* H. The MSS show a variety of forms. Meyer reads *Scélín* against Murphy's *Screllín. Scélín* may be a diminutive form of *scél* 'story' used as a nickname and may therefore be more appropriate in the context of satire. Cf. *a uí Scandail* no. 45.

scuitemail. This adjective is otherwise unattested and is taken as a derivative of *scuit* 'buffoon, laughing-stock' in *DIL* s.v.

minn. Rhymes with *chinn.* Meyer takes *minn* as genitive singular of the adjective *menn* 'stammering'. Since *chinn* (OIr. *chiunn*) ends in a broad consonant, the rhyming word must be genitive plural of *minn* 'diadem'. Murphy, *op. cit.* 116, suggests 'venerated object, (religious) relic'.

34. *MV* III §78.

The metre is *carrannaigecht mór ocus carrannaigecht becc i cummusc* '*carrannaigecht mór* and *carrannaigecht becc* in a mixture' (9^1 11^2 11^1 11^2), classified as *gnáthaiste.* It consists of alternating, extended lines of *rannaigecht mór* (ending in a monosyllable) and *rannaigecht becc* (ending in a disyllable). As noted by Meyer (1909, 15 note 1) and Thurneysen (1891, 131), the terms *carr* and *carn* in names of metres appear to be synonymous. Meyer (*op. cit.*) states of the metre *carnrannaigecht mór* that the 'addition of *carn* (*carr*) to the name of a metre denotes that an original metre of six or seven syllables has been extended to eight syllables'. It is clear from the present stanza, however, that lines can be extended to more than eight syllables. *Carr* is also applied to an extended form of *dechnad* in no. 57 below. Thurneysen (1891, 85) prints this stanza as continuous prose.

liúin. *leoin* BME. I have emended to *liúin* for *aicill* rhyme with *siúil.* This form is not well attested, however, and *aicill* rhyme is not obligatory in this position.

ar argat. E reads *arargad*, rhyming with *charpat*, while BM omit this reading. *A chuing ar argat* seems to be a metaphor for an unequal bargain; for other examples see p. 34 above.

sirthe. I take this as genitive singular of *siriud*, verbal noun of *sirid* 'wanders', used here in the sense of 'a (light) reconnoitoring or raiding party'.

a gait. *icait* BM, *agaid* E. This is the only stressed word in line *c* which is not fixed by rhyme with a word in line *d*. I follow E for alliteration with *gerrfile* since this is a feature of lines *a* and *d*.

a gait balláin etir dá scrín. An entry in *Corm.* Y §48 states that it was customary for kings to leave silver drinking vessels beside wells for passers-by to drink from. If the vessels were not stolen, this was a sign that law and order was being upheld during their reign: *Fri hōl tra do dāinib scīthaib esib dobertis na lestair-si forsna tibradaib ⁊ ba ō rīgaib dobertis forra do promad a cāna* 'These vessels used to be placed on the wells for weary people to drink from them and they used to be placed by kings in order to test their rule'. I am grateful to Liam Breatnach for this reference.

A description of a well in the poem *Echtra Mac Echdach Mugmedóin* also seems to allude to the presence of drinking vessels. Here the editor translates the phrase *conaca in tiprait túagaig n-escraig* as 'he saw the fountain's falling arch of waters', suggesting (note 2) that *escrach* may be from *escor* 'fall' (Joynt 1908–10, 100 §34). *DIL* s.v. *escrach* is probably correct, however, in taking this as an adjective from *escra* 'vessel', since *escor* 'fall' is normally used of a fall from horseback (as in *láir is láech ic léim íar n-escur uirre* 'a mare with a warrior jumping onto her after falling off' no. 75).

Although neither text states that the drinking vessels were tied in place, some such usage may lie behind the phrase *a gait balláin* in our poem. By likening the subject to something fragile and easily broken like a withe tied to a goblet, the poet may be hinting that he will be short-lived. A similar idea is conveyed by comparing him to an old wooden helmet among flames (line *d*).

chrannáin. *cran curudaibh* B, *crandain* ME. B's reading is corrupt, since this word rhymes with *balláin*. *DIL* cites two examples of *crannán*, a diminutive form of *crann* 'tree, spearshaft', but omits the present example.

35. *MV* III §84.

Edition: Meyer (1919, no. 83).

The metre is *ochtrannaigecht chorránach becc* 'eight-fold hooked [extended] *rannaigecht becc*' (4 x [7^2 7^2]), classified as *gnáthaiste.*

A Gilla Duinn. *Gilla* qualified by an adjective can be used as a personal name or nickname; see *DIL* s.v. (e). Other examples of nicknames incorporating *Gilla* are *Gilla inn Ime* 'the Butter Lad' (*Ann. Conn. s.a.* 1276) and *in Gilla Ballach* 'the Spotty Boy' (*ibid., s.a.* 1412 §11). Cf. also *Gille in Chataig* no. 38 below. *Gilla* is normally qualified by a saint's name (O'Brien 1973, 229–30), e.g. *A Gilla leóchaill leccaig Mo Laise* no. 36, *Gilla Cellaig* no. 64 and *Gilla Pátraic* no. 78; cf. also *Gilla in Naím* no. 59. Meyer reads *A gilla duinn* 'du brauner Bursche' 'you brown lad'.

Dermaig. Meyer incorrectly renders *Dermag* 'Durrow' as 'Derry'.

bruinn. *bruigh* B, *bruind .i. brondaigh* M, *bronnaigh* E. Rhymes with *Duinn.* Meyer follows B (which omits *mías*) and reads *a bruig*, vocative singular of *brod* 'straw, splinter, speck', with confusion of *-gh* and *-dh.* This gives only six syllables, however. Based on M's suprascript gloss *.i. brondaig* and E's reading *bronnaig*, I take *bruinn* as genitive singular of an otherwise unattested word **bronn* 'chaff'; cf. Modern Irish *bronnach* 'husks'.

a thonn do cheólaib cléirig. The description of the subject as an 'outpouring of melodies of a cleric' and as *cailech d'Úíb Cellaig* 'the cock of the Uí Cellaig' may allude to his voice. Clerics would have been required to sing the Mass and Office and presumably not all liturgical singing would have been of a high standard. Alternatively, he may be a poet who is being criticised for his style of poetry or performance, although it is impossible to be certain due to the lack of context. Note, however, the reference to *dúan* 'poem' in line *d.*

a dúan ar airech n-ellaig. *DIL* s.v. 1 *ellach* 'joining', col. 122, l. 20, suggests that *ar aireach n-ellaig* may mean 'on a harnessed horse'. I take *ellaig* as genitive singular of 2 *ellach* 'goods, property', lit. 'you poem in exchange for a pack-horse of goods' (i.e. a loaded pack-horse). This may be another metaphor for an unequal bargain, since a praise poem would have commanded a more valuable award. For similar examples see p. 34 above. Meyer translates 'du Lied auf einen Packgaul' 'you song to a pack-horse'.

a fertas áraid. The sense here may be that a rung of a ladder is useless on its own; cf. *fíacail círe* 'a tooth of a comb' no. 73. There are several other references to useless objects and undertakings in our poems: *a* *tholltimpáin* 'you pierced *timpán*' no. 41; *a glas cam* 'you crooked bolt' no. 44; *a chris cen scín* 'you belt without a knife' no. 50; *a ól íar n-ítaid* 'you drink after thirst' no. 51. *Fertas* is also used in an insulting sense in no. 43 below, although the context is less clear.

36. *MV* III §106.

Editions: Meyer (1909, 22 §54); Murphy (1961, [38]).

The metre is *sétrad gablánach* 'branched *sétrad*' ($10^2\ 9^1\ 10^2\ 9^1$), classified as *gnáthaiste.* The adjective *gablánach* 'branched' indicates that two syllables have been added to each line of *sétrad mór* ($8^2\ 7^1\ 8^2\ 7^1$).

Gilla Mo Laise. Murphy follows Meyer in taking *leccaig* as the first element of a placename *Lecach Mo Laise.* I have not found any examples of such a placename and therefore take *leccaig* as an adjective qualifying the personal name *Gilla Mo Laise.*

leóchaill. *leochaille* B, *lecchuille* M, *leochaille* E. I follow Murphy in emending to *leóchaill* as this gives a line of ten syllables. Meyer retains *leochaille.*

a lecca cuirre garbglaise grían. For *corr* 'heron, crane' as an abusive epithet see p. 36 above. *Corr* is sometimes qualified by *glas* 'grey' and *grían* 'of river bottoms' and Stokes (1906–07, 185) notes that *corrghlas* corresponds to 'stork' while *corrghrian* corresponds to 'heron' in the Irish translation of the Bible. Both terms are combined here.

ar másaib. *armaslaidh* BE, *armaslaid* M. Meyer, *op. cit.*, reads *maslaid,* dative singular of *masla/maslad* 'insult', declined as a feminine noun. A long vowel is required for *aicill* rhyme with *fásaig,* however (Meyer 1909, 21 note). I follow Murphy in emending to *másaib,* dative plural of *más* 'buttock'.

folta. Murphy (1961, 108) suggests that this is genitive singular of a verbal noun *folad* 'moulting', citing the examples *ag fola, folta* and *folaim* from Modern Irish.

dar fíad. Cf. *cú dar céisib* 'a hound mounting piglets' no. 58. Murphy takes *fíad* to mean 'wild land'.

37. *MV* III §119.

Edition: Meyer (1919, no. 84).

The metre is *rinnard* ($6^2\ 6^2\ 6^2\ 6^2$), classified as *gnáthaiste.*

Dergáin. I take this as a personal name; cf. *A Dergáin deirg díultadaig* no. 28. Note that for E's *Ahudinnimh dergain,* Mackechnie (1973, Vol. 1, 115) incorrectly reads *A hudinnim dergain dergam (?).*

a rann. I take *rann* as referring to a part of the body, possibly in an obscene sense.

a chertaig. This is the only example given in *DIL* s.v. 2 ?*certach*, where Meyer's translation is cited ('du Lumpenkerl aus Cork!' 'you ragged lad from Cork!'). It is a substantival use of an adjective from *ceirt* 'rag'.

38. *MV* III §126.

The metre is *rinnard chorránach becc* 'hooked [extended] *rinnard becc*' (5^2 5^2, 5^2 ; 5^2 5^2, 5^2), classified as *gnáthaiste.*

a errmór. *Aere mor* B, *Ahermor* M, *Aṡearr mor* E. Rhymes with *mellṡrón.* I take this as a compound of *err* 'point' and *mór* 'big'. T. F. O'Rahilly (1927, 238) notes that compound adjectives, like other adjectives, may be used poetically as nouns, citing as an example *a shlisgheal* 'o bright-sided one'. The first element of E's reading appears to be *serr* 'sickle'.

athbruit. *aahbruit* BE, *athbruit* M. I take this as genitive singular of *brot* 'goad' and the prefix *ath-* 'worn-out'; cf. *a athbró íchtair* 'you worn-out lower quern' no. 51.

a ithe imme re harán secail. The significance of this phrase may lie in the fact that butter was a luxury food (see p. 205 above), while rye was associated with the nobility (Kelly 1997, 219 and 221). The implication may be that the subject is not entitled to such foods.

a Gille in Chataig. I take this as a nickname ('Lad of the Treaty'), reading *Gille* for rhyme with *imme* in line *c.* For other examples of nicknames incorporating *Gilla* see note on *Gilla Donn,* p. 220 above.

39. *MV* III §140.

Edition: Murphy (1961, [136]).

The metre is *ochtḟoclach becc* (5^2 5^2, 5^2 4^1 ; 5^2 5^2, 5^2 4^1), classified as *gnáth medónda.* Thurneysen (1891, 93) and Murphy (*op. cit.*) present this poem as eight short lines, which is the normal convention for this type of metre. *Aicill* rhyme, end-rhyme and internal rhyme are highlighted by presenting the examples of *ochtḟoclach* in *MV* III as four extended lines (as in no. 19 above). Note the rhyme between voiced and voiceless stops in *laic* (b) : *cait* (d). For other examples see p. 198.

is. *ocus* BM. The reading of the MSS gives one extra syllable.

do chossa. *darcosa* B, *darcossa* M. I follow Murphy in emending *dar* to *do* and read *cáela do chossa* 'skinny your feet'. This echoes the structure of the preceding phrase *beca do bossa* 'small your hands'. The reading *dar* may have arisen through the influence of *dar cossa,* which is written in the following line in both manuscripts.

barr. This is an example of the use of nominative for vocative; see p. 127 above.

rossa. As Murphy notes (1961, 120), the treatment of *ros* as a *u*-stem is unusual.

40. *MV* III §160.

The metre is *sechtbricht* 'sevenfold *bricht*' (18^5 18^5 17^5 23^5), classified as *anaichnid.* The lines have been divided on the basis of end-rhyme between *caratgréchánaig* (b) and *canatgréchánaig* (d) and alliteration. Metres with pentasyllabic endwords are highly unusual and there are no examples of such types in the standard reference works on metrics by Meyer (1909) and Murphy (1961). Ó Cuív (1967–68, 275–6) draws attention to varieties of *ceanntrom na ceanntruime* illustrated in *IGT* V which have hepta- and pentasyllabic end-words.

The metrical structure of this stanza is particularly complex and there is frequent alliteration, internal rhyme, *breccad* rhyme and consonance. Note the repetition of *bodur-*, *comar-*, *-gréchánaig*, *-lúpánaig* and *-grúcánaig*, which is a feature of *breccad.* It also contains a number of adjectives ending in *-ánach* which seem to have been coined specifically for metrical purposes; see p. 126 above.

doburlúpánaig. *DIL* cites both instances of *-lúpánaig* in our text (*doburlúpánaig* and *cuarlúpánaig* line *d*) s.v. *lubanach.* The meaning 'grizzled' is given and the reader is referred to *luban* 'tassel'. The metre requires a long vowel, however, and I take *-lúpánach* as an adjective from *lúp* 'loop, circle' plus the suffix *-ánach.*

-métlánaig. This word is not cited in *DIL.* I take it as an adjective derived from *métal* 'a paunch' plus the suffix *-ánach.* The first element in the compound is the adjective *bodur* 'deaf', which can be used of harsh or grating sounds; see *DIL* s.v. *bodar* col. 133, ll. 38–42 and 59–60.

chomargrúcánaig comardídánaig. *comorgruganaigh comordidanaigh* B, *comorgruanigh chomar ditanaigh* M. I take *comar-* in these compounds as *com* 'equally' plus the intensive prefix *ar.* I take *-dídánaig* as dative singular of the adjective *dánach* 'skilled' plus the negative prefix *dí.* Note that M reads *comorgruanigh.*

caratgréchánaig. I take the first element as the composition form of *carae* 'friend' and the second element as an adjective derived from *gréch* 'a scream' plus the suffix *-ánach. DIL* cites this line s.v. 2 *cara* 'haunch, leg; side'.

a uí airim. *ahua airim* B, *ahua bairb* M. I follow B against M, which appears to be corrupt. I have also emended the nominative form *úa* in the MSS to vocative.

brocṡalaig. M reads *broc sadhail*, a compound of *broc* and *sádail* 'ease, comfort'.

amarmícháanaig. I tentatively take this as genitive singular of a compound of *amar* 'singing; wailing' with the pejorative particle *mí* and *cánach*, an adjective from *cáin* 'law, regulation'. *Amarmíchánaig* qualifies genitive singular *airim*. I have found no other examples of an adjective *cánach*, however.

aladlíacánaig. *DIL* cites this line s.v. *ladlíacanach*, suggesting that the first element may be *ladg* 'snow'. This is impossible on metrical grounds, since the lines end in words of five syllables. I take the first element to be *alad* 'variegated' and the second element as an adjective formed from *líacán* 'stone pillar'.

gaillín. I take this as genitive singular of *gaillín*, with the diminutive suffix *-ín* for earlier *-én* (*GOI* §272). *Gaillén/gaillín* 'capon' is derived from Latin *gallus* 'cock' (Kelly 1997, 103). The present example is not cited in *DIL*.

detbudánaig. This form is not cited in *DIL* and I have found no other examples. I take it as containing the same first element as in the word given in *DIL* as *detfadach, detbudach* 'smoky, misty (?)' with the suffix *-ánach* rather than *-ach*.

caladgríantrágthaig. *caladgriantragthaigh* B, *caladgriantragthanigh* M. I follow the reading of B which rhymes imperfectly with *aladlíacánaig* and, like many of the compound adjectives in this stanza, has five syllables. The first element is *calad* 'hard'. I take *-trágthaig* as an adjective from *trágud* 'ebbing, drying up'. M's reading *-thanaigh* may have come about due to the large number of adjectives ending in *-ánaig*. I take the second element as *grían* 'gravel' rather than *grían* 'sun' on the grounds that gravel is referred to elsewhere in *MV* III in contexts which suggest that it was associated with harsh or rasping sounds and the subject of this stanza is described as screeching (*caratgréchánaig*) and wailing (*amarmíchánaig*). Two stanzas refer to the sound of horses' hooves on gravel: *A fogar ingen ngobar ar grenaig* 'O sound of horses' hooves on gravel' (*MV* III §93) and *A ṡeinm na n-ingen ngabar ar grenaig* 'O sound of the horses' hooves on gravel' (*MV* III §94). Note that *seinm* is normally used of the sound of musical instruments. Gravel is associated with the playing of foreign pipes in a difficult text which may be satirical: *cor ṡén de grían gaillfetána* 'so that he charmed foreign pipes with [the sound of] gravel' (*MV* III

§116b). The final reference does not allude to sound but nevertheless is interesting in the context of satire. The phrase *ac íarraid na gile a grenaig* 'seeking the brightness from gravel' (*MV* III §87) is a metaphor for a futile undertaking (i.e. grasping at the sparkles of light reflected in gravel at the bottom of a river or lake). A similar idea is expressed in phrases such as *a gleic im thuinn* 'you wrestling with a wave' no. 42, *is glac um ghath gréine* 'it is grasping at a sunbeam' (Hyde 1899, 86) and *dorn im diaid* 'grasping at smoke' (O'Dav. §1586; note that Stokes mistakenly translates this as 'a fist after me'). Lists of such futile undertakings are found in a number of texts, including the *Fodlai Aíre* tract on satire; see p. 66 above.

canatgréchánaig. I take the first element as a composition form of *cano* 'whelp'. The second element is the same as in *caratgréchánaig* (line *b*).

41. *MV* III §165.

Edition: Meyer (1919, no. 62).

The metre is *débricht* 'twofold *bricht*' (7^2 8^2 12^2 8^2), classified as *anaichnid.* The stanza has been divided into lines on the basis of end-rhyme *aílig* (b) : *saíbḟir* (d) and imperfect *aicill* rhyme between *Alcáin* (c) : *ardáin* (d). *Ardáin* (d) also rhymes with *Thadcáin* (c).

srethḟíar. *sreathar* B, *srathfiar* M. I follow Meyer in taking this as a compound of *sreth* 'row, line' and *fíar* 'crooked'. *DIL* s.v. *sreth* col. 372, l. 46 suggests 'with distorted features (?)'.

a uí Thadcáin. *atadgain* B, *aahui tadhgain* M. In B the victim and his father are identified, while in M his father and grandfather are named. Either manuscript reading is possible, since the stanza is syllabically irregular.

a thoilltimpáin. *DIL* s.v. *timpán* suggests '(a) timbrel, drum; (b) some kind of stringed instrument'. The sense is that a perforated skin on a drum would render the instrument useless. *Timpán* refers to a stringed instrument in the phrase *tiompán dhá théd* 'a two-stringed lute' (Quin 1965, 33 q. 39), also used in the sense of something useless.

ardáin. It is difficult to establish if this word is a personal name, place name or the noun *ardán* 'drinking vessel'. I take it to mean 'drinking vessel', since there are four other references to goblets or drinking vessels in our poems: *a gait balláin* 'you withe of a goblet' no. 34; *a choss escra* 'you stem of a goblet' no. 45; *linn i mbleide* 'ale left in a goblet' no. 65; *ballán i mbí bainne lomma* 'a goblet in which there is a drop of milk' no. 66. Meyer takes it as a placename: 'du Pech auf der Tafel voṅ Ardān!' 'you pitch on the border of Ardán'. This is on the assumption that the verse should contain the triad *ainm 7 us 7 domgnas* 'name and lineage and abode', all of which are the characteristics of *lánáer* 'full satire'; see p. 88 above.

Meroney (1950, 124 note 2) agrees with Meyer's interpretation of *ardán* as a placename but notes that *ainm* is missing. *DIL* cites this line under three head-words: *ardán* 'drinking vessel' col. 389, l. 26, *bord* 'edge, border' col. 146, l. 5, where it is translated 'handle on the side of a drinking vessel (?)' and *bí* 'pitch' col. 92, l. 64. In the latter case, however, *ardán* is taken as a personal name and the phrase is translated 'thou pitch on Ardán's table', based on Meyer's edition.

42. *MV* III §183.

Edition: Murphy (1961, [58]).

The metre is *aí idan* 'pure poetry', classified as *écoitchenn*. Murphy analyses the syllabic structure as $9^2\ 9^2\ 9^2\ 9^2$, although it could also be interpreted as $4^1 5^2$, $4^1 5^2$, $4^1 5^2$, $5^2\ 4^1$ (Thurneysen 1981, 147; de Búrca 1971–72, 140). In the latter case, there is linking alliteration between the half-lines, each of which consists of two stressed words. For the repetition of the victim's name in satire see p. 14.

cella do chobair. Lit. 'churches are your help'. This, together with the description 'sparks around churches' in line *c*, suggests that the subject of this satire is a beggar who relies on charity; see p. 30.

a gleic im thuinn. For an explanation of this metaphor see pp. 66 and 225.

a thenga thamain. I take this to refer to one of the sub-grades of poets, for which see p. 29. In no. 8, however, *taman* seems to be used in the primary sense of 'trunk of a tree' or 'stump' in the phrase *a thamain chrín fo choiss cháich* 'you withered stump under everyone's feet'; cf. also *cenn tamain* no. 68 'a block-head'. Note the following definition of the term in the glossary *Dúil Dromma Ceta*: *Tamon .i. fográd filed, fo cosmuilus tamoin .i. crann dia mbenar a barr; síc ille cin manchuine, ní dlig díre acht aithgein* '*Taman*, i.e a sub-grade of poet, like the trunk of a tree, i.e. a tree from which the top is cut off. He is thus without attendants. He is not entitled to honour-price but only to restitution' (CIH ii 620.17–8).

43. *MV* III §189.

Edition: Meyer (1919, no. 86).

The metre is *táescad Segsa* 'outpouring of Segais' (6^2 13^3 5^2 11^2), classified as *écoitchenn*. The metrical structure is unusual in that the main rhyme is between *messair* (a) : *Bressail* (d). The mystical hazels of *Segais* were believed to be a source of poetic inspiration (T. F. O'Rahilly 1946, 322–3; L. Breatnach 1981, 86).

A máelscolb. Although Thurneysen (1912, 87) includes Mael Scolp among a list of unidentified persons in *MV* III, he also notes the possibility that the subject of this stanza may be named at the end (Bressal). This is an argument against interpreting it as a personal name and I follow Meyer in taking it as a compound for alliteration with *messair*.

a eclas crainn. I follow Meyer in taking *eclas* as 2 *eclas* 'stomach' rather than 1 *eclas* 'church'. Describing someone as a 'wooden church' could hardly be construed as an insult, since churches were commonly built of wood.

ḟertas. Cf. *a ḟertas áraid d'Éilib* 'you rung of a ladder from Éile' no. 35.

a braind. *abraind* BM. Meyer emends to *a ḟertas a broinn* 'du Stange aus dem Leibe' 'you pole out of the belly'. I follow the MSS and read *braind* rather than *broinn*, although I have not been able to establish a meaning for this. An alternative is to read a single word *abraind*, alliterating with *ḟertas*. *Aprainn*, which is normally used with the copula as an interjection in the sense 'bad, evil', does not fit the context here, however.

bicire. *bicire* B, *bicere* M. This is the only example cited in *DIL*, where it is described as 'a term of contempt'. The reader is referred to *bigirecht*, which is attested once in a context suggesting that it is a type of game. The form in our text appears to be genitive singular, but I have not been able to establish the meaning from the context.

a Bressail. *abreassail* B, *abresail* M. Meyer reads *a Brēnaind* against the MSS.

44. *MV* III §190.

Edition: Meyer (1919, no. 61).

The metre is *áenḟoclach* 'one-phrased [metre]', classified as *écoitchenn*. This stanza can be analysed either in terms of syllable count (4^2 3^1 4^1 3^1 3^1) or stress, in which case there are two stresses in each of the five phrases (including *uí*). Note the rhyme between *láir mall* and *gáir gall*. Meyer prints it as two lines of 4^2 3^1, 4^1 3^1 3^1.

The victim is described as being as useless as a one-legged goose or a crooked lock in the face of an attack by foreigners. By contrast with the latter metaphor, a stanza in *MV* III §30 praises its subject by addressing him as *a glass ar oscaraib Ērenn* (Meyer 1917, 46; 1919, §31): 'you lock against the enemies of Ireland'.

a glas cam. *aglais cham* B, *aglas cham* M. I follow Meyer in taking this as an example of nominative for vocative of a masculine *o*-stem, since a nominative form of the adjective *cam* rhymes with *mall* and *Gall.* For other examples of nominative for vocative see p. 127. Note that B shows the regular vocative form in the noun (*aglais*), but not in the adjective. Both MSS show lenition of *cam.*

45. *MV* III §191.

Edition: Meyer (1919, no. 73).

The metre is *toirrches sestáin* 'clamorous offspring' (4^2 4^2 4^2 4^2), classified as *écoitchenn.*

Scandail. *scandail* B, *scandlain* M. *Scandal* 'quarrel, contention', from Latin *scandalum,* is found both as a personal name and as an epithet. For *Scandal* and the diminutive *Scandlán* as personal names see *Corp. Gen.* 730 and note that both forms are represented in the MSS. For its use as an epithet cf. *Fearghus Scandal .i. scandal roferadh imme ind aidhchi genair é . . .* 'Fergus Scandal, that is, a quarrel (*scandal*) was raised about him the night he was born . . . ' (Stokes 1897, §51).

46. *MV* III §193.

Edition: Meyer (1919, no. 63).

The metre is *bricht nathrach Néde* 'Néde's venomous incantation' (6^2 6^2 6^2 6^2 6^2 6^2), classified as *écoitchenn.* I take *nathrach,* genitive singular of *nathir* 'snake, serpent', to be used here in the sense of 'poisonous, venomous'; cf. the adjective *natharda* 'serpent-like, venomous, deadly'. *Bricht* is also used as a metrical term; see p. 207 above.

a thigaill. *athigaill* BME. I take this as a compound of 1 *tiug* 'last' (found only in compounds) and 2 *all* 'rein, bridle'. Meyer reads *a thicáill,* which gives an extra rhyme with *gipáin,* and suggests that this may be a compound of *tiug* 'thick' and an unattested word *gáill,* comparing Modern Irish *gáilleach* 'gills; open mouth, jowl'. Meyer's line division differs from the present edition in that he reads *A meic dūir daill iffirnn, a thicāill, / a graphainn ar gairdi do gipāin* 'Du harter blinder Sohn der Hölle, du mit der dicken Backe, du Rennreiter mit deinem kurzen Lumpenkleide' 'You harsh, blind son of hell, you with the thick cheek, you jockey with your short, ragged garment'. This gives a syllabic structure of 9^2 9^2 6^2 6^2

6^2 6^2. Thurneysen (1912, 87) suggests that *tigall* may be a personal name *Tigall (?) hua Bregaig (?) Britain.*

ar graphainn. Meyer emends *ar* to vocative *a* against the MSS. *DIL* s.v. *grafand* suggests that this word may have originally been a neuter noun which later became feminine. I take the form in our text as dative singular of a feminine *ā*-stem; cf. *ar grafainn scaílte sciathcha MV* III §97 (Murphy 1961, [105]).

gipáin. Rhymes with *Britáin.* This is the only example attested in *DIL* s.v. *gibán,* where the meaning 'short ragged garment' is suggested. The adjective *gipánach* 'in ragged garb (?)' occurs in a difficult text in *MV* III §159 which may also be satirical. Cf. *gibach* (Modern Irish *giobach*) 'shaggy, rough'.

a geóid íarna gabáil. Cf. *a dronn geóid íarna gabáil* 'you hump of a captured goose' no. 49.

a feóil tarra togáin. *DIL* s.v. *togán* suggests 'some small animal, sometimes kept as pet; squirrel (?)'. *Togán* 'pine marten' is the shortened form of an older term *togmall* (Kelly 1997, 130 note 202); cf. *dobrán* for *doborchú* 'otter' (*GOI* §270). The pine marten was kept as a pet and a passage of miscellaneous legal material includes a note which indicates that it was not considered appropriate to eat it: *Cach esreacht allaid immorro na domelar, is leth in smachta no na eneclainni fil isin esreacht ceannaigh is cosmail fris, is edh doberar ind-sium .i. amail ro gab sinnach 7 toghan, .ui.id neineclainne indtibh.* 'Every wild pet moreover which is not eaten, it is half the penalty or the honour-price which is [due] for the domesticated pet which is similar to it, it is that which is given for it, i.e. as, for example, a fox and a pine marten: one sixth honour-price [is due] for them' (*CIH* v 1585.28–30).

a ithe i míl étaig. *a ithi imil edaig* B, *a ithi imbil etaigh* M, *aithi inmil etaig* E. *DIL* cites this line s.v. *ithe* (col. 326 l. 24) and translates 'thou that gnawest the edge of clothing?', taking *imil, imbil, inmil* of the MSS as genitive singular of *imbel* 'edge'. Reading *imbil* would give a line of seven syllables, however, whereas all the other lines have six. I follow Meyer in reading the preposition *i* 'in' and 2 *mil* (b) 'louse', which gives six syllables as in the other lines. The phrase 'you eating of a clothes' louse' is also in keeping with the reference to the flesh of a pine marten in the previous line. With this use of *i* cf. *longud i scellaib scibair* 'dining on grains of pepper' (*Fodlai Aíre* tract §3).

47. *MV* III §197.

The MSS give the metrical name as *Eisce feris .i. firesca* (suprascript gloss) B, *Esce feris inso .i. bricht nadrach* M, *Eisce feris .i. far esca* (suprascript gloss) *.i. bricht natrach* E. It is classified as *écoitchenn*. *DIL* s.v. *eisce* suggests that this word may be *ésca/éisce* 'the moon' rather than *eisce* 'intention to damage, slay or wound'. In the context of satire, however, the latter meaning is more appropriate, particularly since the phrase is glossed *.i. bricht nadrach* in M and *.i. bricht natrach* in E; cf. *bricht nathrach Néde* 'Néde's venomous incantation' no. 46. I do not understand *feris*, which is explained in an etymological gloss as *fír* 'true' in B and *far* in E. The syllabic structure is irregular (3^1 9^2 9^2 9^1 10^2) but there is a regular stress pattern which consists of units of two stressed words (including *uí* in line *a*). Aside from the first line, these are grouped together into longer lines of two units each. There is alliteration between each two-unit line (*daim* and *drochḟir*, *gair* and *glám*, *omda* and *ibes*, *clíabaig* and *cinn*), as well as between *Chuinn* and *chossa*.

in gair. *ingair* BM, *in gair* E. *DIL* cites this line s.v. 2 *ingor* 'undutiful'. The pattern of alliteration suggests that the intended form is *gair*, however, and this word also rhymes with *daim* in the preceding line. I tentatively take *gair* as genitive singular of *gor* 'pus', although I have not found any other examples of this spelling.

cen glám. Lit. 'without satire'. A palatalised final would be expected after the preposition *cen* and *glám* may be an instance of the confusion between nominative and accusative singular of feminine *ā*-stems in Middle Irish (*SG* III §5.6).

cen gráda. Since the subject is addressed as *a drochḟir dána* 'you bad poet', I take *gráda* here to be used in the sense that he is unqualified and does not belong to any of the seven grades of poets.

a chongna clíabaig. *DIL* s.v. 1 *clíabach* suggests 'name of some wild animal. Wild boar (?)', while Meyer (1906b, 386) suggests 'deer' and cites examples from *MV* III. Meyer's suggestion seems more likely, since *clíabach* is found in contexts which suggest that one of its distinguishing features was great speed, a characteristic of a deer rather than a wild boar. In *Táin Bó Cúailnge*, for example, a chariot is described as moving *co lūas faindle nō clīabaigi allaid* (Strachan and O'Keefe 1912, l. 2553): 'with the speed of a swallow or a wild *clíabach*'. Similarly, in *Comhrag Fir Diad ⁊ Chon Culainn* the speed of horses is described as *go luas faindli no eirbi no iarann no cliabhaighi allaidhi* (Best 1915, 298 §42): 'with the speed of a swallow or a doe or a squirrel or a wild *clíabach*'. In both of these instances *clíabach* is treated as a feminine noun. There are three other examples in our text, all of which are in the genitive singular and treat the word as an *o*-stem: *cnám clíabaig caim úa Cuinn* 'the bone of a crooked deer is the grandson of Conn' no. 61; *seche chon fo chom chlíabaig* 'a hound's hide under the breast of a deer' no. 63; *cnám do chnámaib clíabaig* 'one of the bones of a deer' no. 68. It is noteworthy that in three of the four examples in *MV* III *clíabach* is associated with bones.

i cinn do chnáma. This may allude to the subject's hands and feet (i.e. the extremities of his bones) being mis-shapen, so that they resemble antlers.

48. *MV* III §198.

Edition: Meyer (1919, no. 74).

The metre is *gobal immarind dé-ind for ardchasbairdne* 'a two-pointed, greatly rhymed (?) branch on *ardchasbairdne*', classified as *écoitchenn.* E reads *casbairni* against *ardchassbairdni* B, *ardcasbairnde* M. The term *immarind* (*imairnd* B, *imairind* M, *imarind* E) is cited in *DIL* s.v. ?*immairnd,* where it is the only example and no meaning is given. The first element may be the intensive prefix *immar* and the second *rinn* 'point', used here of rhyme. Alternatively, it may be a corruption of the term *imrinn* 'having rhymes all around'. *DIL* s.v. *gabul* (j) suggests 'name of a metre in which there is triple alliteration', although there are four alliterating words in line *b.* The stanza is highly alliterative and each stressed word either rhymes or consonates with another word. Although the syllabic structure is irregular (10^3 13^3 8^3 11^3), the pattern of stress is regular (three stressed words in lines *ac* and four in lines *bd*).

A number of adjectives in the second couplet are otherwise unattested; see p. 126 above. Some of these are formed from words for various types of containers: *pait* 'skin bottle' > *paitech*; *píanán* 'bag' > *píanánach*; *tíagán* 'little bag' > *tíagánach*; *aite* 'case' > *aitech.* Similarly, *pít* 'light meal' > *pítech. Pít* is used of meagre rations of monks and nuns (Kelly 1997, 343). The overall effect is to portray the subject as a beggar who carries all his possessions with him as he scrounges around bags and bottles in search of scraps. Various types of beggars and paupers are described in legal sources. In *Córus Béscnai,* for example, *puipir* 'paupers' is glossed *.i. qui pera pascitur .i. sastar o teigh* 'i.e. who are fed from a bag' (*CIH* ii 524.32). *Míadślechta* describes a landless freeman known as a *sindach brothlaige* 'fox of a coooking pit' as someone who scrounges around for food: *.i. bruar cach bidh do iter dilis 7 indilis; no cuma lais* *cidhbedh bruidhes nó domeala* 'i.e. crumbs of all food for him, both lawful and unlawful; or he does not care what he crunches or consumes' (*CIH* ii 585.30–1; Kelly 1988, 425).

A Dalláin. I take this as a personal name, although it seems to be used in the sense of 'little blind man' in the phrase *dallán Dromma Bó* no. 66.

dígrádaig. This word is not cited in *DIL.* I take it as an adjective from *dígrád*; see *DIL* s.v. 3 *dígrád* 'dishonour, disgrace', where only one example is cited. Note that the subject of no. 47 is described as being *cen gráda.*

a chammáin. *Cammán,* a stick for playing ball games, is used here metaphorically to describe a crooked or twisted person.

cúaránaig. This is the only example cited in *DIL,* where the reader is referred to *cúarán* 'shoe, sock'.

49. *MV* III §200.

Edition: Meyer (1919, no. 59).

The metre is *súainem Domangairt* 'Domangart's thread [of poetry]', classified as *écoitchenn. Súainem* 'rope, thread' is used of versification in the pseudo-historical prologue to the *Senchas Már,* where it is stated that the poets Fergus and Dubthach tied a *súainem filidechta* 'thread of poetry' around the law (*CIH* v 1654.32). It is also found in the metrical name *sūainem Segsa* (Meyer 1913, 56 §36). This stanza can be divided into two five-line sections and there is a regular pattern of end-rhyme between *gabáil* (b) : *chamáir* (g); *demain* (c) : *crebair* (h) and between *brait* (d) : *laic* (i); *caíche* (e) : *saíthe* (j). *Domangairt* (a) rhymes with *chonadmairt* (f), while *chícaraig* (f) is the only end-word not involved in rhyme. In view of the pattern of end-rhyme, one would have expected a heptasyllabic first line ending in a trisyllabic word which rhymes with *chícaraig,* and it is noteworthy in this regard that a space has been left after *Domangairt* in BE. The syllabic structure is irregular (4^3 7^2 6^2 6^1 7^2; 7^3 7^2 7^2 7^1 7^2) and the stanza is probably to be interpreted as consisting of a slightly more regular pattern of stressed words (1 3 3 3 3 ; 2 3 3 3 2). There is linking alliteration between most lines.

chonadmairt. *conadhmairt* BE, *connadh mairt* M. BE agree against M in reading a form with single *-n-*. The second element is *mart* 'ox'. The first element in M seems to be *connad* 'firewood', but this is unsuitable metrically as *chonadmairt* rhymes with *Domangairt.* I follow Meyer, who reads *a chonadmairt chīcaraig* 'du gieriges gefräßiges Stierkalb' 'you greedy, voracious bull-calf', taking the first element as *conadh* 'a greedy appetite, rage, fury'. *Conad* is not well attested, however, and Meyer's suggestion is based on the meaning given in O'Brien's Irish-English dictionary and on an entry in *AU s.a.* 1357. In the latter case, the word is not translated. *DIL* s.v. *conadmairt* suggests that the first element may be *cú* 'hound' and the compound is also cited s.v. ?*admairt*.

chrúachaide. *cruachaidhi* B, *acruachaiti* M, *cruachaidi* E. *DIL* cites this line s.v. *crúachaige*, where it is the only example, based on Meyer's reading *a chrūachaigi* 'geschwollener Bauch'. The MSS point to the form being *crúachaide* rather than *crúachaige*, however. I take this as an adjective from 1 *crúach* 'stack of corn; heap', meaning 'heap-like' or 'swollen'; cf. *gerc-aide* 'grouse-like' from *gerc* 'grouse' no. 28 and *sinnchaide* 'fox-like' from *sinnach* 'fox' no. 55. *Crúachaide*, used here as a substantive, may refer to a swollen part of the body, possibly the stomach, as translated by Meyer. With the phrase *a chrúachaide lenaim laic*, cf. *a charpat lenaim liúin* 'you gum of a pathetic child' no. 34 and *a lenaim laic* 'you weak child' no. 39.

50. *MV* III §18.

Edition: Meyer (1919, no. 69).

The metre is *dían airṡeng comthrom* 'balanced *dían airṡeng*' (4^3 8^3 4^1 8^3), classified as *gnáthaiste*. This stanza has the same syllabic structure and rhyming pattern as the illustration of *dían airṡeng ina cirt chóir cen impód* '*dían airṡeng* in its proper order without inversion' cited in *MV* III §21. The adjective *comthrom* 'even, balanced' may be used here in a similar sense, i.e. to illustrate an opposition to *dían airṡeng impóid* 'inverted *dían airṡeng*', an example of which is cited in *MV* III §20 (no. 4 above). G gives the name as *dian fereng cenntrom*.

A ḟetánaig, a chornaire etc. For other references to entertainers see p. 25.

a chléraige. *acliaraige* B, *acleraige* M, *acliaraide* E, *acliaraighe* G. I follow Meyer in reading *cléraige* for rhyme with *scélaige*, although the majority of the MSS point to *clíaraige*. *DIL* cites the first couplet s.v. '*clíaraige* also *cléraige*' and gives the meaning 'member of a *clíar*, one of a poetic band', citing one other example.

51. *MV* III §127.

Edition: Meyer (1919, no. 60).

The metre is *ochtrinnard becc* 'eight-fold *rinnard becc*' (4 x [5^2 5^2]), classified as *gnáthaiste*. The metrical structures of *ochtrannaigecht mór* no. 8 and *ochtrannaigecht becc mór* no. 13 are similar.

a chrebair chuilig. *DIL* cites this line s.v. *cuilech* = *colach* and suggests 'unclean horsefly(?)', while Meyer translates 'du geile Schmeißfliege' 'you lecherous bluebottle'. *Crebar* can also mean 'woodcock' (Kelly 1997, 298) and I take *chuilig* as vocative singular of an adjective *cuilech* 'flea-ridden' from *cuil* 'fly, flea'. Cf. *snedach* 'nitty' from *sned* no. 41, *rónach* 'abounding in seals' from *rón* and *íascach* 'abounding in fish' from *íasc.*

a airbe ibair. For an explanation of this insult see p. 39.

a inair uidir. Cf. *inar odar* 'a dun-coloured tunic' no. 20. For an explanation of this insult see p. 23.

52. *MV* III §151.

The metre is *int anaichnid dona druimnib suíthe* 'the unfamiliar [one] of the summits of learning' (8^3 11^3 10^3 12^3 10^3 15^3), classified as *anaichnid.* G has a different metrical name: *Ise so intanaichnidh donadruimnibh suithibh* B, *Ise seo autem intanaichnidh donadruimnibh suithibh inso* M, *Druimni saitheadh andseo* G. This poem consists of three couplets with end-rhyme between *dromlaige* (b) : *longaire* (d) : *cornaire* (f).

According to *MV* III §150, there are two types of *druimne suíthe*: *im-garb* 'very rough', for which see no. 69 below, and *anaichnid* 'unfamiliar'. It is stated in *MV* II §1 that *druimne slan suídhe* is the most appropriate metre for the highest grade of poet (*dilsem dodoen .i. ollam* 'most suitable for a tutor, i.e. an *ollam*'). The treatment of a stanza in *MV* I, II and III shows confusion over the use of the term, however. In *MV* I §66 (Meyer 1919, no. 133), the stanza is cited as an illustration of the metre *bricht,* of which it is stated: *Brict da, is hé drumni suide na bairdne* '*bricht,* then, is the summit of learning of bardic craft'. Here *druimne suíthe* is not used as a metrical name, but means simply 'summit of learning'. The same stanza is cited in *MV* II §88, where *druimne suithe na bardne* has become a metrical name. Finally, it is cited in *MV* III §161 as an example of *sébricht,* while *druimne suíthe* is used as the metrical name for *MV* III §§150–1.

uime. BM omit this word, which makes *breccad* rhyme with *uidre.* I take it as genitive singular feminine of the adjective *om* 'raw; crude, unrefined'.

ibraide. For an explanation of this insult see p. 39.

a ingaire. These words are omitted in BM.

luinne. *luinde* B, *luindi* M, *lughe* G. I follow BM and read genitive singular of *lonn* 'fierce'.

tréise. Rhymes with *céise.* I take this as genitive singular of a poorly attested word *tréis* 'guile, treachery'; see *DIL* s.v.

tibride. *thibhraide* B, *tibrige* M, *thibhrighe* G. This is the only example cited in *DIL* s.v. ?*tibraide* and no meaning is given. I take it as genitive singular of an adjective from *tibre* 'smile; laughing-stock, fool'.

baise. *Bas* 'palm of the hand' may be used here with the extended meaning 'handle, blade', possibly referring to part of a *céis*; see *DIL* s.v. *bas* (b).

céise. The exact meaning of *céis* is uncertain, although it is generally taken to refer to part of a musical instrument, particularly a harp; see *DIL* s.v. 2 *céis*. The phrase *is cruit cen chéis* 'it is a harp without a *céis*' is used to describe something useless, which suggests that the *céis* was an important part of the instrument (Stokes 1899, §20; O'Donoghue 1921–23, 48 §22; 54 note 9). Given its occurrence in the context of satire, it is interesting to note that *céis* sometimes has negative associations in literary sources (Toner 2007, 154).

53. *MV* III §162.

The metre is *cúicbricht* 'five-fold *bricht*' (10^2 10^2 $10^2 17^2$), classified as *anaichnid*. The lines have been divided on the basis of rhyme between *cossaib* (a) : *fossaid* (b) : *chossaib* (e). The satire is in three sections, each beginning with the phrase *A drúith na hAlla* and each referring to the subject's feet. Ó Máille (1973, 84 §11) draws attention to *breccad* rhyme in this verse.

na hAlla. Hogan (1910) gives a number of placenames with the elements *Alla* and *Aill*. It is impossible to establish which is the intended form in our text, however, as *Alla* could be genitive of either. Note the common formula of *drúth* qualified by a placename in the genitive, for which see p. 26 above.

breccánaig. Rhymes with *senáraig*. I take this as a substantive use of the adjective *breccánach*, from *breccán* 'speckled thing'. This is the only example cited in *DIL*, where the phrase is translated as 'wearer of motley (?)'.

a dord im dronda. This phrase is difficult to interpret. Both MSS read *dronda* and I follow the suggestion in *DIL* (s.v. *drong* col. 406, l. 6) in taking it as a variant of *drong* 'crowd', although only one other example is given. This seems to make more sense than reading *dronn* 'hump' ('you buzzing around humps') and a similar idea is conveyed by the phrase *a chrithre im chella* 'you sparks around churches' no. 42. Alternatively, one could read *dord* as a variant of *dorn* 'fist', but this form is also poorly attested (see *DIL* s.v. *dorn* col. 360, l. 6) and it is difficult to see how it could be interpreted in the present context.

54. *MV* III §185.

The MSS differ in the metrical name of this stanza. B reads *laidh frecnairc* 'a poem in one's presence' (*laíd frecndairc*), while M reads *laeidh f-cair* 'a poem of violation (?)' (*laíd forcair*). The syllabic structure is 12^3 8^2 5^3 8^2 and the metre is classified as *écoitchenn.*

A diripi talman. *a dhiripi talmhun* B, *aidrip bi talman* M. The beginning of this line seems to be corrupt in the MSS. The context suggests that *dhiripi* B, *drip bi* M is a noun in the vocative. It may be a type of small creature, possibly an insect, since it is described as being 'of the ground' and 'fleeing from a little trout'.

breccóice. This is the only example cited in *DIL* s.v. *brecóigi*, where it is suggested that it may be a diminutive form of *brecc* 'trout'. The form is genitive singular, as noted in *DIL*, which would suggest a nominative singular **breccóc.*

eógainn. *eogaing* BM. Rhymes with *feórainn.* I tentatively take this as a compound of *eó* 'point' and *gainn* 'scurf'; see *DIL* s.v. ?*gainn* and cf. *gainech* (*gainnech*) 'scurf, scab on the skin'.

fetóice. This example is not cited in *DIL.* The plover (the English name for which ultimately derives, through French, from Latin *pluvia*) was associated with rain; see *Oxford English Dictionary* s.v. According to Nicholson (1996, 445), a week in early Spring was called *Feadag* ('the Plover or Whistle') in Scottish Gaelic tradition 'probably because of the piping winds then prevalent'. A rhyme describing the periods known as *Feadag* and *Gearran* 'gelding' suggests that the plover was associated with harsh weather conditions: *Is mis' an Fheadag lóm, luirgneach, luath / Marbham caora, marbham uan; / Is mis an Gearran bacach bàn, / 'Us cha mhi aon bhonn a's fhearr* 'I'm the bare swift leggy Plover, I can kill both sheep and lamb; I'm the white lame Gelding, And not one bit better' (Nicholson *ibid.*, 446). With the description *Feadag lóm luirgneach,* cf. the phrase *a luirgne fetóice ar feórainn* 'you shins of a plover on a river bank' in line *d* of our poem.

55. *MV* III §186.

The MSS give the name of this metre as *tedm leoda* B, *teidm leodha* M and it is classified as *écoitchenn.* The syllabic structure is 10^3 10^3 8^3 8^3 8^3 8^3 8^3 10^3. *Teidm léoda* could be taken to mean 'a fit of hacking/hewing'. This stanza is followed in the tract by examples of *imbas forosnai* (*MV* III §187) and *deilm laíde la díchetal* (*MV* III §188; see no. 56 below), however, which suggests that the compiler had in mind the triad *teinm láedo, imbas forosnai* and *díchetal di chennaib.* These were types of divination associated with poets but they are also used as names of metres in *MV* II (Carey 1997, 52–3).

M omits everything between *gataile* (e) and *in lecaile* (g) and there are also many textual difficulties, such as rare or otherwise unattested words and compounds. Excluding the article, prepositions and the vocative particle, ten out of the twenty remaining words are unattested elsewhere: *mairbthine* (a); *sailchide* (b); *sinnchaide* (b); *clecaire* (c); *gataile* (e)*; cetaile* (e, f); *lataile* (g); *lecaile* (g); *acaite* (h); *anachluim* (h). The lines have been divided on the basis of end-rhyme and alliteration. The main rhyme is between *salachluim* (b) : *anachluim* (h). There is rhyme between the end-words *chlecaire* (c) : *becaige* (d) : *cetaile* (e) : *cetaile* (f) : *lecaile* (g). There is internal rhyme between *mairbthine* (a) : *ṡailchide* (b) and *minchuile* (a) : *ṡinnchaide* (b) (in the latter instance the rhyme is imperfect). There is *breccad* rhyme between *gataige* (c) : *brataire* (d) : *gataile* (e) : *gataile* (f) : *lataile* (g) : *apaide* (h) : *acaite* (h).

mairbthine. *mhairbhthene* B, *marbthene* M. This word rhymes with *ṡailchide* and I have normalised the spelling accordingly. It is not cited in *DIL* and Thurneysen (1912, 87) suggests that *Mairbthene* may be a personal name. The first element may be the adjective *marb* 'dead'. *DIL* cites one example of a form *marbtine* which occurs in commentary on *Córus Fine.* This is defined as *cin inndethbiri* 'an avoidable liability' in an interlinear gloss (which Binchy states is in a different hand): *tola marfiach .i. cinta dethbiri marbtine .i. cin inndethbiri .i. imat fiach mor do dlesdain de* 'a *marbtine,* i.e. an avoidable liability, is an abundance of great penalties, i.e. unavoidable liabilities, i.e. an abundance of great penalties is due for it' (*CIH* ii 730.9–10). It is difficult to establish if this is the same as the word in our text, however.

mongthige. I follow *DIL* s.v. *mong* col. 165, l. 71 in taking this as a compound of *mong* 'hair' and *tige* 'thickness, density'.

ṡailchide. This is the only example cited in *DIL,* where it is suggested that it may be an adjective from *sailche* 'dirtiness', used substantively.

ṡinnchaide. This is the only example cited in *DIL,* where the meaning 'fox-like, stinking' from *sinnach* 'fox' is suggested. Cf. *gercaide* 'grouse-like' no. 28.

a rith. *imarith* B, *arith* M. I follow M as this gives a pattern of four consecutive lines beginning with the vocative particle.

chlecaire. This is the only example cited in *DIL* and I have not been able to establish the meaning from the context. The first element cannot be *clé* 'left', since a short vowel is required.

becaige. *inbecuidhi* B, *inbecuidhi* M. The context suggests that this is a noun in the genitive singular rhyming with *clecaire, cetaile* etc. On this basis, I have emended the MSS to *becaige*, a compound of the adjective *becc* 'small' with genitive singular of *ag* 'cow'.

gataile, cetaile, lataile. The only examples of these words cited in *DIL* are from our text and I have not been able to establish the meanings. Note also *lecaile* in line *g*. For other examples of words ending in *-aile* see p. 126 above.

lecaile. *DIL* s.v. *lecc* col. 68, l. 65 'flagstone' suggests that this may be a compound of *lecc* and *aile* 'fence' in the sense 'fence of flat stones (?)'. Cf. *nochtaile* 'bare fence', *tondaile* 'wave fence', *lochaile* 'lake-fence' and *tartaile* 'drought-fence' (Kelly 1997, 376–7). It is difficult to establish if this is the intended meaning, however, and it may simply be another example of the suffix *-aile* as found in *gataile* etc.

a apaide. Note that both MSS omit the vocative particle. I take this as a substantival use of the adjective *apuide/apaide* 'very yellow'. Cf. *airem apaide* 'a sallow ploughman' no. 20.

acaite. *acaite* B, *accaite* M. This is the only example given in *DIL* s.v. ?*acaite*. The context suggests that it is vocative singular of an adjective, alliterating with *apaide* and *anachluim*, but the meaning is uncertain.

anachluim. *anachlaim* B, *anachluim* M. Rhymes with *salachluim*. I tentatively take this as a compound of *enach* (later *anach*) 'bog' and *lom* 'bare'.

56. *MV* III §188.

The metre is *deilm laíde la díchetal* 'sound of a lay with incantation'. The syllabic structure is irregular (10^3 6^2 5^3 9^2) and the stanza is probably to be analysed as a stressed metre (4 3 2 3). It is classified as *écoitchenn*. This occurs after illustrations of the metres *teidm léoda* and *imus forosnudh* and appears to have been coined from the terms *teinm láedo* and *díchetal di chennaib*; see note on no. 55.

bennimle. *beand imle* BM. I take this as a compound for rhyme with *gerringne* (d) and alliteration with *bruit, broinn* and *balbduine*. The first element is the noun *benn* 'peak, prong'. I take the second element as Middle Irish vocative plural of *imbel* 'edge'.

Charnmaige. Carnmag in Thomond (Hogan 1910, 162).

gamnaige. Kelly (1997, 40 note 99) defines a stripper (*gamnach*) as 'a cow which has not come into calf in a particular year, and is still accompanied by the calf of the previous year'.

57. *MV* III §45.

The metre is *carrdechnad* (8^2 8^2 8^2 8^2), classified as *gnáthaiste*. For *carr-* in names of metres see note on no. 34. Note rhyme between voiced and voiceless stops in *focul* : *cocur*; for other examples see p. 198.

focul i mbít rainn co rigne. Lit. 'a phrase in which there are verses with stiffness'. This may allude to a badly constructed poem or phrase. *Rigne labartha* 'stiffness of delivery' is listed as one of the seventeen signs of bad pleading in *Tecosca Cormaic* §22, while in the *Triads* §179 it is described as a flaw in speech: *Trí miscena indsci: rigne, dlúithe, dulbaire* 'three hateful things in speech: stiffness, obscurity, a bad delivery'. Meyer notes (1906, 24 note 1) that in Modern Irish *righneas labhartha* means 'an impediment in speech'.

tri aibne. Lit. 'on account of whips'. *DIL* notes s.v. *abann* that there are no certain examples of a nominative singular form of this word.

tairnge. *traigne* B, *trai* <. . .> B^b, *tairnge* MH, *tairgni* E. *DIL* cites this line (with a query) s.v. *tragna* 'corncrake', based on the reading of B.

tidle. *DIL* cites this line s.v. ?*tidle* and no meaning is given. The form *tidle* also occurs in *MV* III §37, where Meyer (1919, no. 44) takes it as a placename: *trīall dar Tidle* 'ein Marsch über die Gebiete von Tidel' 'a march over the regions of Tidel'. *Tidle* in both instances could also be taken as accusative plural of *tidel* 'bunch of corn stalks'; cf. *tideal no barr bláithe* 'a bunch of corn stalks (?) or a flowering branch' (Binchy 1973b, 80 §11 and 85–6; Charles-Edwards and Kelly 1983, 190).

58. *MV* III §57.

Edition: Meyer (1919, no. 65).

The metre is *cummasc rannaigechta móire ocus lethrinnairde* 'a mixture of *rannaigecht mór* and *lethrinnard*' (7^1 4^2 7^1 6^2), classified as *gnáthaiste*. E gives the name of the metre as *cumasc rannaigechta ⁊ lethrannaigechta*.

mant capaill chróin. The use of the adjective *crón* 'reddish-brown' may be significant, as it is stated in *Bretha Nemed Dédenach* that colour is one of four criteria used for judging a horse: *mesir eocha ar a méd sgéo crotha, dathaib sgēo rethaib* 'may you judge horses by their size and shape, by their colours and runnings' (Kelly 1997, 91 note 197 = *CIH* iii 1131.6). According to Kelly (*ibid.*, 92), white appears to have been the most prestigious colour. In view of this, it is interesting to note that both the horse and cow referred to in our text are described as being of mixed colours (i.e. reddish-brown and speckled).

dar céisib. Note the Middle Irish use of the dative after *dar*. Cf. *a reithe folta fásaig dar fíad* 'you moulting desert ram mounting deer' no. 36.

59. *MV* III §63.

The metre is *lethrannaigecht mór chorránach* 'hooked [extended] *lethrannaigecht mór*' (4 x [5^1 5^1]), classified as *gnáthaiste*.

Gilla in Naím. *Gilla na naem* B, *Gillananaem* E, *Gilla innaim* MH. The reading of MH is stematically superior and also gives a line of five syllables. *Gilla* is a common element in personal names (O'Brien 1973, 229–30) and BE read the well-attested form *Gilla na Náem*. I have found no other examples of a form *Gilla in Naím*.

fíacla lega i lis. *fiacla gela nó lega illiss* B, *fiacla lega iliss* M, *fiacla leadha alis* E, *fiaclai lega hillis* H. *DIL* cites this line s.v. ?*lega* and the reader is referred to *lecc* 'flagstone'. *Lis* rhymes with *cris*, so the intended word must be *les* 'enclosure' (with broad -*s*-) rather than *les* 'buttock, haunch'. The metrical structure suggests that *lega* rhymes with *ela*, and I take it as genitive singular of *líaig* 'leech'. B corrects *fiacla gela* to *no lega* in a suprascript addition. The phrase 'teeth of a leech in an enclosure' seems to be another instance of the victim of satire being described as something useless, i.e. teeth that have fallen out or possibly false teeth.

dlochtán. Cf. *a chos dlochtáin* 'you stem of a little bunch' no. 8 and *dlocht crema* (Meyer 1881–83, 202 §24).

drúth Lemna. I take *Lemna* as genitive of the placename *Líamain*, several examples of which are given in Hogan (1910, 488) The prevalence of Leinster placenames in *MV* III suggests that this may be Newcastle Lyons in Co. Dublin, although it is impossible to establish the location for certain. Cf. also *A meic Con Lemna* 'O son of Cú Lemna' no. 31 and *lon ic longaire i Líamain* 'a blackbird screeching in Líamain' no. 63. *Drúth* qualified by a placename in the genitive is a common formula in our poems; see p. 26 above.

chlérech. *clerigh* B, *clereach* M, *cler-* E, *clerech* H. B reads a genitive singular form, while E has a suspension stroke.

fo gerrga nglas. *fa gearrga nglas* B, *fogerga nglas* M, *fogerrga glas* E, *fogerr ganglas* H. E differs from BMH in omitting Middle Irish nasalisation of the adjective. *Glas* 'green, blue' is often used of metal; see *DIL* s.v. 2 *glas* (d) and cf. *crenaid claidbiu glassu* 'he buys blue swords' (*Fodlai Aíre* tract §10; p. 54 above).

60. *MV* III §64.

Edition: Meyer (1919, no. 64).

The metre is *cummasc lethrannaigechta móire ocus rinnairde* 'a mixture of *lethrannaigecht mór* and *rinnard*' (6^1 6^2 6^2 6^2 6^1 6^2), classified as *gnáthaiste*.

For an example of *rinnard* (6^2 6^2 6^2 6^2) see no. 37. The syllabic structure of *lethrannaigecht mór* is 5^1 5^1 5^1 5^1 (Murphy 1961, [69]). The name *cummasc lethrannaigechta móire ocus rinnairde* would seem to indicate a mixture of 6^2 and 5^1, whereas the syllabic structure of our poem resembles a mixture of *rinnard* (6^2) and *dá trían rannaigechta móire* (6^1 6^1 6^1 6^1). For an example of the latter see no. 61. The pattern of end rhyme is unusual in that there is rhyme between *pundainn* (b) : *cundail* (f) and *cairig* (c) : *aílig* (d).

lára. E's reading *lara bana* is hypermetrical.

phuint. *phuint* B, *puint* M, *puinnt* E, *phuit* H. Meyer follows H and reads *pút* 'a block, stump?', suggesting that it may derive from Old Norse *bútr* 'block' or Welsh *pwt* 'stump'. The only example of *pút* 'a block, stump?' cited in *DIL* is from our text. BME read a form with -(*n*) *n*- and an *n*-stroke may simply have been omitted in H. I take the reading of BME to be genitive singular of *pond* 'a pound weight' (from Latin *pondus*). *DIL* s.v. cites one example from the Old Irish Glosses (Sg. 70[a]9).

pundainn. Kelly (1997, 238–9) suggests that the occurrence of the Old Norse loanword *punnann* 'sheaf of corn' in *Saltair na Rann* may be evidence of Norse influence on Irish farming practice. The earlier practice was to cut corn just below the ear.

lúa ri lúag. *luige* B, *lue .i. luac* M, *lue* H. The reading of B (*luige* 'oath') is hypermetrical. I read *lúa* for rhyme with *úa* , while Meyer reads *lúe fri lúag*. *DIL* s.v. 1 *lúa* (c) cites other examples of *lúa* used with the preposition *fri* in the sense 'kicking against' and suggests the translation 'one who tramples on (spurns) his wages (?)'.

61. *MV* III §70.

Edition: Murphy (1961, [68]).

The metre is *dá trían rannaigechta móire* 'two thirds of *rannaigecht mór*' (6^1 6^1 6^1 6^1), classified as *gnáthaiste*.

eidnén. Only H preserves this reading, which rhymes with *deidblén* in line *b* and gives a line of six syllables. For the significance of the phrase *sonnach eidnén* see p. 40 above.

dán ina díamair daill. *danma diamair dhaill* B, *dan madiamair daill* ME, *dán inadiamair daill* H. Lit. 'a craft in its state of being a dark, obscure thing'. I take *daill* as dative singular feminine of the adjective agreeing with *díamair*, which is used here as a substantive. Thurneysen gives the reading of H as *dán mad diamair*, although there is a hair-stroke on the first minim and there is only one *d*. Murphy, following Thurneysen's edition, emends to *dán* [*dona*] *díamair daill*, stating that 'for the missing two syllables of line *c*, one of the two MSS has *mad*, the other *ma'*. The reading of H (*ina*) gives the required number of syllables, however, and *ma* in BME could have easily come about as a result of the confusion of minims.

clíabaig caim. Murphy reads *clíabaig chaim*, although *c* is delenited after final *-g* (*GOI* §231). For *clíabach* see p. 230.

62. *MV* III §71.

Edition: Meyer (1919, no. 66).

The metre is *cummasc slaite brechte ocus rinnairde ocus lethrannaigechta móire* 'a mixture of *slat brecht* and *rinnard* and *lethrannaigecht mór*' (5^3 5^3, 5^1 ; 6^2 5^1, 5^1), classified as *gnáthaiste.* As the name suggests, the stanza is composed of a mixture of three metres: *slat brecht* [*becc*] (5^3 5^3 5^3 5^3), *rinnard* (6^2 6^2 6^2 6^2) and *lethrannaigecht mór* (5^1 5^1 5^1 5^1). B gives the metrical name as *cumasc slaite breachte ⁊ lethrannaigechta moire.*

methmac. Meyer takes the first element as *méth* 'fat', noting that *meth* 'decadent' is also possible, while Thurneysen (1912, 86) suggests that *meth* could be either a personal name or an adjective. Reading a compound *methmac* gives imperfect rhyme with *breccar* and *screpall.*

mesce chírmaire. Lit. 'drunkenness of a comb-maker'.

screpall ar ḟeóil n-aige. For an explanation of this phrase see p. 34.

breccar claime i cinn. Only one other example of *breccar* is cited in *DIL.* Taunting someone who suffered from *claime* 'leprosy, scabies' was an offence; see p. 19.

63. *MV* III §77.

The metre is *merugud rannaigechta bice ocus rannaigecht móire* 'a confusion of *rannaigecht becc* and *rannaigecht mór*' (10^2 7^2 7^1 7^2), classified as *gnáthaiste.* Thurneysen (1891, 85) prints this stanza as continuous prose. The lines have been divided on the basis of end-rhyme between *clíabaig* (c) and *Líamain* (e) and *aicill* rhyme between *chreche* : *seche* and *chrod* : *lon.* The name suggests that this metre should consist of a mixture of *rannaigecht becc* (7^2 7^2 7^2 7^2) and *rannaigecht mór* (7^1 7^1 7^1 7^1) and this is reflected in the syllabic structure of lines *b, c, d.* If the last two words of line *a* were omitted, this would give a line of 7^1, with *aicill* rhyme between *om* and *chon.*

chlíabaig. For *clíabach* see p. 230.

longaire. *DIL* s.v. cites two examples of *longaire* referring to the voices of women and boys and it may be used in the present context to suggest that the subject speaks in a high-pitched or shrill voice. In no. 52 above *longaire* describes the noise made by a cow: *a ingaire bó luime luinne longaire* 'you herding of a bare, fierce, screeching cow'.

64. *MV* III §85.

The metre is described as *cuntabairt etir dechnaid ⁊ rannaigecht mbic ⁊ imdeliugud fair ⁊ is dechnad a bunad* 'Uncertainty between *dechnad* and *rannaigecht becc* and [there is] a division on it and its basis is *dechnad*' (8^2 6^2 8^2 6^2 ; 8^2 8^2 6^2 6^2 7^2 8^2). It is classified as *gnáthaiste.* As the name suggests, it consists of a mixture of *dechnad mór* (8^2 6^2 8^2 6^2) with one line of *rannaigecht becc* (7^2 7^2 7^2 7^2). This is the only example of *imdeliugud* 'separation' in *DIL*, where it is taken as the verbal noun of a poorly attested verb *imdeligid* 'divides'. It may refer to the break after line *d*, since line *e* begins with a capital letter in all three MSS. The second section reinforces what has been said about Gilla Cellaig in the first, i.e. that the person in question is not Gilla Cellaig simply because he is not 'scum of flitches of bacon' or 'a snail with two horns' etc. For the repetition of the subject's name in satire see p. 14.

Gilla Cellaig. For a suggestion as to his identity see p. 118.

cenn. *ceann* B *cenn* ME. This may be an example of a poorly-attested word *cenn* 'skin' (Greene 1958b, 45). It does not appear as a separate head-word in *DIL* (Greene 1975, 175 note 1) and a nominative singular form has not previously been attested. The examples cited by Greene are in compounds and the present example is of interest in that it may provide evidence of a nominative singular *cenn.* Greene notes (1975) that in the Book of Armagh *scamae* (*squamae*) 'scales' is glossed *cenni aut bloscc aut lanna* 'skins or a membrane or scales' (*Thes.* i, 497.1). In the context of our poem, a meaning such as 'scum' would be appropriate. I am grateful to Liam Breatnach for these references.

seilche. In an Early Modern Irish satire, a dead pig is described as *seilche fliuch fúar* 'cold slimy snail' (Quin 1965, 30 §13); see p. 37 above. It is also interesting to note that *selche* is the term used to describe a thin, niggardly slice of bacon in the tale *Erchoitmed Ingine Gulidi*: ... *la selche salli seingbline, la tana táib na blinmuici* ... '... with a snail of thin lean bacon, with the thin side of a lean pig ...' (Meyer 1894, 66 §9).

finna ar. *finn ar* B, *find ar* ME. I have restored *finna* on the basis of *finna ar gúaire* (line *g*).

cullaig allaid. *Cullach* 'boar' may be used in both a laudatory and contemptuous sense; see *DIL* s.v.

challaig. This word occurs in lines *d* and *i.* Meyer (1906b, 310) cites the form from our text (with a query) but no meaning is given. *Callach* may be a variant of the adjective *collach* 'corpulent', showing Middle Irish alternation between *a* and *o* in stressed syllables before a broad consonant (*SG* III §3.6). This meaning would suit the context in line *d*. The context in line *i* is less certain, but since *challaig* is the subject of what appears to be a Middle Irish preterite plural passive form *tucait*, it may be used as a substantive in the plural. *Collach* is used as a substantive in heptad 3, where it is stated that an excessively fat man (*fer rochollach*) can be divorced on the grounds that he cannot satisfy his wife sexually: *ni tualaing toile nach rochollach* 'any excessively fat man is not capable of sexual intercourse' (*CIH* i 5.24–5; see Kelly 1988, 74).

apair. Rhymes with *acaib*. This word is omitted in M. I tentatively take it to be Middle Irish second singular imperative of *as-beir*. If this is the intended form, the use of the singular form of the imperative with the plural prepositional pronouns *cucaib* and *acaib* is noteworthy. In no. 5 above, a singular prepositional pronoun is used with a plural imperative form.

ar gúaire. *a* BME. *Ar* has been restored on the basis of *ar guaire* line *c*.

cucaib. *cubaidh* B, *chugaib* M, *cuccaib* E. I follow ME on the grounds that line *j* also contains a second person plural prepositional pronoun (*acaib*). B reads *cubaid* 'fitting'.

65. *MV* III §90.

Editions: Meyer (1919, no. 82); Murphy (1961, [77]).

The metre is *rannaigecht becc becc* (4^2 4^2 4^2 4^2), classified as *gnáthaiste*. M gives the name of the metre as *randaigecht bec*.

díltad dona. Murphy (1961, 103) s.v. *díltad* translates 'bad refusing', suggesting that the phrase is 'an exclamatory remark indicating that Finn was generous'. The description of Finn as *íchtar eime* 'the base of a handle' is hardly complimentary, however, and Meyer's classification of the stanza under the heading 'Spott- und Schmählieder' is more appropriate.

66. *MV* III §108.

Editions: Meyer (1919, no. 79); Murphy (1961, [39]).

The metre is *sétrad baccach* 'limping *sétrad*' (8^2 5^1 8^2 5^1), classified as *gnáthaiste*. Murphy suggests (1961, 84) that the adjective *baccach* 'limping' in the metrical name *sétnad mbacach* refers to the shortening of the second line by two syllables. *Baccach* is also found in the metrical name *rannaigecht baccach mór*, an illustration of which is cited in *MV* III §49. Here the first line has been shortened from seven to three syllables. The term is not used of metres in *MV* I or *MV* II. G gives the name of the metre as *sednaidh gairidh bhacach*, for which see p. 107.

Goll Mena. Cf. *Goll Mena mún cromgabair* no. 67. Thurneysen (1912, 86) suggests that this may be a nickname, while Murphy (1961, 130) takes *Mena* as genitive singular of an unidentified placename. Hogan (1910, 537) cites two examples of *Men*, anglicized Main or Myn, one of which is a river in the barony of Toome Upper, Co. Antrim. Meyer suggests that this may be the placename in our text, noting that *Druim Bó* is near Strangford Loch, Co. Down.

gall ic cnúasach cnó. *gall acnuasach cno* B, *gall icnuasach cno* M, *gall achnuasach cno* E, *gaill icnuasach cno* G. *DIL* cites the first two lines s.v. 5 *gall*, preceded by a question mark, and no meaning is given. I follow Meyer, who translates '(wie) ein Wikinger, der Nüsse sammelt' '(like) a Viking collecting nuts'. O'Brien (1938, 369 §9) rejects this translation on the grounds that it 'gives no sense' and suggests reading *gall i cnúasach cnó* 'an empty husk in a cluster of nuts', stating that '*Goll* (*gall*) has exactly the same meaning as *cáech*'. O'Brien's suggestion is followed by Murphy (1961, 109) s.v. 2 *gall*. While *cáech* 'blind' is found in the phrase *cnú cháech* 'blind nut' as a metaphor for something useless, I have found no examples of *gall/goll* used in a similar sense. On the other hand, *gall* 'foreigner' occurs frequently as an abusive epithet in our poems; see p. 31. Note the word-play between the personal name *Goll* and *gall* 'foreigner'.

dallán. This is unlikely to be a personal name, since the subject has already been named at the beginning of the stanza. Meyer suggests the meaning 'blind man', an allusion to the subject's name Goll 'blind in one eye'. I take *Dallán* as a personal name in no. 48, however. With the phrase *dallán Dromma Bó*, cf. the formula *drúth* qualified by a placename in the genitive; see p. 26.

67. *MV* III §115.

Edition: Meyer (1919, no. 80).

The metre is *ochtchasbairdne chorránach* 'hooked [extended] eight-fold *casbairdne*' (4 x [7^3 7^3]), classified as *gnáthaiste.* G differs from BME in reading *don casbairdni corranaigh aichillich* 'concerning hooked [extended] *casbairdne* with *aicill*' (the normal form is *aiclech*).

Goll Mena. See note on no. 66 above.

mún. Meyer reads *'mun*, a reduced form of the preposition *im* plus article, and takes the phrase to mean 'on the crooked horse'. Reading *mún* 'urine' gives alliteration with *Mena.* For other metaphors involving animal imagery and excrement see p. 34.

deidblénach. An adjective from *deidblén* 'an invalid'. This is the only example given in *DIL.*

stiúir d'fid lim. The insult lies in the fact that a rudder made of a softwood would not be durable. *DIL* cites this line s.v. 1 *lem* 'elm tree'. Describing the subject as 'an elmwood rudder' would be less insulting, however, since elm is a hardwood and is therefore suitable for use in boat building.

brocairecht. Rhymes with *stocairecht.* This is the only example cited in *DIL.* Meyer translates 'der Spottvogel der Gesellschaft bei der Dachsjagd' 'a satirist of the company at the badger-hunt', while *brocaireacht* is given as the Modern Irish word for 'badger baiting' in Ó Dónaill s.v. I take this as a verbal noun formation from *broc* 'badger' and the agent suffix *-aire,* meaning 'acting like a badger'; cf. *stocairecht* 'trumpeting' line *c, cornairecht* 'horn-playing' no. 63 and *bechairecht* 'bee-keeping' no. 86. Binchy (*CIH* iii 1100 note h) suggests reading *brocairecht* for *brachairecht,* which is cited alongside *cortacht* 'swarthiness' and *brenanalche* 'having bad breath' as examples of nicknames in Middle Irish legal commentary; see p. 21 above. In describing the subject as *cáinte búaile ic brocairecht* 'a satirist of the cowshed acting like a badger', the poet portrays him as a mean and filthy person who runs away and hides at the approach of guests, just as a badger runs and hides in its set when anyone approaches. A similar depiction of inhospitality is found in the poem *Tithe Chorr an Chait* by Séamas Dall Mac Cuarta. Here the poet describes the unwelcoming people of Corr an Chait as badgers who hide from everyone: *Béasa an bhroic bheith ag tochailt faoi / i ndorchadas oíche is lae; / ar ar cruthaíodh ó neamh go lár, / i gceann cháich cha dtig sé* 'It's the badger's habit to burrow down night and day in the dark. For the world from Earth to Heaven he wouldn't come to greet you.' (Ó Búachalla 1976, 17). The translation is by Ó Túama and Kinsella (1981, 131). The *cáinte* is also depicted as a mean and inhospitable householder in the tale *Erchoitmed Ingine Gulidi* (Meyer 1894, 65–9).

68. *MV* III §123.

The metre is *ochtrinnard chorránach* 'hooked [extended] eight-fold *rinnard* (4 x [6^2 6^2]), classified as *gnáthaiste.* The following words are omitted in B: *cnám* (line *b*); *i ndairib* (line *c*); *dér do* (line *d*).

cenn tamain. I take *taman* here and in no. 8 above to be used with the primary sense of 'trunk of a tree' or 'stump'. In no. 42, however, it seems to be used with the secondary meaning of one of the sub-grades of poets in the phrase *a thenga thamain* 'you tongue of a *taman*'; see p. 29.

dám etir dá dámaib. *damh etir damhaibh* B, *tarb etir danaibh no damaibh* M, *dam no tarb etir damaib* E. As it stands in the MSS this line is one syllable short. B has *dam*, M has *tarb* 'bull', while E corrects *dam* to *tarb* in a suprascript addition. The metaphor of a bull or ox (reading *dam*) 'between oxen' would certainly be in keeping with the animal imagery in this poem and in many other satires in *MV* III. On metrical grounds, however, I read *dám* 'a company', rather than *dam* 'an ox'. The rhyming pattern of other *ocht-* forms of *corránach* metres in *MV* III suggests that there should be *aicill* rhyme between *dámaib* and *cnámaib* and rhyme between *dám* and *cnám*; see, for example, nos. 35 and 67 in the present work. I also emend to *dá dámaib*, since a line of six syllables is required and the letters *da* could easily have been lost through haplography. The phrase *dám etir dá dámaib* 'a company between two [other] companies' could refer to an unexpected or unwelcome company of guests.

lommarc. I take this as a compound of *lomm* 'bare' and *orc/arc* 'piglet', rhyming with *Connacht.*

ettchu. Cf. the similar epithet *a chacc cuirre uidre ittige* 'you shit of a brown wingy heron' no. 43.

69. *MV* III §150.

The metre is *druimne suíthe imgarb* 'very rough summit of learning' (4^3, 4^2 6^2, 4^2 4^2 ; 6^3, 4^2 5^2, 4^2 4^2), classified as *anaichnid.* The MSS read: *Druimni suite annso 7 atat da ernail furre .i. imgharbh 7 anaichnidh. Ise so intimgharbh cepimus* B, *Druimne suithe inso sis 7 ata daernail fair .i. imgarb 7 anaichnid. Ise seo. Ise seo intimgarb cepinnas* M. 'Here is *druimne suíthe* and there are two divisions on it, i.e. "very rough" and "unfamiliar". This is the "very rough" [type] first of all'. For *druimne suíthe,* see note on no. 52 above.

The lines have been divided on the basis of rhyme and alliteration. The stanza consists of two sections, each comprising one short line and two 'extended' lines. There is rhyme between *Dall Bóruime* (a) and *cam órbuide* (d). The end-words of the extended lines rhyme with each other: *slabraid* (b) : *tragnaib* (c) : *garlaig* (e) : *cranngail* (f). There is also rhyme between *gopluim* (b — imperfect) : *tromguin* (c) : *chorrmaid* (f) and between *senchon* (b) : *gerrchod* (e).

Dall Bóruime. I take this as a personal name, but *Dall* could also be a nickname or an appellative. Cf. *Goll Mena* nos. 66–7, where *goll* could also be taken to mean 'blind of one eye' and *dallán,* which I take as a personal name in *a Dalláin* no. 48 but with the meaning 'little blind man' in *dallán Dromma Bó* no. 66.

a hol cumgucht. *aholchumgucht* BM. This line is cited in *DIL* s.v. *cumgacht* = *cumgae* 'narrowness; difficulty'. *DIL* lists a number of words with the spelling *ol* and *ól*, but it is difficult to be certain which is the intended form in our text since it is not fixed by rhyme and the meaning of the entire line is uncertain.

gerrchod. *gearrchod* B, *gerr chod* M. Rhymes with *senchon.* The form is accusative singular after Middle Irish *ro* < *fri* (SG III §13.14). *DIL* gives this as a headword but no meaning is suggested. The first element may be the adjective *gerr* 'short'. Rhyme with *-chon* means that the second element is *cod* rather than *cúad/cód* 'drinking vessel, cup'. *DIL* gives one example of *codh* (Stokes 1894, 433) and suggests the meaning 'tail', but this occurs in a *rosc* passage and the meaning is uncertain.

ngarlaig. *ngarrlaigh* B, *ngarlaigh* M. This is the only example cited in *DIL* s.v. ?*garrlach,* based on the reading of B. I follow M in reading a form with single *-r-* and take this to be an early example of the word *garlach* 'child, brat'. This word exists in Modern Irish; see *Dinneen* s.v. The form is genitive singular.

ro chorrmaid. *rochomraidh* B, *rocorrmaidh* M. I take M's reading *rocorrmaidh* as *ro maid,* Middle Irish third singular preterite of *maidid* 'breaks', with the adjective *corr* 'pointed' inserted between *ro* and the verbal form. The resulting compound *corrmaid* rhymes with *gopluim* (b – imperfect) and *tromguin* (c). Another example of an adjective prefixed to a verbal form is *ro fírchrap* no. 22; see p. 208 above. *DIL* cites this line s.v. 2 *comraid,* based on the reading of B. The form is preceded by a query and the reader is referred to the verb *con-reith,* later *comrithid* 'rushes'.

70. *MV* III §163.

The metre is *cetharbricht* 'four-fold *bricht*' (3^2 7^2 5^2 6^2 7^3 7^2), classified as *anaichnid.* For *bricht* in names of metres see p. 207.

Úa Mesen. *Ua mesean* B, *Ua me sean* M. Thurneysen (1912, 86) suggests reading *ua Mesean mac Gobal* (?).

líathglas. This seems to be an allusion to a mottled or discoloured complexion. In no. 74, the adjectives *líath* and *glas* are used to describe the appearance of a blacksmith: *mac don gabainn glasléith* 'a son of the wan, grey smith'.

gort íchtair ḟaithche. *Faithche* normally refers to a green area around a dwelling (Kelly 1997, 369–70). The significance of *íchtair* may be explained by a passage in the tale *Erchoitmed Ingine Gulidi.* Here the low-lying, north-east corner of a field is described as a dark and infertile place: ... *la ceithri scribline scremloiscthi do choirci iarmair airthir ichtair tuaiscirt athguirt lena frisna roben gaeth 7 frisna rotaitin grian* '... with four nasty burnt little scruples of oats left in the low bitter north-east (corner) of a field on which wind never blew nor sun ever shone' (Meyer 1894, 66 §9). In our poem, the phrase *gort íchtair ḟaithche* 'a field of the lower part of a green' seems to used in a similar sense to describe a low-lying field which gets little or no sun. The subject of no. 77 below is described in similar terms as *gort fossaid férmar mara* 'a level grassy field by (lit. 'of') the sea', i.e. a field which would be unproductive for growing crops because of its proximity to the sea.

gall bladach. *gallblach* B, *gallbladhach* M. *DIL* cites this line s.v. *bluch* 'salt meat', based on the reading of B. *Bluch* is not well attested and in any case the reading of M is superior, as established by rhyme with *dabach* (line *f*). For *gall* as an abusive epithet see p. 31.

dabach ibairglic aithne. Lit. 'a yew-skilled vat of a deposit', i.e. an item of little value deposited with someone for safe keeping. The regulations governing deposits are discussed by Kelly (1988, 120).

71. *MV* III §171.

The metre is *menmarc Mongán* 'Mongán's desire' (6^2 6^2 7^2 5^2), classified as *écoitchenn.* The Mongán in question may be Mongán mac Fiachna, who incurred the wrath of the poets through his display of superior knowledge. In one instance, he disagrees with the poet Forgoll over the circumstances of the death of Fothad Airgdech (Meyer 1895, 46) and Forgoll threatens to satirise him along with his father, mother and grandfather. In a second anecdote he humiliates the poet Eochu Rígéices, who subsequently curses him and his descendants (Knott, 1916). Mongán's name may have become associated with satire on account of these anecdotes. For other examples of personal names in the metrical names of satires in *MV* III see McLaughlin (2005, 128–30).

Cera. Hogan (1910, 228) identifies two such places: the barony of Carra in Mayo and Ceara in Bréifne. The only reference to the latter is 'Ceara in Breifny, Tp.', however, and O'Donovan (1862, xl) identifies this as 'Ceara, now the barony of Carra, in the county of Mayo'. Ceara does occur in a section of O'Donovan's edition entitled *Cuid na Breifne* (*op. cit.*, 46), but this contains many other placenames which are not located in Bréifne. Carney (1943, 120) locates it in Northern Uí Fhiachrach (Co. Mayo). Ó Concheanainn (1971, 91–2) discusses an instance of the placname Cera in Meath and notes that it is sometimes confused with Cermna.

teimnide, tais. *temn detais* B, *temhnidhe tais* M. *DIL* cites this line in the form ?*tenm detais*, based on the reading of B, s.v. 1 *teinm* 'cutting, gnawing', col. 118, l. 26. The metrical pattern suggests that *tais* is to be taken as a separate word for rhyme with *glais.*

deir Mide. *dernidhe* B, *deirmidhe* M. *DIL* cites this line s.v. ?*dernide.* Although the syllabic structure is irregular, the other lines end in disyllabic words and on this basis I tentatively take the second element as the placename *Mide* 'Meath'. There are other examples of placenames being incorporated as elements of abusive epithets, e.g. *a iuchra maigre a Mumain* 'you salmon spawn from Munster' no. 31 and *gruth a Caimlinn* 'curds from Caimlinn' no. 84. The first element may be *deir*, a type of skin disease which *DIL* s.v. translates as 'herpes'. For a similar image, cf. *breccar claime i cinn* 'mangy spots on a head' no. 62.

72. *MV* III §173.

The MSS give the name of this metre as *abachtada* B and *abbata* M. I follow B and read *ábacht fata* 'long humour'. Both the syllabic structure (3^2 5^2 7^3 10^2) and stress pattern are irregular and the metre is classified as *écoitchenn. DIL* s.v. *ábacht* takes the reading of B to be nominative plural and states that *ábacht* is masculine. According to Murphy (1961, 76) it is feminine, however, and the word is also feminine in Modern Irish. *Ábacht* is also used in the metrical name of no. 24 above (*ábacht chummaisc* 'mixed humour'). I can make no sense of M's reading *abbata.* Thurneysen (1891, 100) reads lines *ab* as one octosyllabic line.

Úa Scuirre. *Uas cuirri* B, *Uascuirri* M. This could be either a personal name or a nickname. I have not found any examples of a nominative form, which may be **Scorr* from Latin *scurra* 'buffoon'. A diminutive form Scurríne occurs in *Corp. Gen.* LL 317 bb 3 (O'Brien 1962, 350). *DIL* cites the reading of B s.v. 1 *corr* 'projecting part, end, corner', col. 483 l. 34.

73. *MV* III §179.

The metre is *berraide ar rinn chúaille* 'a chip of wood on the tip of a post' (7^2 8^1 8^2 7^2 7^1), classified as *écoitchenn.*

Gúaire. I take this as a personal name, although it could also be the word *gúaire* 'bristles'; cf. *finna ar gúaire cullaig allaid* 'a hair on the bristles of a fat (?) wild boar' no. 64.

fíacail. *fiacla* B, *fiachail* M. The reading of B ('teeth of a comb') would also be suitable as this word is not fixed by rhyme.

fostán. This word is not well attested and *DIL* s.v. suggests the meaning 'steady, firm'.

gablóc. This is the only example cited in *DIL* s.v. *gablóg* 'small fork'. Dinneen s.v. *gabhlóg* gives the meaning 'a small two-pronged fork made from the limbs of a shrub or furze bush'.

crostál. This is the only example cited in *DIL*. Meyer (1906b, 531) suggests *cross-téll* 'a cross-belt?'. This cannot be the intended form, however, since it rhymes with *fostán*. I take it as a compound of *cros* 'cross' and *tál* 'adze'. A similar compound, *crostúag lethan* 'broad cross-axe', is found in Middle Irish legal commentary (Kelly 1997, 488 note 164).

74. *MV* III §180.

The metre is *anair imrinn scaílte* (8^2 6^2 8^2 6^2), classified as *écoitchenn*.

Lachtnán mac Luchduinn uí Gadra. See note on *Lachtnán úa gormfiaclach Gadra* no. 22. In a note on another occurrence of this name, Gwynn (1903–35, ii, 108 note 21) suggests that *luchdonn* is an epithet rather than a proper name, noting that Thurneysen took the first element to be *luch* 'mouse'. *DIL* s.v. 1 *luch* col. 231 l. 35 also takes the first element as 'mouse'. Meyer (1920, 8) suggests that *luch-* in the name of the subject of our text is used in an insulting sense rather than as a personal name. As McCone points out (1985, 175–6), however, *luchdonn* is generally applied to heroes and the first element is thus more likely to be the word for wolf rather than the word for mouse.

ar cascéith. *arcass geith* B, *arcasceith* M. I take this as a compound of *cas* 'curly' and dative singular of *scé* 'a thorn bush' declined as a dental stem, for which see Binchy (1971, 163 note 65). Meyer (1920, 7) reads *ar cas-scéich* 'auf einem krausen Dornbusch' 'on a gnarled thornbush'. Note that *DIL* cites this line s.v. *géith*, based on B's reading, where it is the only example.

glasléith. Rhymes imperfectly with *cascéith*. Note the use of a feminine form of the adjective with the dative of a masculine consonantal stem, for which see *SG* III §6.4. The adjective *glas* is also used of the mottled complexion of a smith's daughter in a satire in *MV* II §120 (Meyer 1919, no. 70).

75. *MV* III §181.

The metre is *bánrothán* 'little white wheel' (8^2 7^2 7^2 8^2 8^2 8^2 ; 8^2 10^2 8^2 8^2 8^2), classified as *écoitchenn*. This poem is highly ornamented. In addition to the main rhyme between *imme* (f) and *tinne* (k), the end-words of the lines rhyme with each other and also consonate with the main rhyme. There is *aicill* rhyme between *fairre* (b) : *fainne* (c) and internal rhyme between *carpat* (a) : *arcat* (b), *crín* (a) : *lín* (b), *lonna* (e) : *lomma* (f) and *géim* (g) : *léim* (h). There is *breccad* rhyme between *gestul* (g) : *escur* (h) : *estud* (i), *drochbó* (g) : *mochbró* (i) and *finne* (c) : *timme* (e). In the final two lines, there is rhyme between *cuinge* (j) : *cruinne* (k): *cuirre* (j) : *tuille* (k) : *cruimme* (j): *truimme* (k) and these words also rhyme with *cuirre* (a) etc. There is alliteration in every line except *f.*

arcat ar lín. The phrase 'silver in exchange for linen' is used in the sense of a bad or unequal bargain. For similar metaphors see p. 34.

fairre. I follow *DIL* s.v. *farr* 'a post or prop' col. 41, l. 68 in taking this as genitive singular.

láech ic íarraid lomma is imme. For an explanation of this metaphor see p. 205.

láir is láech ic léim íar n-escur uirre. The word order is unusual and one would expect *ic léim uirre* 'leaping onto her'. The position of *uirre* has presumably been dictated by the requirement for rhyme with some of the other end words. Cf. the unusual word order in *upaid i salann suirge* 'a love potion in salt' no. 82, where *suirge* is required for end-rhyme with *uidre. Escar* is used here with the meaning 'a fall from horseback'; see *DIL* s.v. 1 *escar* col. 189, l. 9.

mochbró. The context suggests that this is a genitive plural form. *Bró* is an *n*-stem in Old Irish and a genitive form *brón* (OIr. *broön*) would be expected. The form in our text is fixed by rhyme with *drochbó*, however. A genitive singular form *bró* is attested in Middle Irish commentary on *Bretha Étgid*, where the phrase *Bla muilinn bleith* 'the immunity of a mill is milling' is explained in the commentary as *Slan dono cétsceinm na bro ris cach naen* 'Immune from liability, moreover, is the first slipping of the mill with respect to everyone' (*CIH* 287.28).

pistol cuinge. Kelly (1997, 472) suggests that this refers to 'the peg which secures the yoke to the yoke-beam of a plough or the pole of a cart'.

76. *MV* III §182.

Edition: Meyer (1919, no. 71).

The metre is *gort fo lid* 'distinctive field' (8^2 10^2 12^2 8^2 6^2), classified as *écoitchenn. Gort fo lid* is a type of Ogam alphabet illustrated in a tract known as *In Lebor Ogaim* (*Auraic.* l. 6044) and there is evidence to suggest that this tract was used as a source by the compiler of *MV* III when coining certain metrical names (McLaughlin 2005b, 122–7). McManus (1991, 182 note 19) suggests that *lid* in the phrase *gort fo lid* may be an old dative form of the neuter *s*-stem *leth* 'side'. The repetition of the subject's name, *Dúngal,* is a feature of several other satires in *MV* III; see p. 14.

Máel Inmain. For a suggestion as to his identity see p. 118.

idraid. This is the only example cited in *DIL.* Meyer takes it to be a collective from *id* 'collar, ring' and translates as 'eine abgelebte Nonne, die über kotiges Flechtwerk spaziert' 'a decrepit nun who walks over filthy wickerwork'. *Idrad otraig* 'rings of dung' appears to be used here in the sense of 'cow-pats'.

ar achtaib. *arechtaibh* B, *arachtraibh* M. Meyer reads *ar ēchtaib* and translates the line as ' Dūngal, ein Mensch, der seine Seele auf einem Hügel zu schlechten Taten zum Verkauf ausbietet' 'Dúngal, a man who on a hill offers his soul for sale for bad deeds '. The MS forms together suggest that *achtaib* is a possible reading and this has the advantage of forming consonance with *otraig* (b) and *gortaig* (e). As an alternative, Meyer suggests reading *ḟechtaib,* which would also form consonance.

úrad. The primary meaning of *úrad* is 'act of making fresh, renewing'. The fact that the patch is yellow may be significant in the context of satire, since this colour was associated with individuals of low status; see p. 23.

77. *MV* III §201.

The metre is *meisce Draigin meic Dorndorbied* 'drunkenness of Draigen son of Dorndorbied' (10^2 10^2 10^2 10^2), classified as *écoitchenn.* Meyer (1909, 37) includes Draigen in a list of the poets of Ireland, but it is unlikely that he was an historical personage. He may have been a literary figure, since other metrical names in *MV* III are qualified by personal names of literary characters rather than poets (e.g. Mug Ruith no. 28; Cú Roí no. 29; Néde no. 46; Mongán no. 71).

Goll Gabra. For the alternation *gobra/gabra* as found in the MSS see *SG* III §3.6. I take *Gabra* as genitive singular of a placename *Gabar,* several examples of which are cited in Hogan (1910, 432–3). *DIL* cites this line s.v. *goll* 'blind of one eye' col. 134, l. 17 and suggests 'a one-eyed horse (?)'. Thurneysen (1912, 89) suggests that Goll Gabra may be the same person as Goll Gabráin, who is recorded in *AU s.a.* 1113 as having killed his brother Domnall mac Donnchada, king of Ossory. As is the case in many of the satires in *MV* III, however, it is impossible to establish the identity of the subject due to the lack of context.

ar omna. *aromna* B, *armona* ME. I follow B and read *omna* 'the bole of a tree', which is also found in the sense 'spear, spear-shaft'; see *DIL* s.v. *omna* (c).

gaite. Genitive singular of *gat* 'theft', used attributively.

gotán. I take this as a substantive use of the adjective *got* 'stammering' plus the diminutive suffix. DIL cites line *b* of our poem s.v. the personal name/sobriquet *Gotán*.

gort fossaid férmar mara. *gort fosaigh fear mara* B, *gort fossaig fer mara* M, *gort fosaigh fear no ferrmar mara* E. I follow the suprascript correction in E, which gives ten syllables as in the other three lines. *Fermar mara* could easily have been mis-transcribed as *fer mara* through haplography and this reading also makes better sense than the alternative *gort fossaid fer mara* 'the level field of the men of the sea'. The adjective *fossad* 'stationary; firm, steady' is applied to land of good quality in an Old Irish law tract on land values. This text describes best arable land (*etham remibí ethamnaib*) as *tir fosad a mbi maith cach maith* 'level land in which every good thing (?) flourishes' (Mac Niocaill 1971, 82; see also Kelly 1997, 394). While a *gort fossaid férmar* 'level grassy field' would be ideal for growing crops, such a field by the sea would be unproductive. A similar idea is expressed by the metaphor *gort íchtair ḟaithche* 'a field of the lower part of a green' no. 70 above.

clama. Note the Middle Irish loss of the dative plural ending of an adjective, here fixed by rhyme with *mara*.

78. *MV* III §203.

The metre is *etal ṡeisedach Cruithentúath i Cloich Locha Comra* 'the six-part beam of the Cruithentúatha in Cloch Locha Comra' (8^3 8^3 8^3 ; 8^3 6^3 8^3), classified as *écoitchenn*. The adjective *seisedach* 'consisting of a sixth or sixths' is applied to an example of *rannaigecht becc mór* in *MV* III §87 which also has six lines. It is impossible to establish from the context whether *Cruithentúath* refers to Pictland or to *Cruithentúath* in Ulster (Hogan 1910, 312). Hogan (*ibid.*, 250) cites two examples of placenames containing the elements *Cloch Locha* and on this basis I take *Cloch Locha Comra* as a placename. I have not been able to identify the location, however.

nocon ḟuair slántroit senmaire. Lit. 'he did not get a safe fight of musicians'. *DIL* cites two examples of *senmaire* 'musician' but omits the present example.

ágmuilt. The second element is genitive singular of *molt* 'wether'. If imperfect rhyme with *Pátraic* (line *a*) and *slántroit* (line *b*) is intentional, possibly as a form of *breccad*, this would indicate that the *a* is long. On this basis, I tentatively take the first element to be the noun *ág* 'fight, battle', used in the sense 'fierce'.

fidnaige. *fidhnaigi* B, *idhnaidhe* M, illeg. E. I take this as genitive singular of *fidnach* 'twigs, used for fuel or bedding'.

rodraige. *rodraide* B, *rodraige* M, illeg E. Rhymes with *foglaide* and *cornaire.* I take this as genitive singular feminine of **rodrach*/**radrach,* the base form to which the abstract suffix *-us* is attached in *radrachus.* The latter is a defect in cattle which results in the failure to conceive: *radhracus .i. dairthir í ⁊ ni anand innti* '*radrachus* i.e. she is bulled and it does not stay in her' (*CIH* iii 998.37; Kelly 1997, 201). This would lead to a reduction in the animal's value. I am grateful to Liam Breatnach for this suggestion.

isti. The context suggests that this is an adjective qualifying *cornaire* but I have found no other examples and it is not given as a headword in *DIL.*

ibraide. For the significance of the epithet 'yew-like' see p. 39 above.

79. *MV* III §204.

The metre is *slat airbern* 'rod of defects' (4^2 8^1 7^1 8^1), classified as *écoitchenn.*

i ngill. A pledge (*gell*) or fore-pledge (*tairgille*), left in anticipation of possible injury or trespass, was generally an item of some worth and was often associated with the occupation of the person making the pledge (Kelly 1988, 164–5).

asa maid. *isamhuigh* B, *isamaig* M, illeg. E. I have emended the MSS to read third singular conjunct present indicative of *maidid* (lenited *-d* and *-g* are often confused in the MSS). *Asa maid* qualifies *srón,* i.e. Finn is described as 'a calf's nose ... out of which bursts ... '.

80. *MV* III §59.

Edition: Murphy (1961, [47]).

The metre is *cró cummaisc etir carnrannaigecht móir ocus sruth di aill* (8^1 4^1 8^1 4^1), classified as *gnáthaiste.* The MSS show confusion over the name of the metre in that only B^b has *móir,* only H has *carnrandaigecht,* while G reads *sruth daill.* In H, the suprascript letters *.c.* (written above the second instance of *corr*) and *.d.* (written above *broth*) stand for *carnrannaigecht* and *sruth di aill* respectively. The latter is also the name of a type of bard according to *MV* I §1 and *Bretha Nemed Dédenach* (*UR* 50 l. 7), while in *Míadślechtae* it is given as one of the grades of Latin scholars (*CIH* ii 586.1).

corrmíl corr nó chuil. The subject is likened to biting or stinging insects, possibly an allusion to his use of satire (*felcháinte fir*).

chuil. This word is omitted in BB^{b}ME, which also read an extra syllable in line *b*, i.e. *bro toll tall* BB^{b}E and *bro coll tall* M against *broth oll* GH. It may be the case that in the line of transmission represented by BB^{b}ME, *chuil* was lost and *bró* was then interpreted as the last word in line *a*, *tall* being added to line *b* at a later stage to give four syllables.

bró tholl. A hollow quern is a metaphor for something useless; cf. *a athbró íchtair* 'you worn-out lower quern' no. 51 and *a tholltimpáin* 'you pierced *timpán*' no. 41. Murphy reads *broth tall 'na thig* 'flesh yonder in his house'.

lethbráice. G stands apart from the other MSS in reading *athbraighi* 'of a worn-out shoe', but this does not rhyme with *felcháinte*.

láithir. *laithir* BB^{b}M, <. . .>*hair* E, *leathair* G, *lathir* H. I follow Murphy in taking this as Middle Irish third singular relative present indicative passive of *láid* 'throws'. G reads genitive singular of *lethar* 'leather' used attributively, i.e. 'a thong of a worn-out leather shoe'.

felcháinte fir. Rhymes with *lethbráice*. I take the first element in *felcháinte* as *fell* 'deceit, treachery', which is normally *fel* or *feil* in compounds; cf. *felgabar* 'an evil goat' no. 27. *Fir* is genitive of apposition. Murphy (1961, 106) suggests that *fel* is the same as the element in *felmac* 'pupil, student, apprentice', translating 'the type of man who would make a satirist (?)'. *DIL* cites this line s.v. 2 *fel* 'poetry, science'.

81. *MV* III §73.

Edition: Murphy (1961, [78]).

The metre is *cethramthu* [*rannaigechta móire*] 'one quarter [of *rannaigecht mór*]' (3^1 3^1 3^1 3^1), classified as *gnáthaiste*. This stanza is found in a section of *MV* III which illustrates the following 'fractions' of *rannaigecht mór*: *trían rannaigechta moiré* 'one third of *rannaigecht mór*' (4^1 4^1 4^1 4^1) *MV* III §72; *a cóiced* 'one fifth of it' (1^1 1^1 1^1 1^1) *MV* III §74; *Ní as ḟuilliu bic innás cóiced in só ⁊ ní roich cethramthu* 'This is something which is slightly greater than one-fifth and it does not extend to one quarter (2^1 2^1 2^1 2^1) *MV* III §75.

muine menn. *Muine* 'bush, thicket' can be used of a thicket providing shelter or secrecy and a conspicuous hiding place could be a metaphor for something useless. Alternatively, *muine* may be used here metaphorically of the subject (who is described a *cáinte* 'satirist'), in the same way that *taman* 'trunk of a tree' and *dos* 'bush' are used as names for grades of poets. Since lines *acd* refer to physical defects (*dall* 'blind', *cam* 'crooked', *cen chenn* 'headless'), *menn* could also be taken to mean 'stammering' and *DIL* cites this line s.v. 2 *menn* 'stammering, inarticulate'.

82. *MV* III §83.

Edition: Meyer (1919, no. 88).

The metre is *rannaigecht becc corránach* 'hooked [extended] *rannaigecht becc*' (7^2 7^2, 7^2 ; 7^2, 7^2 7^2), classified as *gnáthaiste*.

Drúth Gailenga cen intliucht. *Druth gaileng cen indtliucht* B, *Druth gaileng ceninthucht* M, *Druth gailing cinindtlecht* E. The MSS read the historical genitive form *Gaileng*. As noted by Meyer, this gives a pentasyllabic line, which is unsuitable metrically. Reading *Gailenga* would give the required number of syllables and Mac Neill notes (1911–12, 63 §28) that a genitive plural form in *-a* is found in Middle Irish: 'As in Airgialla, so in several other plural names with *o*-stems, Middle Irish usage substitutes a strengthened nominative ... The added syllable is occasionally maintained in gp., e.g. septem genera Gailinga'. Unfortunately, he does not give the source of *septem genera Gailinga*. An alternative is to read *cen a intliucht* 'without his intelligence', adding a third singular masculine possessive pronoun. M's reading *inthucht* has probably arisen due to the confusion of the letters *l* and *h*.

sacairt ṡenóir. I follow Meyer in taking *sacairt* as a preposed genitive.

traigle i nach úathad uidre. Lit. 'a shoelace in which dun-colour is not a small amount'. ME both add *taeb* after *traigle*, which gives a line of nine syllables. The colour *odor* 'dun' was associated with low status; see p. 23 above. Note that the subject of no. 80 is described in similar terms as *íall lethbráice láithir do choin* 'a thong of a single shoe which is thrown to a dog'.

upaid i salann suirge. The unusual word order is due to the requirement for rhyme between *uidre* and *suirge*.

83. *MV* III §139.

The metre is *in chethramthanach mór meic Adomnáin* 'the great lined [metre] of the son of Adomnán' (7^3 8^3 6^3 8^4 7^3 8^3 8^3 8^3 8^4), classified as *gnáth medónda*. *Cethramthanach* is an adjective from *cethramthu* 'quarter', used here of the lines of a quatrain (Thurneysen 1891, 128). An introductory passage in *MV* III states that this metre is the same as a combination of *rathnúall bairdne* and *slat brecht*, both of which are illustrated in the preceding section of the tract: *Forba na slat mbrecht for óenscél in só ocus do rathnúall bairdne, conid óenaiste fásas díb ocus in chethramthanach mór meic Adomnáin só sís* 'This is a culmination of the *slat brecht* [metres] on a single narrative and of *rathnúall bairdne*, so that the same metre grows from them as the following [example of] *in cethramthanach mór meic Adomnáin*'. The similarity seems to lie in the fact that the examples of *rathnúall bairdne* and *slat brecht* illustrated in *MV* III §§128–38 also end in words of three and four syllables, while in *rathnúall bairdne* the main rhyme is between lines *cf* rather than between the couplets. Thurneysen (1891, 159) notes that this metre resembles types such as *laíd luibenchosach* and *eochraid.*

There is a complex metrical pattern, with main rhyme between *casbúarote* (d) and *nglasfúarote* (i) and rhyme between the endwords of the first lines of both sections, *slimabaill* (a) and *finnArainn* (e). All of the other trisyllabic words consonate with each other (sometimes imperfectly). The only exceptions are *senubull* and *fannadall,* which themselves form imperfect consonance. There is also a pattern of *breccad* rhyme (sometimes between voiced and voiceless stops) in *slat* (f) : *gat* (g) : *cnap* (g): *glac* (h).

The first section is difficult to interpret, although the phrase *senubull for slimabill* 'an old apple on a slender apple tree' is clearly meant as an insult; cf. *ubull buide bís for abaill* 'a yellow apple on an apple tree' no. 74 above. The second section describes a visit to Arran in Scotland in terms of a series of useless or worthless items, a theme which is quite common in the satires in *MV* III; see p. 66. The final line may allude scathingly to the fruits of this visit: a short, grey fleece. This would certainly have been considered an inappropriate gift or reward for a poem. A fleece was the honour-price of an apprentice (*inol*), the lowest grade of freeman, and grey fleeces were less valuable than white (Kelly 1997, 70–1; 77). Perhaps this is what the poet is referring to in the phrase *selb chronaigim* 'property which I claim'.

chronaigim. *tronaigim* B, *cro andoghaimh* M. M's reading is probably a copying error as a result of the scribe's eye having wandered to the letters *ndogaim* of *rith rindogaim* in line *f.* I have found no examples of a verb *tronaigid* as in B, but M reads a form beginning with *c* and both letters are easily confused. I follow *DIL* which suggests reading *cronaigim* for B's *tronaigim* (s.v. *cronaigid* col. 547, l. 56). Although this verb is not well attested, it occurs several times with the meaning 'claims' in a fourteenth-century legal text attributed to Giolla na Naomh mac Duinn Shléibhe Mhic Aodhagáin (*Companion* 30). In one instance it is used with *selb,* as is the case in our text: *masa innraic cronaigus ag innraic, sealb don innraic aga cronaigter...* 'if it is an honest person who claims against an honest person, possession [is granted] to the honest person against whom it is claimed' (*CIH* ii 693.24–5).

cellinill. *cheillinill* B, *chellinill* M. *DIL* takes this as a compound of *cíall* 'sense', citing B's reading s.v. *cíall* col. 177, l. 3, preceded by a query. A short vowel is required for the metre, however. The first element is *cell* 'church' and the second may be a substantive use of *inill* 'safe, secure'.

cennḟolaim. *ceandfolaim* B, *cendolaim* M. The palatal ending in both MSS suggests that this is a genitive singular form of the adjective *folam* 'empty'. While the individual elements are clear enough, the precise meaning of the phrase *cellinill cennḟolaim* is difficult to construe and I have left the phrase untranslated. An 'empty-ended church sanctuary' may be a description of an unguarded or unsafe sanctuary.

chamḟulang. *camfolang* B, *chambolang* M. *DIL* s.v. *camm* col. 63, l. 30 suggests a compound of *camm* 'crooked' and *fulang* 'support, prop'. This could be another metaphor for something useless, but the precise meaning in the present context is unclear.

casbúaróte. Rhymes with *glasfúaróte*. The first element may be *cas* 'curly, furred' and the second *búar* 'cattle'. It is difficult to interpret the meaning of the compounds *chamfulang casbúaróte*, however. The suffix *-óte* is unusual and is also found in *glasfúaróte* (line *i*). It may be a genitive singular form of the suffix *-óit*, which occurs in Latin loanwords such as *umaldóit* 'humility' and *tríndóit* 'trinity' (*GOI* §294 (a)). A collective *cethardóit* is found in the legal text *Bechbretha* and the editors suggest that this is a compound of the compositional form *cethar* 'four' plus a suffix *-dóit* abstracted from *tríndóit* (Charles-Edwards and Kelly 1983, 95). *Casbúaróte* and *glasfúaróte* in our poem may be similar *ad hoc* formations. The suffixes *-aile* and *-ánach* also seem to be peculiar to *MV* III; see p. 126 above. Meyer (1906b, 322) cites this line s.v. *casbúarot?*

finnArainn. Rhymes with *slimabaill.* I take this as a compound of *find* 'fair' and dative singular of the placename *Arann* 'Arran' in Scotland (with short *-a-* as required by the metre), for which see Meyer (1920, 3) and T. F. O'Rahilly (1927, 113).

rindogaim. *DIL* cites this line s.v. *rind-* col. 73, l. 29 and suggests 'a species of Ogham?'. McManus (1991, 160) draws attention to the use of *rindaid* 'cuts' and *do-foirndea* (from **to-fo-rind*) 'expresses, marks out' to refer to the writing of Ogam in Early Irish sagas.

fo gallseminn glac gallṡalainn. Here the insult appears to lie in the fact that imported salt, a valuable commodity (Kelly 1997, 341), is wasted by being sprinkled on rushes. A similar image is found in *Aislinge Meic Conglinne*, where *ba salond for luachair* 'it would be salt on rushes' is included among a list of useless things (Jackson 1990, 28, l. 862). For other references to foreigners in satire see p. 31 above.

glasḟúaróte. *glasfuarrote* B, *glasfuarothe* M. I take the first two elements as the adjectives *glas* 'grey' and *fúar* 'cold'. For the suffix *-óte* see note on *casbúaróte* (line *d*).

84. *MV* III §172.

The metre is *scem scaílte* 'scattered yelp' ([12 x 4^2] + 5^2 6^2), classified as *écoitchenn. Scaílte* appears to be used here with the basic meaning 'scattered' rather than as a technical term to indicate a lack of consonance. The poem consists of two sections, each of which comprises seven phrases. The main rhyme is between the end-words of each section *Caimlinn* (c) : *cairling* (f). In the first section, there is rhyme between *demain* (a) : *lenaim* (b), *Domnaill* (a) : *comrainn* (b) and *duiblinn* (a) : *chuibrinn* (b). The metrical structure of the second section is unusual in that here the rhyme is between words in the same line: *lomgaill* (d) : *mondaill* (d) : *lomraim* (d) and *mergaill* (e) : *Cerbaill* (e). There is internal rhyme between *luch* (b) : *gruth* (c) and *breccad* rhyme between *buirbrind* (e) : *duiblinn* (a) : *chuibrinn* (b) and *drúth* (a) : *lúth* (e) : *drúth* (e). Although this poem is difficult to interpret, it is clearly satirical since the subject is described as a *drúth* 'fool', *dall* 'blind man' and *gall* 'foreigner', all of which are common terms of abuse.

gruth. *Gruth* 'curds', unlike butter (for which see p. 205), would not have been associated with high status and a type of cheese known as *grus* (from the same root as *gruth*) is included among the food-entitlements of low-ranking individuals (Kelly 1997, 328).

Caimlinn. Caimlinn here would seem to be located in the barony of Upper Massareene, Co. Antrim (Hogan 1910, 140).

bérla in lomgaill. For other references to the speech of foreigners in satire see p. 32.

merga. I take the first element of this compound as *mer* 'demented, crazy' and the second as *ga* 'spear', possibly referring to a spear cast by a blind man (*in mondaill*) performing tricks or feats. Alternatively, one could read *mér* 'finger' (in the sense of a small or finger-like spear) as the first element for rhyme with *bérla.*

mondaill. I tentatively take this to be a compound of *mon* 'feat, trick' and genitive singular of *dall* 'blind man'.

lenga. *DIL* cites this line s.v. ?*lenga* and no meaning is given. The context suggests that this is genitive singular of an adjective but I have not been able to establish a meaning. The vowel length is also uncertain, although rhyme between *Bérla* : *mérga* : *lénga* may be intended.

lomraim. *lomraimh* B, *loraim* M. The reading of M may have arisen through the loss of an *m*-stroke.

in buirbrinn. *inuirbrind* B and *inbuirbrind* M. Rhymes with *duiblinn* (a), *chuibrinn* (b). I follow M and read genitive singular of a compound of *borb* 'rough' and a poorly attested adjective *renn*, used substantively, for which *DIL* s.v. suggests the meaning 'swift, hasty?'.

mergaill. *mearbaill* B, *mergaill* M. I follow M in view of the frequent use of *gall* as an abusive epithet in *MV* III. B's reading may reflect the confusion of lenited *b* and lenited *g* or may be due to anticipation of *Cerbaill* in the following phrase.

Cille Cerbaill. Hogan (1910, 686) identifies this as Kilcarrol in Kilrush, Co. Clare.

cairling. Rhymes with *Caimlinn. DIL* cites this line s.v. *cairling* 'hag', of which it is the only example. According to Meyer (1906b, 306), *cairling* 'hag' is from Old Norse. An alternative interpretation would be to take *cairling* as the placename *Cairlind* in Co. Louth (Hogan 1910, 141), although the use of the definite article would be unusual in this context. Note that the final *-ing* of *chairling* forms a *dúnad.*

85. *MV* III §194.

The metre is *gáir gaill* 'cry of a foreigner' (3^2 7^1 8^1 7^1), classified as *écoitchenn.* The MSS give the metrical name as *Gair gaill* B, *Gair guill* M, *Gair gaill nó guill* E.

Drúth Dala. I take *Dala* as the same element as in the placename *Slige Dala* near Borris-in-Ossory (Hogan 1910, 613). Hogan reads *Slige Dála,* but an example in *MV* III §143 (which he omits) indicates that the *-a-* is short, since here *Dala* rhymes with *mara* and *chara. Drúth* is often qualified by a personal name or placename; see p. 26.

saillige. Rhymes with *chaillige.* This is the only example cited in *DIL* s.v. ?*saillech* and the reader is referred to *saill* 'salted meat'. The form is genitive singular, qualifying *colptha.* A shank of salted meat served between two meals is probably a metaphor for something pointless or excessive (i.e. an unwanted or unnecessary meal).

86. *MV* III §199.

The metre is *mellgal filed* 'blind fury of a poet' (8^2 4^1 6^2 4^1), classified as *écoitchenn*. Cf. the phrase *plág mellgaile* 'a plague of blind fury' no. 78 above.

térnuma. *ternumtha* B, *ternamtha* M, *ternumha* E. Rhymes with *brénulcha*. This line is cited in *DIL* s.v. ?*ternumtha*, where it is the only example, and the reader is referred to *térnam*, verbal noun of *do-érni* 'escapes'. I take *térnuma* as genitive singular of *térnam*, qualifying *corp cáerach* (lit. 'body of a sheep of escaping of a wether'). This construction is commonly found with transitive verbs, e.g. *fer dénma bairgine* 'a man of the making of bread' (*GOI* §250(b); Vendryes 1917–19, 328–30).

bechairecht. This is the only example cited in *DIL* s.v. ?*becairecht* and the reader is referred to the preceding entry ?*becaire*. The example of *becaire* is also from *MV* III (§130), where rhyme with *brethaile* indicates that the *-c-* is lenited. I take *bechairecht* as a verbal noun formation from *bech* 'bee' and the agent suffix *-aire* by analogy with formations such as *cornairecht* from the agent-noun *cornaire* no. 63 and *stocairecht* from *stocaire* no. 67. Note also *brocairecht* 'acting like a badger' no. 67. *Beachaire* is given as the Modern Irish word for 'beekeeper' and 'beehive' in Ó Dónaill and Dinneen but I have not come across any early examples aside from the forms in *MV* III.

bai. This word is missing in B, which has a blank space sufficient for 4 or 5 letters. There is also a larger space than normal before and after *bai* in M, which suggests that some letters may be missing. Line *a* has eight syllables and *bai* may have formed part of a trisyllabic word. It is impossible to be certain of this, however, since many metres in the *écoitchenna* section of the tract are syllabically irregular. The form as it stands in ME (*bai*) may be genitive singular of *báe* 'profit', although the description *bechairecht baí* 'profitable bee-keeping' seems unsuitable in the context of satire.

buide. The adjective *buide* 'yellow' is used of bees in *Táin Bó Cúalnge*, where hair is described as *samalta* ... *re buidi mbech* 'like the yellow of bees' (C. O'Rahilly 1976, ll. 2962–4).

Indexes

First Lines in Miscellany of Satires

Abusive Epithets in Miscellany of Satires

This index comprises epithets which occur more than once. See also Index of Animal Invective.

aball 'apple-tree': *ubull buide bís for abaill* no. 74; (in compd.) *senubull for slimabaill* no. 83.

airem 'ploughman': *airem apaide* no. 20; *a uí airim brocsalaig* no. 40.

bél 'mouth': *nochon acca béolu eich / amail béolu in Líathainig* no. 3; *a bél chaillige caíche* no. 49; *a bél mná uidre uime ibraide* no. 52; *bél daim dona Déisib* no. 58; *bél gaill gopluim* no. 69.

ben 'woman': *a bél mná uidre uime ibraide* no. 52; *a ben drúth i ndabaig* no. 56; *ben chamlámach chomdálach* no. 67; *ben ic coistecht ri toirm tuinne* no. 75.

bró 'quern': *bró tholl 'na thig* no. 80; (in compd.) *a athbró íchtair* no. 51; *estud mochbró itir muille* no. 75.

buide 'yellow': *a bolgán buide* no. 19; *co n-arm cháembuide chírmaire* no. 29; *a uí chúic patán pellbuide* no. 52; *fíacail cam órbuide* no. 69; *ubull buide bís for abaill* no. 74; *úrad buide ar brat gamna* no. 76; *bechairecht bai buide* no. 86.

cacc 'shit': *a chacc ar másaib* no. 36; *a chacc cuirre uidre ittige* no. 43; *cacc na ndrúth* no. 85.

caillech 'hag, nun': *a bél chaillige caíche* no. 49; *cáith chaillige* no. 85; (in compd.) *athchaillech ic imthecht idraid otraig* no. 76.

cáinte 'satirist': *cáinte búaile ic brocairecht* no. 67; *cáinte cam* no. 81; (in compd.) *felcháinte fir* no. 80.

cam 'crooked': *a glas cam* no. 44; *senáraig . . . chama fot chossaib* no. 53; *cnám clíabaig caim úa Cuinn* no. 61; *fíacail cam órbuide* no. 69; *cáinte cam* no. 81; (in compd.) *robo lór a cambuirbe* no. 16; *ben chamlámach chomdálach* no. 67; *do chamfulang . . . cnap cammuilind* no. 83. Cf. also *a chammáin* no. 48.

carpat 'gum; upper beak': *a charpat lenaim liúin* no. 34; *carpat bó bricce for benn* no. 58; *carpat crín cuirre* no. 75.

clérech 'cleric': *a thonn do cheólaib clérig* no. 35; *láir cháel chlérech ar cúairt chros* no. 59; (in compd.) *a chorann maccléirig minn* no. 33.

cornaire 'horn-player': *a chornaire* no. 50; *a imlige baise céise caise coise cornaire* no. 52; *cornairecht chornaire ar chrod* no. 63; *cornaire isti ibraide* no. 78.

cos 'foot': *a chossa daim* no. 47; *a chossa cromma crebair* no. 49; *at cranda i cossaib* no. 53; *senáraig corra, chromma, chamma fot chossaib* no. 53; (in compd.) *a lethchoss geóid* no. 44.

crossán 'jester': *crossán líath ic linn* no. 62; *crossán machaire ic merle* no. 82.

cuing 'yoke': *a chuing ar argat* no. 34; *pistol cuinge* no. 75.

dabach 'vat': *a ben drúth i ndabaig* no. 56; *dabach ibairglic aithne* no. 70.

dall 'blind': (adj.) *A meic dúir daill iffirnn* no. 46; *Duine dall* no. 81; (subst.) *a daill Charnmaige* no. 56; *cocur daill dar draigne* no. 57; *dán inad díamair daill* no. 61; *merga in mondaill* no. 84. Cf. also *dallán Dromma Bó* no. 66.

deman 'devil': *a gemm dubgorm demain* no. 49; *a delb in demain* no. 51; *ingen demain* no. 84.

díabal 'devil': *a díabail omda ibes in linn* no. 47; *dér do déraib díabail* no. 68.

dronn 'hump': *a dronn geóid íarna gabáil* no. 49; (in compd.) *gédglac dronngerr gopdub* no. 70.

drúth 'fool': (adj.) *a ben drúth i ndabaig* no. 56; (subst.) *Ní mó as ráiti rit, a drúith* no. 8; *A drúith, cid taí dom airbire?* no. 23; *a drúith chaíl ar clocthaig* no. 37; *drúth uí Domnaill* no. 84; (with population group) *A drúith na nDéise* no. 19; *ócdrúth odur d'Éoganacht* no. 72; *Drúth Gailenga* no. 82; (with placename) *A drúith na hAlla* no. 53; *drúth Lemna* no. 59; *drúth Durlais* no. 73; *drúth Cille Cerbaill* no. 84; *drúth Dala* no. 85; cf. also *dallán Dromma Bó* no. 66.

fíacail 'tooth': *a fíacla con ar cloich aílig* no. 41; *fíacla lega i lis* no. 59; *fíacail cam órbuide* no. 69; *fíacail círe* no. 73; (adj.) *Lachtnán úa gormfíaclach Gadra* no. 22.

gall 'foreigner': *gall cas a cnápluing* no. 5; *gall ic cnúasach cnó* no. 66; *bél gaill gopluim* no. 69; *gall bladach ar bilairlic* no. 70; *gáire gaill* no. 73; *gall cen chenn* no. 81; (in compd.) *do gelugud galluirge* no. 16; *snáith glais ri gallat* no. 71; *Gúaire na ngallbróc* no. 73; *fo gallṡeminn glac gallṡalainn* no. 83; *Bérla in lomgaill* no. 84.

gat 'withe': *a gait balláin etir dá scrín* no. 34; *gat gerrinnill* no. 83; (in compd.) *a folt gobann gatbéimnig* no. 33.

gobae 'smith': *a folt gobann gatbéimnig* no. 33; *mac don gabainn glasléith* no. 74.

gop 'mouth, gob': *a gop in gair* no. 47; (in compd.) *bél gaill gopluim* no. 69; *gédglac dronngerr gopdub* no. 70.

gort 'field': *gort íchtair faithche* no. 70; *gort fossaid férmar mara* no. 77.

ibar 'yew': *a airbe ibair* no. 51; (in compd.) *dabach ibairglic aithne* no. 70; (adj.) *a bél mná uidre uime ibraide* no. 52; *cornaire isti ibraide* no. 78.

imm 'butter': *Ith imm is uige* no. 19; *salann ar arán cen imm* no. 26; *a ithe imme re harán secail* no. 38; *láech ic íarraid lomma is imme* no. 75.

inar 'tunic': *inar odar* no. 20; *a inair uidir* no. 51.

lenam 'child': *a charpat lenaim liúin* no. 34; *a lenaim laic* no. 39; *a chrúachaide lenaim laic* no. 49, *tinme lenaim* no. 84.
linn 'ale': *a díabail omda ibes in linn* no. 47; *crossán líath ic linn* no. 62; *linn i mblede* no. 65; *linn deidblénach drolmánach* no. 67.
merugud 'going astray': *do-cúadas ar merugud* no. 16; *a-tá ar merugud* no. 20; *nocho gairit a merugud* no. 29.
odar 'dun colour': (adj.) *tráill odor ulchach ar echtra* no. 12; *inar odar* no. 20; *a chacc cuirre uidre ittige* no. 43; *a inair uidir* no. 51; *a bél mná uidre uime ibraide* no. 52 ; (subst.) *traigle i nach úathad uidre* no. 82.
salann 'salt': *salann ar arán cen imm* no. 26; *upaid i salann suirge* no. 82; *glac gallṡalainn* no. 83.
scían 'knife': *a scían espa* no. 45; *a chris cen scín* no. 50.
taman 'stump; blockhead': *a thamain chrín fo choiss cháich* no. 8; *Rí Connacht, cenn tamain* no. 68; a sub-grade of poet: *a thenga thamain* no. 42.
toll 'hollow': *pistol cuinge ... tuille ...* no. 75; *bró tholl 'na thig* no. 80; (in compd.) *a tholltimpáin* no. 41.
ubull 'apple': *ubull buide bís for abaill* no. 74; (in compd.) *senubull for slimabaill* no. 83.

Animal Invective in Miscellany of Satires

ag 'bullock': *screpall ar feóil n-aige* no. 62.
airech 'packhorse': *os muing airig aicedphellaig* 32; *a dúan ar airech n-ellaig* no. 35.
arc/orc 'piglet': (in compd.) *lommarc ar dá charaid* no. 68.
bó 'cow': *a ingaire bó luime luinne longaire* no. 52; *carpat bó bricce for benn* no. 58; *gestul im géim drochbó duinne* no. 75; *adarc bó rodraige* no. 78.
boc 'buck goat': *brénulcha buic* no. 86.
breccóc 'little trout': *A diripi talman ic teiched breccóice* no. 54.
broc 'badger': *sceith bruic ar beraib* no. 72; (in compd.) *a uí airim brocṡalaig* no. 40. Cf. also *cáinte búaile ic brocairecht* no. 67.
cáera 'sheep': *cenn crúaid con ar caírig* no. 60; *Corp cáerach corraige duibe* no. 86.
cailech 'cock': *gúaille cranda cailig* no. 22; *is tú in cailech d'Uíb Cellaig* no. 35.
cana 'whelp': (in compd.) *a ulcha gaillín . . . canatgréchánaig* no. 40.
capall 'horse': *serthe capaill íarna chor* no. 22; *Muiredach, mant capaill chróin* no. 58.
catt 'cat': *a chos dlochtáin ria catt* no. 8; *a barr feóir rossa / 'dar cossa cait* no. 39.
céis 'piglet': *a chloicenn chéise* no. 19; *cú dar céisib* no. 58.
cerc 'hen': *cerc i cill* no. 67.
cerc usce 'water-hen': *a cherc usce* no. 45.
clíabach 'deer' (?): *a chongna clíabaig i cinn do chnáma* no. 47; *cnám clíabaig caim úa Cuinn* no. 61; *seche chon fo chom chlíabaig* no. 63; *cnám do chnámaib clíabaig* no. 68.
colpthach 'heifer': *a cholpthach i cennach ndaim* no. 31.
corr 'heron': *ocus corr dlúith ina díaid* no. 8; *a lecca cuirre garbglaise grían* no. 36; *a chacc cuirre uidre ittige* no. 43; *Úa Cléirig, carpat crín cuirre* no. 75.
corrmíl 'midge': *Ní mó iná corrmíl corr nó chuil* no. 80.
crebar 'woodcock': *a chossa cromma crebair* no. 49; *a chrebair chuilig* no. 51.
cú 'hound, wolf': *a chú chlechtas ar cnámaib* no. 35; *a fíacla con ar cloich aílig* no. 41; *cú dar céisib* no. 58; *cenn crúaid con ar caírig* no. 60; *seche chon fo chom chlíabaig* no. 63; *guth senchon ar slabraid* no. 69; *íall lethbráice láithir do choin* no. 80; (in compd.) *a chammáin . . . confathmannaig . . .* no. 48.
cuil 'flea, gnat': *Ní mó iná corrmíl corr nó chuil* no. 80; (adj.) *a chrebair chuilig* no. 51.

cullach 'boar': *finna ar gúaire cullaig allaid* no. 64.
dam 'ox': *a cholpthach i cennach ndaim* no. 31; *a chossa daim* no. 47; *géim daim arathair tri aibne* no. 57.
ech 'horse': *óinmit ar eoch mall* no. 62.
ela 'swan': *net is ela as* no. 59.
én 'bird': *a eóin ré n-ossaib* no. 43; *én is ettchu d'énaib* no. 68.
erp 'doe': *erp d'erpaib i ndairib* no. 68.
fetóc 'plover: *a luirgne fetóice ar feórainn* no. 54.
fiach 'raven': *a cháith lín i lladair ḟiaich* no. 8; *Gilla in Naím, gnúis ḟiaich* no. 59.
fíad 'deer': *a reithe folta fásaig dar fíad* no. 36.
gabar 'goat': *felgabar* no. 27; *mennán oc deól gabair gaite* no. 77; (compd.) *Goll Mena, mún cromgabair* no. 67.
gadar 'hound': *a rigthe gerra glassa gadair* no. 42.
gaillín 'capon': *a ulcha gaillín* no. 40.
gamnach 'stripper' (type of cow): *a gerringne gamnaige galair* no. 56.
gamuin 'calf': *sút srón gamna ar guin i ngill* no. 79.
géd 'goose': *a lethchoss geóid* no. 44; *a geóid íarna gabáil* no. 46; *a dronn geóid íarna gabáil* no. 49; (in compd.) *gédglac dronngerr gopdub* no. 70.
gercc 'grouse': (adj.) *It durn bís do gop gercaide* no. 28.
goblán 'swift': *a goblán gorm* no. 4.
láir 'mare': *A meic Con Lemna, a láir gerr* no. 31; *a láir mall* no. 44; *láir cháel / chlérech ar cúairt chros* no. 59; *Adastar lára i lláim* no. 60; *láir is láech ic léim íar n-escur uirre* no. 75.
lon 'blackbird': *lon ic longaire i Líamain* no. 63; (in compd.) *a ingaire bó luime luinne longaire* no. 52.
luch 'mouse': *luch i comrainn* no. 84.
maigre 'salmon': *a iuchra maigre a Mumain* no. 31.
mart 'ox': (in compd.) *a chonadmairt chícaraig* no. 49.
matad 'dog': *a melṡrón mataid* no. 38.
mennán 'kid': *mennán oc deól gabair gaite* no. 77.
míl 'louse': *A-táit na míla co mer* no. 15; *a ithe i míl étaig* no. 46.
minchuil 'midge': (in compd.) *a mairbthine mongthige minchuile* no. 55.
molt 'wether': *Corp cáerach ... térnuma muilt* no. 86; (in compd.) *tlám do tharr ágmuilt ḟidnaige* no. 78.
muc 'pig': *Goll Gabra, gréch muice mairbe ar omna* no. 77; (in compd.) *a mucṡúil* no. 38.
os 'deer': *a eóin ré n-ossaib* no. 43.
patán 'leveret': *A uí chúic patán pellbuide* no. 52.
reithe 'ram': *a reithe folta fásaig dar fíad* no. 36.

scatán 'herring': *a scatán demnaide for druim dromlaige* no. 52.
seilche 'snail': *seilche co ndíb mbennaib* no. 64.
sinnach 'fox': (adj.) *a ṡailchide ṡinnchaide ṡalachluim* no. 55.
sned 'nit': *A-táit sneda cona clainn / it chorainn* no. 15; *ima agaid séolanart co snedaib* no. 72; (adj.) *a brollach snedach srethḟíar* no. 41.
togán 'pine marten': *a feóil tarra togáin* no. 46.
tragna 'corncrake': *brú arna tromguin / itir tragnaib* no. 69; *tragna co cossaib clama ar cnocán* no. 77.

Metres in Miscellany of Satires

Personal Names in *Fodlai Aíre* Tract

Adde: gen. (*Broccán mac*) *Addi* §13.
Artrí: gen. (*Rechtabrae mac*) *Artrach* §12.
Bran: acc. *la Bran*; gen. *Brain* §11.
Broccán mac Addi: nom. §13; gen. *Broccáin maic Addi* §13.
Cellach mac Cumascaig: nom. §12.
Cenn Fáelad: gen. *Cinn Fáelad* §17.
Cíanán: nom. §15.
Cíarán: voc. *a Chíarán* §16.
Cormac: nom. §3.
Cumascach: gen. (*Cellach mac*) *Cumascaig* §12.
Derglega: gen. *aue Derglega* §15.
Fotacán Laídech: nom. §11.
Gartnán: gen. *Gartnán* §14.
Mac Aithcherdae: dat. *do Mac Aithcherdae* §13.
Mac Dá Cherdae: nom. §13.
Paitrén: nom. §7.
Rechtabrae mac Artrach: nom. §12.
Rechtgal aue Síadail: nom. §17.
Rígnach: dat. *do Rígnaig* §17.
Síadal: gen. (*Rechtgal aue*) *Síadail* §17.
Tanaide: voc. *a Thanaidi* §10.

Personal Names in Miscellany of Satires

Where there is doubt about the nominative form of a name, the form in the text is given as the headword. Some of the names may be nicknames.

Adamnán: gen. (*in chethramthanach mór meic*) *Adamnáin* no. 83 (metrical name).
Alcán: gen. (*a meic*) *Alcáin* no. 41.
Bressal: voc. *a Bressail* no. 43.
Brigit: acc. *dar Brigit* no. 28.
Britán: gen. (*a uí brécaig*) *Britáin* no. 46.
Buide: gen. (*Finn úa*) *Buide* no. 65.
Cadla: gen. (*Conchobar úa*) *Cadla* no. 25.
Caíar: nom., acc. and dat. *Caíar* no. 21.

Population Groups in *Fodlai Aíre* Tract

Déise: dat. *donaib Déssib* §15.
Fir Maige Féne: In Co. Cork; gen. *Fer Maige Féne* §13.
Laigin: gen. *Laigen* §11.

Population Groups in Miscellany of Satires

Cáenraige: acc. *Cáenraige* no. 29.
Cíarraige: gen. *Chíarraige* no. 29; dat. *a Cíarraigib* no. 16.
Connachta: gen. *Connacht* no. 68.
Cruithentúatha: gen. pl. *etal ṡeisedach Cruithentúath* no. 78 (metrical name).
Déise: gen. *na nDéise* no. 19; *na nDése* no. 63; dat. *dona Déssib* no. 30; *dona Déisib* no. 58.
Éoganacht: dat. *d'Éoganacht* no. 72.
Galenga: gen. *Gailenga* (see note) no. 82.
Múscraige: acc. *Múscraige* no. 29.
Uí Chellaig: dat. pl. *d'Uíb Cellaig* no. 35.

Placenames in *Fodlai Aíre* Tract

Placenames which can refer to more than one location have been left unidentified.

Cell Aithcherdae: dat. *do Chill Aithcherdae* (*i tír Ḟer Maige Féne*) §13.
Cell Chomair: In Fermoy, Co. Cork; dat. *do Chill Chomair* §13.
Cell Dá Chellóc: Kilmallock, Co. Limerick; dat. *a Cill Dá Chellóc* §15.
Clúain Iraird: Clonard, Co. Meath; dat. sg. *i Clúain Iraird* §7.
Clúain Mac Nóis: Clonmacnoise, Co. Offaly; gen. *Chlúana Mac Nóis* §12.
Currech: The Curragh, Co. Kildare; gen. *Churrig* §11.
Les Mór Mo-Chutu: Lismore, Co. Waterford; gen. *Lis Móir Mo-Chutu* §3.
Life: The plain of Liffey; gen. *Liphi* §11.
Loch Léin: Lakes of Killarney; gen. *Locha Léin* §17.
Mag Lacha: nom. §3.
Mag nUlad: dat. *i Maig Ulad* §3.
Temair: Tara, Co. Meath; gen. *Themra* §10.

Placenames in Miscellany of Satires

Placenames which can refer to more than one location have been left unidentified. In cases where there is doubt about the nominative form of a placename, the form in the text is given as the headword.

Alla: gen. *na hAlla* no. 53.
Arann: Arran in Scotland; dat. *i finnArainn* no. 83.
Bóruime: Near Killaloe; gen. *Bóruime* no. 69.
Caimlinn: In barony of Upper Massareene, Co. Antrim; dat. *a Caimlinn* no. 84.
Carnmag: In Thomond; gen. *Charnmaige* no. 56.
Cell Cherbaill: Kilcarrol in Kilrush, Co. Clare; gen. *Cille Cerbaill* no. 84.
Cell Dá Chellóc: Kilmallock, Co. Limerick; dat. *a Cill Dá Chellóc* no. 30.
Cera: In Northern Uí Fhiachrach, Co. Mayo; gen. *Cera* no. 71.
Cloch Locha Comra (?): dat. (*etal ṡeisedach Cruithentúath*) *i Cloich Locha Comra* no. 78 (metrical name).
Corcach: Cork; dat. *ó Chorcaig* no. 37.
Dala (?): gen. *Dala* no. 85.
Dermag: dat. *a Dermaig* no. 35.
Druim Bó: gen. *Dromma Bó* no. 66.

Rare Words in Miscellany of Satires

The symbol + before a word indicates that the form is otherwise unattested.

+acaite: meaning uncertain; voc. sg. *acaite* no. 55.
+aitech: adj. from *aite* 'case'; voc. sg. *aitig* no. 48.
+bechairecht: 'bee-keeping'; nom. sg. no. 86.
+bicire: meaning uncertain; gen. sg. *bicire* no. 43.
brataire: 'robber'; voc. sg. *a brataire* no. 55.
+breccánach: 'freckled'; as subst. voc. sg. *a breccánaig* no. 53.
breccar: 'spots'; nom. sg. no. 62.
+breccóc: 'little trout' (?); gen. sg. *breccóice* no. 54.
brígrad: 'powers' (coll.); nom. sg. no. 25.
+brocairecht: 'acting like a badger'; dat. sg. *brocairecht* no. 67.
+bronn:'chaff' (?); gen. sg. *bruinn* no. 35.
+cairling: meaning uncertain; dat. sg. *'sin cairling* no. 84.
céis: part of a musical instrument; gen. sg. *céise* no. 52.
cenn: 'skin, scum'; nom. sg. no. 64.
+certach: 'ragged'; as subst. voc. sg. *a chertaig* no. 37.
+cetaile: meaning uncertain; no. 55.
+clecaire: meaning uncertain; acc. sg. *im chlecaire* no. 55.
+clocaile: meaning uncertain; acc. sg. *clocaile* no. 9.
comdálach: 'gregarious'; nom. sg. no. 67.
cornairecht: 'horn-playing'; nom. sg. no. 63.
+crúachaide: 'swollen stomach'; voc. sg. *a chrúachaide* no. 49.
+cúaránach: 'sandal-wearing'; voc. sg. *cúaránaig* no. 48.
+cuilbir: meaning uncertain; no. 26.
+cuilech: 'flea-ridden'; voc. sg. *chuilig* no. 51.
+cumgucht: meaning uncertain; no. 69.
+deidblénach: 'weak'; nom. sg. no. 67.
deir: 'herpes' (?); nom. sg. no. 71.
+detbudánach: 'smoky-coloured'; gen. sg. *detbudánaig* no. 40.
+dígrádach: 'degraded'; voc. sg. *dígrádaig* no. 48.
dlochtán: 'little bunch'; nom. sg. no. 59; gen. sg. *dlochtáin* no. 8.
+drenntaide: 'quarrelsome' (?); nom. sg. no. 28.
+dretránach (or **dretnánach**): 'drunk' (?); nom. sg. no. 28.
dulus: 'voraciousness' (?); acc. sg. *dulus* no. 13.
eidnénach: 'ivy-covered'; nom. sg. no. 67.
+etránach: 'interfering' (?); nom. sg. no. 28.

+**folta:** 'moulting'; gen. sg. *folta* no. 36.
fostán: 'steady'; nom. sg. no. 73.
+**gablóc:** 'little forked branch'; nom. sg. no. 73.
gaillín/gaillén: 'capon'; gen. sg. *gaillín* no. 40.
+**garlach:** 'brat'; gen. sg. *garlaig* no. 69.
+**gataile:** meaning uncertain; no. 55.
+**gelugud:** 'brightening'; acc. sg. *gelugud* no. 29; dat. sg. *do gelugud* no. 16.
+**gercaide:** 'grouse-like'; nom. sg. no. 28.
+**gipán:** 'ragged tunic'; gen. sg. *gipáin* no. 46.
+**idrad:** 'rings' (coll.); gen. *idraid* no. 76.
+**imdeliugud:** 'separation'; nom. sg. no. 64 (in description of metre).
+**isti:** adj. (?) meaning uncertain; no. 78.
+**lataile:** meaning uncertain; no. 55.
lenga: adj. (?) meaning uncertain; gen. sg. *lenga* no. 84.
lorcán: 'little mite'; voc. sg. *a lorcáin* no. 8, *a lorcán* no. 19.
+**mairbthine:** meaning uncertain; voc. sing. *a mairbthine* no. 55.
+**ocaile:** meaning uncertain; nom. sg. no. 9.
ogmóir: 'oghamist, man of learning'; nom. sg. no. 5.
+**paitech:** adj. from *pait* 'skin bottle'; voc. sg. *phaitig* no. 48.
+**píanán:** 'bag, sack'; nom. sg. no. 30.
+**píanánach:** adj. from *píanán* 'sack'; voc. sg. *phíanánaig* no. 48.
+**pítech:** 'starving'; as subst. voc. sg. *a phítig* no. 48.
pond: 'pound weight'; gen. sg. *phuint* no. 60.
+**rodrach:** variant of **radrach*; cf. abstract *radrachus* 'failure to conceive (of cow)'; gen. sg. *rodraige* no. 78.
+**sailchide:** 'dirty'; as subst. voc. sg. *a ṡailchide* no. 55.
+**saillech:** 'salted meat'; gen. sg. *saillige* no. 85.
+**scuitemail:** 'ridiculous'; voc. sg. *scuitemail* no. 33.
senmaire: 'musician'; gen. pl. *senmaire* no. 78.
+**senugud:** 'old age'; acc. sg. *senugud* no. 20.
+**sinnchide:** 'fox-like'; voc. sg. *ṡinnchaide* no. 55.
+**tíagánach:** adj. from *tíagán* 'little bag'; as subst. voc. sg. *a thíagánaig* no. 48.
+**tibride:** 'foolish'; gen. sg. *tibride* no. 52.
tidel: 'bunch of corn stalks' (?); acc. pl. *tidle* no. 57.
tréis: 'guile'; gen. sg. *tréise* no. 52.
uime: 'crudeness'; gen. sg. *uime* no. 52.

Concordance of Miscellany with *MV* III

No. 1 = *MV* III §3
No. 2 = *MV* III §5
No. 3 = *MV* III §6
No. 4 = *MV* III §20
No. 5 = *MV* III §31
No. 6 = *MV* III §44
No. 7 = *MV* III §53
No. 8 = *MV* III §54
No. 9 = *MV* III §67
No. 10 = *MV* III §68
No. 11 = *MV* III §82
No. 12 = *MV* III §88
No. 13 = *MV* III §89
No. 14 = *MV* III §96
No. 15 = *MV* III §102
No. 16 = *MV* III §111
No. 17 = *MV* III §120
No. 18 = *MV* III §121
No. 19 = *MV* III §141
No. 20 = *MV* III §146
No. 21 = *MV* III §155
No. 22 = *MV* III §164
No. 23 = *MV* III §170
No. 24 = *MV* III §176
No. 25 = *MV* III §178
No. 26 = *MV* III §192
No. 27 = *MV* III §196
No. 28 = *MV* III §202
No. 29 = *MV* III §205
No. 30 = *MV* III §210
No. 31 = *MV* III §12
No. 32 = *MV* III §15
No. 33 = *MV* III §56
No. 34 = *MV* III §78
No. 35 = *MV* III §84
No. 36 = *MV* III §106
No. 37 = *MV* III §119
No. 38 = *MV* III §126
No. 39 = *MV* III §140
No. 40 = *MV* III §160
No. 41 = *MV* III §165
No. 42 = *MV* III §183
No. 43 = *MV* III §189
No. 44 = *MV* III §190
No. 45 = *MV* III §191
No. 46 = *MV* III §193
No. 47 = *MV* III §197
No. 48 = *MV* III §198
No. 49 = *MV* III §200
No. 50 = *MV* III §18
No. 51 = *MV* III §127
No. 52 = *MV* III §151
No. 53 = *MV* III §162
No. 54 = *MV* III §185
No. 55 = *MV* III §186
No. 56 = *MV* III §188
No. 57 = *MV* III §45
No. 58 = *MV* III §57
No. 59 = *MV* III §63
No. 60 = *MV* III §64
No. 61 = *MV* III §70
No. 62 = *MV* III §71
No. 63 = *MV* III §77
No. 64 = *MV* III §85
No. 65 = *MV* III §90
No. 66 = *MV* III §108
No. 67 = *MV* III §115
No. 68 = *MV* III §123
No. 69 = *MV* III §150
No. 70 = *MV* III §163
No. 71 = *MV* III §171
No. 72 = *MV* III §173
No. 73 = *MV* III §179
No. 74 = *MV* III §180
No. 75 = *MV* III §181
No. 76 = *MV* III §182

Concordance of *MV* III with Miscellany

MV III §3 = no. 1
MV III §5 = no. 2
MV III §6 = no. 3
MV III §12 = no. 31
MV III §15 = no. 32
MV III §18 = no. 50
MV III §20 = no. 4
MV III §31 = no. 5
MV III §44 = no. 6
MV III §45 = no. 57
MV III §53 = no. 7
MV III §54 = no. 8
MV III §56 = no. 33
MV III §57 = no. 58
MV III §59 = no. 80
MV III §63 = no. 59
MV III §64 = no. 60
MV III §67 = no. 9
MV III §68 = no. 10
MV III §70 = no. 61
MV III §71 = no. 62
MV III §73 = no. 81
MV III §77 = no. 63
MV III §78 = no. 34
MV III §82 = no. 11
MV III §83 = no. 82
MV III §84 = no. 35
MV III §85 = no. 64
MV III §88 = no. 12
MV III §89 = no. 13
MV III §90 = no. 65
MV III §96 = no. 14
MV III §102 = no. 15
MV III §106 = no. 36
MV III §108 = no. 66
MV III §111 = no. 16
MV III §115 = no. 67
MV III §119 = no. 37
MV III §120 = no. 17
MV III §121 = no. 18
MV III §123 = no. 68
MV III §126 = no. 38
MV III §127 = no. 51
MV III §139 = no. 83
MV III §140 = no. 39
MV III §141 = no. 19
MV III §146 = no. 20
MV III §150 = no. 69
MV III §151 = no. 52
MV III §155 = no. 21
MV III §160 = no. 40
MV III §162 = no. 53
MV III §163 = no. 70
MV III §164 = no. 22
MV III §165 = no. 41
MV III §170 = no. 23
MV III §171 = no. 71
MV III §172 = no. 84
MV III §173 = no. 72
MV III §176 = no. 24
MV III §178 = no. 25
MV III §179 = no. 73
MV III §180 = no. 74
MV III §181 = no. 75
MV III §182 = no. 76
MV III §183 = no. 42
MV III §185 = no. 54
MV III §186 = no. 55
MV III §188 = no. 56
MV III §189 = no. 43
MV III §190 = no. 44
MV III §191 = no. 45
MV III §192 = no. 26
MV III §193 = no. 46
MV III §194 = no. 85
MV III §196 = no. 27

Types of Satire

(References are to page numbers)

Bibliography

Abbott, T. K., and Gwynn, E. J. (1921): *Catalogue of Irish Manuscripts in the Library of Trinity College, Dublin* (Dublin).

Arbuthnot, Sharon J. (2002): 'A Context for Mac Mhaighstir Alasdair's *Moladh air Deagh Bhod*' in *Rannsachadh na Gàidhlig* 2000 (ed. Colm Ó Baoill and Nancy R. McGuire, Aberdeen) 163–70.

Atkinson, Robert (1887): *The Book of Ballymote: a Collection of Pieces (Prose and Verse) in the Irish Language, Compiled about the Beginning of the Fifteenth Century* (Facsimile) (Dublin).

Atkinson, Robert and Bernard, J. H. (1898): *The Irish Liber Hymnorum*. 2 vols (London).

Bergin, Osborn (1916): 'Metrica', *Ériu* 8, 161–9.

— **(1921–23):** 'Nominative for Vocative', *Ériu* 9, 92–4.

— **(1938):** 'On the Syntax of the Verb in Old Irish', *Ériu* 12, 197–214.

Bergin, O., Best, R. I., Meyer, K. and O'Keeffe, J. G. (1907–13): *Anecdota from Irish Manuscripts*. 5 vols (Halle).

Best, R. I. (1905): 'The Tragic Death of Cú Roí mac Dári', *Ériu* 2, 18–35.

— **(1905b):** 'The Graves of the Kings at Clonmacnois', *Ériu* 2, 163–71.

— **(1915):** '*Comhrag Fir Diad 7 Chon Culainn*, *ZCP* 10, 274–308.

Best, R. I., and Bergin, O. (1929): *Lebor na hUidre, Book of the Dun Cow* (Dublin, reprinted 1992).

Best, R. I., Bergin, O., O'Brien, M. A. and O'Sullivan, A. (1954–83): *The Book of Leinster, formerly Lebar na Núachongbála*. 6 vols (Dublin).

Bieler, Ludwig (1963): *The Irish Penitentials*, Scriptores Latini Hiberniae 5 (Dublin, reprinted 1975).

Binchy, Daniel A. (1941): *Críth Gablach* (Mediaeval and Modern Irish Series 11, Dublin, reprinted 1970).

— **(1952):** 'The Saga of Fergus mac Léti', *Ériu* 16, 33–48.

— **(1962):** 'The Old-Irish Table of Penitential Commutations', *Ériu* 19, 47–72.

— **(1966):** '*Bretha Déin Chécht*', *Ériu* 20, 1–66.
— **(1971):** 'An Archaic Legal Poem', *Celtica* 9, 152–68.
— **(1972):** 'Varia Hibernica', in *Indo-Celtica* (ed. H. Pilch and I. Thurow, Munich) 29–41.
— **(1973):** 'Distraint in Irish Law', *Celtica* 10, 22–71.
— **(1973b):** 'A Text on the Forms of Distraint', *Celtica* 10, 72–86.
— **(1978):** *Corpus Iuris Hibernici.* 6 vols (Dublin).
— **(1979–80):** 'Bergin's Law', *Studia Celtica* 14/15, 34–53.
Black, Ronald (1986): *Mac Mhaighstir Alasdair: The Ardnamurchan Years* (Inverness).
— **(2001):** *An Lasair: Anthology of 18th Century Scottish Gaelic Verse* (Edinburgh).
Borsje, Jacqueline (2002): 'Approaching Danger: *Togail Bruidne Da Derga* and the Motif of Being One-Eyed' in *Identifying the 'Celtic', CSANA* Yearbook 2 (ed. J. F. Nagy, Dublin) 75–99.
Bracken, Damian (1995): 'Latin Passages in Irish Vernacular Law: Notes on Sources', *Peritia* 9, 187–96.
Breatnach, Caoimhín (1996): *Patronage, Politics and Prose* (Maynooth).
— **(2000):** 'The Transmission of *Ceasacht Inghine Guile*: Some Observations', *Éigse* 32, 138–45.
Breatnach, Liam (1980): 'Tochmarc Luaine ocus Aided Athairne', *Celtica* 13, 1–31.
— **(1980b):** 'Some Remarks on the Relative in Old Irish', *Ériu* 31, 1–9.
— **(1981):** 'The Caldron of Poesy', *Ériu* 32, 45–93.
— **(1983):** 'Varia IV. On the Agent Suffix *-e* in Irish', *Ériu* 34, 194.
— **(1984):** 'Addenda and Corrigenda to 'The Caldron of Poesy', *Ériu* 35, 189–91.
— **(1984b):** 'Canon Law and Secular Law in Early Ireland: the Significance of *Bretha Nemed*', *Peritia* 3, 439–59.
— **(1986):** 'The Ecclesiastical Element in the Old-Irish Legal Tract *Cáin Fuithirbe*', *Peritia* 5, 36–52.
— **(1987):** *Uraicecht na Ríar: the Poetic Grades in Early Irish Law* (Early Irish Law Series 2, Dublin).
— **(1988):** 'An Aoir sa Ré Luath', *Léachtaí Cholm Cille* 18, 11–19.
— **(1989):** 'An Edition of *Amra Senáin*', in *Sages, Saints and Storytellers: Celtic Studies in Honour of Professor James Carney* (ed. D. Ó Corráin, L. Breatnach and K. McCone, Maynooth) 7–31.
— **(1989b):** 'The First Third of *Bretha Nemed Toísech*', *Ériu* 40, 1–40.
— **(1994):** 'An Mheán-Ghaeilge' in *Stair na Gaeilge* (ed. K. McCone *et al.*, Maynooth) 221–333.

— **(1996):** 'Poets and Poetry' in *Progress in Medieval Irish Studies,* (ed. K. McCone and K. Simms, Maynooth) 65–77.

— **(1996b):** 'On the Original Extent of the *Senchas Már*', *Ériu* 47, 1–43.

— **(1997):** 'On the Flexion of the *ā*-stems in Irish' in *Dán do Oide: Essays in Memory of Conn R. Ó Cléirigh* (ed. A. Ahlqvist and V. Čapková, Dublin) 49–57.

— **(1998):** '*Cáin Ónae:* An Old-Irish Law Text on Lending', in *Mír Curad: Studies in Honor of Calvert Watkins* (ed J. Jasanoff *et al.*, Innsbruck) 29–46.

— **(2003):** 'On Words Ending in a Stressed Vowel in Early Irish', *Ériu* 53, 133–42.

— **(2004):** 'On Satire and the Poet's Circuit' in *Unity in Diversity* (ed. C. Ó Háinle and D. E. Meek, Dublin) 25–35.

— **(2005):** *A Companion to the Corpus Iuris Hibernici* (Early Irish Law Series 5, Dublin).

— **(2006):** 'Satire, Praise and the Early Irish Poet', *Ériu* 56, 63–84.

Breatnach, Pádraig A. (1997): 'The Poet's Graveside Vigil: a Theme of Irish Bardic Elegy in the Fifteenth Century', *ZCP* 49–50, 50–63.

— **(2000):** 'The Metres of Citations in the Irish Grammatical Tracts', *Éigse* 32, 7–22.

Breatnach, Risteard A. (1941–42): 'A Pretended Robbery', *Éigse* 3, 240–4.

Byrne, Francis J. (1973): *Irish Kings and High Kings* (London, revised ed. 1996).

Byrne, Mary E. (1908): *Airec Menman Uraird maic Coisse, Anecdota* 2 (ed. Bergin *et al.*, Halle) 42–76.

Calder, George (1917): *Auraicept na n-Éces: the Scholars' Primer* (Edinburgh, reprinted Dublin 1995).

Campbell, J. L. (1933): *Highland Songs of the Forty-Five* (Edinburgh).

Campbell, J. L. and Thomson, D. (1963): *Edward Lhuyd in the Scottish Highlands 1699–1700* (Oxford).

Carey, John (1997): 'The Three Things Required of a Poet', *Ériu* 48, 41–58.

Carney, James (1943): *Topographical Poems by Seaán Mór Ó Dubhagáin and Giolla-na Naomh Ó Huidhrín* (Dublin).

— **(1945):** *Poems on the Butlers of Ormond, Cahir and Dunboyne* (Dublin).

— **(1955):** *Studies in Irish Literature and History* (Dublin).

— **(1964):** *The Poems of Blathmac, Son of Cú Brettan, together with the Irish Gospel of Thomas and a Poem on the Virgin Mary* (Irish Texts Society 47, Dublin).

— **(1969):** 'The Ó Cíanáin Miscellany', *Ériu* 21, 122–47.

— **(1971):** 'Three Old Irish Accentual Poems', *Ériu* 22, 23–80.
— **(1980–81):** 'Linking Alliteration ('*fidrad freccomail*')', *Éigse* 18, 251–62.
— **(1989):** 'The Dating of Archaic Irish Verse', in *Early Irish Literature: Media and Communication, Mündlichkeit und Schriftlichkeit in der frühen irischen Literatur, Scriptoralia* 10 (ed. S. Tranter and H. Tristram, Tübingen) 39–55.
Carney, Maura (1943): 'Agreement between Ó Domhnaill and Tadhg Ó Conchobhair concerning Sligo Castle (23 June 1593)', *Irish Historical Studies* 3, 282–96.
Charles-Edwards, Thomas (2000): *Early Christian Ireland* (Cambridge).
Charles-Edwards, Thomas and Kelly, Fergus (1983): *Bechbretha: an Old Irish Law-Tract on Bee-Keeping* (Early Irish Law Series 1, Dublin).
Clancy, Thomas Owen (1993): 'Fools and Adultery in Some Early Irish Texts', *Ériu* 44, 105–24.
Crumlin-Pedersen, Ole (1997): *Viking-Age Ships and Shipbuilding in Hedeby/Haithabu and Schleswig* (Schleswig & Roskilde).
Danaher, Kevin (1972): *The Year in Ireland* (Cork).
De Búrca, Seán (1971–72): 'The Metron in Celtic Verse', *Éigse* 14, 131–51.
Dillon, Myles (1932): 'Stories from the Law-Tracts', *Ériu* 11, 42–65.
Dobbs, M. E. (1950): 'A Poem on the Uí Dega', *Journal of Celtic Studies* 1, 227–31.
Etchingham, Colmán (1999): *Church Organisation in Ireland AD 650 to 1000* (Maynooth).
Forbes, A. R. (1905): *Gaelic Names of Beasts, Birds, Fishes, Insects and Reptiles* (Edinburgh).
Freeman, A. M. (1944): *Annála Connacht: the Annals of Connacht* (Dublin, reprinted 1983).
Gray, Elizabeth A. (1982): *Cath Maige Tuired: the Second Battle of Mag Tuired* (Irish Texts Society 52, London).
Greene, David (1945–47): '*Mac Bronn*', *Éigse* 5, 231–5.
— **(1958):** 'The Analytic Forms of the Verb in Irish', *Ériu* 18, 108–12.
— **(1958b):** 'Miscellanea: W. *kenn*: Ir. **cenn*', *Celtica* 4, 44–7.
— **(1968):** 'A Satire by Cathal Mac Muireadhaigh' in *Celtic Studies: Essays in Memory of Angus Matheson 1912–62* (ed. D. Greene and J. Carney, London) 51–5.
— **(1973):** 'Synthetic and Analytic: a Reconsideration', *Ériu* 24, 121–33.
— **(1975):** 'Varia III: *ceciderunt ab oculis eius tamquam squamae*', *Ériu* 26, 175–8.
— **(1978):** 'The *é*-Future in Modern Irish', *Ériu* 29, 58–63.

Greene, David and O'Connor, Frank (1967): *A Golden Treasury of Irish Poetry, A.D. 600 to 1200* (London).

Gwynn, Edward J. (1903–35): *The Metrical Dindshenchas.* 5 vols (Dublin, reprinted 1991).

— **(1913–14):** 'An Irish Penitential', *Ériu* 7, 121–95.

— **(1931):** 'Some Irish Words', *Hermathena* 21, 1–15.

— **(1942):** 'An Old-Irish Tract on the Privileges and Responsibilities of Poets', *Ériu* 13, 1–60; 220–36.

Hall, Edith (1989): *Inventing the Barbarian: Greek Self-definition through Tragedy* (Oxford, reprinted 1991).

Harrison, Alan (1984): '*Séanadh Saighre*', *Éigse* 20, 136–48.

— **(1989):** *The Irish Trickster* (Sheffield).

Hayden, Mary (1912): 'The Songs of Buchet's House', *ZCP* 8, 261–73.

Hogan, Edmund (1910): *Onomasticon Goedelicum* (Dublin, reprinted 1993).

Hull, Vernam (1940): 'Miscellanea: The Ancient Irish Practice of Rubbing the Earlap as a Means of Coercion', *ZCP* 21, 324–9.

Hyde, Douglas (1899): *Eachtra Cloinne Rígh na hIoruaidhe* (Irish Texts Society 1, London).

Jackson, Kenneth (1990): *Aislinge Meic Con Glinne* (Dublin).

Jaski, Bart (2000): *Early Irish Kingship and Succession* (Dublin).

Joynt, Maud (1908–10): '*Echtra Mac Echdach Mugmedóin*', *Ériu* 4, 91–111.

— **(1941):** *Tromdámh Guaire* (Mediaeval and Modern Irish Series 2, Dublin).

Kelleher, John (1988): 'The Battle of Móin Mhór, 1151', *Celtica* 20, 11–27.

Kelly, Fergus (1976): 'The Old Irish Tree-List', *Celtica* 11, 107–24.

— **(1986):** 'Varia III. Old Irish *creccaire*, Scottish Gaelic *kreahkir*', *Ériu* 37, 185–6.

— **(1988):** *A Guide to Early Irish Law* (Early Irish Law Series 3, Dublin, reprinted 1991).

— **(1997):** *Early Irish Farming* (Early Irish Law Series 4, Dublin, reprinted 1998).

Kenney, J. F. (1929): *The Sources for the Early History of Ireland: Ecclesiastical* (New York, reprinted with addenda by L. Bieler: New York 1966 and Dublin 1978).

Knott, Eleanor (1916): 'Why Mongán was Deprived of Noble Issue', *Ériu* 8, 155–60.

— **(1936):** *Togail Bruidne Da Derga* (Mediaeval and Modern Irish Series 8, Dublin, reprinted 1975).

— **(1952):** 'An Index to the Proper Names in *Saltair na Rann*', *Ériu* 16, 99–122.

Koch, J. T. and Carey, J. (1997): *The Celtic Heroic Age: Literary Sources for Ancient Celtic Europe and Early Ireland and Wales* (Andover, Massachusetts).

Leach, Edmund (1964): 'Anthropological Aspects of Language: Animal Categories and Verbal Abuse' in *New Directions in the Study of Language* (ed. E. H. Lennenberg, Cambridge, Massachusetts) 23–63.

Macalister, R. A. S. (1941): *The Book of Uí Maine otherwise called 'The Book of the O'Kellys',* The Irish Manuscripts Commission, Facsimiles in Collotype of Irish Manuscripts 4 (Dublin).

Mac Cana, Proinsias (2002): 'The *Ingen Moel*', *Ériu* 52, 217–27.

McCaughey, Terence (1989): 'Bards, Beasts and Men' in *Sages, Saints and Storytellers: Celtic Studies in Honour of Professor James Carney* (ed. D. Ó Corráin, L. Breatnach and K. McCone, Maynooth) 102–21.

McCone, Kim (1985): 'Varia II: OIr. *Olc, Luch-* and IE **wĺ̥k^{w}os, *lúk^{w}os* "wolf"', *Ériu* 36, 171–6.

— **(1987):** *The Early Irish Verb* (Maynooth).

— **(1989):** 'A Tale of Two Ditties: Poet and Satirist in *Cath Maige Tuired*' in *Sages, Saints and Storytellers: Celtic Studies in Honour of Professor James Carney* (ed. D. Ó Corráin, L. Breatnach and K. McCone, Maynooth) 122–43.

— **(1990):** *Pagan Past and Christian Present in Early Irish Literature* (Maynooth).

— **(2007):** 'Die Spottwettkämpfe in der Geschichte von Mac Da Thós Schwein', *Keltische Forschungen* 1, 149-61.

Mac Eoin, Gearóid (1974): 'Genitive Forms as Nominatives in Irish', *ZCP* 33, 58–65.

— **(1981):** 'The Dating of Middle Irish Texts', Sir John Rhŷs Memorial Lecture, *Proceedings of the British Academy, London* 68 (1982) (Oxford).

Mac Giolla Léith, Caoimhín (1992): *Oidheadh Chloinne hUisneach* (Irish Texts Society 56, Dublin).

McGrail, Seán (1993): *Medieval Boat and Ship Timbers from Dublin. Medieval Dublin Excavations 1962–81.* Ser. B vol. 3 (Dublin).

Mackechnie, John (1973): *Catalogue of Gaelic Manuscripts in Selected Libraries in Great Britain and Ireland.* 2 vols (Massachusetts).

Mackinnon, Donald (1909): 'Unpublished Poems by Alexander Macdonald (Mac Mhaighstir Alastair)', *The Celtic Review* 5, 20–30, 116–28, 225–35, 294–303.

— **(1912):** *A Descriptive Catalogue of Gaelic Manuscripts in the Advocates' Library Edinburgh and Elsewhere in Scotland* (Edinburgh).

McLaughlin, Roisin (2005): 'A Threat of Satire by Tadhg (mac Dáire) Mac Bruaideadha', *Ériu* 55, 37–57.

— **(2005b):** 'Metres in *Mittelirische Verslehren* III', *Ériu* 55, 119–36.

McLeod, Neil (1987): 'Interpreting Early Irish Law: Status and Currency (part 2)', *ZCP* 42, 41–115.

— **(1992):** *Early Irish Contract Law,* Sydney Series in Celtic Studies 1 (Sydney).

— **(2000):** 'Kinship', *Ériu* 51, 1–22.

— **(2000b):** 'The Not-so Exotic Law of *Dian Cécht*', in *Origins and Revivals: Proceedings of the First Australian Conference of Celtic Studies* (ed. G. Evans, B. Martin and J. M. Wooding, Sydney Series in Celtic Studies 3, Sydney) 381–99.

McManus, Damian (1991): *A Guide to Ogam* (Maynooth).

— **(2004):** 'The Bardic Poet as Teacher, Student and Critic: A Context for the Grammatical Tracts' in *Unity in Diversity* (ed. C. Ó Háinle and D. E. Meek, Dublin) 97–123.

Mac Neill, Eóin (1923): 'Ancient Irish Law: the Law of Status or Franchise', *PRIA* 36 C, 265–316.

Mac Neill, John (1911–12): 'Early Irish Population Groups: Their Nomenclature, Classification and Chronology', *PRIA* 29 C, 59–114.

Mac Niocaill, Gearóid (1971): '*Tír Cumaile*', *Ériu* 22, 81–6.

Mac Piarais, Pádraig (1908): *Bruidhean Chaorthainn: Sgéal Fiannaidheachta* (Dublin).

Marstrander, Carl J. S. (1915): *Bidrag til det Norske Sprogs Historie i Irland* (Kristiania).

— **(1915–16):** 'Remarques sur le "Zur Keltischen Wortkunde I–VI" de Kuno Meyer', *RC* 36, 335–90.

— **(1962):** 'Review of J. Vendryes, *Lexique Étymologique de l'Irlandais Ancien: A*', *Lochlann* 2, 196–226.

Mercier, Vivian (1962): *The Irish Comic Tradition* (Oxford).

Meroney, Howard (1949): 'Full Name and Address in Early Irish', *Philologica: The Malone Anniversary Studies* (Baltimore) 124–31.

— **(1950):** 'Studies in Early Irish Satire: I. "*Cis lir fodla aíre?*"; II "*Glám dícind*"', *Journal of Celtic Studies* 1, 199–226.

— **(1953):** 'Studies in Early Irish Satire: III. "*Tréfhocal fócrai*"', *Journal of Celtic Studies* 2, 59–130.

Meyer, Kuno (1881–83): '*Macgnímartha Find*', *RC* 5, 195–204.

— **(1892):** *Aislinge Meic Conglinne: the Vision of Mac Conglinne, a Middle-Irish Wonder Tale* (London).

— **(1894):** *Hibernica Minora* (Oxford, reprinted New York 1989).

— **(1895):** *The Voyage of Bran son of Febal to the Land of the Living* (London, reprinted Llannerch 1994).

— **(1898):** 'Irische Bardennamen', *Archiv für celtische Lexikographie* 1, 160.

— **(1901):** '*Brinna Ferchertne*', *ZCP* 3, 40–6.

— **(1904):** 'The Death of Conla', *Ériu* 1, 113–21.

— **(1905):** 'Mitteilungen aus irischen Handschriften', *ZCP* 5, 495–504.

— **(1905b):** *Cáin Adamnáin: An Old-Irish Treatise on the Law of Adamnan.* Anecdota Oxoniensia, Mediaeval and Modern Series 12 (Oxford, reprinted New York 1989).

— **(1906):** *The Triads of Ireland* (Todd Lecture Series 13, Dublin).

— **(1906b):** *Contributions to Irish Lexicography* (Halle).

— **(1906–07):** 'Neue Mitteilungen aus irischen Handschriften', *Archiv für celtische Lexikographie* 3, 215–46.

— **(1908):** 'Mitteilungen aus irischen Handschriften', *ZCP* 6, 257–72.

— **(1909):** *A Primer of Irish Metrics* (Dublin).

— **(1909b):** *Tecosca Cormaic: the Instructions of King Cormac mac Airt* (Todd Lecture Series 15, Dublin).

— **(1910):** 'Mitteilungen aus irischen Handschriften', *ZCP* 7, 297–312.

— **(1911):** *Betha Colmáin maic Lúacháin: Life of Colmán Son of Lúachan* (Todd Lecture Series 17, Dublin).

— **(1912):** 'Mitteilungen aus irischen Handschriften', *ZCP* 8, 102–20.

— **(1913):** *Über die älteste irische Dichtung 1. Abhandlungen der königlich preussischen Akademie der Wissenschaften. Phil.-Hist. Klasse.* Nr. 6. (Berlin).

— **(1914):** *Über die älteste irische Dichtung 2. Abhandlungen der königlich preussischen Akademie der Wissenschaften. Phil.-Hist. Klasse.* Nr. 10. (Berlin).

— **(1917):** *Miscellanea Hibernica* (Urbana).

— **(1919):** *Bruchstücke der älteren Lyrik Irlands. Abhandlungen der preussischen Akademie der Wissenschaften. Phil.-Hist. Klasse.* Nr. 7 (Berlin).

— **(1920):** '*Miscellanea Celtica*' in *Aufsätze zur Sprach- und Literaturgeschichte. Wilhelm Braune zum 20. Februar 1920 dargebracht von Freunden und Schülern* (Dortmund) 1–10.

Mhág Craith, C. (1967): 'Anomalous Rime in Irish Bardic Poetry', *Studia Celtica* 11, 171–95.

Mulchrone, Kathleen (1939): *Bethu Phátraic: the Tripartite Life of Patrick* (Dublin).
— **(1954):** '*Macalla as Cluain-mhac-Nóis* A.D. 1050', *Galvia* 1, 15–17.
Murphy, Gerard (1940): 'Bards and Filidh', *Éigse* 2, 200–7.
— **(1956):** *Early Irish Lyrics* (Oxford, reprinted 1998).
— **(1956b):** '*Te; Tét; Téith*', *Celtica* 3, 317–19.
— **(1961):** *Early Irish Metrics* (Dublin).
Nagy, Joseph Falaky (1999): 'The Irish Herald' in *Ildánach Ildírech — a Festschrift for Proinsias Mac Cana* (ed. John Carey, John T. Koch and Pierre-Yves Lambert, Andover and Aberystwyth) 121–30.
Nicholson, Alexander (1996): *A Collection of Gaelic Proverbs and Familiar Phrases* (Edinburgh; first published 1881).
Ní Dhomhnaill, Cáit (1975): *Duanaireacht: Rialacha Meadarachta Fhilíocht na mBard* (Dublin).
Ní Shéaghdha, Nessa (1967): *Catalogue of Irish Manuscripts in the National Library of Ireland. Fasciculus 1* (Dublin).
— **(1977):** *Catalogue of Irish Manuscripts in the National Library of Ireland. Fasciculus 4* (Dublin).
Ó Briain, Máirtín (2006): 'Satire in Seventeenth- and Eighteenth-century Gaelic Poetry' in *Memory and the Modern in Celtic Literatures, CSANA* Yearbook 5 (ed. J. F. Nagy, Dublin) 118–42.
O'Brien, Michael A. (1938): '*Miscellanea Hibernica*', *Études Celtiques* 3, 362–73.
— **(1952):** 'The Birth of Áedan mac Gabrán', *Ériu* 16, 157–70.
— **(1962):** *Corpus Genealogiarum Hiberniae* (Dublin, reprinted 1976).
— **(1973):** 'Old Irish Personal Names': Rhŷs lecture notes, 1957 (ed. R. Baumgarten), *Celtica* 10, 211–36.
Ó Buachalla, Breandán (1976): *Nua-Dhuanaire* 2 (Dublin).
Ó Cathasaigh, Tomás (1986): 'Curse and Satire', *Éigse* 21, 10–15.
— **(2005):** 'Cú Chulainn, the Poets and Giolla Brighde Mac Con Midhe' in *Heroic Poets and Poetic Heroes in Celtic Tradition, a Festschrift for Patrick K. Ford, CSANA* Yearbook 3–4 (ed. J. F. Nagy, Dublin) 291–302.
Ó Concheanainn, Tomás (1971): 'Topographical Notes – 1', *Ériu* 22, 87–96.
— **(1975):** 'The Scribe of John Beaton's "Broad Book"', *Ériu* 26, 99–101.
— **(1981):** 'The Book of Ballymote', *Celtica* 14, 15–25.
Ó Corráin, D., Breatnach, L. and Breen, A. (1984): 'The Laws of the Irish', *Peritia* 3, 382–438.
Ó Corráin, Donnchadh (1971): 'Topographical Notes II: Mag Femin, Femen, and Some Early Annals', *Ériu* 22, 97–9.

— **(1984):** 'Irish Law and Canon Law' in *Irland und Europa: Die Kirche im Frühmittelalter* (ed. P. Ní Chatháin and M. Richter, Stuttgart) 157–66.
Ó Cuív, Brian (1952): *Párliament na mBan* (Dublin).
— **(1967–68):** 'Some Developments in Irish Metrics', *Éigse* 12, 273–90.
— **(1973):** 'Two Items from Irish Apocryphal Tradition', *Celtica* 10, 87–113.
— **(1973b):** 'The Linguistic Training of the Mediaeval Irish Poet', *Celtica* 10, 114–40.
— **(1980–81):** 'Some Gaelic Traditions about the Wren', *Éigse* 18, 43–66.
— **(1988):** 'Personal Names as an Indicator of Relations between Native Irish and Settlers in the Viking Period' in *Settlement and Society in Medieval Ireland: Studies Presented to F. X. Martin* (ed. J. Bradley, Kilkenny) 79–88.
— **(1989):** 'An Ornamental Device in Irish Verse', *Éigse* 23, 45–56.
— **(2001):** *Catalogue of Irish Language Manuscripts in the Bodleian Library at Oxford and Oxford College Libraries. Part 1: Descriptions* (Dublin).
O'Curry, Eugene (1873): *On the Manners and Customs of the Ancient Irish* Vol. 3 (London, reprinted 1996, Dublin).
O'Daly, Máirín (1946): 'The Verbal System of the LL Táin', *Ériu* 14, 31–139.
Ó Domhnaill, Caoimhín (2005): *Talland Étair: a Critical Edition with Introduction, Translation, Textual Notes and Vocabulary* (Maynooth).
O'Donoghue, Tadhg (1921–23): 'Advice to a Prince', *Ériu* 9, 43–54.
O'Donovan, John (1852): *The Tribes of Ireland* (Dublin).
— **(1862):** *The Topographical Poems of John O'Dubhagain and Giolla na Naomh O'Huidhrin* (Dublin).
O'Grady, Standish Hayes (1926): *Catalogue of Irish Manuscripts in the British Library* [*formerly British Museum*] (London, reprinted Dublin 1992).
Ó hAodha, Donncha (1991): 'The First Middle Irish Metrical Tract' in *Metrik und Medienwechsel / Metrics and Media, ScriptOralia* 35 (ed. H. Tristram, Tübingen) 207–44.
— **(2000):** 'Rechtgal úa Síadail, a Famous Poet of the Old Irish Period' in *Seanchas: Studies in Early and Medieval Irish Archaeology, History and Literature in Honour of Francis J. Byrne* (ed. Alfred P. Smyth, Dublin) 192–8.
— **(2002):** 'The First Middle-Irish Metrical Tract: Two Notes', *Peritia* 16, 232–41.
O'Keeffe, James G. (1905): '*Cáin Domnaig*', *Ériu* 2, 189–214.
—**(1911):** 'Mac Dá Cherda and Cummaine Foda', *Ériu* 5, 18–44.

— **(1931):** *Buile Ṡuibhne* (Mediaeval and Modern Irish Series 1, Dublin, reprinted 1975).

O'Leary, Aideen M. (2001): 'Mog Ruith and Apocalypticism in Eleventh Century Ireland' in *The Individual in Celtic Literature, CSANA* Yearbook 1 (ed. J. F. Nagy, Dublin) 51–60.

O'Leary, Philip (1991): 'Jeers and Judgments: Laughter in Early Irish Literature', *Cambridge Medieval Celtic Studies* 22, 15–29.

Ó Macháin, Pádraig (1991): 'The Early Modern Irish Prosodic Tracts and the Editing of "Bardic Verse"' in *Metrik und Medienwechsel / Metrics and Media, ScriptOralia* 35 (ed. H. Tristram, Tübingen) 273–87.

Ó Máille, Tomás (1973): *Breacadh: Ornáid ar an Duanaireacht* (Dublin).

O'Neill, Patrick (1982): 'A Middle Irish Poem on the Maledictory Psalms', *Journal of Celtic Studies* 3, 40–58.

O'Rahilly, Cecile (1976): *Táin Bó Cúailnge Recension 1* (Dublin).

O'Rahilly, T. F. (1922): *A Miscellany of Irish Proverbs* (Dublin).

— **(1927):** *Measgra Dánta.* 2 vols (Cork).

— **(1942):** '*-genn* for *-chenn*', *Ériu* 13, 140–3.

— **(1946):** *Early Irish History and Mythology* (Dublin, reprinted 1984).

O'Sullivan, Anne (1968): 'Verses on Honorific Portions' in *Celtic Studies: Essays in Memory of Angus Matheson 1912–62* (ed. D. Greene and J. Carney, London) 118–23.

O'Sullivan, Anne and Ó Riain, Pádraig (1987): *Poems on Marcher Lords* (Irish Texts Society 53, Shannon).

O'Sullivan, William (1989): 'The Book of Uí Maine, formerly the Book of Ó Dubhagáin: Scripts and Structure', *Éigse* 23, 151–66.

Ó Tuama, Seán and Kinsella, Thomas (1981): *An Duanaire 1600–1900: Poems of the Dispossessed* (Dublin).

Petrie, George (1845): 'The Ecclesiastical Architecture of Ireland, Anterior to the Anglo-Norman Invasion, Comprising an Essay on the Origin and Uses of the Round Towers of Ireland' (second ed., Dublin).

Quiggin, E. C. (1910): 'The *S*-Preterite in Middle Irish', *Ériu* 4, 191–207.

Quin, E. G. (1965): '*Truagh Truagh an Mhuc*', *Hermathena* 101, 27–37.

— **(1981):** '*Ochtfoclach Choluim Chille*', *Celtica* 14, 125–53.

Robinson, Fred Norris (1912): 'Satirists and Enchanters in Early Irish Literature', *Studies in the History of Religions Presented to Crawford Howell Toy* (New York) 95–130.

Sims-Williams, Patrick (1984): 'Gildas and Vernacular Poetry' in *Gildas: New Approaches* (ed. M. Lapidge and D. Dumville, *Studies in Celtic History*, Woodbridge) 169–92.

Smith, Roland M. (1932): 'The Advice to Doidin', *Ériu* 11, 66–85.

Stokes, Whitley (1860): *Irish Glosses: a Mediaeval Tract on Latin Declension* (Dublin).

— **(1862):** *Three Irish Glossaries* (London).

— **(1887):** 'The Siege of Howth', *RC* 8, 47–64.

— **(1889):** 'The Voyage of Mael Dúin (2)', *RC* 10, 50–95.

— **(1893):** 'The Voyage of the Húi Corra', *RC* 14, 22–69.

— **(1894):** 'The Prose Tales in the Rennes Dindṡenchas', *RC* 15, 272–336; 418–84.

— **(1895):** *Félire Húi Gormáin* (London).

— **(1897):** '*Cóir Anmann* (Fitness of Names)' in *Irische Texte* 3, 2 (Leipzig) 285–444.

— **(1899):** 'The Bodleian Amra Choluimb Chille', *RC* 20, 30–55, 132–83, 248–89, 400–37.

— **(1900):** 'O'Mulconry's Glossary', *Archiv für celtische Lexikographie* 1 (Halle) 232–324.

— **(1900b):** *Acallamh na Senórach* in *Irische Texte* 4, 1 (Leipzig).

— **(1904):** 'O Davoren's Glossary', *Archiv für celtische Lexikographie* 2 (Halle) 197–504.

— **(1905):** 'The Colloquy of the Two Sages', *RC* 26, 4–64.

— **(1905b):** *Félire Óengusso Céli Dé: The Martyrology of Oengus the Culdee* (London, reprinted Dublin 1984).

— **(1906):** 'The Birth and Life of St. Moling', *RC* 27, 257–312.

— **(1906–07):** 'The Glossary in Egerton 158', *Archiv für celtische Lexikographie* 3 (Halle) 145–214, 247–8.

— **(1907):** 'The Fifteen Tokens of Doomsday', *RC* 28, 308–26.

— **(1908):** 'Poems ascribed to S. Moling', *Anecdota from Irish Manuscripts* 2 (Halle) 20–41.

Stokes, Whitley and Strachan, John (1901–03): *Thesaurus Palaeohibernicus.* 2 vols (Cambridge, reprinted Dublin 1987).

Strachan, John (1905): 'Contributions to the History of Middle Irish Declension', *Transactions of the Philological Society* 202–46.

Strachan, John, and O'Keeffe, James G. (1912): *Táin Bó Cúailnge from the Yellow Book of Lecan with Variant Readings from the Lebor na hUidre* (Dublin).

Thurneysen, Rudolf (1891): 'Mittelirische Verslehren', *Irische Texte* 3, 1 (Leipzig) 1–182.

— **(1912):** 'Zu den mittelirischen Verslehren', *Zu irischen Handschriften und Litteraturdenkmälern* 1, 59–90.

— **(1913):** 'Nachträge zur ersten Serie', *Zu irischen Handschriften und Litteraturdenkmälern* 2, 22–4.

— **(1918):** 'Zu irischen Texten', *ZCP* 12, 398–407.

— **(1925):** 'Aus dem irischen Recht III [4. Die falschen Urteilssprüche Caratnia's], *ZCP* 15, 302–70.

— **(1925b):** 'Cóic Conara Fugill: Die fünf Wege zum Urteil'. *Abhandlungen der preussischen Akademie der Wissenschaften. Phil.-Hist. Klasse.* Nr. 7 (Berlin).

— **(1927):** 'Aus dem irischen Recht IV', *ZCP* 16, 167–230.

— **(1928):** 'Zu Verslehre II', *ZCP* 17, 263–76.

— **(1931):** 'Irisches Recht. I. Díre. Ein altirischer Rechtstext. II. Zu den unteren Ständen in Irland', *Abhandlungen der preussischen Akademie der Wissenschaften. Phil.-Hist. Klasse.* Nr. 2 (Berlin).

— **(1935):** *Scéla Mucce Meic Dathó* (Mediaeval and Modern Irish Series 6, Dublin, reprinted 1986).

Toner, Gregory (2007): *Bruiden Da Choca* (Irish Texts Society 61, Dublin).

Tranter, Stephen (1997): *Clavis Metrica: Háttatal, Háttalykill and the Irish Metrical Tracts* (Frankfurt).

Ua Ceallaigh, Seán (1927): *Trí Truagha na Scéaluidheachta* (Dublin).

Uhlich, Jürgen (2002): 'Verbal Governing Compounds (Synthetics) in Early Irish and Other Celtic Languages', *Transactions of the Philological Society* 100, 403–33.

Van Hamel, A. G. (1917–19): 'Poems from Brussels MS. 5100–4', *RC* 37, 345–52.

Vendryes, Joseph (1917–19): 'Le Génitif de Destination en Celtique', *RC* 37, 327–34.

— **(1959–):** *Lexique Étymologique de l'Irlandais Ancien* (Dublin and Paris).

Wasserschleben, Hermann (1885): *Die irische Kanonensammlung* (2nd ed., Leipzig).

Watkins, Calvert (1962): 'Varia II: Old Irish *-antar*', *Ériu* 19, 116–18.

— **(1963):** 'Indo-European Metrics and Archaic Irish Verse', *Celtica* 6, 194–249.

— **(1976):** 'The Etymology of Irish *Dúan*', *Celtica* 11, 270–7.

Williams, Nicholas (1980): 'Gnéithe den Aoir i Litríocht na Gaeilge', *Studia Hibernica* 20, 57–71.

— **(1981):** *Pairlement Chloinne Tomáis* (Dublin).

Wincott Heckett, Elizabeth (1997): 'Textiles, Cordage, Basketing and Raw Fibre' in *Late Viking Age and Medieval Waterford. Excavations 1986–1992* (Waterford) 743–61.